THE RAZORBACKS

THE RAZ

A Story

ORVILLE HENRY and **JIM BAILEY**

With a *Foreword by* J. WILLIAM FULBRIGHT

ORBACKS
of Arkansas Football

NEW EDITION

THE UNIVERSITY OF ARKANSAS PRESS   *Fayetteville   1996*

Designed by Alice Gail Carter

Library of Congress Cataloging-in-Publication Data
Henry, Orville.
    The Razorbacks : a story of Arkansas football / Orville Henry and
Jim Bailey : with a foreword by J. William Fulbright. — New ed.
        p.   cm.
    Originally published : Huntsville, Ala. : Strode, 1973.
    Includes index.
    ISBN 1-55728-429-6 (alk. paper). —
    ISBN 1-55728-430-X (pbk. : alk. paper)
        1. Arkansas Razorbacks (Football team)—History.
    2. University of Arkansas, Fayetteville—Football—History.
    I. Bailey, Jim, 1932–   . II. Title.
    GV958.A74.H46   1996
    796.332'63'0976714—dc20   96-8602
                                                          CIP

TO ALL THE RAZORBACKS

CONTENTS

FOREWORD

Razorback football has come a long way since my playing days, when the games were played on a dirt field with only a sprig of grass, and the small crowds sat on primitive wooden bleachers or, on a cold or wet day, watched from a few cars parked nearby. In those days in the early twenties, the squad rarely exceeded twenty. Except for injury or exhaustion, there were few substitutes, and most of us usually played the full sixty minutes. There were no offensive or defensive teams as we now have. There was a head coach and one assistant coach and sometimes a trainer to take care of injuries. There was no special dormitory and no scholarships for players.

Now, tens of thousands see every Razorback game—often, because of television, the viewers number in the millions. There still is no grass on the field, but instead of a bumpy dirt surface, there is artificial turf to ensure optimum playing conditions at all times.

Today's players tend to be much larger, more experienced, and their uniforms and equipment are sleek and streamlined, with several coaches and offensive and defensive specialists numbering at least forty.

Yet despite these dramatic changes, much has remained the same through the years, and it is these constants, these unchanging factors which I believe account for much of the sport's appeal in the fast-moving and often turbulent times.

Each September brings new hope, a clean start, visions of a championship. For the Razorbacks it is always an uphill struggle—the lone non-Texas team in the Southwest Conference. Even though the Razorbacks have beaten the Texas schools with some regularity in recent years, many still think of the Arkansas teams as underdogs, a role the Razorbacks have always relished.

The most remarkable thing about the Razorbacks is the way in which they have served as a rallying point for our state's citizens. Arkansans from all walks of life, many who have never even seen the Fayetteville campus, join students and alumni in following the Razorbacks. In the fall months, and especially on Saturdays, from the Ozarks to the Delta, Razorback football is the prime subject of conversation. The team is truly a source of unity and pride for the state.

I can readily testify that the Razorbacks, with their reputation for fierce competition, are known far beyond the state's borders, as is the famous "Calling the Hogs" yell, which symbolizes fervent loyalty.

The history of the Razorbacks and their struggle for football supremacy is an exciting one, not without setbacks and crushing defeats, but full of dramatic victories, with individual heroics and outstanding teamwork.

No one is better able or more qualified to tell the story of the Razorbacks than Orville Henry and Jim Bailey, who for years have chronicled their ups and downs for the *Arkansas Gazette* and are among those most responsible for building the great interest in and support for Razorback football.

> BILL FULBRIGHT
> University of Arkansas Athlete, 1921–24
> University of Arkansas President, 1939–41
> United States Senator, 1945–74

EDITOR'S NOTE: The late Sen. J. William Fulbright wrote this foreword to the original edition of *The Razorbacks* in 1973.

PREFACE

Almost all football games contain remarkable plays, but most are fated to be forgotten in a week. Just those few that seem to alter the immediate or long-range future take on a life of their own.

When J. J. Meadors made his diving catch of Barry Lunney's touchdown pass against Alabama early in the 1995 season, the Arkansas Razorbacks instantly shed five years of encrusted mediocrity and brought back their fans in sellout numbers.

That was for the short haul. Much more time will be necessary to determine if Meadors's play has the durable impact of John Hoffman's touchdown against Rice in 1946 (which made the building of War Memorial Stadium necessary); Buddy Bob Benson's pass to Preston Carpenter against Ole Miss in 1954 (which led to 30 years of full stadiums at Fayetteville and Little Rock); Lance Alworth's two-point conversion run against SMU in 1959 (starting a streak of championships in the Frank Broyles era); and, of course, Teddy Barnes's 1975 catch against Texas A&M that produced an improbable Cotton Bowl bid.

The Razorbacks' moderate successes of 1995 do not guarantee total restoration. However, the public's response affirms that old formulas remain valid in an age of ever-mounting competition for the sports entertainment dollar.

Winning may not be the only thing, but the first century of Arkansas football leaves no doubt it must always be the main thing.

THE RAZORBACKS

– 01 –

FIXATION AND FULFILLMENT

The date happened to be October 5, 1957, a football night in War Memorial Stadium, but it could have been any such evening during the past five decades.

High in the west stands sat a fervent fan. He and his wife were annoyed by a juiced-up, loud, offensive patron in a seat behind them. The man in front finally let his attention be distracted from the field long enough to say the drunk's remarks should not be made in mixed company.

So the drunk pulled a knife and slashed at the neck and throat of his neighbor in front.

"And do you know," stadium manager Allan Berry told reporters later, "that we couldn't get the man to leave the game. He kept sitting there with his throat cut, insisting he wasn't going to miss a play. We finally got him down in the first-aid station in the end zone. They took four stitches and grudgingly let him go back to his seat. He agreed to check in for more treatment at a hospital—after the game."

The drunk was removed, of course, and police officers came back after the game to obtain a statement from the fan who had been slashed. Arkansas beat Texas Christian, 20-7, and the fan was so pleased with the game he refused to press charges.

When the story came out, people were shocked by the attack but not surprised at the victim's reaction. That was the season's Southwest Conference opener, after all, and TCU had a tough team in those days.

Now let us move on to October 15, 1960. The Razorbacks were playing the University of Texas in a regionally televised game at Austin. One man could not stay close to his set; his business forced him to drive through central Arkansas that afternoon. He followed the game on his car radio until the station flickered out of range with Texas holding a 23-21 lead late in the fourth quarter. Twisting his dial frantically, cursing the static, he drove into Malvern.

"It looked deserted," he said. "Nobody on the streets, nothing. Then it just exploded, like everybody in town yelled at once, and some came running out on the sidewalks. I knew Arkansas had won, but I had no idea how. I felt like the loneliest and least informed man on earth. The rest of the day I was ashamed to let on that I didn't know. I saw in the papers the next morning that Mickey Cissell kicked a field goal with 25 seconds left and the score was 24-23."

Arkansas and Texas met in "Big Shootout I" at Fayetteville on December 6, 1969. With the whole country locked in on television, with President Richard Nixon and an unsuspected future president George Bush in the stands, the Razorbacks and Longhorns played for a national championship. Underdog Arkansas led 14-0 after three quarters but lost 15-14.

The tape of the telecast was replayed several times in Arkansas markets during the ensuing years. One Razorback rooter always watched until the end of the third period and then called the Hogs and shut off his set.

"That game broke my heart once," he says. "It's not ever going to hurt me again."

We could go on, but you get the idea: Razorback fans—the real ones, not front-runners and bandwagon climbers—take seriously an old quip that a game "is not a matter of life or death; it's more important than that."

Football fulfillment came late to Arkansas, some 20 to 50 years behind other powers in the south and southwest. Waiting tends to sharpen appreciation.

As writer Dan Jenkins once explained to *Sports Illustrated* readers:

> Arkansas is a curious state, one that saw part of its people in support of the Union, and a state that elected a Fulbright and a Rockefeller at the same time it voted for Wallace. Figure that out. What brings it all together, however, is football.

That was on the mark as written in 1969, when all resources, energy, prayers, and passion were poured into a single sport. Today, "what brings it all together" is football *and* basketball and any other activity likely to flag national recognition or cause teeth-gnashing in the camps of the Razorbacks' natural rivals.

For a relatively small state, 27th in size among 50, Arkansas has a diverse topography—mountains, hills, woodlands, plains, delta—that naturally breeds conflicting commercial, social, and political priorities. The Razorbacks transcend all that. It is only at their games that the whole state assembles in anything approaching total accord.

John Barnhill, a wise man from Tennessee, started cultivating the impression in 1946 that a University of Arkansas football game was an urgent defense of the state's honor rather than merely an athletic contest. Barnhill's strategy came to full flower with consistent success under the coaching of Frank Broyles in the 1960s.

In 1990 Arkansas withdrew from the fading, malaise-stricken Southwest Conference and cast its lot with the burgeoning Southeastern Conference. The Texas members jeered briefly, then started a frantic search for new affiliations of their own. By 1994 the SWC was ready for the archives.

At the time of the rupture, only Arkansas, Texas, and Texas A&M retained gate appeal in football, and the conference basketball tournament unabashedly depended on Arkansas partisans to fill Reunion Arena in Dallas.

The Razorbacks had outgrown a league that once considered them a drag on the operation and departed to assure their program's continued progress. No hard feelings; just hard facts. And plenty of irony.

As the only non-Texas team in the Southwest Conference, and mostly a loser for the longest, Arkansas had suffered with a terrible stepchild complex. Up to the time of Broyles, Texans asked the rhetorical question: "Now, what the hell is Arkansas doing in this league, anyway?"

Ultimately Arkansas put that question to itself and found no satisfactory answer.

INSTANTLY IN THE RED

Princeton and Rutgers played the first intercollegiate football game in 1869. The Arkansas General Assembly passed enabling legislation that created the University of Arkansas in 1871. The two events did not catch up with each other until 1894.

Only three areas showed interest in securing the location of the school, and bond elections were held. Fayetteville and Washington County won by approving $130,000 in financing. Batesville bid $50,000. Voters in Little Rock and Pulaski County rejected the issuance of bonds.

The first record of sports activity of any kind was furnished by W. M. . Harrison, a member of the class of 1878.

"On Saturday afternoons," he wrote in an alumni publication in 1923, "we went out on the commons, where Arkansas Avenue is now located, and played baseball in ball season, without gloves, masks, shin guards, et cetera, the catcher taking the ball on the bound, frequently the score being 30-odd to 20-odd."

By the early 1880s students and faculty members were petitioning for something better. In 1884 the school set aside two and a half acres on campus for baseball and football, but neglected to allocate any money for development.

During the 1891–92 term, students began talking about athletic teams which would represent the entire school. An athletic association was formed in the fall of 1892, with officers and separate "managers" for football, baseball, and tennis, as well as a general athletic club. The project was entirely student controlled and not sponsored by the school.

After a few years of intramural-style football, the association was successful in arranging a three-game schedule in the fall of 1894. It consisted of a two-game, home-and-home series with a team nominally representing Fort Smith High School (members were adult Fort Smith citizens, including two blacksmiths) and a Thanksgiving visit to the University of Texas at Austin. Texas had played its first game against outside competition the previous year.

John C. Futrall, then a young Latin professor and later (1913–39) U of A president, agreed to meet with the 1894 players three times a week for practice.

At the University of Virginia, Futrall had been exposed to football, but it is not clear if it was as participant or spectator. No matter. In the 1890s, just a tiny percentage of Americans had seen a football game, much less played in one. A good guess would be that Futrall served more as manager, disciplinarian, and cheerleader than as tactical coach.

Futrall was offered $400 or 80 percent of the gate receipts for the Texas game. Fearing a bad break in the weather and a sparse crowd, he accepted the $400 guarantee.

The Arkansas team turned the Fort Smith games into encouraging tune-ups, 42-0 and 38-0. A squad of 14 players and Futrall left Fayetteville on Monday, November 26, by train, presumably with high hopes. They reached Dallas late Tuesday night and Austin early Thursday morning, just in time for their first test against another college team.

They were beaten, 54-0.

A crowd of 1,500 turned out, and the receipts reached $700. Futrall had guessed wrong by taking the guarantee; the trip ran $35 in the red. Futrall made up the difference out of his pocket and was reimbursed by the student athletic association.

These were the original 14 players:

Ends . . . . Edward Mook and H. Dade Moore
Tackles . . . . Raleigh Kobel and LeRoy Campbell
Guards . . . . Tommy H. Rogers and J. C. Braswell
Center . . . . Frank D. James
Quarterback . . . Wright Lindsey
Halfbacks . . . . . W. W. Haydon and Arthur J. McDaniel
Fullback . . . . . . Herbert Y. Fishback
Subs. . . . . Jim Brown, E. Carney, and W. S. Norman

Only two were enrolled in the college division of Arkansas Industrial University (the school's name until 1899); the others studied in the AIU preparatory department, doing basic high school work. It makes sense the Arkansas neophytes found the Texas players "bigger, older and more numerous," as described later by a member of Futrall's squad.

Herbert Fishback was the first campus football hero at Arkansas. A three-time team captain, son of a former Arkansas governor, he died while still a student in 1898, a few weeks after catching cold during a football trip to Springfield, Missouri.

These early teams were called Cardinals, and the school's first yearbook, the 1897 *Cardinal,* editorialized against the inadequacies of the program. "The legislature of our state seems to cling to the antiquated and moss-grown idea that an appropriation—even a small one—for athletics is not only a waste of money but a positive detriment to the welfare of the students, arguing from the standpoint that too much time and energy spent in athletics would lead to a corresponding diminution of mental labor."

Futrall managed the team through three sketchy schedules. He gave way in 1897 to B. N. Wilson, another professor, who would later serve as the U of A's faculty representative on athletics. Years after his coaching stint, Wilson relished quoting an unfriendly review by a Fort Smith newspaper, following a game against the Fort Smith team. "Thugs, pug-uglies, and roughnecks. Such are B. N. Wilson and the University of Arkansas football team."

The 1901 *Cardinal* recorded the school's first popular cheer (an elaborate piece of gibberish that opened with "Boom-a-lacka, boom-a-lacka") and also the boast that "one of our athletes already holds the Southwestern record for the 100-yard-dash (10 seconds) and the running broad jump (21 feet)." It neglected to mention the name of the athlete.

College football was anything but an overnight sensation. Adapted from rugby and soccer, particularly the former, it gradually moved from its cradle, the East, to other regions of the United States. At most schools, Arkansas included, baseball outweighed it in popularity until well into the 1900s.

Across the nation, football evolved at different speeds, depending on factors such as size, location, and financial support. The University of Arkansas scarcely had a prayer on any of the three counts.

John C. Futrall, later U of A president, was a young Latin professor when he volunteered to coach the school's first football team in 1894.

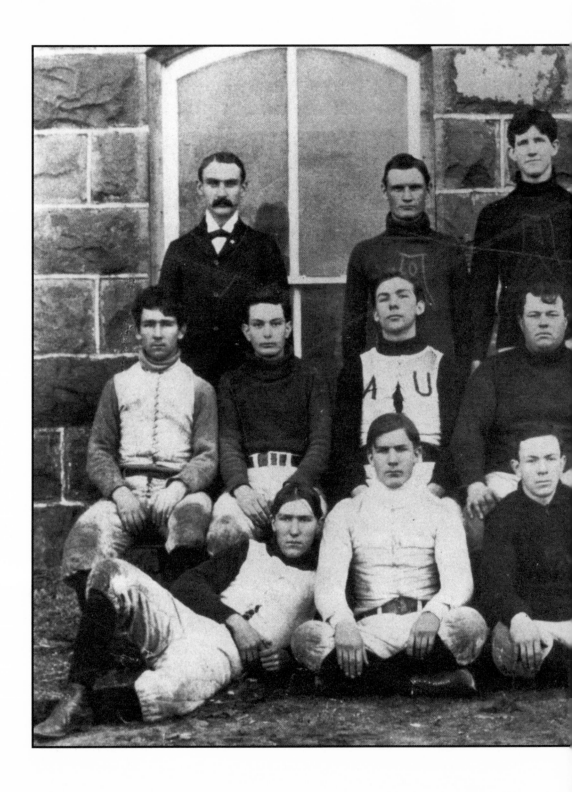

THE RAZORBACKS

The 1896 Arkansas football squad

– 03 –

WILL F. THOMAS

The late Will F. Thomas was not a remarkable football player in the fall of 1901, he said once, but by the 1970s he was—as far as he knew, as far as anyone knew—the oldest surviving former University of Arkansas athlete.

At the age of 94 in the spring of 1973, Thomas sat in his living room at Fayetteville and told an interviewer how things were nearly three-quarters of a century before.

"Now, don't misrepresent what I was," he said. "Nobody ever called me a great player or anything like that."

Thomas was the quarterback when the 1901 Cardinals played an eight-team schedule against Pierce City College, Drury College, Fort Scott (Kansas), a Little Rock athletic club, Henry Kendall (later Tulsa University), the Kansas City Medics, Louisiana State, and Louisiana Tech. They won three, lost five. It was the largest schedule they had attempted.

"We only took eleven men to Little Rock," Thomas said. "Right at the first of the game, on the second or third down, Bill Ellis got hurt and couldn't play anymore. Fred Brown, our captain and manager, told the other manager that the game was off. 'We can't play our ten against your eleven.' The other captain said, 'Who's that sitting there on the bench?' We told him it was our coach, Charlie Thomas. They said, 'Aw, hell, play him. We'd just as soon have him as anybody else.' So we played the rest of the game with our coach." Arkansas lost, 5-0.

Charlie Thomas, a former Michigan football player, was the first Arkansas coach who was not a regular U of A faculty member or a part-time, volunteer helper.

"He was the first one paid as a coach," Will Thomas said. "We elected a student management, what they called an athletic board, to help promote the football team."

What sort of support did the football team have from the student body in 1901?

"None. We played our home games over there where the Fine Arts Building is now, around in there somewhere. They graded it up a little but they had no bleachers. If they could sell enough tickets, they drove stakes and put up a rope and sent marshals out there with signs to keep the crowd back.

"If you had 50 people to look at you, you felt fortunate. They'd pay 25 or 35 cents for a tag, and it kind of served as a ticket. Those who didn't have tags would take advantage just like they would today. But most of the students didn't care much about football then, and the people downtown didn't manifest much interest in it, either.

"The way football worked then, they'd pick out the first team. Then all the other boys who had tried out—maybe there'd be 10 or 15 or 20 of them—would play on the scrub team, the Cubs. We played against them in practice.

"If you were selected to play, you bought your own shoes, pants, shirt, equipment, everything. You bought it all yourself. If you weren't able to buy it, you just didn't play.

"When they picked the team for 1901, the coach named a man for every position except quarterback. Then he turned to me and said, 'Thomas, you're the only one left. Looks like you're gonna be the quarterback.' Well, you know, I didn't have any qualifications. But what they did, they gave us a position and developed us from there. Quarterback was open because Ashton Vincenheller, who had been a good player for us through the 1900 season, had dropped out.

"The coach, Charlie Thomas—he was no kin to me—had been a good tackle at Michigan, they said. He taught us to be rough. We practiced our signals with 15 or 20 scrubs lined up against us. We worked on everybody firing off at the same time, with the scrubs trying to break it up. Normally the quarterback called signals, but when they had a new man, like me, trying to learn, the captain, Fred Brown, called 'em most of the time.

"We were invited down to Baton Rouge to play LSU, and 13 players and the coach made the trip on the train. Because I was new at quarterback, they took an extra quarterback along and it turned out to be a good thing, because I got sick on the trip. The train stopped in a town somewhere, and a man was running up and down the sidewalk selling ham sandwiches, hot dogs, things like that. I made a bad mistake. I ate one.

"We got to Baton Rouge and there was no bridge over the river. A ferry took us across, and some streetcars pulled by mules took us to the hotel.

"The game was played on the campus. They didn't have a field or anything, but it was an especially nice campus. Plenty of grass. We thought it was a mighty nice place to have a game. Maybe 125 people—a small crowd of citizens—stood around and watched the game, and they beat us, 15-0.

"On the way home we stopped off at Ruston to play Louisiana Tech, and we beat them, 16-0.

"You had to have an appointment from your county judge—a certificate from him—before they'd take you at the University," Thomas said. "When I applied, I found Sevier County had issued all its certificates. So I went over to Nashville in Howard County and talked to the county judge there. He said, 'Well, you were born in Howard County, and we'll just claim you as one of our citizens.'

"So I enrolled in September of 1900, a week late because of the way I had to go about it.

"The best I can recall there were only two high schools in the state at that time, Little Rock and Fort Smith. You could go to about the eighth grade in most other towns. I hadn't been to the ninth grade, and when I stood the entrance exam, I needed it pretty bad. They listed me in the preparatory department."

Had he ever played football before he enrolled at Arkansas?

"No, no, I had never been around anything like that. I had played baseball. In fact, I pitched all but four innings of the baseball played at the university while I was out for it. Baseball was much better accepted than football then.

"I roomed at Buchanan Hall. It was the only building on the grounds that was worth anything at that particular time. It was always full; the first year I had to go into a room with four beds in it. There was no bathroom in the building at all, but there was a bathhouse on the outside where we cut our wood.

"The student union ran the school, and Buchanan Hall had a student union management. If they wanted beef for the next week, they bought a cow and dressed it. They'd ring the bell for the boys to line up and eat. If a boy couldn't eat what was put on his plate, he was out of luck. He didn't have much choice. Buchanan Hall didn't have an outstanding menu, but they had enough to sustain all the boys, and you were glad to stay there.

"They didn't charge any tuition at all. What they called a matriculation fee cost $10 to $15 and $100 would cover everything else, room and board, for nine months. There were about 820 students when I enrolled."

Thomas left school in 1902. His father had been elected sheriff of Sevier County and needed his son to help him as a tax collector.

"The coach wrote me an awfully ugly letter about dropping out of school," he said. "He wanted me to return all my stuff I had carried home—my pants, shoes, coat. He wanted my jacket that had UA on it. Of course I had bought all that stuff myself; everybody bought their own stuff. He wrote me several letters and ate me up pretty bad. I finally ignored him."

Thomas became a keen follower of the Razorback teams of Hugo Bezdek, Francis Schmidt, Fred Thomsen, John Barnhill, Bowden Wyatt, and Frank Broyles. Not many people saw them all.

Looking back from 1973, Thomas found it hard to relate his own era to what came afterward.

"It grew in inspiration considerably," he said.

The 1907 Razorbacks, then called Cardinals, summoned a businesslike pose for a photographer.

– 04 –

"HUGO, YOU HAVE
A WONDERFUL TEAM"

Amos Alonzo Stagg is credited with nearly 30 football innovations, and some are rather important to the game as we know it: the huddle, the unbalanced offensive line, the backfield shift, cross-blocking, the reverse, the man in motion, wind sprints, the direct pass from center, the lateral pass, even the awarding of letters and the numbering of players.

Stagg's inventiveness helped football swing from a rowdy semi-sport to a complex spectacle. The University of Arkansas was fortunate to secure the services of a Stagg pupil in 1908.

Hugo Bezdek was 24 years old when he took the job at Fayetteville. Born in Prague, Bohemia, he migrated to Chicago with his parents when he was five years old. He graduated from the University of Chicago in 1907, after playing fullback four years for Stagg and also serving as his student assistant.

Even before Bezdek earned his degree, he took off one year and coached the University of Oregon to a 5-0-1 record in 1906.

Until Bezdek's time, Arkansas students elected a senior as student manager of athletics and hired a coach. The students guaranteed the coach a sum for his season's work, and if the gate receipts (25 cents a head) failed to cover it, the manager had to coax the difference out of the students' pockets or pay it himself.

Bezdek was hired by the school. He represented a new order in more ways than one. "He sort of woke things up," Will F. Thomas said.

Bezdek was a round, powerful man ("twice as broad as tall," went one obvious exaggeration) who combined a large measure of charm ("blue eyes, big smile") with energy, ambition, and shrewdness. He was the first Arkansas coach to register on the public at all. He had impact, presence, charisma.

"He was a driver," said the late Phil C. Huntley, who at 88 in 1973 was the only living member of Bezdek's undefeated 1909 football team. "Playing the other team on Saturday was the easiest thing we did all week."

"He coached everything," Huntley said of Bezdek. "Football—great success. Baseball—great success. He tried to get track started. He was all things to all men. He understood the importance of placing his program in front of the public. He had cards printed and distributed in towns like Rogers, Springdale, and Fort Smith advertising his home games. It was the first athletic advertising the school did."

He would be important now even if he had been less successful. It was Bezdek who changed the team from Cardinals to Razorbacks.

"We were on a trip in Texas, getting off the train for a stroll—I think in Dallas," said Huntley, Bezdek's center from 1908 through 1911 and his graduate aide in 1912. "Somebody yelled, 'Here come the hogs.' See, there were a lot of jokes about Arkansas at that time.

The undefeated Razorbacks of 1909, with quarterback Steve Creekmore in front and coach Hugo Bezdek (big "C") at far right

"Bezdek stopped and thought a minute. He said, 'Hmmm, boys, I like that. We're the Razorbacks from now on.' I've heard and read a lot of ways it was supposed to have come about, but that's how it really was. It took a year or two for it to catch on with everybody, but it started right there."

Another account has Bezdek telling the student body, in a pep-rally setting, that the team "played like a band of wild razorbacks" in a stirring 1909 victory over Louisiana State. Probably he did; the story is not necessarily in conflict with Huntley's version.

Evidently Bezdek had seen some of the wild hogs that roamed Arkansas, and the lean, evil-tempered razorback impressed him. When he made up his mind he was coaching Razorbacks rather than Cardinals, he did his best to spread the word.

When did the mascot change become official? We can only tell you for sure that the school yearbook remained the *Cardinal* through 1915. It became the *Razorback* in 1916. By the 1920s the Woo Pig Sooie (properly, Whoooo PIG! Sooie) cheer had been established, as had the logo of the snorting, charging red razorback.

In 1894 students picked cardinal (deep red) as a school color over heliotrope, a shade of moderate purple. A small but crucial decision. Could purple razorbacks have been taken seriously, even by themselves?

Huntley arrived at the University ahead of Bezdek.

"I grew up in the woods down around Camden. Know where Louann is? Near there. There were four of us boys in a little neighborhood school that ran two months of the year in the summer. When I say neighborhood, I might be talking about a 10-mile area of timber and farm land.

"Anyway the teacher said it was important to achieve more than your forefathers, to rise above your surroundings. Well, I'd seen all these boys in my area get married at 19, raise a slew of kids, and work hard all their lives for a bare living. So the four of us went off to the university. Two of us stayed.

"F. C. Longman was the coach. He says, 'Huntley, you're a good-sized fella, you ought to come out for football.' I said, 'Hell, I don't have time.' See, I was working all the time to make my way. But I changed my mind and tried it, and when Bezdek came I said, 'Coach, I'm your center—from now on.' He said, 'Fine, fine.'

"I talked Dan Estes into coming out. Dan was from Alpena and, like me, never gave football a thought before he got there. Dan weighed 240, and he could move and play. It was a long time before they had another football player as big as Dan Estes. In those days he seemed like a giant. Nicest, sweetest-natured fella you ever met, and I guess everybody was lucky on that account."

Recruiting was almost unknown. Almost, but not quite.

"Bezdek brought down a player or two from Chicago, but they didn't work out too well," Huntley said. "One of our best linemen was Stanley Phillip, a half-Indian from South Dakota, great 190-pounder. Longman got him down there; they were related."

How many seasons could a player be eligible?

"As long as you lived," Huntley said. "Of course you had to be enrolled in school, but you could be a graduate coming back to take some courses. Clifton Milford, one of our good backs, lettered six years, from 1904 through 1909. There weren't that many eligibility rules, and not all of them were strictly enforced everywhere."

The quarterback who would tie everything together for Bezdek was, like Huntley, already on campus when the new coach arrived.

Steve Creekmore had participated in a couple of sandlot football games organized by two teachers back home in Van Buren, but he did not go out for the team when he enrolled at the University of Arkansas in 1907. Bezdek picked him out of intramurals, worked him into his 1908 plans, and installed him at quarterback in 1909.

Bezdek's teams were light and furiously quick, and no foe on their seven-game schedule could handle them in 1909. Contemporary accounts express amazement at the speed, endurance, swarming defense, and kicking-game efficiency of Arkansas that year.

Creekmore, weighing 148 stripped and under six feet tall, became a regional name for play selection, fast and slippery running, blocking, and passing. He was an artful punt returner (vital in an era of 20 to 30 kicks a game) and a deadly tackler at safety.

Bezdek coached Creekmore to call plays as rapidly as possible— nobody ever huddled then—and so the Razorbacks would run a play, chase the ball, put it in play immediately when it was downed, and drive as far as they could as quickly as they could.

"I guess it was a forerunner of Oklahoma's hurry-up style in the split-T days under Bud Wilkinson," Creekmore told an interviewer in 1960. "I know we'd often run four or five plays and then find the official had penalized us back down field for the first one. He'd catch up, and we'd have to go back. The LSU coach protested our system, but it was legal."

The Cardinals went 5-4 in 1908 while Bezdek was fitting everything together, and in 1909 the Cardinals beat Henderson (24-0), Ouachita

(56-0), Drury (12-6), Fairmont (23-6), and Oklahoma (21-6) to set up the first real football showdown the school had known.

Arkansas and LSU were scheduled at Memphis, November 13. LSU had a 4-1 record to that point, and romantic lore that has grown up around the game insists they were playing for the "mythical championship of the South." If they were, it was indeed mythical, since LSU's earlier loss was to Sewanee, which was about as southern as one could get.

Arkansas beat LSU, 16-0. Creekmore "played rings around" LSU veteran star W. E. Fenton and was acclaimed "the south's best quarterback." By loose (and probably generous) estimates, the crowd at Memphis reached 4,000. Hundreds jammed around the Western Union office at Fayetteville for reports on the game.

"Not an Arkansas man was called upon single-handed," according to the game account in the *Arkansas Gazette,* "for each time that a crimson runner started with the ball, he was well protected by perfect interference established by his teammates."

In less formal terms, apparently they blocked the devil out of LSU.

Arkansas had an open date the next weekend, but Bezdek did not slacken his practice schedule. He was gunning for a November 25 game at Little Rock with Washington University of St. Louis, a season's capper on Thanksgiving Day.

The state realized something extraordinary was happening at that remote school up in the mountains. It was Bezdek's big moment, and he was not a man to waste it.

A series of newspaper stories out of Fayetteville claimed unofficial championships of both the South and Southwest. The pitch was, Arkansas beat Oklahoma by 21-6 when Oklahoma was fresh and rested, and Texas A&M (undefeated that year) beat Oklahoma 14-8 when the Sooners were frazzled by two hard games. And Washington would be going to Little Rock off a respectable 12-0 loss to Vanderbilt, a southern powerhouse.

Arkansas would not only be after a perfect season on Thanksgiving; it would also be trying to beat Vanderbilt's score against the same target.

By this time the Arkansas team was occasionally called Razorbacks in newspaper articles but with quotation marks around the new nickname.

Bezdek heightened interest by bringing in his teacher, A. A. Stagg, to referee the Little Rock game. Coaches often officiated games in those days, but it was rare for a coach of Stagg's stature to travel that far to lend his prestige to an event.

An *Arkansas Gazette* reporter visited both teams when they reached Little Rock on Wednesday, November 24, and filed this account.

The maroon and myrtle warriors from St. Louis arrived early in the afternoon and at once proceeded to the Hotel Marion. A little later the undefeated gladiators from Fayetteville arrived and were quartered at the same hostelry.

The lobby of the Marion was packed last night with a football-crazy crowd. The big, husky gladiators of both elevens were much in evidence early in the evening, surrounded by a little knot of admiring football fans. They soon disappeared, however, for the watchful coaches sent their charges off to bed shortly after nine o'clock.

Both teams worked out at West End Park during the afternoon. Arkansas arrived on the field first. As soon as the cardinal-clad Razorbacks lined up for their first play, it was evident that Coach Bezdek had an edge for the final and most important game of the season. Their speed was a revelation to the little group who watched the practice.

Before Quarterback Creekmore had finished shrieking the signals, the whole eleven, a solid mass of cardinal, was under motion. Up and down the gridiron they raced, going through play after play with lightning-like rapidity. The men lined up on the dead run, and before they had fairly come to a stop Creekmore had shrieked another signal and the whole team was sprinting through another play.

With the possibility Washington adherents might be looking on, Coach Bezdek allowed his men to uncork none of the special plays he had prepared, and only the simplest sort of forward passes were attempted.

Arkansas execution of the forward pass is a revelation to those who have seen only local teams play. The quarterback shoots the ball low and straight while on the dead run, and the end receives it also on the run. There were none of the high, soaring tosses such as local football fans are accustomed to seeing.

After the regular backfield had raced up and down the field a few times, Coach Bezdek sent in his sub pony backs with Sib Ward, the Little Rock boy, at quarter, and practice continued with unabated vigor.

At the conclusion of the signal session Stanley Phillip, the husky Indian captain, spent a quarter of an hour attempting goals from the field. Then the players wrapped themselves in their heavy sweaters and hurried off the field.

The writer stayed for Washington's workout, but was much less impressed. He noted the visiting players were small in comparison to Arkansas and "were evidently still feeling the effects of their recent hard encounter with Vanderbilt." The Washington coach, Francis M. Cayou, staged a little signal work and kicking and then asked all the spectators to leave. He wanted to rehearse some trick plays behind closed gates.

"We are hopeful rather than confident," Coach Cayou told the press.

The Razorbacks' 34-0 conquest of Washington ran on the front page of the *Arkansas Gazette*. Inside was a play-by-play account and even a crude forerunner of a dressing-room story. (The post-game quizzing of contestants is a modern staple of sports journalism, but it was a rare procedure in 1909 and for a long while afterward.)

"At last, after years of waiting, the University of Arkansas has come into her own," the front-page article proclaimed.

"As the referee's whistle blew signaling the conclusion of yesterday's gridiron battle between the University of Arkansas and Washington of St. Louis, the frenzied students from Fayetteville leaped over fences, smashed down those that could be smashed, and in a frantically cheering mob gathered about their unbeaten warriors . . . By administering the St. Louis eleven such a crushing, overwhelming defeat, the cardinal-clad gladiators have raised the University of Arkansas—so long an underdog in the athletic world—to a place among the leading elevens of the South."

It turned out that Creekmore did not have much more trouble charging up and down the field against Washington than he had had in signal drill the previous day.

"It was a corking game," Bezdek was quoted as saying. "It was the cleanest game that has been seen for years. The officials and spectators on the sidelines who observed the plays closely were unanimous in their praise of the tactics used by the elevens.

"Washington fought hard and gamely, but they were fighting against too great odds. Yes, we will meet them again next year, if they can be persuaded to schedule another game with us."

"I am not surprised at the defeat of Washington today," said the super-realist, Coach Cayou. "In fact I was fearful that the score against our team would be in the nature of an avalanche.

"In the first place the team is crippled. The regular backs are out and anybody who knows anything about football knows the strength of a team centers in the backs."

He declined to be drawn into any comparisons. "The Washington team that went against Arkansas was not the same that went against Vanderbilt."

As A. A. Stagg prepared to catch a train back to Chicago, he told Bezdek, within earshot of a reporter, "Hugo, you have a wonderful team. You have three great men in Creekmore, Phillip, and Milford. I cannot say I would feel safe to put my bunch of warriors against Arkansas tomorrow."

"There weren't that many of us," Huntley said 64 years later, when he was the only one left. "Ray Davis and W. E. Bradford were the ends; Stanley Phillip and T. S. Ellington the tackles; Dan Estes and Pat Wright, the guards; me at center. Creekmore was the quarterback—the kind who led by doing things himself, setting the example instead of doing a lot of talking. Creekmore was no prima donna. Clifton Milford and Joe Allen were the halfbacks, and W. H. Phillips was the fullback. The top subs were Percy Hinton and G. T. Blakely. Hinton was a good player for us then, and later he made quite a name for himself as a regular starter. And that was about it; just 13 or 14 men."

Arkansas had played football only 15 seasons, but tributes to the unbeaten 1909 team stressed "years of waiting." The wait for another perfect season would consume 55 years.

Fifty years after the fact, 1909 heroes Phil Huntley, center, *and Steve Creekmore,* right, *are honored at an Arkansas game. George Cole handles the presentation.*

— 05 —

SPRINGTIME EXPERIMENTS

In the spring of 1910 Hugo Bezdek invited A. A. Stagg down to Fayetteville for a series of daily football experiments. It is a firmly rooted belief in Arkansas that that was the nation's first spring football practice.

Maybe yes, probably no. But this may have been the first that was more than a scuffle to determine who would make the team the following fall.

"Stagg brought his great Chicago quarterback, Walter Eckersall, down to Arkansas with him," Phil Huntley said. "Bezdek tried to get as many boys to come out for spring football as he possibly could, but the response was no better than it was in the fall. Maybe we had 20 boys show up, or 25.

"One of the new rules changed football from 35-minute halves to 15-minute quarters. Bezdek and Stagg wanted to see what effect that had. Mainly they were testing a bunch of rule changes. They did some work on passing, although passing wasn't brand new. They tried everything."

Five years earlier, college football seemed on the verge of brutalizing itself into extinction. In 1905 the public grew edgy when 18 football deaths and 149 serious injuries were reported nationally. The crisis came when President Theodore Roosevelt looked at a photograph.

Swarthmore had a gifted 250-pound lineman named Bob Maxwell in 1905, and Penn decided the best way to handle Swarthmore was to concentrate on Maxwell. The punished Swarthmore star lasted the entire game, but he was a scary sight as he tottered off the field afterward. A photographer took his picture, and the president was horrified when he saw it. Roosevelt's ultimatum: Clean up football, or see it banned by presidential edict.

A meeting was held in New York City in January of 1906. You can regard it as the first session of what became the Football Rules Committee. A neutral zone the length of the ball was placed between opposing lines. First-down yardage was raised from five yards to 10. A minimum of six men was required to be on the line of scrimmage. The forward pass was legalized on a limited basis.

The 1906 changes accomplished part of their purpose. Requiring six men up front put a crimp in dangerous mass momentum plays like the flying wedge. The neutral zone made the line of scrimmage more civilized. The extra five yards to gain in three downs made punts and field goals important.

Bezdek's time at Arkansas coincided with constant, refining change. In 1909 the value of field goals was reduced from four points to three. Rule changes kept coming in bunches, always for the better. Seven men were required on the offensive line. Pushing or pulling the ball carrier was prohibited. Crawling was barred and so was interlocked interference.

In 1912, the value of a touchdown was increased from five points to six. The fourth down was added, the length of the field was set at 100 yards, and the kickoff was moved from the 50 to the 40. The lid was removed from the forward pass in 1912. The end zones were added as pass-catching territory, and the 20-yard distance restriction on the pass was lifted.

Bezdek found himself badly overscheduled in 1912, his fifth and final season at Arkansas. He took one of his typically thin squads (16 men) to Madison, Wisconsin, to play the University of Wisconsin, four teams deep. Wisconsin kicked him, 64-7.

"I was helping him that year, and I begged him to call off the Wisconsin trip," Huntley said. "He was a good coach, but coaching can only do so much. We had some good men in 1911 and 1912 but not the same quality we'd had in 1909 and 1910. That was the big thing we had going for us in 1909. We were a true team then.

"We had some prima donnas later on. Like when we went down to play the University of Texas in 1911. That was my last season as a player, and we should have won the game. Texas beat us, 12-0. The Texas coach came by afterward and said, 'You know something, Hugo? Five of your men damn near beat my 11.' He knew."

The Razorbacks' reputation improved in 1909–10, but not their home facilities.

"We played to one wooden grandstand that held about 200 people—not much more," Huntley said. "The field wasn't too good even though we worked on it, graded it, carried water from the creek to wet it down before every game."

Bezdek lost several important regulars off the 1909 team, but had Creekmore, Estes, Huntley, and Hinton to build around. The Razorbacks were almost as good in 1910. A 5-0 loss to Kansas State cost them a second straight perfect season. On the positive side, they scored a 5-0 win over otherwise unbeaten Texas A&M.

Russell May, a freshman halfback from Little Rock, had arrived as the state's first high school football star. He weighed 190 and could cover 100 yards in 10.2 seconds—an awesome combination in 1910.

On October 22 at Fayetteville, Texas Southwestern scored to take a 12-8 lead with two minutes to play. Russell May, searching his memory in 1963, takes it from there.

"Their kickoff was a bad one, low and wobbly, and Brunce Tunnah fell on it at our 30 near the sideline.

"I was on the other side, 'laying out'—you could do that then—and Creekmore threw me a long lateral pass. I went 75 yards and had to get away from five men to do it. That has to be my best game, wouldn't you think?"

The Arkansas-Texas game of 1911 almost filled the stands at Austin, without creating a parking problem.

THE RAZORBACKS

Newspaper accounts said May stiff-armed three defenders on the trip down the sideline. He was knocked down at the goal but fell with the ball shoved across for a touchdown that won it, 13-12.

"I couldn't spend a dime in Fayetteville that night," May said.

From the start of the 1909 season through mid-season of 1911, Bezdek's Razorbacks went 17-1 and outscored the combined opposition 617-42. They finished 1910 by beating LSU 51-0 at Little Rock and started 1911 with a school-record, 100-0 romp over Southwest Missouri at Fayetteville.

They were never as good after the 1911 Texas game, and from there through 1912 they lost 8 of 16. Then Bezdek left.

"He would have stayed," Huntley said, "if he had known John C. Futrall was going to get the president's job in 1913. He was having a lot of trouble with the administration, particularly an acting president they had. Certain people around the school were jealous of athletics and were determined to keep his program cut down to size."

Bezdek compiled a long and remarkable career. He had coached at Oregon in 1906 when he was 22 years old, and Oregon welcomed him back in 1913. His 1916 Oregon team beat Penn in the Rose Bowl, 14-0. He was so successful as a college baseball coach that the Pittsburgh Pirates hired him as manager in 1917. He tried three years to stir the Pirates, then settled in at Penn State as football and baseball coach.

Bezdek's Penn State football teams went 65-30-11 through 1929, and he retired to a teaching and administrative position with the school. In the late 1930s, he un-retired to coach the Cleveland Rams of the National Football League. In 1938 he had a rookie end from Arkansas, Ray Hamilton.

"He was an elderly man by then, and he was a gentleman," Hamilton said. "On the side he raised fancy chickens up in Pennsylvania. He retired at the end of my first season, and some of those big lugs just cried."

Bezdek died at Doylestown, Pennsylvania, in 1952. His teacher, A. A. Stagg, by then 90 years old, was still coaching on the field, helping his son Alonzo at Susquehanna College.

"I got a picture postcard from Stagg when he had his 100th birthday," Huntley said. "He wrote, 'Dear P. C., This is what a 100-year-old man looks like and this is what he writes like.'"

In his later years Bezdek named Glenn Killinger of Penn State, Johnny Beckett of Oregon, and Steve Creekmore of Arkansas as the three greatest players he had coached.

Creekmore, who became a Fort Smith business and civic leader and a notable amateur golfer, was once asked what gave Bezdek the most satisfaction as an Arkansas coach.

"You never know what moves a man the most," Creekmore said. "But I'm quite sure our 16-0 win over Louisiana State in 1909 meant a great deal to him, and so did beating Oklahoma the same year.

"I'll always remember this about the Louisiana game. It was the only time he ever advised us before a game that we might like to make some wagers on ourselves."

— 06 —

A CONFERENCE IS BORN, SORT OF

As football gained in scope and acceptance, the stakes naturally climbed. Colleges became less willing to leave the arrival of winning athletes to mere chance. Crowds grew more unruly toward game officials, and alumni grew less patient toward coaches.

The years approaching World War I found colleges quibbling over eligibility rules. In practical effect there were none. A national organization with broad authority and carefully defined standards, such as the National Collegiate Athletic Association (NCAA), was still beyond imagination. Regulations were administered by regional affiliations as unwieldly as they were impotent.

The Southern Intercollegiate Athletic Association (SIAA), formed about 1895, originally spanned the territory later occupied by the Southwest, Southeastern, Southern, and Atlantic Coast Conferences. Southwest teams were first to pull away.

The University of Arkansas had its first public squabble with another institution in 1905. The Cardinals lost to Rolla (Missouri) School of Mines, 16-0, and Arkansas thought it detected home cooking in the officiating. President John Tillman said, "The Arkansas eleven was given no chance to win" and announced the severing of athletic relations with Rolla. They were resumed a couple of years later, and Arkansas won by 7-5 at Fayetteville.

On the face of it, Arkansas's most disputed games were against the University of Mississippi in 1914 and Tulsa University in 1922.

Ole Miss and Tulsa still list those games as wins—which they were, on the field. Arkansas still claims both games as wins by forfeit. In both cases, the argument involved summertime baseball activity. The era's administrators apparently worried most that a college athlete might make a few semi-pro baseball dollars.

Something that happened to Arkansas in 1913 would generate spectacular controversy today. At the time it was too commonplace to stir a ripple.

Arkansas had a promising freshman quarterback from Fordyce, J. L. (Nick) Carter. The Razorbacks played Ole Miss in Little Rock and lost, 21-10, on November 15, 1913. E. T. Pickering, the Arkansas coach, received an offer to ride a train down to Arkadelphia and play Ouachita Baptist College before returning to Fayetteville.

Scheduling could be that casual then, and Pickering accepted. The game was played on November 17, and Arkansas won, 14-3. In the long run, though, the Razorbacks lost.

Eating dinner in a hotel dining room and waiting for the team's departure, Nick Carter answered a page and walked outside to confront "a big touring car" driven by one of Ouachita's best-heeled backers. Nick was impressed; in a re-telling 50 years later, he reckoned there probably were not more than a dozen automobiles in Arkadelphia at that time. He was driven to a caucus of Ouachita boosters, who invited him to transfer. They spelled out how much help they could give him and in what form.

On October 10, 1914, Carter quarterbacked Ouachita to a 15-9 win over Arkansas at Fayetteville. Later, as a retired Arkadelphia businessman, Carter explained the circumstances that prompted him to switch schools.

"I had nothing against the University of Arkansas; they had treated me well up there. But I was having a financially hard time of it and had just about made up my mind I was going to leave after one year and go into professional baseball. If the Ouachita people hadn't offered me a campus job that would cover all my expenses, I couldn't have gone on in school."

Transfers were instantly eligible in Carter's time. So were freshmen and, for that matter, graduate students. Some players at some schools enrolled only during football season, and some players at some schools may not have bothered to enroll at all.

When the University of Texas hired Theo Bellmont as athletic director in 1913, he surveyed the loose structure and determined to tighten it. After consulting officials of his school, Bellmont initiated contact with the larger state-supported and denominational schools of the region, asking if they would be interested in a new league. The University of Arkansas received one of the letters.

Arkansas had been invited to join a widespread Southern Conference as far back as 1902, but wisely declined at that time due to lack of traveling funds, playing facilities, and public interest.

Before Hugo Bezdek left Fayetteville, he advocated membership in a conference. John C. Futrall, the former professor-coach who became U of A president in 1913, thought the Texas proposal worth exploring.

Arkansas was one of eight schools represented at a meeting on May 6, 1914, at the Oriental Hotel in Dallas. The others were the University of Oklahoma, the University of Texas, Baylor, Oklahoma A&M, Texas A&M, Southwestern (Texas) University, and Louisiana State University.

They agreed to form the Southwest Intercollegiate Athletic Conference (SIAC). "Ringers" would be controlled by rules that limited a regularly enrolled student to three years of varsity competition following a freshman year of residence. And, of course, the competitors would be strictly amateur.

Arkansas, Texas, Texas A&M, Baylor, Southwestern, Oklahoma, and Oklahoma A&M became charter members during a follow-up meeting on December 18, 1914, at Houston. LSU attended but did not join. Rice was accepted, then withdrew from the league in 1916–17.

From 1894 through 1914, Arkansas had played 138 football games. Only eight of those were against Texas, only three against Baylor, only three against Texas A&M. Plainly the Hogs did not do much nosing around in Texas before the SWC was organized, although you can see a trend in Bezdek's 1912 schedule. He played Texas A&M, Baylor, and Texas that season, plus two other charter members, Oklahoma A&M and Southwestern.

Until this time, the University of Arkansas was not quite sure if its natural roots were southern, southwestern, or midwestern. Its Fayetteville location contained natural geographic ties to Missouri and Oklahoma, but the state as a whole seemed most excited when Arkansas played distinctly southern teams like LSU and Ole Miss.

There was a Southwest Conference race of sorts in 1915, and Oklahoma and Baylor led it with 3-0 records. Arkansas beat Oklahoma A&M and lost to Oklahoma in its only league games that first year.

In a decade, 1914–24, the Southwest Conference restructured itself for the long haul. Southwestern bowed out after two seasons. Southern

Methodist entered in 1918, the year Rice came back to stay. Oklahoma's last year was 1919, and Texas Christian's first was 1923. Oklahoma A&M withdrew after 1924.

By 1925 the SWC meant six Texas teams and Arkansas. It remained that way until a seventh Texas team, Texas Tech, was accepted in 1956, and an eighth, the University of Houston, in 1971.

The Southwest Conference had little impact on Arkansas football until a full round-robin schedule was established in the 1930s. It was longer still before Arkansas football had much impact on the Southwest Conference.

– 07 –

THE TURBULENT TIMES OF FRANCIS SCHMIDT

Francis Schmidt raged against the world with an unswerving singleness of purpose. All he demanded was perfection.

The public Schmidt became famous for sideline tirades, slave-driving practice sessions, a world-class vocabulary of swear words to express nearly constant displeasure, and a total absorption with football that made him comically and dangerously absent-minded on any other subject.

The private Schmidt seems to have been something of an elegant gentleman, classically educated, a parlor piano player, and completely at home in polite society. His athletes could have never guessed it.

For Tulsa (1919–21), Arkansas (1922–28), TCU (1929–33), Ohio State (1934–40), and Idaho (a sad swan song in 1941–42), Schmidt won 158 games, lost 57, and tied 11.

Some friend or foe dubbed him "Francis (Close the Gates of Mercy) Schmidt." He enjoyed seeing a lot of points on his side of the scoreboard and hated to see any on the other side.

At Tulsa, he whipped hapless opponents by margins like 152-0, 151-0, 121-0, 92-0, 89-0, 88-0, 75-0, 70-0. Those particular scores were posted against Oklahoma Baptist, Oklahoma Mines, Shawnee, Kingfisher, Chilocco Independents, East Central Oklahoma, Northwest Oklahoma, and Trinity.

A Nebraska man, Schmidt first attracted the attention of the University of Arkansas by taking his Tulsa team to Fayetteville in 1919 and stomping the Razorbacks, 63-7. Three years later, he had the U of A job. Arkansas did not play Tulsa again in the meantime.

He coached Arkansas to a 42-20-3 record in football and got the

Razorbacks away and winning in intercollegiate basketball competition, 83-18.

Schmidt showed opponents Fayetteville was a good place to avoid for reasons other than difficult travel. His football teams went 24-3-2 at home.

In the nine seasons between Bezdek and Schmidt, Arkansas football had sort of bumbled along under five different coaches. Two years proved maximum, even for such a personally popular coach as young George McLaren, Schmidt's immediate predecessor. McLaren had been a Pittsburgh All-American in 1917 under Pop Warner.

Gene (Sodie) Davidson, a multi-talented backfield star who lettered each season from 1915 through 1919, was the outstanding player of this transitional period. The 1920 school yearbook was dedicated to him as "Arkansas's greatest athlete." Temple Hardin, James Rudd, James Coleman, Chris Reichardt, and Ben Winkelman were other top Razorbacks of the seasons around and during World War I.

In 1917 Arkansas fielded the lightest team in its history, averaging 157 pounds per man. In 1918 the Razorbacks lost nearly the entire squad to military service after two games. A result was the school's most one-sided loss, 103-0 to Oklahoma. Rank-and-file students were asked to come out for football three days prior to the game so the schedule could be met.

The next year, Arkansas drew considerable satisfaction from a 7-6 victory over Oklahoma.

John C. Futrall became president of the university in 1913, starting a 26-year tenure that would end with his death in an automobile accident in 1939. His interest in athletics ran deeper than lip service. As a 21-year-old, first-year professor in 1894, he had coached the school's first team. He had been a firm faculty friend of Bezdek's efforts. As president he continually sought the right man to stabilize and build the athletic program. He thought the search ended with Schmidt.

When Schmidt agreed to switch to Arkansas, he brought from Tulsa Ivan H. Grove, who became Arkansas's first "regular" assistant coach. Predecessors in the role had been volunteers or part-timers.

Grove left in 1924 to head up athletics at Hendrix College, where he retired as a revered father figure in the 1950s. Incidentally, some old-time Hendrix people insisted that the small Methodist-sponsored school at Conway was directly responsible for Schmidt going to Arkansas. When Hendrix forced a 0-0 tie on Arkansas in 1921, the reasoning went, it prompted Arkansas to look for a coach who would not have to settle for a tie with Hendrix.

It is ironic, considering Schmidt's sarcastic comments on the mental

*Francis Schmidt convinced opponents that
Fayetteville was a good place to avoid in the 1920s.*

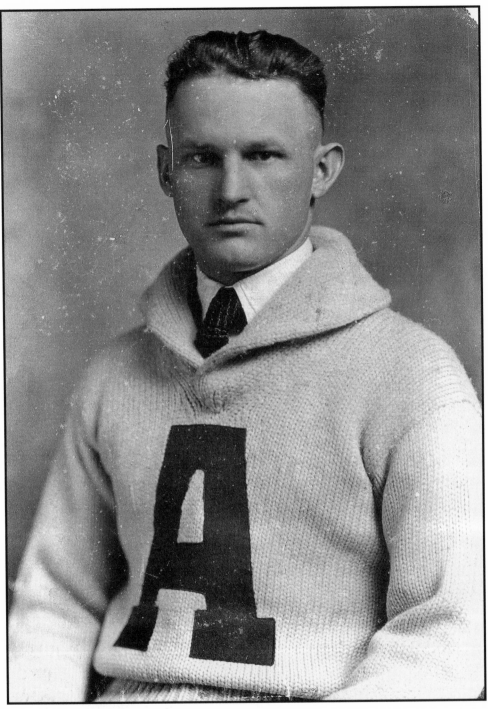

Gene (Sodie) Davidson, the brightest Razorback star of the World War I era, was saluted by the 1919 school yearbook as "Arkansas's greatest athlete."

capacity of his players, that his hitch at Arkansas started with one remarkable student-athlete, Bill Fulbright, and ended with another, Wear Schoonover.

Fulbright, later a Rhodes scholar, later U of A president, and still later one of the most widely praised, bitterly assailed thinkers ever to serve in the United States Senate, was a sophomore halfback in 1922. Arkansas played its first homecoming game that season, against Southern Methodist, and Fulbright turned it into a personal vehicle. He passed to Homer Berry for the game's only touchdown, played well on defense, and kicked a 32-yard field goal to sew up a 9-0 win.

Schoonover's brilliant senior year accrued to Fred Thomsen, Schmidt's successor, in 1929. A four-sport letterman from Pocahontas, Schoonover was so consistently good his final season that he became the Razorbacks' first football All-American. He played every minute of nine straight games at end. He had a record 96-yard pass interception return against Centenary; he caught 13 passes against Baylor; he saved a 14-13 victory over Texas A&M by blocking an extra point.

Schmidt's first three Arkansas football teams were modest winners (5-4, 6-2-1, 7-2-1) and a frame gymnasium, "Schmidt's Barn," went up in 1923 to house the infant basketball program. But the football Razorbacks slipped to 4-4-1 and 5-5 in 1925–26.

"I remember distinctly," Glen Rose said, "that when I enrolled in school, you'd walk around the campus and see where students had written 'Fire Schmidt' all over the sidewalks."

Schmidt was building toward a big finish. His 1927 Razorbacks (8-1) lost only to one of the great Dana X. Bible teams at Texas A&M. After a 7-2 season in 1928, Schmidt surprised and angered Arkansas followers by resigning to take a job at TCU.

"President Futrall stuck right by him and believed in him when he was under pressure," Rose said, "and I think it made Futrall a little mad when he left."

Schmidt found his winning Arkansas quarterback—his Creekmore —in the person of 5-7, 150-pound George Cole, a Bauxite boy. They met in the office of C. G. (Crip) Hall, a rabid U of A partisan who, later as secretary of state, would lend vital political assistance to the building of War Memorial Stadium in Little Rock.

Hall and another Razorback enthusiast, Boyd Cypert, had a line on Cole as a promising athlete, and they persuaded Schmidt to come and look him over. This was what recruiting amounted to at the time. The term "athletic scholarship" had not been invented.

"How much money can you get from home, son?" Schmidt asked.

Cole had already obtained a county judge's certificate which would cover his tuition. He estimated he could get $35 a month from home. Schmidt practically embraced him.

"Son, on that you can live like a king."

"When I got to Fayetteville," Cole said, "I found that room and board came to $32.50 a month. I made it all right and so did everybody else. We all worked at odd jobs."

In three seasons as a tailback in the short punt and single-wing formations, and as a passer, runner, punter, place kicker, and signal-caller, Cole scored 185 points: 22 touchdowns, 32 extra points, seven field goals. His one-season record of 85 points in 1927 lasted until 1965, Bobby Burnett's senior year. His career total was a school record until Bill Burnett's 1968–70 exploits.

Bill Fulbright kicks a field goal against SMU in 1922.

THE RAZORBACKS

"We had one solid team in 1927, but Coach Bible had three at A&M, and we played two of them," Cole said. "We were down just 13-6 at half-time, but they beat us bad in the fourth quarter." (Final: 40-6.)

"To start the second half I remember asking Eusell Coleman, our captain, who I should kick to. He told me to kick it to that little one down in the corner. That was Joel Hunt, and we hadn't tackled him yet. We didn't know him—you didn't scout much then, if at all—and he scored 128 points that year."

For their biggest wins, the 1927 Razorbacks upset LSU, 28-0, at Shreveport, and prevailed over a stubborn TCU team at Fort Worth, 10-3. Cole scored 21 points and passed for a touchdown against LSU. He kicked a field goal and threw a 35-yard touchdown pass to Rose to see Arkansas safely past TCU.

As quarterback, Cole bore the brunt of Schmidt's fury. George's ears burned for three years.

"He was one of the greatest of the passing coaches, but he believed in running first," Cole said. "He always wanted a big, strong fullback. We had Ox Smith first and Bevo Beavers next, and he'd say they could take care of the inside and we (tailbacks and wingbacks) could take care of the outside.

"He'd tell me, and I still think it's good strategy, if you find a play that makes four yards, try it again. We'd run the sweep until they stopped it. He'd say, 'When they stop it, find out if they stopped it to the inside or outside and then go where they came from. If the halfback stopped it, throw over him—he's up too close. When they stop a play, there's another that's bound to work.' You have to remember that was before game films, before press-box spotters, before systematic scouting, before in-and-out (message-carrying) subs."

As a sophomore in 1925, Cole kicked three field goals for a 9-7 home-coming win over Oklahoma A&M. The third field goal was a one-for-the-book stunner.

"Lloyd Dhonau, our holder, jumped up and pulled down a high snap and placed it where I could kick it," Cole said. "Most holders would have tried to run with the ball or pass it after a high snap. I couldn't prove it, but in my mind he didn't ever get back on his knees in placing the ball."

The winning kick, spotted barely in bounds, was variously reported as covering 42 to 47 yards. The visiting coach supposedly turned to the stands and screamed his frustration.

Wear Schoonover, the Razorbacks' first All-American football player (1929), also excelled in basketball and academics.

"Anybody might kick the ball 42 yards for a field goal," Cole said, "but not many could save the play the way Lloyd did."

In addition to Cole, Rose, Beavers, Fulbright, and Schoonover, Schmidt's most outstanding players in his seven years at Arkansas were end Harry Hansard (1922), end Clifford Blackburn (1924), halfback Herman Bagby (1925), tackle Gus Japp (1925), guard Brad Scott (1926), and guard Clyde Van Sickle (1928).

Schmidt had the services of two of the three Coleman brothers from Strong who captained U of A football teams. He missed James (1916–19), but Sam (1921–24) and Eusell (1925–27) were among his leaders.

After the TCU game of 1927, Fort Worth sportswriters accused Schmidt of all sorts of skullduggery, including changing uniform numbers.

"I wore 23," Cole said, "but the week before, it got torn up and I wore 22. We just had one set of uniforms. I was the smallest man out there, so I don't think they could have mistaken me.

"I was so short I couldn't see much over the line, but Glen was so tall I could always see him and he sure could catch it."

"You know Schmitty had to be a good coach," Rose said. "He built fine records everywhere he went—Tulsa, Arkansas, TCU. He had a good record at Ohio State, too, but they fired him. He got on a streak where he couldn't beat Michigan."

After Schmidt moved to TCU, Cole went to visit him at the TCU-SMU game at Fort Worth in 1930.

"He said they were so close on complimentary tickets he would have to slip me and Tom Spaulding in," George said. "Just before we reached the stadium, Coach Schmidt opened his trunk, and Tom and I rode in with the trunk locked."

Luckily Schmidt was not struck by one of his spells of absent-mindedness. He remembered to free his guests promptly.

— 08 —

POLITICS AND FOOTBALL

A University of Nebraska decision to change coaches triggered a chain reaction that resulted in the big break of Fred Thomsen's career.

Then a national power approximating its later successes under Bob Devaney and Tom Osborne, Nebraska hired Dana X. Bible away from Texas A&M. Under Bible, a courtly, pink-cheeked Tennessean, A&M had won five Southwest Conference championships in the period from 1917 to 1928.

To replace Bible, A&M reached for and got Madison (Matty) Bell of Texas Christian.

TCU reacted in kind. Wealthy Fort Worth publisher Amon Carter dangled his bankbook before Arkansas's Francis Schmidt, promising him a new stadium and other facilities impossible to obtain at Arkansas. Schmidt moved to TCU, completing the triple coaching switch in the winter of 1928–29.

The Arkansas job fell to Thomsen, Schmidt's assistant just two years out of a high school post at Gothenburg, Nebraska, where his teams had a two-year record of 18-1. Thomsen was to remain Arkansas head coach 13 years, a longevity record finally broken by Frank Broyles, and he was to become the first man to deny the Southwest title to Texas teams—twice, in fact.

Schmidt had also coached Razorback basketball, not only introducing the sport to the U of A, but also claiming four straight conference titles, hardly ever losing a league game. Basketball was not Thomsen's thing. He needed someone who could coach basketball and also serve as his line coach.

Bible and Bell knew this. They had just the man for Thomsen, a Texas A&M aide who did not fit into Bible's Nebraska plans and who was not going to be retained by Bell. The two of them pushed Thomsen to take the A&M assistant to Arkansas. His name was Charles Bassett, and while he did almost maintain Arkansas's dominant basketball program, he was not what Thomsen was looking for as a football helper.

"They built him up to me," Thomsen said years later, "and he didn't pan out as advertised."

He never let Matty Bell forget it.

"When Matty and I were together, I'd remind him of the favor I'd done for him, and what he'd done to me. It became kind of a laughing matter between us, the result of which he agreed he owed me a favor in return."

The favor Thomsen eventually collected turned out to be the cornerstone of the U of A football program, a full-fledged membership in the Southwest Conference.

Through the friendships he developed with Bell (who went from TCU to A&M to SMU), Rice's Jimmy Kitts, and others, Thomsen persuaded all six league opponents to grant Arkansas home-and-home dates. An agreement was reached in December of 1931, and Arkansas joined the full round robin in 1934.

"Schmidt had never been able to get games at Fayetteville," Thomsen said. "We didn't have any crowds, about 4,000 would be tops. The trip took three or four days. It had always been the goal of President Futrall to join the round-robin schedule, but we just hadn't been able to make any headway."

Arkansas became a charter member of the Southwest Conference in 1914. During Schmidt's seven years, 1922–28, he could schedule only 19 league games. Arkansas competed for the title, if at all, only because games with LSU, Centenary, and others were sometimes designated substitute conference games. The Razorbacks never played more than three or four real league games in a season.

The fact that visiting teams had great difficulty winning at Fayetteville did not help Schmidt's scheduling problems. Of the eight SWC games played there in his seven seasons, Arkansas lost two against five wins and a tie. On their 10 trips to Texas, they won just once. It was not until Broyles's coaching time that rapid air travel and night games in Texas finally eliminated disparities between playing in Fayetteville and at steamy Texas sites.

Thomsen and his predecessors existed largely on their fan and booster support from Fayetteville and Fort Smith and the northwest Arkansas area generally, almost the limit of their horizon.

"They were indispensable to me, especially the good people of Fort Smith," Thomsen said. "I never asked them for the money until I spent it. They'd raise it somehow."

Home crowds for the TCU and SMU games of the 1933 season were announced at 4,000 and 6,000. "I know better," Glen Rose said. "Those stands and bleachers wouldn't seat but 2,500."

Not until after John Barnhill came in 1946, and really not until Bowden Wyatt filled War Memorial Stadium with the Mississippi game of 1954 did the Razorbacks reach a receptive statewide audience. Thomsen and his business manager, Boyd Cypert, coveted this essential interest even though tedious transportation doomed their efforts.

The central fact of life for Thomsen in his 13 years at Arkansas was this: whether by train (the Frisco to Fort Smith, the Missouri Pacific down the river) or by unheated car over winding concrete and gravel, it took eight hours to get from Fayetteville to Little Rock. And Little Rock was where the job of recruiting, raising money, and currying favor began.

In Little Rock, Thomsen would drop in on Tom Spaulding, who ran a sporting goods store, or mosey through the lobby of the Hotel Marion. If Spaulding was heading out in the state that day, Thomsen would go with him, making the rounds of high school coaches. He would also hitch rides with political candidates.

To put together his 1933 team, Thomsen mortgaged his home and sank $2,500 into ALL, the Arkansas Loyalty League, precursor of the Razorback Club. ALL pins sold for $1.

To advance his program onto the next plateau, he got into politics.

"This helped us," Thomsen said, looking back from the vantage point of the 1960s. "We got our stadium in Fayetteville. But it made me enemies, and politics hurt me in the end."

He recalled hitching a ride with Cypert, who was leaving Little Rock that day to make a speech in his unsuccessful candidacy for attorney general.

"I walked into that hotel lobby with Boyd, and there was his opponent. Later on this man gained some influence. I don't think he ever forgave me."

Thomsen tied in with Carl E. Bailey, who served first as attorney general and then, 1937–41, two terms as governor. Under Bailey, Thomsen had the help of the state highway department in construction and the state police in recruiting. When the present Razorback Stadium opened in 1938, it was (temporarily) named Bailey Stadium.

Thomsen said the basic 12,500-seat structure was built for $68,000 in university funds. Federal money did the rest. The highway department sold shovels to the school for which it was receiving $100 per shovel in WPA funds. The school sold the shovels back to the highway department for $3,500 at the completion of the job.

Razorback Stadium was so soundly engineered that it could be expanded repeatedly after World War II to its 1985-expansion capacity of just beyond 50,000.

"I had to hook up with Bailey," Thomsen said, "and then came Homer Adkins (who defeated Bailey in a bitter race for governor in 1940) and everybody got fired—the school president (future U.S. senator J. William Fulbright) and three deans. Adkins nipped at me but I had a contract and the American Legion saved me once."

Thomsen got his first three-year contract after the championship season of 1936.

"President Futrall called me in and said I hadn't needed a contract until now, but that I'd better have some protection. He could see it coming."

Thomsen had an eager ally in Boyd Cypert. A baseball and football player under Hugo Bezdek, Cypert entered the practice of law at Little Rock where his reputation for baseball heroics helped make him a popular figure. Along with C. G. (Crip) Hall, longtime secretary of state, and a few others, Cypert labored as a Razorback booster and recruiter. He sought to promote U of A football games in Little Rock, where the Hogs had played intermittently since the time of Bezdek. When Cypert lost a race for attorney general, a friend helped him become the U of A's business manager of athletics.

So Thomsen and Cypert scrounged for funds and players and, for a time, almost made it work.

— 09 —

SAY IT AIN'T SO, HEINIE

Rummaging through an old trunk in his home at Springfield, Missouri, years ago, Fred Thomsen ran across a stack of 3 x 5 cards that brought back memories.

"The cards showed money I put out and never got back," he said. He counted it well spent. Much of it went for the assembling and maintenance of the 1933 Razorbacks, the first and least celebrated Arkansas squad to dominate the Southwest Conference standings.

"We had a fine ball club in 1929 (7-2), my first year as head coach," Thomsen said. "But the 1930 and 1931 teams were too thin and too small to compete in the new round-robin schedule that was coming up.

"We did a fairly good job of recruiting for our 1932 freshman squad. We set up the first athletic dormitory in old Hill Hall, and that summer I went to practically all the canning factories in northwest Arkansas and bought canned food of all description for our supplies.

"Every athlete was compelled to find some kind of work to defray his expenses. Scholarships didn't exist. We got room and board down to approximately $17 a month. Some of the athletes lived and got wages in the Fayetteville Fire Department. Two or three, I think Taft Moody and Milan Creighton were included, slept in rooms at some of Bill Sonneman's theaters. Bill always gave some of the boys jobs, $6 a week.

"After the 1932 season and the following spring practice, I could see we were going to have a fairly good team, but one that a few gaps had to be filled to make it a really solid squad. I got in my car and started driving.

"I went to Monticello JC (Arkansas A&M and later UA-Monticello) and got Bill Spivey, John Measel, and Doug Locke. Locke didn't stay—not enough credits. From Russellville JC (Arkansas Tech) I got Oliver

Criswell, Mickey Spencer, and Curtis Henderson. There were several from out of state, too. I got Ulysses Schleuter from Kemper Military Academy at Lexington, Missouri."

Spivey, Measel, and Criswell proved to be outstanding additions. Schleuter's presence cost Arkansas the official Southwest Conference championship.

These were the 1933 stalwarts:

Ends . . . . Paul Rucker, Howard (Muddy) Lake and much-injured captain Lewis (Red) Johnson, backed by two sophomores who were to be great, Jim Lee Howell and Ike Poole.

Tackles . . . . W. R. (Footsie) Benton and Jack Haden, with help from John Measel, who also played guard.

Guards . . . . Bill Spivey, Measel, and Charles Black, with help from Gus Eidson, 29-year-old Emil (Dutch) Beopple, and Earl Fulton.

Center . . . . Jack Newby, rated by Thomsen as second only to TCU's Ki Aldrich at his position in the SWC during the 1930s, and Mark Sherland. Newby died of pneumonia after the 1934 season, his junior year.

Backs . . . . Tom Murphy, Clark Jordan, and Al Harris at quarterback. Murphy was a gifted all-purpose athlete, a star in basketball, and the SWC's most valuable football player of 1933. Criswell and Joe Biddle were the fullbacks. Choice Rucker and George Jordan split time at one halfback spot, with Elvin Geiser and game-wrecker Ralph LaForge at the other.

"Murphy was like a coach," Thomsen said. "He hated a loser and he got 'em told if they weren't getting the job done. LaForge had that speed and running ability at tailback. When he was in there, they had to spread out and open up the inside game for us. Choice Rucker was the best 170-pound blocking back I ever had. Jack Dale (1929) was probably better down the field, but Choice, who had speed, came through in 1933 at the position that worried me the most.

"Without Spivey and Measel we could not have won. Spivey was probably the finest offensive guard we had in my time, and I can still see him in the LSU game. He came out on the off-tackle play and hit Gus Tinsley, their All-American, and they carried Gus off the field. Measel

Tom Murphy did everything right for the unrecognized champions of 1933.

played both guard and tackle. When he was the inside tackle, we pulled him to lead weak-side plays. A terrific blocker.

"Benton and Haden played 90 percent of it at the tackles, both outstanding. Newby had that extra sense on defense, and we got great leadership from Johnson, even though he didn't play much."

The 1933 Razorbacks tuned up with 40-0 and 42-7 wins over College of the Ozarks and Oklahoma Baptist. Francis Schmidt scouted the Oklahoma Baptist game at Fayetteville and saw LaForge return a kickoff all the way. "He'll never do that against a good team," Schmidt told Arkansas publicist Walt Lemke, sitting next to him.

The next week, also at Fayetteville, Schmidt was on the field with his TCU players, pointing to Murphy lined up in deep position with LaForge. When Schmidt turned his back and hastened to the bench, Murphy and LaForge swapped places. The skittery LaForge raced 95 yards into the end zone.

Early in the third quarter the Hogs came out of a huddle on the TCU 40, and six linemen positioned themselves to the right of center. The backs lined up to the left. LaForge caught the Horned Frogs overshifted and confused and dashed 40 yards for another touchdown and a 13-0 win.

Schmidt had accepted an invitation for dinner at the home of Mrs. Roberta Fulbright, a newspaper publisher and a friend from his Arkansas days. Instead, he disappeared into the visitors' dressing room, packed all the TCU luggage himself, went with it to the station, and sat on it until the train came.

Murphy's kicking was a decisive factor in Arkansas's 19-7 win over Baylor; he pulled the Hogs from a deep hole with a 69-yarder out of bounds. LSU deflated Arkansas at Shreveport, 20-0. But the SMU game, back at Fayetteville, proved the key to the whole season. It was a 3-0 epic.

That afternoon Murphy twice pulled down SMU runners from behind in the open field. The Mustangs were equally tenacious. They forced Arkansas to waste a couple of touchdown opportunities.

The Razorbacks threatened on a 37-yard pass interception return by LaForge to the SMU 41. Murphy shot a 24-yard pass to LaForge on the 17, but a 15-yard penalty turned Arkansas back.

An interception by Newby put the Razorbacks in business at the SMU 47. Murphy aimed a quick pass at end Paul Rucker, but it was batted away and Choice Rucker caught it before it hit the ground at the 25. Two plunges by Murphy brought a first down, and then Tom faked a pass and went around end for an apparent score. The officials ruled he had stepped out of bounds on the one. SMU held and fought back.

George Jordan set up the last-period field goal on a 60-yard sprint off tackle to the Mustangs' 11. With Murphy holding, Geiser delivered the three points.

"It was a terrible day on the old field up on the hill," Thomsen said. "The wind was blowing from the west at about 50 miles an hour. Well, it felt like 50 miles an hour. Sitting on that bench we were in perfect line with the uprights. It was that bad an angle. The ball went through the east uprights by about three inches. When the ball hit the ground, it was way over in the corner of the field. Two or three of the SMU players gave the referee a big rush. A lot of confusion, but I've never doubted the kick was good."

The Razorbacks lost a blah game to Rice, 7-6, and then won their final meeting with Hendrix, 63-0. The way was clear for the conference closer with Texas in Austin, and winning there would put Arkansas on top with a 4-1 record.

Texas was nothing special that year (4-5-2), but the Longhorns had never lost to Arkansas in 14 meetings. It looked like the same old story when Texas went quickly ahead, 6-0.

Criswell slammed in with the first Arkansas touchdown, and LaForge kicked the extra point, 7-6. In spite of a hobbling injury, Murphy kept Texas at bay with tremendous kicking until the Longhorns cracked deep in their territory.

Arkansas covered a fumble on the Texas 35, and on the next play Murphy threw to Muddy Lake for a touchdown. LaForge converted for 14-6, and the clincher followed immediately.

Paul Rucker put a tough rush on the Texas passer, and LaForge intercepted and ran it back 45 yards for a touchdown that made it 20-6. It ended that way.

"That one game meant so much to Arkansas," Thomsen said. "When our train pulled into the Frisco station at 'Shulertown' on Sunday night (the game had been on Friday afternoon), the whole town turned out along with the fire department. The band played, and President Futrall got up on the baggage trucks and made a great speech."

But trouble was already in the air.

The Arkansas-Texas game was played on November 24. The Schleuter story had broken on Sunday, November 19, out of Dallas. Rumors about Schleuter had spread over the SMU campus, Thomsen was informed. Dr. J. S. McIntosh, the SMU faculty representative, made public a telegram to Julian S. Waterman, founder and dean of the U of A Law School and the Arkansas faculty representative, apprising Waterman of SMU's suspicions.

Ulysses S. Schleuter, sometimes mistakenly listed as Ulysses H. Schleuter, called Heinie or Dutch by teammates and friends, had neglected to inform U of A officials that he had captained the Nebraska freshman team in 1931 and played regularly on the Nebraska varsity in 1932.

An SMU player who had opposed Schleuter in the Nebraska-SMU game of 1932 recognized him from a photo, and that was the beginning of it. Once it started, the facts were easy enough to sift out. Schleuter took all the blame and fled to his parents' home in Fremont, Nebraska.

When the news broke, everything added up for the other Arkansas players. The day they posed for a team picture, Dutch showed up with a piece of tape over his mouth. He had an ankle injury off and on, but when somebody would rile him in practice he'd take the place apart. It was like he was playing hard enough to save his place on the squad, but not hard enough to make the first team. He ducked away from any publicity. He did not show up for the SMU game, giving some excuse about an ill aunt.

"But trying to hide the Dutchman," said teammate Al Harris, "was like trying to cover the Eiffel Tower with a butterfly net. You couldn't miss him—a big blond guy with all the tools."

According to Harris, when Glen Rose, the line coach, heard the truth about Schleuter, he said, "Hell, I should have known a junior college athlete couldn't be that good."

Schleuter had played only about seven minutes all fall, consisting of a few downs in the TCU, Baylor, and Rice games. "That's all," said Rose, who handled the subbing for linemen. "You could see he had a lot of ability, but we thought he was having trouble adjusting to our system."

TCU coach Francis Schmidt, Thomsen's former boss at Arkansas, called for forfeiture of the three games in which Dutch played. That would have given TCU and Baylor 5-1 SWC records and a cochampionship, a fact that did not elude Arkansas students and fans. Their resentment soon focused on Schmidt, not Schleuter.

Schmidt was quoted as saying there seemed to be a "New Deal" at Arkansas (thanks to Franklin D. Roosevelt, New Deal was a hot term in 1933) and of course those games should be forfeited. The response from Arkansas was furious, and a few days later Schmidt wrote a letter to Crip Hall. He said his remarks had received "the worst possible interpretation" from "a sensation-seeking reporter" and he had not meant to imply the school administration had any knowledge of the player's ineligibility.

Schleuter sent the following telegram to the Associated Press in Dallas:

I mentioned nothing about Nebraska to officials of the University of Arkansas. I wanted an education, but I had no money. I knew I had football ability. It just didn't pan out as I had hoped.

Many years later Schleuter expanded his explanation in an interview.

"You see, I went five years to Kemper—a great school, by the way. I went through high school there and two years of junior college. We played teams at every level, even senior colleges. Then I enrolled at Nebraska. Players in my situation had been allowed three seasons. I played a freshman season, then a varsity season. The Big Six Conference checked me out and said I had no more eligibility. D. X. Bible called me in and put it this way: 'Heinie, you're finished.'

"So I got in touch with Kemper and had them transfer my credits to Arkansas. I did all the covering up that was done."

The Schleuter case was the number-one item on the Southwest Conference business meeting scheduled for December 10, 1933. TCU faculty representative E. W. McDiarmid, vice-president of the conference, said he fully expected forfeiture of all three games in which Heinie appeared.

Thomsen asked permission to plead Arkansas's case before the conference fathers, seven faculty men. His contention was that the mistake had been an honest one on the school's part and that Arkansas had won its games on merit, without appreciable help from the ineligible player.

Arkansas declined to let its coach appear before the group. The reasons were well understood by Thomsen. Arkansas had just gained the full round-robin schedule, to be implemented the following season. Rather than jeopardize this long-sought goal, Arkansas would rather make a routine plea and take its chances.

In every decade until the 1960s, there always existed some sentiment for dismissing unhandy, unappealing Arkansas from what had otherwise become an all-Texas league. This feeling dictated a passive role by the U of A in SWC politics.

The conference took a middle ground in 1933. No games would be forfeited. Arkansas's 4-1 record would continue to lead the standings.

But no championship would be awarded.

A clause in the league by-laws permitted the latter action. To soften the immediate impact of the ruling, the league gave Arkansas permission to play a January 1, 1934, game against Centenary, which had badly beaten three SWC schools. This was Joe Utay's Dixie Classic, previously a college all-star game but now becoming the forerunner of the Cotton Bowl. It was the Razorbacks' first post-season appearance, and it settled nothing. Arkansas and Centenary tied, 7-7, in the Texas State Fair stadium at Dallas.

Later rules required accounting for every year's lapse on a transcript. The SWC put this in after the Schleuter case, but the U of A faculty people were partly at fault for carelessness and so was Thomsen.

"I was in the room with Schleuter for an hour on the day he left," said Harris. "He was working on a pint of moonshine in the window and he unburdened to me. His family had had a hard time of it in the 1920s. Until 1917 they had made a good living selling mules to Kaiser Wilhelm's German Army."

Schleuter returned in honor 37 years later to a reunion and reception in conjunction with the Arkansas-Stanford game in Little Rock on September 12, 1970. He laughed when someone asked about the pint of booze.

"It must have been applejack," he said. "That's all we could get up there in those days.

"These guys are great. They're my friends. They tell me I'm one of them, and I feel like I am."

"Oh, we were a loose bunch," Harris said. "Somebody called us, 'plumb nonchalant.'

"Spivey and Papa John Measel were in the gym one afternoon when Tommy [Thomsen] came in. They decided they'd flip him—the coach! —on the wrestling mat. Tommy flipped them so quick they didn't have time to figure out what happened. Tommy hated to lose.

"Tommy and Glen complemented each other. Tommy coached the backs. He'd talk up a storm. He doted on offense. Glen coached the line, and he doted on defense. He could go through an entire practice without saying more than 'let's go.'

"Paul Rucker popped a blister on his heel in the Texas game. He walked through the hotel lobby barefooted and told a lady it was a hill-billy custom to go barefooted when you win and he'd been barefooted most of the season.

"When you had guys like Footsie Benton and the Jordan twins and Red Johnson together in a room, even a southerner would need an interpreter.

"Until his knees went out, Johnson was quite an athlete. The ol' Prescott Curly Wolf. He could play anything, and he could convince us that the other team didn't have a chance. On the way to Austin he kept telling us what was going to happen to those Longhorns and all the good things that would happen to us after we won. He said Tommy was going to buy us all gold footballs with diamonds in them as big as horse droppings."

The Rootin' Rubes, then the student booster organization, commissioned a bronze football engraved simply "1933" a few days after the conference denied the official title to the Hogs. The trophy was mounted on a concrete slab outside the upper end of Razorback Stadium and seemed fated to be the only memento to the uncrowned champions.

But in 1994, with the Southwest Conference at the verge of extinction, revisionist historians surfaced. They included Arkansas athletic director Frank Broyles.

"The 1933 team didn't forfeit any games," Broyles said. "It led the standings. It was permitted to play in a bowl game. It won the championship. We should claim it."

Consider it claimed.

– 10 –

THE PASSINGEST TEAM
IN THE NATION

When Walt Lemke, the U of A's journalism professor and first publicity director, reported for duty on January 1, 1928, Francis Schmidt hardly cared. The less publicity about his team the better, believed this pre-occupied, eccentric genius.

A year later Lemke found a taker in Fred Thomsen, the freshly installed head coach.

"Make any statement you want," Thomsen told Lemke, "and I'll back you up."

With student aides Ernie Deane and Johnny Erp, Lemke was off and running. He laid the groundwork for the naming of the school's first All-American (also one of the Southwest Conference's first), end Wear Schoonover, in 1929.

By 1936 Thomsen had given Lemke something juicier to promote. The Hogs were putting the ball in the air 300 times. They were the Passing Porkers, the passingest team in the nation. Lemke spread the word. Win, lose, or tie, the hurling Hogs were guaranteed never to be dull.

First you must appreciate what the Southwest Conference was like in the 1930s. Offense ruled. The coaching staffs spent most of their time fashioning trick plays, which, before the era of all-revealing game films, could be executed successfully over a long period of time.

Passing had been popularized by the SMU teams of Ray Morrison in the mid-1920s. The terms razzle-dazzle and aerial circus came into wide use.

The Southwest Conference seldom knew a gaudier time than that from 1934 to 1939. It began one October day in 1934 when Texas toppled Notre Dame and Rice felled Purdue. That stunned the smug, mighty

Midwest. TCU, coached by Leo R. (Dutch) Meyer, and SMU, coached by Matty Bell, took 11-0 records into their season-ending showdown in 1935. SMU won the game—and some national championship citations—on a famous Bobby Wilson pass and went on to lose to Stanford in the Rose Bowl, 7-0.

The 1935 TCU team rode the arm of Sammy Baugh to the Sugar Bowl, and TCU made another New Orleans trip following the 1938 season, in which 145-pounder Davey O'Brien passed and ran the Frogs to a national championship, the league's second in four years. Texas A&M came along with John Kimbrough and a perfect season and another national title for the SWC in 1939.

Jim Benton, Thomsen's All-American end from Fordyce, said in 1994: "There's no question in my mind the Southwest Conference was at least equal to any other league in the country from 1934, the year I enrolled, certainly through 1937—I can personally vouch for that much—and probably right on to the outbreak of World War II. It was a rough proposition every week."

Fred Thomsen at work in his office, surely drawing pass patterns.

So the people Tommy Thomsen was asked to beat had not (as Darrell Royal might have phrased it) "come to town on a load of wood."

And even in the pass-happy Southwest, they said Thomsen drew the prettiest patterns.

He had one passer, Jack Robbins, wristy, for a dry day, and another, Dwight (Paddlefoot) Sloan, who had a sure touch on a wet ball, for rainy games. The Razorbacks had ample targets at ends in Benton and Ray Hamilton, and Thomsen also liked to throw to his backs the way pros do nowadays.

Thomsen used short punt and single-wing formations, as did most teams in those days. A tailback like Robbins was always in position to run, pass, or kick. And Robbins was a superb athlete, perhaps the most under-rated back who ever played at Arkansas. Thomsen ran the standard spinners, reverses and power plays, but he stayed up nights diagramming passes.

"Francis Schmidt used to keep a pencil under his pillow," Glen Rose said, "so if he thought of a play in the middle of the night he could get up and write it down. Tommy was the same way, except he'd say, 'Let's try something I dreamed about last night.'"

The passers and receivers came off Rose's basketball teams; he had only two basketball players who were not also involved in football, and he usually won the conference basketball title.

"I never thought we were going to win any (football) championship in 1936," said Rose, who coached the line. "Looking back, I believe we had a stronger team in 1933, when we won it and they didn't give it to us.

"To tell the truth I could never tell what kind of a team we'd have or what we'd do because Tommy used so many passes. We couldn't break a plate of glass with our running. I don't know why, because we had running plays. I guess we just didn't practice them or use them enough. Tommy doted on passing, and he was way ahead of his time, even ahead of the pros. If he sent a play into the game, you could bet it was a pass.

"Many a game we'd get ahead with our passing and then lose because we couldn't control the ball. You'd be afraid to pass, and you couldn't run. We'd need two or three first downs to kill the clock, and we couldn't make them. Rice beat us that way [1937, 26-20], and so did A&M [1938, 13-7], and so did Texas [1939, 14-13]."

By Thomsen's own recollection he lost 14 games in the final two minutes.

But in 1936 most of these disappointments were still ahead. Thomsen secured Arkansas's first official Southwest Conference title

The 1936 Porkers didn't always pass, as Dwight Sloan proves with this field-goal attempt.

with these key men: Robbins or Sloan at tailback (quarterback, in effect); Ralph Rawlings and Allen Keen at halfbacks; Vann Brown, Marion Fletcher, and Lloyd Montgomery for good depth at fullback; Benton and Hamilton, backed mostly by Billy Hunter, at the ends; Ken Lunday or Lloyd Woodell at center; Percy Sanders and B. A. Owens at guard; Ed Lalman and Cliff Van Sickle at tackle.

Robbins, 6-2, and Benton, 6-4, two gifted, intelligent, nonchalant naturals, had established themselves as a formidable passing combination as sophomores in 1935.

Still, few considered the Razorbacks a serious contender in 1936, especially after they lost their league opener, 18-14, to TCU. Robbins outpassed Sammy Baugh that day, but Baugh's pin-point punting and the inside running of a fullback called Donkey Roberts carried the day for the Frogs.

The Hogs' chances looked even slimmer as they trailed Baylor late in the game, 10-0. Three days before the game Robbins hurt one of his knees in the "classroom." Glen Rose taught the class, "Theory of Basketball," and his basketball players, including several who doubled

A gifted competitor, Jack Robbins ran almost as well as he passed.

as football players, usually demonstrated the theories, sometimes for the full hour at full speed. Since Rose also coached football and served as the football trainer, he found himself in Thomsen's doghouse the rest of the year.

Robbins's mishap, however, became a break for Paddlefoot Sloan, who stepped in to save the Baylor game. He hit Ray Hamilton on four short passes, then pitched out to Keen, who went 55 yards for a touchdown. The winning touchdown, 14-10, came on Sloan's 25-yard pass to Benton.

Thereafter, in the 1936–37 seasons, Thomsen alternated Sloan and Robbins and also used them together, throwing to each other.

"Jack gripped the ball," said Hamilton. "Sloan had small hands and palmed it and could throw on a wet day. Jack was better on short passes, Sloan on long ones. Jack was the better runner."

Benton caught 35 passes in 1936. In 1937, his All-American season, he caught 48 for 814 yards, while Hamilton was catching 29. Even Texans acknowledged they were the best pair of all-purpose ends in the league and maybe in the country. The rangy, rugged Hamilton, Glen Rose said, was a burning competitor who "thrived on physical contact."

Benton's 48 catches in 1937 remained the SWC record until Lawrence Elkins of Baylor grabbed 70 in 1963. Benton held the U of A record until Mike Reppond caught 56 in 1971.

LSU tried hard to recruit Benton out of Fordyce. He said he probably would have enrolled at Arkansas even if his brother, W. R. (Footsie) Benton, hadn't preceded him there. "Playing for Arkansas seemed like the natural thing," he said. "It was what I wanted to do."

From Fordyce through an outstanding career in the NFL, nobody kept Jim from catching the ball.

The 1936 Razorbacks suffered mid-season losses to George Washington University and LSU and stood only 2-3 going into the stretch run of the season. They gained new life by surprising previously unbeaten Texas A&M, 18-0, at College Station. They added momentum by downing Rice, 20-14, on homecoming. They shut out SMU at Dallas, 17-0, and whipped Tulsa, 23-13, in their Thanksgiving Day grudge match.

TCU had lost early to A&M and was tied by SMU, 0-0, the Saturday after Thanksgiving. The Frogs stood 4-1-1, and Arkansas took a 4-1 league record into a December 5 game with Texas at Little Rock, arranged in the then-new high school stadium as part of the state's centennial celebration. Texas, 2-6-1, didn't look scary. Arkansans smelled a championship.

Rain fell all day. The new sod had not been set, and the teams slogged it out in a quagmire. There had been much pre-game excitement about tickets, and they might have pulled 8,000 to 10,000 people in good weather. Nobody knows exactly how many spectators sat through it. Some say 6,000. It may have been as few as 3,000.

The teams traded fumbles, and Texas dominated the statistics, but Arkansas scored the only touchdown and won, 6-0. Late in the third quarter Hamilton and Sanders covered a fumble just inside the Texas 20. From the 13 Sloan pitched to Benton for the touchdown.

"The play call was 'Benton over center,'" Benton said. "That's the way Tommy Thomsen's terminology was set up. If it had been another player, it would have been his name over center. The pattern was to cut across the middle. If the linebackers played deep, you caught the ball in front of them. If they played close, which they did on this play, you went between them.

"I got through the crease, and Paddlefoot drilled the ball perfectly. I got doubled—hit on both sides—as I caught the ball. The safety and somebody else cracked me, and one of them tried to take the ball from me, but I pulled it back and put it away before I hit the ground."

Hamilton considers the Texas game the best he played defensively.

"It was fun, especially after we scored. You'd just scoot along in that mud."

How did they celebrate the championship?

"I don't know what some of them did," said Hamilton, "but on Monday morning about half of us reported to the Black Hawk for basketball. That's what we called Glen. He wore a black suit and a black hat."

Arkansas's per-game passing average in 1936, when half the games were played in rain and mud, was 12 of 28 for 143 yards. That dazzled spectators accustomed to three plunges and a punt.

— 11 —

ON THE ROAD

In common usage today, an intersectional game is any that is not against a conference opponent. Originally an intersectional game meant exactly that—a match-up with a foe out of your territory, North vs. South, East vs. West.

Until Fred Thomsen took over at Arkansas, the school's only true intersectional games were Hugo Bezdek's disastrous trip to Madison, Wisconsin, in 1912 (a 64-7 humiliation) and Francis Schmidt's ill-advised venture into Iowa in 1925 (a 26-0 loss).

Thomsen scheduled coast to coast: George Washington University, Fordham, Villanova, Santa Clara, and Detroit. The Razorbacks would leave home by train Tuesday or Wednesday and certainly no later than early Thursday morning.

George Cole scouted opponents for Thomsen, as he later would for John Barnhill, Otis Douglas, Bowden Wyatt, and Jack Mitchell. In 1938 Thomsen dispatched Cole to check out Santa Clara in a game at Phoenix, Arizona. "You can go any way you want to," Thomsen said. "Just be back here by Sunday afternoon."

"I had never been in an airplane, but I didn't have much choice," Cole said. "The game was being played on a Saturday night. I rode the train out there and then, after the game, I went out to the airport. First thing I knew I had a picture of Mim [his wife] and the family out, sub-consciously taking a last look, I guess. I got on the plane, one of those Ford trimotors, and it was a sleeper. I didn't know anything like that existed.

"They had my berth ready, and I had all the newspapers I could find to read, but there was a big commotion. Some big-shot woman was raising all kinds of the devil. She said she couldn't sleep on an upper berth. I didn't expect to sleep at all, so to keep the peace, I offered to switch. So we did, and I read and read and read and I must have dozed off because I woke up smelling gasoline. I peeped around and nobody else seemed excited. I drew the curtains and looked out and we were gassing up in El Paso.

"I switched planes in Dallas and got off in Tulsa, where I had left my car. I got to the office about 3 P.M., just in time to give my scouting report.

"For the Santa Clara game," Cole said, "We had a special train that left Fayetteville for San Francisco on Tuesday morning. Players, coaches, fans, and school people lived on that train about four days. We'd stop awhile and practice and then ride until time to practice the next day. A seven-day picnic, coming and going. People had a big time and they talked about the Santa Clara trip (a 21-6 loss) for years."

Cliff Van Sickle had an unusual experience in the George Washington game of 1936. Van Sickle's blocking assignment was a big lineman who kept staring at him and finally asked his name.

"Oh, yeah, I remember you," the GWU player said. "I played against you when you were with Green Bay."

"He was a former pro, back in college getting his law degree," Van Sickle said. "I don't know how he arranged it, but there he was, a pro in a college game and he thought I was pulling the same trick. He had me confused with my brother."

Clyde Van Sickle, Cliff's older brother, had played four years for the Green Bay Packers after leaving Arkansas. Clyde, incidentally, was one of the last college players to go at it without a helmet. Lining up for his first pro game, he disdainfully tossed his helmet to the sideline.

"You're gonna need that," somebody yelled.

"Never have," Clyde shrugged. Then the legendary Bronko Nagurski hit him.

"You know," Clyde always said in retelling the story, "I ran and caught that helmet before it quit rolling. And if it had been possible, I woulda wore two of 'em."

— 12 —

SUNBEAM SPEAKS UP

If Fred Thomsen had left Arkansas after the 1936 season, his place of honor in fans' memories would have been as secure as Bezdek's. Instead he left in 1942—just a step ahead of the posse, one might say.

Thomsen did not lack for job opportunities in the mid-1930s. Syracuse made him a good offer. At one point he was set to go to Tulsa for nearly double his Arkansas salary, but he permitted a fervent booster, Bill Sonneman, to talk him out of it.

"I was getting a haircut and Bill barged in and literally climbed all over me," Thomsen said. "I was defenseless. He had been such a great supporter, I couldn't turn him down."

Sonneman came on that way. A businessman of substance, he owned the Fayetteville movie theaters much of his life and billed himself "the original No. 1 booster," a claim nobody disputed.

Things started to turn sour for Thomsen in 1937. Arkansas played as a pre-season Southwest Conference favorite for the first time and kicked away a chance to become the first team to win consecutive SWC titles. (That distinction was left to Homer Norton's Texas Aggies of 1939-40-41.)

The 1937 Razorbacks lost to Baylor in the last minute, 20-14, and to Rice in the last minute, 26-20. Rice won the championship with 4-1-1; Arkansas landed third with 3-2-1.

"We were just unlucky," Jim Benton said. "Dwight Sloan got blocked into a punt that was rolling around, and Baylor recovered and scored.

"We were leading Rice, 20-19, and had the ball on our 40—first down, I think. I can still hear Jack Robbins saying in the huddle, 'We've got it won—don't fumble.' And we fumbled.

Sunbeam and Fred Thomsen

"Rice still had a fourth-and-10 situation on our 20. We knew what they were going to call. It would be a flat and up (pass) to Ollie Cordill from Ernie Lain. And Robbins had Cordill covered all the way; covered perfectly in the end zone. But Cordill was 6'3" and Robbins was tired. Cordill outjumped him for the ball.

"Jack always blamed himself for losing that game. I don't think he ever really got over it. And it wasn't his fault. He did everything he could, and Cordill just outjumped him and made a great catch on a high pass.

"That pass grazed my middle finger. I felt it. I didn't deflect it in any way, but I touched it. If my middle finger had been an inch longer, we could have won the championship. We might as well put the blame on that. It's all over and done with."

After that, Thomsen's Razorbacks went down, down, down.

Take the homecoming game against Rice at Fayetteville on November 5, 1938, scoreless into the last minute. Rice lined up for a field-goal try with Jake Schuehle kicking from the 27.

Ralph Atwood, Dwight Sloan, Jack Robbins, and Lloyd Montgomery, left to right, *drink up after a 1937 workout.*

His try went wide, but a Rice substitute had appeared on the field, and referee Alvin Bell of Little Rock had blown his whistle. They lined up for Schuehle to try again. This time the pass from center was fumbled. Schuehle picked it up and was chased backward 20 yards before lobbing an impromptu incomplete pass. Arkansas players argued Schuehle had intentionally grounded the ball, but the incompletion ruling stood. Schuehle kicked again, and this time hit it for a 3-0 Rice win.

The game ended a few seconds later. Bell, a top official in the Southwest and Southeastern conferences for years, was furiously booed. He made the mistake of stopping and replying to his critics and was instantly surrounded. Thomsen intervened, calling some of his players to escort Bell to safety. Combined efforts of the players, the school's ROTC unit, and some policemen finally got the referee off the field without harm.

"Actually," Glen Rose said 35 years afterward, "Bell was right under the rules. But the fans didn't like it. Some guy called him an SOB and he started up in the stands. Boy, if they hadn't had a lot of police, there would have been trouble—bad trouble. After that we could never use him. Yet he worked all the bowl games out of the Southeastern Conference—really a great official."

Triple-threater Kay Eakin gave Thomsen his last hopes. No one knows how good Eakin might have been, for by 1939 the Razorbacks could offer him little protection. He took his poundings and carried on.

The 1939 Hogs beat defending national champion TCU, 14-13, but a mid-year loss to Texas knocked Arkansas out of the race. The 1939 Arkansas-Texas game at Austin turned into another of Thomsen's snakebit classics.

Arkansas led the Steers, 13-7, with 30-odd seconds to play, before Jack Crain caught a flat pass and ran 60 yards to save it for Texas, 14-13. Dana X. Bible, who had switched to Texas from Nebraska in 1937, always counted that as the play and the game that turned around the football fortunes of Texas, which had been down through much of the 1930s.

The Razorbacks won one conference game in 1940 and none in 1941. Thomsen entered the army as a captain after the Japanese attack on Pearl Harbor. He was assigned immediately to China.

As the U of A program floundered, Little Rock sportswriters voiced fan yearnings for a "name" coach to head a postwar renaissance. Sunbeam Thomsen, the coach's wife, hit the ceiling.

Tommy was six months away by letter, and Sunbeam was working in Fayetteville. She allowed herself to be quoted in the *Northwest Arkansas*

Times to the effect that Arkansas already had a "name" coach and he had a year left on his contract.

Ben Epstein, then sports editor of the *Arkansas Gazette,* had once been close to Thomsen. They drifted apart in Tommy's later years at Arkansas, but Epstein admired Sunbeam's spunk in taking up for her husband. He urged her on.

The senate of the Arkansas legislature subpoenaed the coach's wife for a hearing. She testified. A bill was drawn up to pay Mrs. Thomsen the difference between the coach's salary and a captain's salary for the remaining year of his U of A contract. Both houses of the general assembly passed it, and Governor Homer Adkins (an old political enemy of Thomsen's) signed it. The next day the state treasurer handed Mrs. Thomsen her check. It was for $1,500.

"Not until the matter was over did Tommy know anything about it," Sunbeam Thomsen explained years afterward. "Perhaps I was too sentimental in my indignation when I heard the Board of Trustees might be

All-American Jim Benton caught 48 passes for the 1937 Hogs. He made this catch for the 1946 Los Angeles Rams.

proposing to replace him when he was in a foreign country, fighting in a war, and unable to defend himself. I acted impulsively. I was half-scared to tell him."

The lingering bitterness of 1937–41 kept Thomsen in limbo with Arkansas followers for more than 20 years. After leaving the service, he settled into private business at Springfield, Missouri. When enough time had passed, his achievements were re-examined and appreciated by many of his old Arkansas detractors.

His outstanding contribution is that he fought for, and achieved, the full SWC round-robin schedule, without which the U of A program could never have grown in the direction it took under Thomsen's post-war successors. And he helped hustle up the means of building Razorback Stadium.

He coached the school's first Southwest Conference champions in 1933 and 1936 and the school's first All-Americans, Wear Schoonover and

Arkansas ends Ray Hamilton, Jim Benton, and Howard (Red) Hickey, left to right, *were ideal NFL types. Here they are seen as Los Angeles Rams veterans in the late 1940s.*

Jim Benton. His teams outpassed the pros of their time and in the process provided the school's first real recognition.

But what he could not do, ultimately, was consolidate the gains of his good years and close the state to outside recruiters.

"I remember when Tommy was trying to get summer jobs for players, and they were building Highway 71," Rose said. "He set up a summer camp down there in the mountains, below Winslow, and all our athletes worked for the Highway Department. But our Highway Department was paying two-and-a-half a day and the Louisiana Highway Department—LSU's bunch—paid three or four dollars a day for the same kind of job."

"It was strictly a catch-as-catch-can operation, and Tommy was always aware every nickel counted," said a man who was a U of A student in the Thomsen years. "I remember one big game, Tommy came running out on the field, leading the team's charge the way coaches do, and he spotted a kid climbing the fence for a free look. He veered off and chased the kid away."

Thomsen was proud to be the passingest coach of the passingest team in the nation, even though he admittedly could go beyond the bounds of logic.

He booked a game with George Washington University in 1936 at Washington, D.C., mainly to court eastern publicity. GWU was a big-timer then. It rained hard on game day, but Arkansas still threw 40 passes, completing 10. One was intercepted for GWU's winning touchdown, 13-6. And the Arkansas touchdown came on a flip of just a few inches to Jim Benton.

A half-yard away, why not take a routine plunge at the goal line?

That was not Thomsen's way. These were the Passing Porkers. They had an image to uphold.

– 13 –

GLEN AND GEORGE

As hard as it is to imagine, thousands of Razorback fans past voting age have no frame of reference for appreciating what Glen Rose and George Cole meant to the University of Arkansas athletic program.

In the 1920s, Cole surfaced as a short, triple-threat quarterback from Bauxite, and Rose as a tall, reliable end from North Little Rock. From their playing years until the early 1970s, only two school terms slipped by without Cole or Rose or both (mostly both) filling vital and often thankless roles in the evolving U of A structure.

Obviously, the 1920s were a long time ago. Come to think of it, the 1970s are beginning to be a long time ago.

Cole coached at Warren High School and College of the Ozarks before rejoining Arkansas in 1934 as an assistant to Fred Thomsen. He was there for the rest of his life, with time out for navy duty during World War II.

Coaching, scouting, and recruiting under five head coaches over the better part of three decades, George became a familiar, trusted figure all over Arkansas long before he left the field for administrative work in 1958. He served as a good right arm to both Frank Broyles, who had just been hired to coach, and athletic director John Barnhill, by then in failing health.

"It's hard to define what George did," Broyles said. "He did everything, large or small. He did what needed to be done.

"One day he might map out some far-reaching policy alternatives for Barnie's consideration, and the next he might drive to Little Rock or Texarkana or Lake Village to reassure some anxious parents or put a

George Cole

Glen Rose

wounded booster in a good humor. He was the detail man supreme, the troubleshooter supreme. But don't leave anybody with the idea he was just a reliable detail man. He was so much more than that."

Cole became Barnhill's successor as athletic director in 1967. He retired in 1973.

Rose coached one year at a Baptist junior college in Jonesboro and went back to Fayetteville as Thomsen's B-team coach in 1929. Glen took over the basketball program in 1933 and had fabulous success with it until he entered the army in 1942. He also coached Thomsen's linemen all the while; coaches doubled up then, the same as most athletes.

It was Glen Rose who explained exactly what "average" meant.

"If you've got one foot in the fire and the other foot in a bucket of ice," he said, "well, on the average, you're warm."

The sportswriters pegged him Gloomy Glen, but that missed the mark. Glen was never gloomy, only realistic. Another tag was Plain Glen, and that was better. No less pretentious man ever involved himself in sports.

Cole and Rose were both asked to keep the University of Arkansas football program afloat at different times during the war years. Being very dutiful men, they both accepted.

On September 3, 1942, the third day of fall practice, T. C. Carlson, the number-two man in the U of A administration, called in Cole and told him he was going to be the head coach.

"I told him I would, if it was an order," Cole said. "A man wouldn't have much of a chance on such short notice, the way things were. About two days later he told me it was kind of an order."

Fred Thomsen had left for military duty, and his program had been on the skids several years. As one of Thomsen's aides, Cole knew exactly what he was up against.

He had one assistant coach, Clyde Van Sickle, just fired from Little Rock (later Central) High School. Cole shopped around for help among other coaches he knew, and they declined. So he signed John (Bud) Tomlin out of an Oklahoma school. It turned out to be a break of sorts for Tomlin. He became the interim head coach in 1943, when Cole went to the navy.

Cole's 1942 team finished 3-7, beating Mississippi, Detroit, and Wichita State. The Hogs' lean roster that fall included a tough linebacker and blocking back from Atkins and Arkansas Tech, Wilson Matthews. The next year Matthews played for a Monticello Navy squad that beat Arkansas, 20-12.

The war years represent a bewildering period in college football, bearing little resemblance to what went on before 1942 or what would start happening in 1946.

One military trainee played for three Southwest Conference schools during a season, and two switches in a college season became fairly common nationally.

Some schools became overnight powers or dropped from sight overnight. Some schools had to discontinue football. Others just limped along, and Arkansas fell into this category. On-campus military units, in various training programs, made the difference.

"Our problem during the war years," Rose said, "was that we had Air Force, and the Air Force didn't let their boys take part in college athletics. The Navy, which a lot of schools had, thought it was okay. The Navy let 'em play and the Air Force didn't, and that was a big handicap for us. We had a lot of talent on campus but couldn't use it. If you didn't have a military program for your team to draw from, you played with 17-year-olds and physical rejects."

Glen coached football at Camp Grant, Illinois, in 1942.

"They called me in and wanted me to take the team. I asked about the schedule and damn if they didn't have the Philadelphia Eagles, the Chicago Bears, and some other pro team on there. I said, 'What are you gonna use to play 'em with?' They said, 'Well, we've got this reception center—we'll just pull out some players and you can have them.' I kept objecting to the schedule, and they took the Eagles off.

"We lost to the Chicago Bears, something like 33-6, and I think all of 'em fell down one time and let us make a touchdown. We lost to Great Lakes Naval Training Station and to Iowa and Wisconsin, but we won seven games. We played Fort Campbell (Kentucky) in Chicago for what was billed as the championship of the Army, and we beat them, too."

Rose was discharged from the service at about the time the Navy assigned Cole to help coach Iowa Pre-flight. As Arkansas basketball coach, Glen had won five Southwest Conference titles in a seven-year period, 1935–42, but Hog basketball was going well under his replacement, Eugene Lambert. The Arkansas administration wanted Rose to take over as football coach.

In 1944, his first season, he got the Hogs up to 5-5-1 overall and 2-2-1 in the conference, their best records either way since 1937, but they fell back to 3-7 and 1-5 in 1945.

Glen's star back, Alton Baldwin of Hot Springs, was one of those "physical rejects," although he certainly did not look 4-F on the field.

"He had a big bunion on one foot," Rose said. "We had to make an iron brace to protect it. It fastened on to the cleats and became kind of a stirrup.

"Bob Fenimore, the great player at Oklahoma A&M, had a bone spur—a calcium deposit in the thigh—I think as a result of an old bruise. He carried 'em to two bowls."

Rose was assisted by Clyde Van Sickle and Bud Tomlin. Van Sickle remained more of a physical force than many of the wartime players. He was serious to a fault, especially when demonstrating blocking and tackling techniques.

"Now here's the way you want to block a man," Clyde would say, flattening a freshman player he had pulled in for a target.

One of the regulars, like Earl (Red) Wheeler, would say innocently, "Coach, can we see that again?"

"Sure."

BLAM! Down went the poor freshman again.

"Just one more time, please, Coach," an upperclassman would say. "I've just about got it now." Clyde would dump the freshman again. And again. And again.

Both of Rose's teams beat Ole Miss, possibly because Glen knew a special incentive-builder. Over and over he showed his squad a film of the riotous 1938 Arkansas-Mississippi game, and his Razorbacks charged over to Memphis and beat the Rebels in 1944, 26-18, and in 1945, 19-0.

But when Texas beat Arkansas by 34-7 in Little Rock on October 20, 1945, it made up the minds of several important boosters. Glen's football days were numbered.

— 14 —

A PLEA FOR UNITY

The war had interrupted Arkansas's search for a "name" coach, but the clamor started fresh as the 1945 season ran its course.

Herbert L. Thomas Sr., chairman of the University of Arkansas Board of Trustees, heard the talk. He had already done some deep thinking on the subject. An insurance executive and a serious, far-sighted man, Thomas concluded Arkansas must drastically upgrade all aspects of its football program to survive in the postwar period.

"The choice," he told an interviewer in 1973, "was to stay in the conference and compete on an equal basis, or be forced to drop out."

Since 1934 the University of Texas had insisted on playing Arkansas in Little Rock instead of in Fayetteville. Thomas knew, or sensed, it would be a matter of time until other SWC members followed UT's lead and refused to make the tedious trek into the hills. Pressing the line of thought to its ultimate conclusion, he could see a day when they would not want to play Arkansas at all.

He could find no enthusiasm for big-time athletics among the U of A's administrators. But he received encouragement from business leaders and long-suffering alumni, so he appointed a screening committee to find a new coach and recommend him to the board.

The nine-man committee represented a financial, political, and geographical consensus: Tom Cutting of Fort Smith, Jack East Sr. of Little Rock, Allan Dunaway of Pine Bluff, Sheldon Vinsonhaler of Little Rock, Milan Creighton of Hot Springs, Herschel Lewis of Little Rock, and state legislators Roy Milum of Harrison and Frank Williams of Osceola.

Gordon H. Campbell of Little Rock became the chairman and guiding force.

By then 65 years old, Campbell was a go-getter, a mover-and-shaker, an effective leader of any cause he joined. Born in Kansas, raised in Illinois, he played football at Lake Forest (Illinois) College and was a bicycle-riding phenomenon before the turn of the century. Representing Lake Forest in the bike races at the 1899 Western Collegiate spring meet, he came away with 17 first places and 8 second places.

Campbell served for a time as a high school football coach in Illinois and then moved to Arkansas at the urging of a former college roommate. That was in 1903.

He coached football for Arkansas Military Academy at Little Rock. He applied his fervor and drive to tennis and became a state champion. He was a pioneering game official in football.

As general agent in Arkansas for Aetna Life Insurance and as director of a couple of banks, he had stature and clout in the business community. He was perfect for the mission he undertook in 1945. Now the Razorbacks were his cause.

Glen Rose had a contract and was in a position to be difficult. But Glen was an Arkansas loyalist and, as always, a realist.

"I had seen Tommy Thomsen fight with a short stick up here for years," he said. "I had fought with a short stick. If a 'name' coach could get the whole state behind the program, I was all for it. We had to get an adequate program here."

When did he know he would not be retained as football coach?

"I don't remember exactly. Some friends on the Board kept me informed all the way through. I understood their position and they understood mine. I cooperated with 'em."

Word leaked that the committee's early favorite was University of Alabama assistant Harold (Red) Drew, but on December 21, 1945, the Board announced it had hired John Barnhill of the University of Tennessee as head football coach and athletic director.

"Barnhill was selected because he had just what the people of Arkansas want most at the University, a big name," Campbell told the media that day. "We hope those who favored the selection of a man of his type will support him wholeheartedly for it is obvious Barnhill cannot produce winning teams by himself."

Barnhill coached the Tennessee line for General Robert R. (Bob) Neyland through the 1930s and became interim head coach when the general went back on active duty in World War II. Barnhill took the Vols to seasons of 8-2, 8-1-1, 7-0-1, and 8-1, and into the Sugar Bowl and Rose Bowl. He had proved himself, he figured, and had no intention of slipping back into an assistant's role when the general returned to claim his job.

Barnhill was on a hunting trip in eastern Arkansas when he was approached about the U of A opening. It appealed to him instantly. He met with the committee at the Albert Pike Hotel in Little Rock and put on a determined stretch drive to successfully overtake Red Drew.

"I was used to it," he said much later. "I had been competing with Alabama all my life."

Barnhill was a physically impressive man in 1945, still ruggedly youthful at the age of 42, and while he was low-key and laconic with reporters, he could be evangelistic in quests for athletes and support.

Barnhill accepted a five-year contract at $10,000 a year. Rose accepted a five-year contract at $4,000 annually as business manager of athletics, but left after one year to coach basketball at Stephen F. Austin (Texas).

"That was the first year (1946) that we'd ever had any restriction on tickets—Coach Barnhill put that policy in—and in his first year here, we tied for the conference championship. They had that game with Rice in the high school stadium at Little Rock. It only held 10,000, and I got bleachers from Russellville and Magnolia and other places, and we had 3,000 to 6,000 extra seats all over the stadium, and we still didn't have enough. Nobody could understand that policy of priority. Hell, everybody was mad at me. I wasn't suited for that kind of work anyway."

Glen Rose became a victim of circumstance, repeatedly. He went to service in 1942 as a winning basketball coach. When he returned in 1944, he was asked to take over football. Two seasons later he was told to hand it back. When he had his fill of the ticket manager's job, he had no recourse but to leave Arkansas.

His situation was resolved, belatedly but happily, in 1952, when Barnhill invited him back to coach U of A basketball. He retired in 1966.

John Barnhill had played at Tennessee as an "old" student. He always thought most youngsters would do well to take time out between high school and college, "to give them a chance to settle down . . . get straight in their minds what they want to do."

He felt such a break was the making of his own career.

"I had to lay out of high school to help on our farm. I did a lot of thinking. I decided I didn't want to spend the rest of my life behind the plow."

He was born on that farm near Savannah, Tennessee, on February 21, 1903, youngest of what he called his father's "second litter."

He left there in 1922 to resume his schooling at what became Memphis State University. He completed work on his high school diploma and began college work in 1923, when he captained the football, basketball, and track teams.

At the age of 21 he enrolled at the University of Tennessee. He was listed as a freshman in 1924, though he carried some Memphis State credit hours with him, and competed on the varsity teams of 1925–27, taking his degree in 1928.

An indefatigable 160-pounder, Barnhill played some at halfback on the frosh team, then at end, and finally was positioned at guard. He was a running guard.

"We were the first balanced-line single-wing team and the first to flip-flop our personnel to the strength or weakness of the formation. I was the weak-side guard for three years. The reason was, the weak-side guard then pulled and led the sweep and blocked to the outside. I was the only one who could make it. The strong-side guard would turn upfield into the hole. I'd have to go on and block the end outside. Later they changed the play so the weak-side guard didn't have to go so far."

Barnhill captained the first of the great Tennessee teams coached by Neyland, a trail-blazing West Point product.

Neyland believed in defense first and foremost, when most coaches concentrated on offense. Barnhill became the archetype of the slashing Tennessee guard, a hard hitter who blocked kicks and caused fumbles. He played much of the time on the center's nose.

"I was facing a man who had his head between his legs looking back to make that long snap on every down," Barnhill said. "I passed him like ships in the night."

Neyland helped Barnhill get a high school coaching job at Bristol, Tennessee, and kept an eye on him. Neyland also had an eye for Beattie Feathers, a devastating triple-threat back who played across the street at Bristol, Virginia.

"I had instructions from Neyland," said Barnhill, "to come back to Knoxville and take a job on the staff if I could bring Feathers with me. I never told Neyland that I had Feathers all the way, but it was still the hardest thing I ever had to do on Thanksgiving—beat Bristol (Virginia) and still not antagonize Beattie. We did."

Feathers was eventually rated an all-timer at Tennessee and in the National Football League, where he played for the Chicago Bears.

Barnhill was asked once why Tennessee-schooled coaches left such an impact on football.

"We were way ahead of everybody on defense," he said.

"The object of our offense was to cash in the opportunities we'd get with our defense. We were trying to score with our offense, our defense, and our kicking. And there are more ways to score with your defense than your offense.

"A good football team scores on offense. A great football team scores on offense and defense.

"We always believed in field position. It didn't matter who had the ball, but where it was. If it was in their end of the field, and they had it, we could take it away on a fumble, interception, kicking situation, and score easily. If it was in our end of the field and we had it, we had to go 90, 80, 70, 60 yards to score and that was hard to do. It still is.

"Few teams can go 80 yards with the ball even once a game. If you're playing a team you can go 80 yards on, you'll beat 'em anyway. So when you've got it down there and conditions aren't right for your offense, you're better off kicking it, if you kick well, and we always could. Or quick-kicking and covering a fumble on the other end.

"More games are lost than won; that's true in football and most any sport. When we had the ball in our end of the field we were more apt to lose than win. So we'd kick it out of there and try to force mistakes on their end of the field."

Tennessee believed in rigid conditioning, precision blocking and tackling, and usually won with these fundamentals. Barnhill planned to apply all his Tennessee precepts at Arkansas, naturally.

He announced at that initial press conference that Harold (Deke) Brackett, a former Tennessee quarterback and Vol assistant coach, would be on his U of A staff. George Cole, just back from the navy, would be retained as chief scout. Barnhill said he planned at least a five-man staff.

Barnhill knew about Arkansas athletes. He had seen them all over the Southeastern Conference, particularly at Alabama and LSU. "Alabama," he said, "was just saturated with 'em." The potential of one major team in one state fascinated him. You can guess he strongly influenced the board's unity message.

He knew his first, most critical task would be shutting off the state to old friends and enemies in the Southeastern Conference. He needed a break, a bold stroke, an attention-grabbing gesture bordering on symbolism. He needed to fight for a prized Arkansas athlete and win.

The opportunity came sooner than he would have dared hope.

— 15 —

BARNIE AND CLYDE

Clyde Scott scored 110 or 120 or 130 points during his senior football season for the Smackover High School Buckaroos in 1942. No one is certain of the exact total. For the longest time, few were sure of his exact name. Somewhere between the excited Smackover correspondent and careless rewrite people in various newspaper offices, Clyde L. sometimes got garbled into Clydell.

Everyone knew, though, that there was a marvelous athlete at Smackover—a running back with extraordinary speed. He received an appointment to the Naval Academy and spent 1943 at Bullis Prep in Silver Springs, Maryland, boning up for the Academy entrance exam. In 1944 and 1945, he played fullback for Navy, the No. 2 college football team in the nation.

Army, with Doc Blanchard and Glenn Davis and a star-packed squad generally, ruled undisputably as No. 1. Twice the service academies settled the national championship when they met in late November, and twice Army won, 23-7 and 32-13.

Scott scored the Navy touchdown in the 1944 Army game. He gave the Midshipmen a 6-6 tie with Notre Dame by returning a pass interception for a touchdown in 1945. He caught a 61-yard pass for one of Navy's scores in the 1945 Army game.

"That Clyde Scott could fly," Army coach Earl (Red) Blaik put in his memoirs, "and not even Davis could catch him from behind."

By the spring of 1946 Scott was wrestling with a decision to leave Annapolis. A career as a naval officer had lost its appeal. More to the point, he was in love.

Leslie Hampton, Miss Arkansas of 1945, had met Clyde at the

Academy the previous fall. Congressman Oren Harris, who handled Scott's Annapolis appointment, was a friend of the Hamptons of Lake Village. Leslie was a guest of the Harrises in Washington en route to Atlantic City for the Miss America contest, and she expressed an interest in visiting Annapolis. Harris called Clyde.

Scott's resignation from the Academy became official in July 1946. He and Leslie were married the following month.

"I came home for June week and then went back and turned in my resignation," Scott said "A lot of boys were resigning at that time, finding a lot of reasons to be on the outside."

Time spent playing college athletics for the service academies during the war did not count against the player's postwar eligibility. Did Scott plan to play anywhere else when he left Navy?

"Yes, I did, I sure did. I wasn't exactly sure what problems faced me on the outside. I knew I wanted to go back home, back to my folks in Arkansas. I always had a feeling I wanted to play for Arkansas, ever since Glen Rose came to Smackover and talked to me (before the Navy appointment). I wanted to play at home, do something in front of the folks I grew up with."

John Barnhill was at a boys' camp he maintained near Knoxville, Tennessee, resting after six grueling organizational months at Fayetteville.

He had conducted a harsh spring practice. He had combed Arkansas, button-holing prospective athletes and prospective contributors. He had carried his "unity" message to any group that would invite him as a speaker. He was looking forward to a few days off until he picked up a Knoxville paper and discovered that Scott had resigned at Annapolis and was going home to Smackover.

"I packed my bag and left that day," Barnhill said. "I had never met or seen him. I met him at Smackover and went with him to Lake Village. I spent two or three days there, and when I left I was pretty sure he was coming."

Barnhill was a first-rate recruiter. He looked for an edge, an ace in the hole, and found it instantly in Scott's case.

Leslie's father was J. P. Hampton, a prominent cotton broker. Her mother was an Arkansas alumnus who was anxious for Clyde to play there. Leslie had just finished her sophomore year at Fayetteville.

"Bear Bryant came by to recruit Scotty," Barnhill said, "And Mrs. Hampton chewed him out because he had gone to Alabama instead of Arkansas."

"I was slightly confused, to be truthful," Scott said. "A great number of coaches gave me advice, from Bear Bryant right on down. After talking to Barnie for the first time, there wasn't any doubt. It must have been late July or the first of August. I guess they knew about my foot (a 1945 injury that developed into a chronic condition). I didn't take spring practice at Navy or do anything else because of that."

"Everybody was after him," Barnhill said. "He could have gone anywhere because of his Navy background. His foot? No, we didn't know anything about it until fall. But it didn't seem important. Everybody has his own problems.

"Mrs. Hampton proved to be the best friend we had. Scotty didn't have any plans; he was just looking for a home. Les was already at Arkansas. I felt pretty safe.

"Clyde Scott meant more to the Arkansas program than any other athlete," Barnhill said 20 years after the historic recruitment. "His coming to Arkansas convinced other Arkansas boys they should stay home."

Clyde was born at Dixie, Louisiana, in 1924. His father supervised crews that maintained oil wells, and Smackover and El Dorado boomed in the 1920s. The Scotts lived out in what they called the oil fields. There were four boys.

Audie had a promising playing career cut short by a leg injury at Memphis Southwestern. He did not try to play again after the war. Benny, a 125-pounder, made an incredible all-over-the-field run that became a film-room classic while playing for Little Rock Junior College in the 1949 Little Rose Bowl. Tracy, the youngest, followed Clyde to the U of A.

Clyde first practiced at Arkansas on September 1, 1946. He came straight from his wedding, a big one at Lake Village.

"I tried to talk Clyde into rearranging the date a little, but I think that was in the hands of the women—it usually is," Barnhill said.

Scott said, "You can imagine the strain and adjustments. Getting married, and two days later going into two-a-day practices under Coach Barnhill."

– 16 –

"HEY, HEY, WHO WANTS TO PLAY?"

The 1946 Razorbacks were a motley collection of war veterans, fresh-faced kids straight out of high school, and in-betweeners who defy handy classification. They tied for the Southwest Conference championship and put Arkansas in the Cotton Bowl.

How?

"We won it on defense and field position," Clyde Scott said later. Of course they did. That was the patented Tennessee way. But if it worked for John Barnhill in 1946, why did it not work for him in 1947, 1948, and 1949?

Well, Barnhill got his war veterans assembled and ready to play earlier than most of the other conference members. A full year earlier, in some instances. And Barnhill's first Razorbacks formed a great defensive team in a league that had always doted on offense. Barnie picked his regulars for defense. And for the rest of his life, he glowed over their approach to it in 1946.

"They'd hit you. When they hit you, you bounced. And they liked to see you bounce."

All through the spring and early fall workouts, the coach thundered on the practice field, "Hey, hey, who wants to play?" It was not an idle question.

"It may have multiplied in my mind," said one man who was out for football in the spring of 1946, "but it seems there were 200 football players up there. Would-be football players, I mean. I don't know where they all came from. A lot of them left."

Barnie gradually hammered them down to this line-up:

```
LE. . . . . . . . Alton Baldwin, 200
LT. . . . . . . . Charles Lively, 205
LG . . . . . . . Theron Roberts, 205
C. . . . . . . . Billy Ray Thomas, 175
RG . . . . . . . Bill Franklin, 180
RT . . . . . . . Jim Minor, 215
RE . . . . . . . Bud Canada, 170
BB . . . . . . . Joyce Pipkin, 195
TB . . . . . . . Aubrey (Cob) Fowler or Kenny Holland, about 150 each
WB. . . . . . . Clyde Scott, 170
FB. . . . . . . . Leon (Muscles) Campbell, 195
```

The second teamers played all the second quarters and also appeared in spots in the second half. They included Mel McGaha, Ed Hamilton, and Herman Lubker at ends; John Lunney, Steed White, Dale Counce, Henry Ford, and James Hager in the interior line; Harry Carter and Red Wheeler at center, John Hoffman at fullback, Ross Pritchard at wing-back, and Alvin Duke at blocking back.

A talented running back and pass-catcher in 1943–44, Baldwin had been dismissed from the squad by Glen Rose for a too-casual approach to training regulations during the 1945 season. He came back to give Barnhill a great senior season end.

Lively, from Carlisle, had starred at Beebe High School in the prewar days, when Beebe coaching sage Bro Erwin recruited five counties. Lively had first enrolled at Arkansas in 1942.

Minor was one of the rugged Arkansas Tech products, a powerful lineman who never said much. When he spoke on the field, it was usually to Canada, who lined up next to him and who could not be still before the snap of the ball. "Dammit, Bud, stay off my feet this time, will you?"

Canada, later a state senator from Hot Springs, was too nervous to play offense. As a freshman tailback in 1945, he threw five pass interceptions in one game. As an end in 1946, he recovered three fumbles after Baldwin cracked the ball loose from the safety. Canada could not be turned inside. When Southern Methodist's Kyle Rote got around him once in 1948, Bud turned to the bench crestfallen, expecting Barnhill's glare. Just then the officials wiped out the 40-yard gain. Rote had been in motion.

Freshmen were eligible in 1946, a carry-over from wartime conditions, and that meant Campbell, just up from Bauxite High School, was immediately available.

John Hoffman led the SWC in rushing as a 1945 Arkansas freshman. He is pictured here as a Chicago Bears' veteran.

When Muscles exploded an 85-yard kickoff return against TCU, Barnhill knew he must be promptly established as the regular fullback. He was equally anxious to get Campbell in there as a linebacker, teamed with Billy Ray Thomas. Arkansas never had two linebackers who covered more ground or hit with more cheerful abandon.

Campbell was one of the great pure, instinctive football players of all time. He combined a tackle's strength with a tailback's speed and a linebacker's agility. His career was frustrated by bad knees. Barnhill used to claim that, in four years, he was never behind on the scoreboard as long as Muscles was able to play. It was an exaggeration, but only a slight one.

Aubrey Fowler had played junior college football for John Tucker at Arkansas Tech before and after a long military hitch. "In fact," Fowler said once, "I left Dumas for the general direction of the University of Arkansas in 1939 and finally got there in 1946."

Fowler's speed could contribute big plays both offensively and defensively. Also he was a punter who could boom the ball out of the end zone or angle it artfully toward the corner. Barnhill called on him to punt 64 times in 1946 and 53 in 1947.

Scott said he "sort of gravitated" to wingback after a look at Fowler and Campbell.

"Up to then I played fullback in the single wing, although I was a little light. At Navy we had a spinner series and a great variety of things, the buck lateral and a lot of ball-handling by the fullback. Barnie came along at Arkansas, and in his system the spinner series was virtually nonexistent. The tailback was the most prominent man on the team. Fowler had been a national scoring champion (for Arkansas Tech) the year before; he was a tremendous boy who did it all. I don't recall we had anybody for wingback that first season, so I went over there. As time passed I got to where I wanted to play tailback."

In 1946 Scott carried the ball 54 times for 134 yards. Obviously his selection to the all-Southwest Conference team was for his defensive contributions. He became the Razorbacks' first three-time all-SWC player; there would not be another until Loyd Phillips in the 1960s.

"I first thought of playing Scotty at fullback because he was a fullback at Navy," Barnhill said. "But then I took a look at him and changed my mind. He couldn't step right in at fullback or tailback, but he could start at wingback and work into tailback. He was a great pass receiver, too."

If you have any question that the Hogs won with defense, check these offensive figures. Fowler was the scoring leader with 28 points (three TDs, 10 PATs). Alternate tailback Kenny Holland was the rushing leader with 397 yards. They threw about as many passes in a season as Fred Thomsen would on a typical Saturday.

In those first months on the U of A campus, Barnhill had to establish himself as athletic director in fact as well as name.

No matter who had carried the title in the past, the true athletic director, in the matter of expenditures, was T. C. Carlson, vice-president in charge of finance, a firm hand at the purse strings. "You couldn't buy a jock strap without his okay," Glen Rose said, speaking of the pre-Barnhill days.

Barnhill had more expensive things in mind. Game film, for example. Arkansas had been filming on an occasional basis for several years, but Barnhill wanted each game filmed and available for study early the following week. When late deliveries made the project useless, he decided the solution was to have the means of processing film right there on campus. It cost money.

Barnhill figured he could not do anything about playing in the Texas heat, but he tried to reduce the travel time by flying to College Station in 1946. The Razorbacks' first plane ride was a ghastly experience. With all the weather scares and re-routing and layovers, it consumed as much time as the traditional train trip. And, of course, it cost money.

Barnhill had to fight for his program, virtually line item by line item. Carlson refused even to buy a desk for the coach's office.

"Gradually Mr. Carlson changed his outlook," said Herbert L. Thomas Sr., the Board chairman who started the whole thing by appointing a committee to find a coach. "He and others in the administration came to appreciate Coach Barnhill's soundness. When the program started to improve, they could see continued improvement was necessary."

As athletic director Barnhill urged far-off goals. As football coach he pointed his first squad toward an Oklahoma A&M squad that seemed completely out of reach.

The Aggies went 8-0 in 1945, finishing fifth-ranked nationally by the Associated Press. With Bob Fenimore as their most imposing weapon, they opened 1946 regarded as a threat to such as Army and Notre Dame for the national title.

Arkansas bowed in under Barnhill by beating Northwestern Louisiana, 21-14, at Fayetteville on September 21. They faced the fierce Aggies the next weekend at Stillwater.

A&M made 21 points and 21 first downs. Arkansas made 21 points and one first down. (Teams were not awarded first downs on scoring plays then, no matter how far they went.) The speed of Fowler and Scott

New on the job, Coach John Barnhill gets acquainted with key backs Aubrey Fowler (left), Clyde Scott (right), and Joyce Pipken (rear).

equalized matters; the Razorbacks scored with three long plays. Fowler kicked three extra points to force a tie. The outcome was properly regarded as a great upset.

Fenimore, who established seventeen team records during his Oklahoma A&M career, suffered a hip injury on a resounding tackle by Billy Ray Thomas that finished him. When Fenimore was finished, the Aggies were finished. They limped to 3-7-1 and were replaced by OU as the going power in Oklahoma.

The Hogs correctly took the Stillwater game as a grand omen.

"Feeling ran high," Scott said. "Barnie, for instance. He came up to me to shake hands afterward, started to say something and just choked up, tears in his eyes. It's hard to realize what the game did mean. It let everybody know Arkansas had a pretty good team.

"We were a ragged-looking bunch in more ways than one. There was a mix-up in uniforms, and we were out there in our practice jerseys. We were looking forward to wearing our new ones for the first time, but there was a lot of confusion."

The Razorbacks entered the conference race by slamming TCU at Fort Worth, 34-14, and Baylor at Fayetteville, 13-0. Two deflating experiences followed. Texas shut them out at Austin, 20-0, and an Ole Miss team that won only one other game beat them at Memphis, 9-7.

At College Station the Hogs struggled past the Texas Aggies, 7-0. Arkansans awoke to the fact that the U of A had a chance to play in the Cotton Bowl, a possibility that had never crossed their minds before.

The reaction caused more than 16,000 people to jam into the Little Rock High School facility, known as Tiger Stadium then and Quigley Stadium later, for the Arkansas-Rice game on November 9.

Rice came in with five straight wins after a 7-6 opening loss to LSU. The Owls beat Texas, 18-13, the week after Texas beat Arkansas, 20-0.

Coach Jess Neely had the Southwest's first great T-formation team with Virgil Eikenberg, Carl Russ, Huey Keeney, and George Walmsley in the backfield and Weldom Humble and H. J. Nichols backing the line. Barnhill's Razorbacks had a defensive masterpiece in the works.

With four minutes left and the score 0-0, Eikenberg passed on first down from around his 25-yard line. John Hoffman intercepted on the 32, swept left, and rushed into the end zone untouched.

Arkansas won, 7-0.

Hoffman would later say, "Well, the only man who touched me was a wild fan who grabbed me as I circled against the overflow (crowd) in the back of the end zone."

Hoffman, as a Little Rock High School star, had scored dozens of touchdowns on the same field. He had led the Southwest Conference in rushing as a Razorback freshman in 1945, but returned to Little Rock in 1946 as the Hogs' number-two fullback. Muscles Campbell had won the job.

In Barnhill's Tennessee system, fullbacks played "close up," meaning close to the line of scrimmage, and Campbell started faster than Hoffman, the explanation went. An unhappy Hoffman left Fayetteville during the following season for a long and useful career with the Chicago Bears.

Rice's free-wheeling offense foundered in the mud, partly because of an ingenious defense. After Eikenberg called his signals, Arkansas would jump from one defense to another, from an odd to an even front, and vice versa. Later, it would be called stunting.

Barnhill had two swift defensive ends in Baldwin and Canada. They beat punts down field and caused fumbles. They put a pincer on Eikenberg when he wanted to pass.

"They had been passing to their right end, just an 'out' pattern," Hoffman said. "Coach Barnhill sent me in (at linebacker) and had me back up and move to the left. I was looking for the pass. It was under-thrown, and Baldwin probably had something to do with that."

Baldwin also laid the key block on Hoffman's runback.

"After the Rice game, people listened to me," Barnhill said. "They might have had some doubts before; now they figured I might know what I was talking about."

Arkansas clinched the Cotton Bowl bid by beating SMU at Fayetteville, 13-0, with Scott contributing an 86-yard kickoff return and Fowler a 75-yard romp on an off-tackle play.

Rice finished in a blaze, crunching A&M, TCU, and Baylor. The Owls and Razorbacks tied at 5-1, with the Arkansas win over Rice determining the bowl representative. A closing 14-13 loss to Tulsa left Arkansas with an unattractive 6-3-1 record. Rice took its 8-2 team to the Orange Bowl and beat Tennessee.

The Cotton Bowl paired the Razorbacks with an LSU team that had lost only to Georgia Tech. Working out at Waco in unseasonably warm weather after Christmas, Barnhill promised his players they would throw every single-wing trick in the book at the favored Tigers. They prepared buck laterals, reverses, hokey passes.

"It was so hot," said a writer covering the team, "I went to sleep one night with the window open at the hotel. I woke up the next morning with snow all over the floor."

Ends Bud Canada (84) and Alton Baldwin take a look around the Cotton Bowl.

Three honest-to-goodness blizzards chased one another across Texas immediately before New Year's Day. The Cotton Bowl came off as a scoreless tie in ice and snow. Scalpers threw away their tickets and went home early.

Supposedly the Cotton Bowl was sold out to its 45,000-seat capacity, but the weather trapped or turned back many travelers headed for Dallas. Many others decided to stay home and trust the radio.

"There were never more than 25,000 people at the game," insists a witness. "And by halftime it was probably down to 12,000 and sinking fast."

Snow and ice had been scraped off the frozen field and banked around the sidelines. The temperature was in the 20s. People didn't know about "the chill factor" in those days, but the chill factor in Dallas on January 1, 1947, might not have topped zero.

Hardy souls who actually braved conditions in the stadium watched LSU pile up first downs and yards, but no points. Fowler kicked, kicked, kicked. The Tigers marched, marched, marched.

George Cole spent the first half in the end zone to study the Tigers' defensive line adjustments. "What did you find out?" Barnhill asked when Cole reached the dressing room. "Well, I know how they react to quick kicks," Cole said.

The Tigers penetrated the Arkansas 20-yard-line five times. On their fourth threatening push, quarterback Y. A. Tittle flipped a short pass to Jeff Adams, down and out, and Adams caught it at the flag. Clyde Scott almost tore him in half and drove him out of bounds on the correct (scoreless) side of the flag. LSU came that close. The pass was too short to be a first down, and Arkansas held on the one.

This was in the last quarter, and Fowler's foot lofted the ball out again. LSU threatened a fifth time before flubbing a field-goal attempt.

According to one charming legend spread by some Razorbacks, Campbell spent timeouts collecting newspapers and game programs swirling around in the frigid wind and stacking them on the Arkansas goal line. Finally, somebody asked what in the world he was doing.

"If we're gonna camp down here all day," Muscles said, "we ought to build a fire."

LSU made 15 first downs, Arkansas one. LSU rushed for 255 yards, Arkansas for 54. LSU completed five of 17 passes for 16 yards, while Arkansas threw four and completed none.

There was only one trophy, and LSU coach Bernie Moore claimed it at the post-game banquet.

"We made the most first downs," Moore said.

"Yeah, but we made the most tackles," Barnhill said.

The trophy went to Arkansas. During the 1960s a visitor noted it was the only one on display in Barnhill's office. Along with "Cotton Bowl 1947" it is inscribed with "Hey, hey, who wants to play?"

~ 17 ~

GAINS AND LOSSES

John Barnhill figured the team's 1946 success both helped and hurt him. It helped much more than it hurt.

The Rice game did more to point up the inadequate facilities of the Razorbacks than Barnhill himself could have ever done in years of impassioned Razorback Club speeches. Crip Hall helped ease the War Memorial Stadium legislation past doubtful or lukewarm politicians, and Gordon Campbell led the stadium bond drive.

"Gordon beat anything I ever saw in my life," said D. P. (Pete) Raney, a Little Rock bond broker and top-echelon booster who later served on the U of A Board of Trustees. "He was up and down Main Street every day, pushing and persuading, not giving anybody any rest. He'd call me every morning. 'How's it going? Are you doing any good? Let's get after it.' I wouldn't have put up with it from anybody but him."

Barnhill moved the Razorbacks' 1947 game with Texas from Little Rock to Crump Stadium in Memphis. To prove a point to foot-draggers? "No, pure necessity," Barnhill said. "The ticket situation was out of hand. I just had to move the game where there were seats available."

Allan Berry, an old Henderson-Brown and Vanderbilt football player and a former Arkansas high school coach, was in charge of Crump Stadium. Barnhill liked the way he operated.

"I came back and told 'em, 'There's a guy in Memphis you ought to get for the new stadium in Little Rock. Hell, you can't hardly get a *team* into Crump Stadium without a ticket.' So we got Allan over here."

As manager of War Memorial Stadium and secretary of the state Razorback Club organization, Berry became Barnhill's troubleshooter. "It was like this," a U of A insider said. "If something needed to be done,

Barnie called Allan, and Allan got with the people who could do it and made sure it was done."

With War Memorial Stadium going up in Little Rock's Fair Park area (soon to be War Memorial Park), Barnhill had one goal under control. He was ahead of schedule in another vital area. For the first time the U of A fought on even terms or better for any player in the state. Recruiting successes in 1947-48 reduced the outward flow of Arkansas athletes to a trickle.

Part of that trickle, however, stuck deeply in Barnhill's craw. To Ole Miss, he lost John (Kayo) Dottley, a McGehee fullback who would have two 1,000-yard rushing years for the Rebels. Barnhill felt strongly enough about this recruiting struggle to leave Mississippi, an important money game, off the Arkansas schedule from 1948 through 1951—a period of time coinciding with Dottley's collegiate career.

The 1947 Razorbacks had every 1946 starter except Alton Baldwin, but things were not the same. Their 5-4-1 record was not an alarming decline from 6-3-1, but in the conference they fell from 5-1 to 1-4-1. This is where 1946 hurt. Barnhill was without a suitable encore.

Baylor accounted for much of the difference. Floundering in 1946, the Bears came on to be Barnhill's nemesis. He turned to them from a 6-0 conquest of TCU in 1947, and they beat him, 17-9. He whipped TCU impressively in 1948 and 1949, and Baylor followed by trimming him, 23-7 and 35-13. In those days the Hogs went to Waco and died in the heat and tradition of the Baylor "jinx."

Southwest Conference opponents considered Arkansas's Cotton Bowl trip an isolated accident. They were right in the sense that the Razorbacks had not reached a level where they competed, strength-for-strength, with the SWC powers each week.

The disappointing conference record of 1947 was offset somewhat by one of the Porkers' best intersectional showings. They were 4-0 outside their league and they pinned a 19-14 loss on Mississippi's Southeastern Conference champions.

This was Johnny Vaught's first Ole Miss team, and it featured 133 pass completions by Charley Conerly and 52 catches by Barney Poole. The year before, the Rebs had been 2-7 (under coach Red Drew, runner-up to Barnhill for the Arkansas job), but they beat the Razorbacks, prompting the Mississippi student newspaper to suggest Clyde Scott was a sadly overrated athlete. Someone sent a clipping to Scott, and he burned over it for a solid year. Then he went back to Memphis and contributed one of his finest performances to the upset win.

Bowl games were popping up everywhere, and Arkansas, in spite of 5-4-1, was invited to play William and Mary (9-1) in the Dixie Bowl at Birmingham, Alabama.

The Razorbacks came from behind twice, from 0-13 and 14-19, to win, 21-19. Kenny Holland passed 59 yards to Ross Pritchard for one touchdown, Mel McGaha returned a pass interception 70 yards for another, and Arkansas drove 97 yards to pull it out in the fourth quarter, with Muscles Campbell scoring from the seven. Aubrey Fowler kicked the three conversions.

A senior end, McGaha had artfully tight-roped the interception return down the sideline. "In your last game," Barnhill told him, "I find I've had you outta position all this time. You shoulda been a tailback."

There was more advance interest in the 1948 Razorbacks than there had ever been in a U of A football team.

War Memorial Stadium opened for business on September 18, and 27,000 people (a state record football crowd then) watched the Hogs in a 40-6 breather against Abilene Christian on a blazing afternoon. The lights were not ready and neither was the press box; reporters sweltered outside with everyone else. One writer captured the scene by reporting that Scott was "as brilliant as the burning sun."

By then Clyde was an international celebrity in track as well as an All-American football candidate. He had tied the world record in the 110-meter high hurdles (13.7) while beating Bill Porter of Northwestern, the eventual gold medal winner in the 1948 Olympic Games at London. Scott ran second to Porter in the Olympics.

A hurdler and sprinter who never really concentrated on track, Clyde scored 18 points in one Southwest Conference meet. Publicity men had no qualms about billing him "the fastest man in college football."

If Arkansas fans were not sold on Barnhill's Tennessee single wing in 1948, they had no doubts about Clyde Scott's authenticity.

Abilene Christian was followed by another light snack, a 46-7 win at Fayetteville over East Texas State, and then the Razorbacks went to Fort Worth for the opening conference test with TCU. Barnhill especially looked forward to this one, a night game. For the first time the Hogs were escaping the Texas heat that permeated October afternoons.

It was an historic occasion for another reason; a Fort Worth station televised the game. There were not enough privately owned sets to threaten the gate receipts.

TCU had a 7-0 lead in the first quarter. Eight fumbles happened in the first 15 minutes, including two by Campbell and one by Scott. Then

All-American Clyde Scott (12) was billed, probably on merit, as college football's fastest back of the 1940s.

Arkansas settled down and started taking the Horned Frogs apart with Clyde. He gained 140 yards, scored three touchdowns, and hurdled a tackler on one of the scoring runs. Looking the part of a legitimate contender, Arkansas won, 27-14.

Scott said it was probably the best game of his career. "He was running the old Number 10 pretty good that night," Barnhill said. Number 10 in the Tennessee system is the tailback off-tackle, a bread-and-butter play.

Baylor bounced Arkansas at Fayetteville, 23-7. Scott was knocked out of the game after a 41-yard run, and Campbell was literally knocked out by a roundhouse right-hand punch from a Baylor player. Nearly everyone in the stadium saw it except the game officials.

At Austin the Razorbacks caught a slow-starting Texas team that was just beginning to assert itself. The game was not as close as the 14-6 score in favor of the Longhorns suggests.

Arkansas went in front on a 36-yard run by Scott. This is how he remembered it.

"I faked in, and Muscles Campbell knocked the end off his feet, literally knocked him off his feet. I swung wide, and Muscles dropped the linebacker with a shoulder block as he went by. When I crossed the goal line, I looked back and Muscles was blocking the safety.

"Muscles Campbell made whatever I earned in the way of recognition. I could accomplish more with Muscles out there. When he wasn't, I was just another player. Before his knees were injured he was one of the finest fullbacks [in the SWC] before or since. When I went back to call a play, I knew one thing. We could depend on getting that end blocked down every time. We did it with Muscles Campbell."

Out of the race with two losses the Razorbacks rebounded against a weak Texas A&M team at College Station, 28-6. Then they made their second appearance in War Memorial Stadium, and a crowd of about 30,000 responded to watch them play Rice. It was a perfect spot for a captivating win, but Jess Neely was smoothing out what would be one of the great Rice teams in 1949, and he gave Arkansas a chilling preview. The Owls brushed aside a quick Scott touchdown and won as they pleased, 25-6.

The next Saturday, November 13, a Fayetteville record crowd of 23,000 saw Arkansas challenge Southern Methodist. The real lure was Doak Walker and Clyde Scott on the same field, although they did not stay with the script.

Scott went out on the first play of the second quarter with a pulled ligament. He never played another down for Arkansas. Walker was knocked out on the same play. Doak soon reappeared, but this was a day the Mustangs' Heisman Trophy winner would gain nine yards and lose 19.

Arkansas never fielded a more inspired team. No one who was there will forget Frank Lambright making tackles all over the field. Nor will they forget Campbell's 68-yard run. He turned Walker, the safety, over and around and left him sprawled.

Muscles had an earlier touchdown on a two-yard blast, and Arkansas led by 12-0 late in the third quarter. The Hogs' sheer fury unhinged the Mustangs, but SMU had a championship team and they rallied.

SMU came powering back with wild-running sophomore Kyle Rote slamming for a touchdown. Walker kicked the Ponies as close as 12-7 with 12:35 gone in the third quarter. It stayed that way until the final 10 seconds.

Gil Johnson, a climax passer, took the Mustangs toward the Arkansas goal in a desperate race with the clock. SMU was calling two plays at once, lining up without a huddle, and an offside penalty cost Arkansas the game.

Alvin Duke intercepted a pass intended for Walker at the Arkansas two-yard line and ran it back to the 30. The play was nullified. An Arkansas player, who had chased Johnson deep on the previous down, didn't get back before SMU put the ball in play again.

Johnson threw to Phil Page, who took it over his shoulder at the two and scored. Walker's second PAT was not necessary, but he kicked it anyway, for a final score of 14-12. Then he went to the Arkansas dressing room to pay his respects to Campbell.

(Senior reserve tailback Gordon Long, a passer and punter who usually checked in to throw the ball on third-and-long, received the Swede Nelson national sportsmanship trophy for helping escort the game officials past angry, disappointed fans after SMU's improbable comeback.)

The 1948 Porkers finished with two War Memorial Stadium games, beating Tulsa and losing to William and Mary. The 9-0 loss to William and Mary set the record at 5-5 and halted efforts to promote a post-season game in Little Rock featuring a 6-4 Arkansas team. It was just as well.

Scott made All-American the hard way, playing for an undistinguished team and missing a lot of playing time to boot.

"Scott was the fastest man I ever saw in a uniform," Barnhill said. "The uniform never seemed to slow him down, if you know what I mean. Scotty could get outside and go. Aubrey Fowler was the faster of the two over any distance, but Scotty started faster, had better football speed. Like Muscles Campbell, he was at full speed the first five yards.

"Scotty was self-conscious, humble, ill-at-ease to a fault. If he'd had some ego, some cockiness, there never would have been a better football player.

"He was the best defensive back I ever had. An excellent tackler. Even if he made a mistake, he could cover it up. They avoided his zone a little because of his speed.

"He got hurt quite a bit, and that hurt his overall record. He got hurt because he couldn't sidestep anybody. Everybody had an angle on him, and when they hit him, it was the damnedest crash you ever saw because he was going so fast. It was the same in pro ball; that's why he had so many fumbles in the pros."

The Detroit Lions had him on defense when they won the NFL title.

If Scott had appeared a few years later, the pros would have turned him into a flanked receiver, and he might have enjoyed a great career along the lines of, say, Lance Alworth. Instead, for four years (1949-52) his 175-pound body was subjected to conventional running plays against NFL defenders who could literally pick him up and shake him when they made the tackle.

His number-12 jersey was the only one the U of A ever retired. In the 1970s, Frank Broyles asked Scott if he minded it being "un-retired" since kicking prospect Steve Little (then being recruited) insisted on wearing 12. Scott, an executive with a Little Rock insurance firm, said in effect, "Certainly, go ahead, anything for the program." After Little's college career, number 12 was again deactivated.

Some people still believe Clyde Scott was the best athlete who ever came out of Arkansas. Fortunately for Barnhill, he also came back.

– 18 –

"ROUGH" FOOTBALL

By 1949 the Tennessee single wing was deemed outmoded and inflexible, no longer able to keep up in the age of the Chicago Bears' tight-T, the Oklahoma split-T, and jazzy spread formations. Some critics and experts believed that speed had been wasted; for example, Clyde Scott, Aubrey Fowler, Muscles Campbell, and Ross Pritchard.

John Barnhill heard about the demise of the single wing from his trusted inner circle of supporters as well as from the rank and file. He did not agree, but he had a struggling program to maintain, tickets to sell, money to raise. He needed a big year. He would pursue it out of the T-formation.

Barnhill had real hopes for 1949. His 1948 freshman team, one of the most talented ever recruited by Arkansas, would yield "hellacious" sophomore linemen Fred Williams, Dave Hanner, Bob Griffin, Pat Summerall, and Frank Fischel. Theron Roberts, one of the 1946 stalwarts, had missed 1948 because of surgery and was holding over for his senior year. Other lettermen—Buddy Brown, Bill Stancil, Don Riederer, Jack Rushing—promised better line depth than Barnhill had ever had at Arkansas.

Bernie Masterson, a former Chicago Bears quarterback who had just been ousted at Nebraska, was brought in for spring practice to install a T-system that would fit the Razorbacks' personnel. Mostly, Masterson set up blocking for fullback Muscles Campbell, who would be in the corresponding position of a single-wing tailback. Instead of a direct snap from center, he would take handoffs from a T-quarterback and hit any hole. He'd be what they called the "single back" in the 1980s and 1990s.

The trouble was, Campbell's knees did not hold up, and the quarterbacks, Don Logue and Jim Rinehart, were sophomores asked to win in a highly competitive league.

Campbell made 236 yards on just 15 carries in the 33-19 opener with North Texas State at Little Rock. The next weekend at Fayetteville, with Muscles still healthy and romping, Arkansas thoroughly dominated TCU, 27-7.

Dutch Meyer, the TCU coach, filed a formal protest with the conference. Arkansas stood accused of "rough" football.

Meyer was nearing the end of a distinguished career. From 1934 to 1952, he coached the Horned Frogs to an aggregate 109-79-13, to one perfect season and a national title, and to three SWC championships. He had not, however, beaten Arkansas since 1943. And Barnhill's Razorbacks flattened the Frogs in the starting gate four consecutive years.

The roughness charge infuriated Barnhill, and when the conference officially censured Arkansas for rough football, he took it as an unjust personal reprimand. It bothered him the rest of his life.

"When somebody like Muscles Campbell hit you, he hit you so hard you thought there ought to be something illegal about it, but there wasn't," he said.

Meyer's offenses were double-wing sets and spreads, triggered by a tailback. Tennessee defensive theory knew only one way to confront such an attack. Get to the tailback as quickly as you can, with as many men as you can, as hard and unkindly as you can. In the specific case of Arkansas vs. TCU, the system had been unfailingly successful.

As in the Heinie Schlueter case of 1933, Arkansas felt keenly aware of its outsider's position. This time, though, the U of A leadership did not cave in without an effort.

Herbert L. Thomas Sr., chairman of the board of trustees, made public a letter to Southwest Conference executive secretary James H. Stewart. The tone was diplomatic, but the letter firmly stated six points that bothered Arkansas:

1. . . . . We understand that the Faculty Committee made no effort to question the coaches directly concerned in this matter.
2 . . . . We understand the Faculty Committee as a whole did not question, or read reports of, the four officials who handled the game.
3. . . . . We understand the Committee did not give any weight to the fact that no roughness (personal foul) penalties were called during the game.

Leon (Muscles) Campbell, according to John Barnhill, "hit you so hard you thought there ought to be something illegal about it, but there wasn't."

4....... We understand the Committee did not request disinterested experts, other than the secretary of the conference, to view (game film) and then pass judgment on the validity of the charges.

5....... We understand the Committee as a whole did not view (film of) the game in order that they might determine at first hand whether the charges of roughness were, in their opinion, justified.

6....... We understand that virtually the entire responsibility of an official investigation was thrust upon the shoulders of one individual—the secretary of the conference—and that the Faculty Committee subsequently reached its decision without consideration of, or asking for, a written report from that individual.

All that came after the season. Nobody accused Arkansas of rough football against Baylor at Waco, where quarterback Adrian Burk riddled the Porkers, 35-13. Superbly prepared for its conference opener, Baylor once again negated Arkansas's own opening efforts against TCU.

Campbell could not play against Baylor, and the pattern for the season was set. Arkansas would hope all week that Muscles could make it, but ended up going with senior backup fullback Geno Mazzanti.

Mazzanti would pop one long gainer per Saturday and usually wind up with about 100 yards rushing, but he lacked Muscles's speed, power, or dazzling take-off. Where Mazzanti totaled 757 yards, a school record at the time, a sound Campbell might have gained 1,500.

Campbell came back to spur the Razorbacks to a 14-0 lead over Texas in War Memorial Stadium, but he was hurt again, and Texas went on to win, 27-14. For the last half of the season Arkansas's only weapon was Mazzanti. Ross Pritchard, whose swiftness could have been an outside complement to the fullback, missed the season with a broken leg.

Against Vanderbilt, Mazzanti winded himself in a long run to the lip of the goal line. While Geno caught his breath on the sideline, Louis Schaufele, the regular punter, regular linebacker, and extra fullback, came in and leaped over the pile-up for the touchdown. Arkansas held on for a 7-6 win.

The Hogs were able to treat Texas A&M as a routine item, 27-6.

They summoned a grim defensive effort against Cotton Bowl-bound Rice, but lost on sophomorish offensive mistakes at Houston, 14-0.

In SMU's high-riding days of 1947-48, Arkansas twice caught Doak

Walker on sub-par Saturdays and pressed the Ponies to the wire, 14-6 and 14-12. Attrition and everything else caught up with the Ponies in 1949, but Arkansas finally saw Doak at his best. SMU had an easy time, 34-6.

Nothing remained then but to lose to William and Mary again, beat Tulsa again, and go 5-5 again.

Now Barnhill found himself under extreme pressure. Complicated pressure. There was the matter of his health. He had unaccountably fallen from the bench during the Rice game of 1948, his first signal that something was wrong. This did not become general knowledge until years after his active coaching days, but it weighed on his decision to leave the field following the 1949 season.

He also knew he had become an issue to fans. He knew the salvation of the Arkansas program lay in a statewide effort. There could be no warring factions. He said it best in 1952, at the end of the Otis Douglas regime. In context he was removing his own name from a list of possibilities to replace Douglas.

"I still think I am a good coach, but I believe we ought to get a man everybody will be for. There are very likely people who still feel about me like they did in 1949. I could get 50, 60, 75 percent support, and that would not be enough."

After the 1949 season Barnhill asked the board of trustees to relieve him of his coaching duties. He would stay as full-time athletic director. He asked that his salary be reduced from $12,000 to $10,000.

"I had become convinced the job was too big for one individual. My health was going bad. I would rather have hired an assistant administrator and continued to coach, but I realized he couldn't do the job the way I thought I could do it. I thought maybe giving up coaching was the best thing I could do. It was my decision, no one else's.

"I broke up my staff, helped them get jobs. Hell, they got better jobs than they had here."

Muscles Campbell spent a few years among the pros, most notably with the Chicago Bears, and when his knees permitted he did not look at all out of place.

There was a final indignity for Geno Mazzanti, fated to spend time in someone's shadow. He ended his senior season against Tulsa on November 26 with a 97-yard lead on Kyle Rote of SMU for the Southwest Conference rushing championship. Rote had one more game against national champion Notre Dame on December 3.

With Doak Walker hurt, Rote took everything on himself and, in a stunning performance, pushed Notre Dame to the brink of a major upset before the Irish rallied to salvage it, 27-20.

During that epic game, Rote galloped past Mazzanti in the SWC rushing race, 777 to 757.

"BEAT ALL THOSE TEXAS TEAMS"

Maybe he only said it once, and maybe not in these exact words, but the joyous news spread through Arkansas in 1950 that Otis Douglas had pledged to "beat all those Texas teams."

Douglas stayed three seasons and beat five Texas teams: North Texas State (not exactly what fans had in mind) and Baylor in 1950; Texas and Texas A&M in 1951; Baylor again in 1952. He beat nine teams in all against twenty-one losses. He went 2-8, 5-5, 2-8.

He did not win a single game on Texas soil.

The Otis Douglas adventure started when Clyde Scott signed with the Philadelphia Eagles after the 1948 season. The Eagles were then on top of the National Football League, but the NFL remained a poorly established novelty out in the hinterlands. Television and its saturation Sunday coverage of pro football was five or six years away in the lives of most Arkansans. The Scott signing stimulated Arkansas interest in the NFL and particularly in the Eagles.

In 1949 the Eagles visited Little Rock for an exhibition game and played an exciting tie with the Los Angeles Rams. More talk, more interest.

Barnhill had been pressured into the T-formation in 1949, and just another 5-5 season turned up instead of miracles. Suddenly the T was not enough. Important contributors as well as casual fans turned clamorous for a "pro" coach and a "pro" system.

Barnie gave them Otis Douglas. He did not intend it as a joke.

"I knew if we got Douglas, we'd have one of two things," Barnhill said years afterward. "We'd either have a good football team or we wouldn't have anything, and everybody would get their belly full."

Douglas was a jack-of-all-trades on Coach Greasy Neale's Philadelphia staff—trainer, assistant coach, and, into his mid-thirties, emergency substitute lineman. In his spare time he coached some football at Drexel Tech. A William and Mary graduate, he was a big, burly man with a contagious grin, a Tidewater accent ("Well, I don't know a-boot that"), a brisk and positive approach, and an amazing range of knowledge on topics in and out of athletics.

As the NFL's presiding genius of the moment, Greasy Neale was asked for a recommendation. He said he just happened to have the man Arkansas needed.

"If I left the Eagles tomorrow," Neale reportedly said, "Otis Douglas is the man I would pick to take over."

That was good enough for Arkansas.

It should be noted that in 1950 the pros had not advanced to what we would now think of as "pro stuff." Like most new coaches, Douglas looked around for a model. Oklahoma's Sooners had touched off the split-T craze. Douglas visited Oklahoma, conferred with coaches Bud Wilkinson and Gomer Jones, and decided to install the split-T offense and the 5-4 defense.

Long-memoried fans still try to sort out the paradoxes of the Douglas years. There he was, a "pro" coach commanding athletes who later thrived as pros, and he won nine of 30 games.

Dave Hanner, Fred Williams, Pat Summerall, Lamar McHan, Lew Carpenter, and Bob Griffin went on to NFL careers totaling 60-odd seasons among them; Hanner of Green Bay and Williams of the Chicago Bears and Washington Redskins became great NFL defensive linemen and remained so for more than a decade. Late in his career Summerall served the New York Giants as a heroic place-kicker.

In spite of the cream at the top, Douglas's overall squads were ordinary in comparison to some of the SWC teams they were asked to beat. There were still, by and large, more good players on the campuses in Texas.

"Douglas had seven or eight pro prospects," said a writer who watched the Douglas Hogs, "but he never had twenty-five solid, winning college players. There's a lot of difference. He never had the great, game-wrecking type of halfback, for example."

"Douglas," said Barnhill, "put 'em on the scales, and the boys who weighed the most played. The thing to do is get big old boys and trim 'em down—get 'em hungry."

"Douglas," said Summerall, who staked out a second career as an admired sportscaster, "was five years ahead of his time in some of his

Pat Summerall as a star sportscaster

theories about football. But he was at least five years behind when it came to the hiring of assistants. He simply didn't have coaches around him who could teach techniques.

"We lost a lot of games on simple, fundamental things. We didn't get the leadership we should have had, and not necessarily from the players."

"Coach Douglas," said Hanner, "was a fine man and a smart man. He knew a lot of football. I don't think he realized how important discipline was. He took a lot of things for granted."

"We didn't win many games," Fred Williams said, "but we didn't lose *any* parties."

"It's hard to figure, isn't it?" said Summerall. "In my senior year (1951) we had six players who became ten-year men in the NFL. [The six mentioned previously.] It's really amazing when you start thinking about that much professional talent on a college team that couldn't win."

The first play from scrimmage the Razorbacks ran under Douglas was bitterly symbolic. In War Memorial Stadium on September 23, 1950, Ross Pritchard got behind the entire Oklahoma A&M team for an easy touchdown bomb. He dropped it. Arkansas lost, 12-7.

The 1950 Razorbacks kept most of their losses exasperatingly close. After a 50-6 romp at the expense of North Texas State, they lost a 13-6 squeaker to TCU. The best day of halfback Ray Parks's career led them to a promising 27-6 win over Baylor. The promise proved hollow.

They were in contention when they went to Austin to play Cotton Bowl-bound Texas. Although badly outgunned, they struggled ahead by 14-13 late in the game. Texas surged back for a 19-14 victory.

"Bud McFadin and Ken Jackson were really working on me that day," Hanner said. "McFadin was by far the best college player I ever had to line up against."

Vanderbilt beat them, 14-13, in Little Rock. They could not keep Texas A&M close, 42-13. Rice barely got out of Fayetteville with a 9-6 win.

At Little Rock, quarterback Jim Rinehart completed five straight passes in a closing drive that failed, and SMU survived a mud game by 14-7. One of the better Tulsa teams handled the Hogs, 28-13, in the season closer.

In 1951 Douglas had three quarterbacks to pick from: Rinehart, a determined, undistinguished senior; Ralph Troillett, a tight-T ball-handling whiz who had transferred from Little Rock JC; and Lamar McHan, a big sophomore from Lake Village with the tools to do anything. Obviously McHan would be the man over the long haul. The question was, how soon should he be installed?

Fred Williams, who became a 15-year NFL stalwart, said the Otis Douglas Razorbacks didn't win many games, "but never lost a party."

Charged high for the Oklahoma A&M opener at Stillwater, the Hogs demolished the Cowpokes by 42-7. Put in the game for a few plays at fullback, McHan broke 81 yards for a touchdown. Part of the answer was there, and the rest came when Rinehart had to undergo an appendectomy. McHan, the sophomore who had been a single-wing tailback in high school, found himself directing the Otis Douglas split-T.

Arizona State was booked as a Fayetteville breather, and the Razorbacks were able to treat it as such, 30-13. But they lost to TCU (the eventual champ) at Little Rock, 17-7, and to Baylor at Waco, 9-7. Knocked out of the SWC race, they found an ample target for their frustration.

The Texas Longhorns visited Fayetteville on October 20 as the number-4 team in the nation. They had beaten Purdue, North Carolina, Kentucky (Bear Bryant), and Oklahoma (Bud Wilkinson). Kentucky and Oklahoma were coming off the Sugar Bowl game in which UK stopped OU's 31-game winning streak.

Arkansas went with McHan at quarterback, Buddy Sutton and Dean Pryor at halfbacks, Lew Carpenter at fullback, and Jack Troxell and Jiggs Phillips as spare halfbacks. The offensive line had Bill Jurney and Summerall at the ends; Tom Garlington, Sammy Dumas, Williams, and Hanner at the guard and tackle positions, with Griffin at center.

Most of them played defense, too, but Johnny Cole, Jimmy Smith, Frank Fishel, Bob Linebarrier, Buster Graves, Floyd Sagely, and others specialized prominently on the defensive unit.

Physically, this was the most awesome Arkansas team up to that time: big, rugged-looking backs and 240-pound linemen when a 220-pounder was still considered a good-sized tackle.

"If we had a flaw," Summerall said, "it was that some of us had to play both ways." In the peak period of college football's first two-platoon era (1947–52), most Arkansas opponents had quality as well as depth on both sides of the ball.

Arkansas jumped to a 6-0 lead. Douglas hoped to drive Texas out of a nine-man front by using McHan as a tailback in the equivalent of a short punt formation. His early passes were dropped, but McHan found the formation ideal for one of his various talents. He quick-kicked 80 yards, and Texas fumbled it away at the 15. Sutton scored from the 13, and Texas blocked the kick.

Soon Gib Dawson broke 78 yards for a touchdown, and the Steers led, 7-6. With the clock running down before halftime, Arkansas worked the ball to a first down on the Texas five. By now it was ball control with

McHan squirming for most of the yards on tight keepers. It was third and three, then fourth and two.

Douglas decided to go for a field goal. It was not the automatic call it is today, and many in the crowd of 19,500 booed.

Otis had tried to break a 7-7 tie against TCU with a field goal, failed, and ultimately lost the game, but was criticized for not trying one (from a long way out) in the 9-7 loss to Baylor.

The 1951 Razorbacks have just broken a 12-year losing streak against Texas. Santa Clara beat them the following week.

Summerall had kicked two field goals, neither of great importance.

"Really, I shouldn't have been in there against Texas," he said. "The ball was placed on the 10, and that's just (extra-point distance). And I didn't kick conversions. The only reason I was the field-goal man was that I kicked off."

Pat made it, and Arkansas took a 9-7 lead to intermission.

An injury to Sutton was one factor that influenced Douglas to go for a field goal. The Razorbacks came back in the second half with Troxell, a swift Jonesboro sophomore. McHan had been keeping. Suddenly he began pitching out wide to Troxell, who set up a touchdown with a 40-yard run and then scored it from the nine. Arkansas held a 16-7 lead.

Late in the game Texas recovered a fumble on the Arkansas 16, and Dan Page tossed seven yards to Tom Stolhandske for a touchdown. Clinching a 16-14 win, Arkansas kept the ball about five minutes, one climax third-down run by McHan after another.

On defense Williams, Griffin, and Hanner had been stupendous. Aside from Dawson's 78-yarder, the longest Texas run had been five yards. The Longhorns completed one pass out of a dozen.

It was the Razorbacks' first win over Texas since 1938, convincing Arkansas rooters that Douglas's team had finally turned the corner.

Around that corner lurked Santa Clara, a once-proud West Coast power now down and on the verge of abandoning football. Santa Clara was expected to serve as a mid-season breather in War Memorial Stadium, but a flat Arkansas team lost by 21-12. The Texas thriller was quickly and effectively tarnished.

The next week, recharged for homecoming against tough Texas A&M, the Razorbacks won by 33-21. This was the game where McHan made 189 yards keeping on the option. He carried the Hogs on a long, late scoring drive while trying to run out the clock.

The next week Arkansas was shut out by Rice at Houston, 6-0.

Fans were puzzled as well as dismayed. How could a team that looked so good against Texas and Texas A&M look so poor against Santa Clara and Rice? Then the question changed slightly and soured. How could the team that beat the Horns and Aggies lose to SMU by 47-7?

The Razorbacks went to Dallas favored over a Mustang team that had been even less predictable than Arkansas. On their way to a 3-6-1 season, the Ponies still had the trappings—passes and razzle-dazzle—but none of the substance of their Doak Walker heyday. The Razorbacks held them to minus nine yards rushing and lost by 40 points.

Otis Douglas found the SWC lonely at the bottom.

Fred Benners, Jerry Norton, and a couple of other Ponies combined for 431 yards passing against Arkansas. The Hogs threw 41 passes of their own, but SMU intercepted seven.

Angry and shot down, Arkansas followers wrote off the Tulsa game. Naturally the Razorbacks played impressively and won, 24-7.

The Douglas Hogs got away from their up-and-down tendencies in 1952. There were no *ups;* it was *down* all the way.

Arkansas beat Oklahoma A&M in a 22-20 opener and slipped by Baylor in the fourth game, 20-17, both in War Memorial Stadium. The last traces of Douglas support vanished when Texas and Ole Miss stomped Arkansas on consecutive weekends in October, 44-7 and 34-7. The Mississippi game in Little Rock created a traffic jam of departing Hog partisans early in the fourth quarter.

The 1952 Razorbacks gave up 215 points in their last six games. In November, with Douglas plainly a lame duck, they lost to Texas A&M, 31-12; Rice, in a wild thing at Fayetteville, 35-33; SMU, 27-17 (after holding a 17-0 lead); and Tulsa, 44-34.

Otis made it official by handing in his resignation at noon on Friday, November 21, some 26 hours before the Tulsa game.

Arkansas never had a nicer, more personable coach. Or one with less grasp of what confronted him.

– 20 –

ANOTHER MAN
FROM TENNESSEE

John Barnhill made a trip to Wyoming in the summer of 1952 to visit Bowden Wyatt. Otis Douglas still had a season left on his three-year contract, so Barnhill could not and did not offer Wyatt a job.

Barnhill used the visit to bring himself up to date on Wyatt's situation and to alert the Wyoming coach to the probability of a change at Arkansas after the upcoming season. In effect, Barnie was securing his ace in the hole.

With Douglas out, the search turned first in the direction of Paul (Bear) Bryant, the Fordyce native who was as successful at Kentucky as he was unhappy.

(This was not Arkansas's first approach to Bryant. In December of 1941, when Bear was a Vanderbilt assistant, Arkansas backers in Little Rock talked informally to him about succeeding Fred Thomsen. The Japanese bombed Pearl Harbor virtually the next day, and everybody involved suddenly had more pressing matters at hand.)

Barnhill and Bryant liked and respected each other. They got along exceptionally well considering one was a Tennessee man and the other an Alabama man who had also worked at Vanderbilt and Kentucky, also Tennessee archenemies.

Bryant tentatively agreed to replace Douglas at Arkansas but returned to Lexington "to an all-night meeting of the biggest Kentucky boosters," he recalled years later, and finally agreed to stay on one more season and see if he could get along better on the same campus with athletic director and basketball icon Adolph Rupp.

Barnhill turned quietly to his ace in the hole.

Wyatt was a prize Tennessee product, an All-American end and captain on the Vols' 11-0 team of 1938. He grew up in Kingston, Tennessee, about 35 miles from the Knoxville campus. In 1938, he caught six passes for touchdowns, blocked a punt for a touchdown, and kicked two field goals and 16 extra points.

His determination and hard football intelligence made a lasting impression on Barnhill, the Tennessee line coach in Wyatt's playing years. Bowden was big, handsome, dynamic, and demanding, a natural leader of men and thus a prime coaching prospect.

Wyatt captained the 1939 College All-Stars and joined coach Allyn McKeen as an assistant at Mississippi State. He was there four seasons, in the navy three years, and back to Mississippi State in 1946. McKeen's years represent something close to M-State's golden age of football. The teams Wyatt was associated with totaled 42-7-2.

In 1947 he was hired as head coach of the University of Wyoming, which had not had a winning season since 1931. Wyatt gave the Cowboys a six-year record of 39-17-1, although many of his Cowboys came from Brooklyn. His undefeated 1950 team visited the Gator Bowl and beat Washington and Lee.

Arkansas was not thrilled to be returning to the Tennessee single wing, to put it mildly, but Barnhill and Wyatt were spared an organized outcry. Numbed by the Douglas years and deflated by the failure to land Bryant, most Razorbackers were temporarily past caring.

In February of 1953, the *Arkansas Gazette* pressed its Fayetteville correspondent for a profile story on the new coach. Instead of a story, the correspondent submitted a memo to his editor:

> He said he didn't have anything to say. I tried to phrase it a different way, and he said he didn't know enough about the Arkansas situation to talk about it. I told him we'd just forget about football and talk about him, and he said, "Well, let's wait until after spring practice." Don't get the wrong idea—he was real nice—just stuck to his ground and said he always wanted to say as little as possible . . . He used the expression "low limb" when I asked how the boys in high school rated Arkansas. He said the boys want to play for a winner and they figure they have to go out of state to do it. However, he said the situation wasn't as bad as he had feared.

Otis Douglas had tried to supplement the native recruits by working the East, particularly Pennsylvania. Only a few of his Easteners played, and none distinguished themselves. Douglas was quite open in a belief that he had to have an outside source of supply. If Wyatt entertained such a theory, he kept it to himself. In fact, Wyatt kept everything to himself.

Bowden had sufficient reason to avoid talk of recruiting: He reached Arkansas during the hysterical "Sanity Code" period. Some college administrators were moving in on athletics in the manner of Carrie Nation carrying an ax to a saloon.

The North Central Association, to which the University of Arkansas looked for its accreditation, sought to bar subsidization, recruiting, bowl games, and spring practice. It also intended that coaches be hired and paid as true faculty members, with job security based on "contributions as an educator" instead of winning or losing. It intended for coaching salaries to stay in line with the pay of classroom professors.

Texas schools belonged to a southern accrediting agency, which was not rabid on the subject. The threats facing Arkansas did not directly confront other SWC members.

The NCAA major schools eventually resolved the main argument by acknowledging athletic scholarships as a fact of life and moving to standardize and control them. By 1955 or 1956 simon purism was a dead issue, but 1952–53 was a nervous time all around.

"A boy has to want to play football before he can play for me," Wyatt said, and out of his first spring practice came the smallest, thinnest varsity squad to represent Arkansas since the war years.

Fans had whipped up their hopes six consecutive seasons, 1947-52, sometimes for valid reasons and sometimes not, and had been disappointed six times. They did not expect a thing from Wyatt's team in 1953, so Arkansas went through a 3-7 season with carping and second-guessing at a minimum.

Obviously the Razorbacks had only a handful of quality athletes and thus did well to win three games and make five others competitive. Only Ole Miss (28-0) and Rice (47-0) destroyed them on the scoreboard. Rice was headed for the famous Cotton Bowl game where Dicky Maegle would run wild and be tackled from the bench by Alabama's Tommy Lewis.

The Mississippi game at Memphis was one of four to be televised in part that Saturday, a network experiment leading to the NCAA Game of the Week. One day at his desk Barnhill opened a letter and said to a visitor, "Look here, they want to pay $9,000 for televising the Mississippi game." The other man read the letter and gulped. "Barnie, you'd better look again. That's $90,000."

"Looks like television has a future," Barnhill said.

Lamar McHan functioned as a great football player in 1953. Wyatt demanded he prove himself—each player had to start fresh in the spring, with no holdover status—and McHan responded.

As a single-wing tailback he led the Southwest Conference in passing (1,107 yards), total offense (1,516), punting (40.2), and punt returns (11.1 average). He was named national back-of-the-week for his performance in the Hogs' 41-14 stunner of Texas A&M. He probably handled the ball more than any back in the country that fall, en route to becoming the number-one draft pick of the Chicago Cardinals.

McHan threw the ball; Floyd Sagely caught it. Halfback-size and a defensive specialist under Douglas, Sagely led the SWC with 30 catches for 542 yards and three touchdowns.

Around McHan and Sagely, Wyatt broke in sophomore fullback Henry Moore, sophomore blocking back Preston Carpenter (Lew's brother), and sophomore walk-on wingback Joe Thomason. Bobby Proctor, a fierce little junior-college transfer, alternated with Carpenter.

Between Carpenter and Proctor the blocking back position caught 29 passes. The wingbacks, Thomason and Phil Reginelli, split 18 catches.

In this version of the Tennessee single wing, fans noted in surprise and delight, passing was understood to be legal.

"We'll throw the ball a lot more than Tennessee does," Wyatt had promised at the end of spring practice. "We'll average better than twenty passes a game. Passing is the only equalizer in modern football."

Arkansas definitely needed an equalizer in 1953.

Assessing Wyatt's first year, people decided he just might be the type to build a winner. He had a five-year contract, and they were thinking in five-year terms.

They could not guess how much of a hurry Wyatt was in.

Triple-threat tailback Lamar McHan had a great season in 1953.

– 21 –

THE 25 LITTLE PIGS

The University of Arkansas football brochure of 1954 did not pretend to be peddling a contender: "The coming season will not be rose-colored, but its results should be a stimulus to Wyatt's program and offer concrete evidence of a start in the right direction. The burden of battle will be largely in the hands of sophomores . . . Perhaps the most convincing evidence of the newness of the '54 crop is seen in Wyatt's decision to hold up on the election of team captains until early in September. By then, Wyatt says, maybe the boys can get to know one another."

By October everybody knew them. Writers scrambled for clichés to convey an underdog gone wild: the Amazing Razorbacks, the Paradoxical Porkers, the twenty-and-three Little Pigs. When it was over they were known for all time as the 25 Little Pigs, but do not ask for an exact head count.

It was one of the great coaching jobs of all time, and it was more.

Scorched by a summer-long drought and emotionally exhausted by the gubernatorial race in which long-shot Orval Faubus overtook Francis Cherry, Arkansans were desperate for something to cheer in the fall of 1954.

Wyatt's Razorbacks became the first "modern" Arkansas team in terms of an overflowing War Memorial Stadium and overflowing state-wide mania.

They beat Tulsa, 41-0. It was the first shutout achieved by a U of A team in 68 games.

They beat TCU, 20-13. It was the first Arkansas victory at a Texas site in six years.

Bowden Wyatt had a surprise in store for the football world in 1954.

They beat Baylor, 21-20, marking the first time since 1946 a Razorback team survived both TCU and Baylor.

They beat Texas, 20-7, their first win at Austin in 17 years.

They beat Ole Miss, 6-0, in a showpiece game that earned national respect.

They beat Texas A&M, 14-7, proving they could win when all the intangibles rested with the other side.

They beat Rice, 28-15, for the first time in eight years.

They got that far, 7-0 and ranked number four in the polls, but by then they were spent. A good SMU team beat them at Fayetteville, 21-14, and a poor LSU team edged them at Shreveport, 7-6. On form they handled Houston in an anti-climax finale, 19-0.

They went to the Cotton Bowl against Georgia Tech, fought the good fight, and lost, 14-6. Then Wyatt left for Tennessee.

The rules makers moved to restore old-time football after the 1952 season, striking down unlimited substitution that had spawned specialized two-platoon play after World War II. Coaches examined the new limits and decided their best bet was alternate units of two-way players. To most coaches, and especially to Tennessee-trained Wyatt, that meant the most advanced and toughest defensive players went on the first unit.

All season long in 1954, Wyatt maneuvered his second group, offensive types, into spots where they could play offense against the other team's weakest defensive combination. The results outdid his fondest expectations.

The first-unit front consisted of sophomore Ted Souter (172) and junior Jerry McFadden (180) at ends, seniors Eddie Bradford (195 to 200) and Jim Roth (196) at tackle, sophomore Dick Hardwick (220) and All-American senior Bud Brooks (206) at guards, and sophomore Jerry Ford (182) at center. Sophomore George Walker came through in splendid style at tailback and safety, junior Henry Moore (190) took care of fullback, junior Joe Thomason (153) played wingback, and junior Preston Carpenter (186) did a lot of things at blocking back in addition to blocking.

Sophomore Olan Burns (184) and junior Billy Lyons (180) were the second-unit ends, although Lyons and junior Walt Matthews (180) were used as important pass receivers with either unit. Sophomore Billy Ray Smith (200) and junior Bill Fuller (210) were the second-team tackles and defensive pinch-hitters on goal-line stands. Junior Wayland Roberts (190) and junior Bobby Gilliam (190) played guard, with junior-college transfer Harold Steelman (190) at center.

The alternate backfield contained sophomore tailback Buddy Bob Benson (167), a high school star from De Queen and a transfer from Oklahoma; senior Joe Bill Wilson (185) at fullback; sophomore Ronnie Underwood (185) at wingback; and senior Bobby Proctor (163), who came to personify the team's competitive fury, at blocking back.

Nothing went to waste. They would turn a big defensive play to get the ball in scoring range, and then turn a big offensive play and score. "They're living off trash; they're stealing a championship," grumbled a Texas A&M aide in mid-season to head coach Paul (Bear) Bryant, who had stayed that extra year at Kentucky before switching to College Station.

"Don't knock it," admonished Bryant, breaking in at A&M with a 1-9 record. "We'd do the same thing if we could."

Brooks and Bradford, seniors who broke in under Otis Douglas, had been "rendered" from near 250 to 200 pounds. The 1954 Razorbacks were literally a lean and hungry team.

Walker, from Rison, was an exemplary Tennessee-system tailback—meaning poised, smart, and coachable—with the knack of making proper moves under pressure. He could win games passing and kicking. He ran, not with great speed but with an instinct and an alertness that made him more dangerous than some faster men. On defense, with Walker back there, nobody worried about safety.

Moore, who had halfback speed as well as fullback power, and Carpenter, who could have played any position, gave Walker the ingredients for a single-wing offense that could score with jolting suddenness. But as often as not, Benson's alternate unit delivered the points.

"Bowden did the best job of coaching with less material than anybody I ever saw," Barnhill said.

All the elements were present in the Razorbacks' 41-0 Tulsa opener: the exploitation of scoring chances and the balanced workload between units. Fans read no omens into it. They knew Tulsa could not be compared to Southwest Conference contenders and mighty Mississippi.

Texas Christian was rugged and raw in 1954, loaded with sophomores who would give the Horned Frogs two of their all-time best teams in 1955–56. At Fort Worth the Frogs and Hogs stood even at 13-13 when Proctor intercepted a pass and ran it back 63 yards to the TCU six yard line with one minute and 53 seconds remaining in the game.

Benson carried three times, overcoming a five-yard penalty, and Moore covered the last few inches for a touchdown. Walker converted, 20-13, and TCU could only accept the kickoff.

The Hogs had piled up an early 13-0 lead, going 18 yards after a fumble recovery with Walker slashing over from the six and shaking Moore loose down the middle on a 48-yard touchdown run. TCU then dominated the last three periods, during which Arkansas made just two first downs.

Against Baylor at Fayetteville the Razorbacks led early by 18-7. In the fourth quarter they trailed 20-18. Wyatt turned to his alternate unit in the final period, and twice Benson fought for the necessary yardage on third-down situations. Twisting and tearing for extra yards caused him to fumble at the Baylor 12.

Baylor handed the ball back on the next play, with Del Shofner fumbling at the 11. Three downs later Benson and Wilson had the ball at the four, facing fourth down and three. Benson called time, and Carpenter entered.

The Razorbacks had missed three extra points that afternoon, two by Carpenter, but Wyatt sent in Preston for the field-goal attempt. He kicked it for a 21-20 win.

The Texas Longhorns, pre-season SWC favorites, took wins over LSU and Washington State and losses to Notre Dame and Oklahoma into the Arkansas game at Austin. Bookmakers called the Longhorns a 12-point pick over the Hogs.

Wyatt told a reporter in mid-week, "These last two days, I've had more advice and plays in the mail than all the rest of my time up here put together."

Volunteer suggestions did not include a 67-yard quick kick by Walker, but he delivered one that kept Texas bottled up most of the first quarter. And Walker's punting pressure led the Steers to gamble with a pass that Carpenter intercepted at the Texas 20 and carried across for the first touchdown.

With the second units matched up in the second quarter, Benson's blockers cut the Steers down around both flanks, and Bobby Bob ran Texas ragged in a drive that ended with him going the final two yards untouched.

The Longhorns rushed in their number-one unit to face Wyatt's reserves and try to cut into the 14-0 margin before halftime. Texas drove 65 yards to within a foot of the Arkansas goal. When officials turned the ball end-to-end for the next play, it appeared almost to hang over the chalk.

Texas tried to throw for a touchdown. Moore intercepted and returned to the 18. Then Moore galloped 82 yards for a 20-0 halftime lead on a play that started as a routine clock-wasting slam.

The final score was 20-7, which meant that the eternal outsider Arkansas stood 3-0 in the Southwest Conference race.

Long after his playing days, Henry Moore said Wyatt's conditioning standards beat the 'Horns and the Austin heat.

"The shape he had us in," Henry said, "we could have run all the way back to Fayetteville after the game."

That game, incidentally, marked the beginning of the end for coach Ed Price at Texas. Soft spots exposed by the Razorbacks could not be repaired by Price, and the decline deepened during the next two years. Then Darrell Royal was called in.

The day Arkansas beat Texas, Mississippi leveled Tulane by 34-7. The Hogs (4-0) and Rebels (5-0) would be together in War Memorial Stadium the following Saturday.

They kicked off with 38,000 people jammed within seeing distance of the field. It was the first absolute sellout in the stadium's history and would soon lead to the selling out of all reserved seats for Little Rock games in the June mail for succeeding seasons.

"We didn't belong on the same field with 'em," said Wyatt assistant Dick Hitt. "They had outscored their first five opponents like 200-0 (actually, 171-35), and they were leading the nation in offense. We'd scrambled for everything.

"They'd been scoring on runs and passes of 40 to 60 yards. We had a cockeyed defense for that. We put seven men on the wide side of the field and four on the short side. They spotted that right away and began hitting the short side, but we took away their long gainers.

"In the first quarter they made a first down on our 14. Now we were in our goal-line defense and (Ole Miss) hadn't run many plays on the goal line. It came to fourth and two at the six. Johnny Vaught put in a new backfield. He had Slick McCool at fullback. Everybody in the park knew they'd give it to McCool off tackle on the belly handoff. Bill Fuller penetrated, and everybody joined him on the tackle."

Later Vaught said, "I've never seen a team clam up like we did after we got stopped down there."

"They weren't prepared to bleed for six points," Hitt said.

The game rocked on, scoreless. The Arkansas staff regarded Eagle Day, a prototype roll-out threat, as the best passer in the country. But Wyatt had noticed it took Day time to fake the belly, fake the pitch, and set up to throw. Teddy Souter, a tigerish end, did not give him time. Day completed two of 11, and Arkansas intercepted two.

"They were afraid of interceptions," said Wyatt, and indeed Vaught lamented Arkansas's "superior speed in the secondary" and "great pursuit."

Arkansas had an outstanding passer in Walker and good receivers on the first unit, but they often wore out playing defense. On this occasion, Wyatt admittedly used his starters to "smooth the knots off that hot first team from Ole Miss."

With six minutes left in the game, Benson's alternates advanced the ball from the Arkansas 17 to the 30. Hitt, in the press box, phoned Wyatt on the field. "If we're gonna run it, we better run it now," he said. "We may not get the ball again."

"It" meant the Powder River Play.

Wyatt came to Arkansas from Wyoming where the Powder River runs a mile wide and six inches deep. At Arkansas, Wyatt's staff tagged Benson the Powder River runner. They said he'd dash 50 yards across the field to net one yard. When he got the ball, both teams would race toward the sidelines.

"It was an old Alabama play," Hitt said. "A sweep to the weak side with a pass to the number-two back (the blocking back) who would half-heartedly block the end and then play poker into the secondary. It wouldn't work with Walker, our best passer; they'd expect a pass."

Wyatt sent in the play on third and six at the 34.

"Well, it worked like a charm," Hitt said. "When Benson lit out to his left, so did the whole Ole Miss team. Houston Patton, their safety, came up fast. Carpenter slipped right by him. And he was so open I was scared to death Buddy wouldn't hit him. But he did."

It was a 66-yard touchdown play. The ball traveled 33 yards in the air, and Carpenter ran the other 33 unmolested. The Razorbacks won, 6-0.

Arkansas fans were slow to leave the stadium.

"They're still up there," Barnhill told Wyatt in the dressing room, "making sure the numbers don't change on the scoreboard."

The Benson-to-Carpenter pass against Ole Miss in 1954 remains the most often cited single play ever executed by a Razorback team.

"Yeah, it was a great game and a great win and a great call by Coach Wyatt," Benson said 40 years later. "To tell the truth, I sometimes get a little tired of hearing about it, but I don't ever hurt anyone's feelings. I'm proud people remember it."

Texas A&M presented a different kind of challenge. The Hogs had been dismantling favorites; they would be favored at College Station. Bear Bryant had cleaned house and was building from rock bottom. His first Aggie squad could not win, but played like it intended to.

Preston Carpenter catches "The Pass" from Buddy Bob Benson.

The Aggies swarmed Arkansas with a fanatical determination to give nothing away. In the process they fumbled twice, and the Razorbacks turned both bobbles into touchdowns.

Arkansas trailed, 7-0, and only 50 seconds remained in the first half when the first break came. McFadden covered a fumble on the Aggies' 38. Wyatt sent in Walt Matthews at weak-side end. Matthews ran a pattern down the middle, grabbed a Walker pass, and scored. Walker kicked Arkansas into a 7-7 tie.

Bud Brooks smacked into Elwood Kettler to send a pitchout astray, and Souter got it for Arkansas at the Hogs' 46 late in the third period. Moore did most of the running on the 54-yard touchdown drive. Henry popped one down the left side for 26 yards and scored the winning touchdown with one of his typical head-first hurdles from the two. The Razorbacks held on, 14-7.

They returned to War Memorial Stadium to face Rice and another frenzied 38,000 sellout. The Owls still had Dick Maegle, who gained 201 yards the previous fall in helping rout the Hogs at Houston, 47-0.

Jess Neely had whipped Arkansas seven straight times after John Hoffman's pass interception beat him in 1946. It would be Neely's misfortune to catch the 1954 Porkers on their last magical afternoon.

Walker passed for the Razorbacks' key plays on two long touchdown drives, each starting under the pressure of a Rice lead, 6-0 in the second quarter and 15-14 in the final period.

And Walker supplied a humiliating fillip with a 72-yard punt return in the third quarter, made possible when the Owls relaxed on the tackle before a whistle was blown. George just pulled away and kept going.

When it was over, Walker had completed nine of 13 passes for 119 yards (each completion a vital one), punted six times for a 43-yard average, advanced the ball nearly 200 yards on rushing and kick returns, and scored 19 points. Now solidly No. 4 in the national polls, Arkansas whipped Rice by 28-15.

The next weekend, homecoming at Fayetteville, a crowd of 27,300 sat in shocked silence while SMU piled up a 21-0 lead in three quarters, Frank Eidom, a hard-running speedster having a deluxe day, scored the three Mustang touchdowns on that new-fangled play, the inside belly. Walker passed the Razorbacks as close as 21-14 and narrowly missed passing them to a third touchdown and a possible tie.

SMU, with one tie (Texas) and no conference losses, then held the inside track on the Cotton Bowl. Arkansas, finishing its league schedule at 5-1, needed outside help.

It came the next weekend. Baylor beat SMU, 33-21, allowing the Hogs to "back into" a conference title and the accompanying Cotton Bowl bid. It happened while Arkansas was losing to LSU at Shreveport, 7-6.

Benson cashed in a short Arkansas drive with a touchdown pass to Billy Lyons in the second quarter. Benson's conversion attempt missed, leaving it 6-0. "I didn't think anything about it," Benson said. "We felt like we could go on scoring all day." They could not. LSU, 3-6 going into the game, scored once and converted, and that was that.

Back at the Washington-Youree Hotel in downtown Shreveport, eating and waiting for the train ride home (teams flew regularly by then, but Wyatt still favored trains), the Razorbacks found it hard to appear heartbroken over their LSU mishap. They had climbed all the way from pre-season obscurity to a Cotton Bowl bid.

There was laughter and loud, kidding talk in the dining room. Members of the coaching staff sharply reminded them they had lost, and they—the coaches—could locate no humor in the day's events.

Wyatt must have had second thoughts on the way home. Some team members recall that Dick Hitt went around on the train and "did a little public relations work" with players who absorbed most of the scolding.

A close-out win over Houston gave the Hogs an 8-2 record. They tumbled in the polls after SMU week, but they finished in the national Top 10 for the first time—exactly tenth in the Associated Press ranking, eighth in United Press International.

On December 2 Wyatt received a new Cadillac from fans who contributed $17,000 to an appreciation fund for the coach.

On the same day the University of Tennessee fired Harvey Robinson, General Bob Neyland's coaching successor.

Rumors linking Wyatt and his alma mater's vacancy piled up through December. Bowden dodged them as best he could and tried to concentrate on preparing his team for Georgia Tech on New Year's Day.

The Porkers put in a series of new pass plays built around Carpenter, their best receiver, as a weak-side target. Carpenter suffered a pulled back muscle in the first quarter at Dallas and was out the rest of the day. Georgia Tech overturned the Razorbacks' 6-0 halftime lead and won the Cotton Bowl game, 14-6.

A week later Wyatt was officially hired by the University of Tennessee.

"It was the toughest decision I ever had to make," Wyatt said in St. Louis on January 8 en route to Fayetteville from an NCAA convention at New York. "I thought about it and thought about it. Finally I had to make up my mind, and I decided if I was ever going to the job I've always wanted, I'd better go now."

Yes, some Razorback fans ripped him bitterly, but the criticism heaped on Bowden Wyatt came, for the most part, from outside Arkansas. Eastern sports columnists, suddenly outraged about contract-breaking, made an example of him. He "jumped" a Wyoming contract to

Bowden Wyatt and All-American guard Bud Brooks talk strategy before the Cotton Bowl game against Georgia Tech.

go to Arkansas and "jumped" an Arkansas contract to leave for Tennessee in his new Cadillac.

The gap was between standard operating procedure at all schools and the obligation implied by "contract." When Wyatt's successor, Jack Mitchell, was hired, U of A president John T. Caldwell spelled it out in a letter to Mitchell.

"The language of the Board of Trustees' approval, as recommended by me and the Faculty Committee on Athletics, is an intentional departure from the language used in recent years in the appointment of head football coaches. The effect . . . is not to bind you to a five-year 'contract' to the University of Arkansas, but to assure you of a five-year tenure . . . The administration and Board would expect from you the proper courtesy of notice to us should you enter into negotiations with another institution for an appointment."

Wyatt and his Wyoming-Arkansas staffers got Tennessee moving again in 1955 to 6-3-1. In 1956, when the Vols took a 10-0 record to the Sugar Bowl, Wyatt's peers voted him coach of the year. The right man in the right situation, he looked forward to a long, enjoyable dynasty.

Instead, Wyatt's personal and professional life turned chaotic the next few years. Everything came to a boil in 1963 when the University of Tennessee decreed that Neyland's successor as athletic director must hold a college degree. Not an unusual requirement, except that Wyatt, the head coach who expected to become athletic director, did not have a degree.

He was then relieved of his coaching duties at Tennessee on an "interim" basis that became permanent. Worried friends heard stories of excessive drinking and erratic behavior by a deeply troubled man.

He tried a comeback as an assistant coach under Phil Cutchin at Oklahoma State, formerly Oklahoma A&M. That lasted two seasons. His problems worsened, and his health continued to decline. At the time of his death, he was overseer of a Tennessee farm owned by a longtime friend.

And when he died his old Arkansas players did not want to hear the details of his last days. They remembered him as a great man in their lives—a powerful, creative leader.

In 1973 Barnhill was asked, "When you hired Bowden, did you feel he was on the way back to Tennessee?"

"I was so desperate at that time," Barnhill said, "I didn't give it a thought."

The combination of the Douglas failure and the Wyatt success spared Barnhill further quibbling from elements of the booster hierarchy.

His concerns as athletic director were not over, but they changed radically after 1954. It was no longer a question of filling War Memorial and Razorback stadiums; it was finding means to expand the seating capacity of the two plants. The athletic scholarship donors' program, known and copied across college football as the "Arkansas Plan," soon developed a waiting list.

All the things Barnhill mapped out in his mind in 1946 came true after 1954. Wyatt's Little Pigs represent a clean break between old and new.

EMOTION AND THE SPLIT-T

Jack Mitchell neither failed nor succeeded. Inserted between Bowden Wyatt and Frank Broyles in the record book, his three-year hitch at Arkansas looks like a caretaker period, a recess. Examined in context, things that happened under Mitchell were better than that. Especially against Ole Miss.

When his teams went 5-4-1, 6-4, and 6-4, Mitchell became the first Arkansas coach in this century to stay more than two years and get away without suffering a .500 or worse season. We know now this was partly a sign that the program was maturing.

Mitchell coached on emotion. Nobody pitched players higher for specific games, and when the inevitable letdown came, Jack was let down right along with his athletes. *His* enthusiasm waxed and waned, too.

He entered a Southwest Conference justly celebrated for top-to-bottom ruggedness. Texas was ailing, but Abe Martin had a great team at TCU—the Jim Swink crowd—and Bear Bryant was hammering together the John David Crow era at Texas A&M. Baylor was usually strong, and Jess Neely was still on his timetable that produced a championship team for Rice every three or four years.

TCU and Baylor ended Mitchell's first two SWC races before they got started. The Horned Frogs humiliated the Porkers by 26-0 at Fayette-ville in 1955 and by 41-6 at Fort Worth (on national television) in 1956. Baylor followed up by beating Arkansas 25-20 at Waco and 14-7 at Fayetteville.

Both those years the Razorbacks settled and came on strongly but were foiled at the finish by struggling, lightly held LSU teams. They never had much emotion left for the Tigers.

Mitchell's third Arkansas squad, and his best, got to the Texas A&M game on November 2, 1957, with a real shot at the Cotton Bowl. They lost, 7-6. They went to Houston the next Saturday with Sugar Bowl talk in the wind. Rice beat them, 13-7. Gator Bowl scouts saw them lose to SMU at Dallas, 27-22.

One fan was especially distraught on the ride home from the SMU game. "We're the only team," he said, "that ever got put out of the Cotton Bowl, Sugar Bowl, and Gator Bowl in three weeks' time. If some other bowl wants us, we won't have a chance against Texas Tech."

No other bowl wanted them, and they beat Tech easily at Little Rock, 47-26. It was their first meeting with the Red Raiders and also the last game Mitchell coached for Arkansas. Stories that he was negotiating with Kansas were around as early as A&M week. Rumor became fact after the Tech game.

Like Wyatt, Mitchell was going home in a sense, although he was not a KU alumnus. His hometown was Arkansas City, Kansas, where he was a local athletic prodigy before enrolling at the University of Texas in 1942. After three and a half years of military service, he decided to go to Oklahoma instead of returning to Texas.

Jack Mitchell became Oklahoma's first renowned split-T quarterback. Considered the sixth-best passer among six quarterback candidates when he checked in at OU, he made it as a runner and fire-eating leader. For Jim Tatum in 1946 and Bud Wilkinson in 1947–48, he led the Sooners to three straight Big Six championships—the launching of the Wilkinson dynasty.

Jack hit the coaching field in 1949 as a man in a hurry: Blackwell, Oklahoma, high school, a 9-1 record; backfield coach under Buddy Brothers at Tulsa University, an 8-1-1 record; to Texas Tech to help DeWitt Weaver install the split-T, a 14-7 record in two years.

At 28 he was offered Wichita State's head coaching job. It was the kind of gamble young coaches find irresistible. Improve the situation, attract attention, move up. When Mitchell's 28-man squad battled to a 4-4-1 record in 1953, it was an improvement. When the Wheatshockers won the Missouri Valley championship with 9-1 in 1954, Mitchell was ripe to move. Arkansas turned to him as Wyatt's successor.

With his energy, Oklahoma background, and Joe College good looks, Jack could recruit and motivate. His overriding defensive theory was that every play should be met at the line of scrimmage. A forcing defense can stop an opponent sensationally cold one down and give up a home-run play the next, as Mitchell's Hogs occasionally demonstrated.

Jack figured effort, desire, and conditioning conquered all. Sometimes they did, and sometimes they did not.

Under Mitchell the pass almost disappeared. Preston Carpenter led the team with 11 catches in 1955, Ronnie Underwood led with seven in 1956, and Billy Kyser led with 10 in 1957. For perspective's sake, remember passing was de-emphasized everywhere in the middle 1950s, a period dominated by split-T theory and unspecialized athletes. Passing teams were regarded as desperate or sissified.

The 1955 Hogs were only 3-3 going into the last month, and fans were making sour little jokes about an offensive gimmick Mitchell called the pigeon-toed split-T.

Then Arkansas forced a 7-7 tie on A&M at Fayetteville, shut out Rice, 10-0, at Houston, and SMU, 6-0, at Dallas. The Razorbacks had not won at Dallas in 19 years. They had never beaten Rice at Houston in 16 previous trips, scattered back to 1919.

Preston Carpenter played some of the best football of his life, and Henry Moore was rushing toward 701 yards in his senior season. Talk started that Wyatt's holdover Arkansas veterans, now operating Mitchell's split-T, would face Wyatt's first Tennessee squad in the Gator Bowl.

Mitchell was eager for a matchup with his predecessor, but it never happened. A 3-5-2 LSU team was not impressed by the nine consecutive scoreless quarters the Arkansas defense brought to Little Rock for the season's final game. The Tigers won more decisively than the 13-7 score suggests. Arkansas got on the scoreboard because Underwood returned a kickoff 88 yards. The Razorbacks were outgained, 302 yards to 94. So long, Gator Bowl.

Mitchell lost half his starting backfield before Arkansas played a game in 1956. Quarterback George Walker suffered a knee injury in the last full-scale scrimmage before the Hardin-Simmons opener. Don Horton, scheduled to be the regular right halfback, had suffered a broken collarbone a few days earlier. Both men were out for the season.

Again the Razorbacks took their early conference lumps, but they exploded at Austin in a 19-point fourth quarter to overtake and run away with Texas, 32-14. Next came a nearly perfect show against Ole Miss.

Don Christian, a running quarterback after Mitchell's own heart, zipped through the Rebels for 122 yards (without any losses) and a 14-0 Arkansas victory on a sellout night in War Memorial Stadium. Mississippi got into Arkansas territory only twice and past the Hogs' 35 only once. Arkansas controlled the game to an extent; it led in first downs, 17-9. This was one of Jack's peaks.

The next week at College Station, Arkansas caved in to an unbeaten Aggie team, 27-0. (After peaks, valleys.)

Christian, Underwood, Gerald Nesbitt, and sophomore Donnie Stone ran Rice and SMU to death the next two Saturdays, 27-12 and 27-13. Tackle Billy Ray Smith, to be a notable long-term pro, was rounding out a tremendous senior season. Surely these Hogs were ready to end the LSU nonsense. The Tigers would take a 1-7 record to Shreveport Fairgrounds Stadium. Arkansas was shooting confidently for a 7-3 finish.

In the second quarter the Razorbacks crowded in to meet future Green Bay star Jim Taylor at the line. He popped through them and had a clear path to a 75-yard touchdown run. Only 90 seconds later Paul Ziegler intercepted a halfback pass by Underwood and loped 27 yards to score. Those two bolts flattened the Hogs, and they botched everything in a 21-7 loss,

Although he remained as professionally cautious as ever in public statements ("In this league, even a good team can finish last"), Mitchell knew a strong squad was coming in 1957.

He had both Walker, for a delayed senior year, and Christian at quarterback. At the last moment, he decided to redshirt James Monroe, who played well as a sophomore behind Christian the year before. (It was a decision for which Frank Broyles would always be grateful.)

Gerald Nesbitt, a 25-year-old ex-Marine from Big Sandy, Texas, was the real find of the Mitchell years and the fullback around which the 1957 offense was built.

Backing Henry Moore in 1955, Nesbitt made 371 yards. In 1956 Gerald gained 663 (he lost the rushing title to TCU's Jim Swink by two yards) and intercepted four passes. "Gerald Nesbitt?" Mitchell said after a Red-White spring scrimmage. "Why, he even looks good tying his shoes." Jerry Ferguson and Lamar Drummonds were serviceable fullback reserves, but there was no total replacement for Nesbitt on the squad.

Behind halfbacks Donnie Stone, Don Horton, and Don Ritschel, Arkansas broke in the prized south Arkansas sophomores Jim Mooty of El Dorado and Billy Kyser of Camden. Center Jay Donathan was the leader of the line, where other important names were Bob Childress, Richard Bennett, Billy Michael, Jerry Ford, Stuart Perry, Billy Gilbow, Rollie Luplow, Greg Pinkston, Charlie Whitworth, Billy Tranum, Barry Switzer, and Richard Bell.

Combine the regulars with sophomores, redshirts, and freshmen, and you see the Razorbacks had, in the fall of 1957, teams of the future as well as the present. The nucleus was there, below the surface mostly, for Broyles's first two winners, 1959–60.

The 1957 Razorbacks were the first Arkansas team to be praised as "quick" in dressing-room tributes week after week. "Two well-conditioned units," Bear Bryant said, and they opened by swarming over Oklahoma State, 12-0, and Tulsa, 41-14.

When they took their revenge on rebuilding TCU, 20-7, and broke the Waco jinx over Baylor, 20-17, they stood 4-0, a hot Cotton Bowl contender.

They were favored over Texas at Fayetteville, but Mitchell's Oklahoma teammate and quarterback successor, Darrell Royal, was now in charge of the Longhorns. Arkansas moved the ball, but Texas did the scoring and won, 17-0,

"He outcoached me," Mitchell said in the Arkansas dressing room. "Jack's mighty gracious," a grinning Royal responded.

Could Mitchell bring Arkansas back against a great Ole Miss team? Indeed he could. Most Arkansas coaches viewed the Rebs as a disastrous distraction between Texas and Texas A&M, but Jack thrived on the motivational factors of the rancorous Arkansas-Mississippi series. And he won two of three from Johnny Vaught.

The 1957 Rebs had allowed their first five foes just seven points, and they turned to Arkansas from a 50-0 clobbering of Tulane. On a windy, downright cold afternoon in late October, quaint old Crump Stadium in Memphis brimmed with 30,000 anxious, agitated people. Those from Mississippi came expecting a rout. Those from Arkansas unhappily reached the same conclusion after a first quarter in which the Rebs mauled the Hogs for a 6-0 lead.

But then a yard or so past midfield in the second quarter, Arkansas faced third down and inches. Nesbitt, obviously, would get the call. Walker faked a handoff to Nesbitt up the middle, then stepped back and arched a strike to Kyser who was racing in the open near the left sideline at the Ole Miss 27. Kyser lost some time cutting to the middle away from a defender, and Billy Lott nailed him from behind at the 13. The 36-yard bolt set the Hogs on fire. Kyser got the touchdown, looking like a blur on an eight-yard dive play.

In the third quarter, the score 6-6, the hard-pressed Razorbacks held on downs at their 15. Soon they faced third and three at the 22.

"We'd better quick-kick it and get the ball out of there," Mitchell told Walker at the bench.

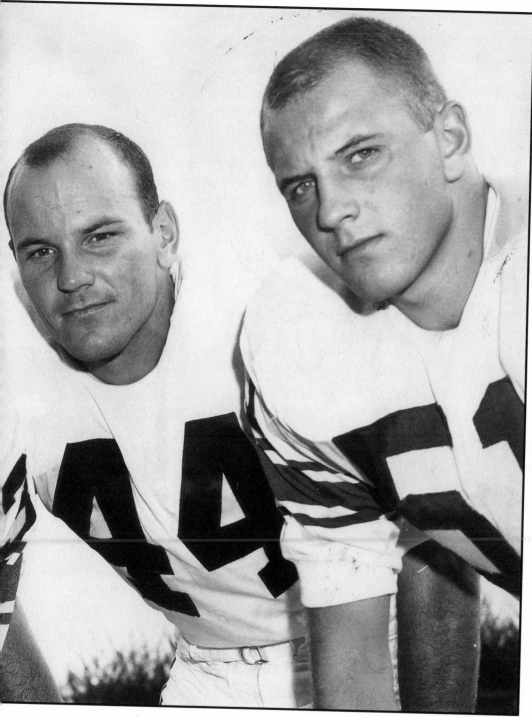

Jack Mitchell and three of his finest: Gerald Nesbitt, George Walker, and Jay Donathan

"Coach, maybe we can run one more play, and then I'll kick it," Walker said.

"Well . . . okay," Mitchell said doubtfully.

Walker's tone was confident and firm. "If we don't make a first down, I'll kick it out of there," he said.

"Well, go ahead," Mitchell said.

Walker gave the ball to Nesbitt off-tackle, who found a huge hole waiting for him. Gerald rambled through, maintained his balance, and started running over and past Rebels. They began to hem him in as he reached the Ole Miss 30, so he started looking for help. Here came Kyser sprinting down the right sideline. Before Nesbitt was tackled, he flipped the ball to Kyser, who carried it on until a Reb shouldered him out of bounds at the three-yard line.

The Nesbitt run and the lateral to Kyser added up to a 75-yard gain, and the ball game went with it. Kyser swept across for the last few inches on fourth down, and Arkansas won, 12-6.

"It was one of those games," a seething Johnny Vaught said in the dressing room. "The damn Hogs got high on us again. They always do."

The Rebels finished 8-1-1 and went to the Sugar Bowl to beat Texas, 39-7. Ole Miss in 1957 was the best team Arkansas beat under Jack Mitchell.

From the sixth-ranked Rebels at Memphis, Arkansas turned to the number-one team in the nation.

Bear Bryant's Texas Aggies were unbeaten in 16 consecutive games when they visited Fayetteville for the Razorbacks' homecoming. There were not that many of them. They had one superior unit—John David Crow, Charley Krueger, Bobby Marks, et cetera—and they were battered and drained. Mitchell intended to wear them down with two units, and it almost worked.

In 1956 the undefeated (9-0-1) Aggies led the SWC but were on probation and ineligible for post-season activity. In 1957, with the sanctions lifted, they had no obstacles except those on the field. They intended to win the national title, the conference title, and snare that elusive Cotton Bowl bid.

All week long, scare stories circulated in Fayetteville about a flu epidemic on the Arkansas squad. The flu was real enough, but most varsity players recovered in time. After the game a reporter asked Bryant if Arkansas appeared to be "flu-weakened." Without hesitating or even blinking, Bryant gestured at the scoreboard, which still showed the 7-6 final score.

"Sure they were flu-weakened," he said. "How the hell else could we have run up the score on 'em like that?"

The Aggies trailed for the first time all season when Don Christian and the second-unit Razorbacks went 46 yards on them the first time they had the ball. Christian scored from the one, and Nesbitt missed the conversion.

A&M put together a 74-yard drive, with Crow scoring on a 12-yard swing around right end. The Aggies had not missed a conversion all year, and Lloyd Taylor kicked them ahead, 7-6. That was the score at halftime, and for all time.

Arkansas controlled the ball the final two periods in an effective execution of Mitchell's two-unit battle plan, but the class of the Aggies enabled them to stand off fourth-quarter Arkansas drives to the five and the 13.

With about seven minutes to play, the Porkers reached a fourth-and-three crisis at the A&M five. Third-string sophomore Freddy Akers was summoned for a point-blank field-goal attempt that went wide to the left.

That, plus a fumble at midfield by Christian, seemed to sew it up for A&M. But with two minutes showing and A&M trying to kill the clock, quarterback Roddy Osborne elected to pass for a first down inside the Arkansas 20. He threw the ball out to the sideline. Don Horton intercepted and took off in the direction of the A&M goal line. A desperate chase ended with Osborne and Taylor tacking him at the A&M 27.

(From that interception sequence came a durable banquet joke. How could a slow runner like Osborne catch the swifter Horton? Easy. Horton was running for a touchdown, but Osborne was running for his life.)

Donnie Stone went for three yards, and George Walker passed to Horton for a first down on the 15. On a sweep to the left, Horton went out of bounds on the 15.

Heisman Trophy winner John David Crow applied the crusher by intercepting a Walker pass at the goal line. Bob Childress crossed over from left end on the pattern, but just as he pivoted for a catch on the run, Crow materialized from nowhere and stole it.

"A big shot of Old Crow," Bryant called it.

More than a decade later, at the end of his distinguished career as an NFL running back, Crow discussed his games against Arkansas in an informal session with Little Rock sportswriters.

"When I was a sophomore (1955), we stayed at Rogers the night before and rode a bus over to Fayetteville. Somebody said something

Ronnie Underwood scores against Texas in 1956, with George Bequette throwing a block near the goal line.

I thought was funny. I snickered. Coach Bryant whirled around and looked, and I felt like jumping under the seat. That was the day when we played a 7-7 tie."

"I had a long conversation with him about you that day," a writer said. "He really downgraded you. And you didn't have that bad a day."

"But we *tied*," Crow said. "The next year, back at College Station, we beat Arkansas bad, 28-0."

"Uh, 27-0," he was gently corrected.

"Yeah? Well, that was a long time ago," Crow said. "In a few years it may be 40-0. Anyway, then we go back to Fayetteville my senior year for a real big game. Okay, it'd been two years since I snickered on that bus ride, and in the meantime we'd beat Arkansas real bad. But Coach Bryant remembered.

"We were getting ready to take the field, and he turned to me and said, 'I think you owe us one at Fayetteville.'"

Drawing each opponent's peak effort week after week, A&M reached 8-0 and yielded everything—national title, SWC title, Cotton Bowl—on losses to Rice, 7-6, and Texas, 9-7. Bryant departed for his alma mater, Alabama, after A&M's Gator Bowl loss to Tennessee.

The bloom was off the Razorbacks, too. Jess Neely's last Cotton Bowl team at Rice stood them off, 13-7. SMU sophomore Don Meredith caught them flat-footed and passed them silly out of a spread formation. SMU had used the spread in spots before, but Mitchell refused to believe it was more than a diversion.

So Meredith completed 19 of 25 for 230 yards and two touchdowns and carried 22 times for 67 yards and two more touchdowns. He made 297 yards of the Mustangs' 348 yards of total offense. Arkansas gained 334 yards but was stopped three times inside the 20. It wound up with SMU yielding a deliberate safety to clinch a 27-22 win at Dallas.

The date was November 16, 1957, and it was an epic football Saturday, nationally and regionally. Notre Dame severed Oklahoma's 47-game winning streak, 7-0. The Rice Owls stopped the Texas Aggies, 7-6, before 72,000 in Houston.

"Oh, boy, this is a crazy day," grinned young Don Meredith in the SMU dressing room. "Oklahoma and A&M lost." He laughed softly. "And ol' Arkansas, too."

"Look at it this way," said a cheery Texas sportswriter to an Arkansas colleague in the press box. "Y'all gonna have the best 6-4 team in the history of the Southwest Conference."

"Thanks," the Arkansan murmured.

The Texas Tech game came off as a no-sweat finale: 575 yards of total offense, 47 points, plenty of playing time for the third unit.

When it became obvious Jack Mitchell was headed for Kansas, there was none of the anguished reaction that followed Bowden Wyatt's departure.

Fans were annoyed that Mitchell considered Kansas a better job, and they were tired of coaches "just passing through," but they had no fear of the future. They were growing up right along with the program.

— 23 —

"BARNIE, WHAT TOOK YOU SO LONG?"

Atlanta Journal columnist Furman Bisher sat with Georgia Tech aide Frank Broyles in a hotel room in Dallas on December 31, 1954, when the Arkansas rooters' first WHOOOO, PIG! SOOOOies began reverberating through the canyons of Commerce and Akard streets. And Bisher said he heard Broyles say, "Can you imagine the feelings of the mother of a football player when they call her son like a hog?"

Frank's policy was to never publicly dispute a writer's word, but he declined to confirm the quote. Maybe it was Bisher who said it, because on the previous night Frank had informally applied to John Barnhill for the Arkansas head coaching post.

"Barnie and I were briefly together at a party the Cotton Bowl gave for the coaching staffs of the two schools," Broyles recalled. "It was common knowledge Tennessee hoped to sign Bowden Wyatt after the bowl game. I told Barnie that for his sake I hoped he didn't lose Bowden, but that if a vacancy did occur I would like to be considered."

The telephone call did not come for three years. When Broyles answered it in Columbia, Missouri, where he was completing his first year as a head coach, he said, "Barnie, what took you so long?"

Broyles said that from the time he first entered the Southwest Conference as a rookie assistant coach at Baylor in 1947 he always wanted to coach at Arkansas. His reasons were the same as those that first brought Barnhill. One school, one state, one goal. He wanted the job all three times it was open after he entered coaching.

Broyles never was interviewed for previous Arkansas vacancies. When the call came he accepted in a matter of seconds. He was always known for quick decisions. "I knew it was a promotion," he said. What he did not know until later was that, while Barnhill always thought well of him, the Arkansas coach-picker made it a policy to never consider anyone who had not had head coaching experience.

The coach who served as window dressing for the actual search to fill the 1958 vacancy was Minnesota's Murray Warmath. He had been one of Barnhill's great linemen at Tennessee. Warmath expressed interest in the job but was then under some duress at Minnesota, and pride insisted he stay and prove himself (which he did, leading Minnesota to the Rose Bowl). Even so Mrs. Warmath phoned Barnhill to intimate that one more call would win her husband over. By then Barnhill had already decided to expose what he had described cryptically to his faculty committee as "my ace in the hole."

Missouri coach Don Faurot had invented or maybe discovered the split-T offense, the basics of which were absorbed by younger coaches Jim Tatum and Bud Wilkinson during a wartime association with Faurot. After the war Missouri suffered much at the hands of Faurot's split-T pupils, especially Wilkinson at Oklahoma. When Faurot was ready to confine himself to full-time athletic director, Broyles was hired as his coaching successor.

"I had known Don Faurot for years," Barnhill said. "Fine coach, but he didn't like to recruit. He had come out for what was known as the Faurot Plan or the Missouri Plan. Everybody would be limited to recruiting in his own state. I knew that when Frank was at Georgia Tech they recruited all over the South. I had some hints he might not like coaching where he'd be limited like that in his recruiting. I thought he'd be ready to come, and he was."

To stunned, hurt Missouri fans, Frank Broyles "fled in the night," in the words of the *St. Louis Post-Dispatch*'s esteemed Bob Broeg.

"Don Faurot never reproached me," said Broyles. "And I will never have anything but gratitude for him. I had despaired of ever getting a head-coaching opportunity; he gave it to me. I wanted the job so badly, and wanted to work under him and at Missouri, which had kept him so long and had not applied great pressures, that I would have agreed to anything.

"And I did agree to the Missouri Plan. Now this did not keep us from crossing the Mississippi River a little or going into Kansas City, Kansas, which we did. Still I thought we ought to be able to go farther, and the fact that the Missouri Plan was forgotten when they hired Dan Devine tells you something.

"Some people said I jumped a contract, but there was none. I had a three-year appointment, and no one knows whether or not it was binding. The Missouri legislature forbade long-term contracts at that time. What I had that was worth something was the word of Faurot that I could leave after one, three or 10 years—whenever I felt unhappy.

"There were some things I was unhappy about after one season. Don went to bat for me, but the committee members pooh-poohed his concern. He warned them of what might happen, but the only thing that could convince them was my departure. Naturally they listened to Devine."

A few years later Devine told a Little Rock writer that Broyles's leaving (as well as some policies Frank instituted in his one year) had helped immensely in his gaining the tools with which to win.

Eventually Frank conceded that Missouri fans could say he had to "eat his words." Thirteen of the freshmen he recruited in 1957 became seniors on Devine's 9-1 (10-0 if you count a forfeiture from Kansas) Orange Bowl team, and they had been rounded up within the framework of the Missouri Plan. And in 1963 Missouri visited Little Rock and out-scrapped Arkansas, 7-6.

Frank never looked back. He had obtained in December 1957, what he called then and afterward "the best coaching job in America."

Twice burnt when Wyatt and then Mitchell left for their native states, Barnhill took one precaution before hiring Broyles. He called his fellow Tennessee alumnus, Bobby Dodd. If Dodd were to retire as head coach of Georgia Tech tomorrow, who would be his successor? Dodd's welcomed reply: Ray Graves, his defensive coordinator. Two years later Graves went to Florida as head coach, and Broyles was to twice decline to return to his alma mater.

Frank's decision to stick with Arkansas would have pleased his father, the late O. T. Broyles, who finished out his life operating an insurance agency. Nothing impressed him more about Frank's new job than the fact Barnhill maintained a $150,000 life insurance policy for the head coach as a fringe benefit, an inducement to stay.

A slight, thin man, O. T. Broyles came from Scotch stock and was cautious and conservative but persevering. Frank inherited many of his qualities but a great deal more came from his mother, a big-boned, forceful woman of German ancestry.

Her will power knew no bounds. When Frank was playing for an Orange Bowl-bound Tech team, Mom Broyles quietly inserted an ad in an Atlanta paper's classified section: "I am Frank Broyles's mother, and I need a ride to Miami." She reached Biscayne Boulevard before Frank and the team did.

When, into her eighties, she suffered a broken leg for the second time and was told she would never walk again, she battled back. She recovered, took a tedious plane trip (seven hours with changes and layovers) from Atlanta to Fayetteville, and spent a month gadding about with Barbara Broyles to teas and school events, often forgetting her cane.

She bequeathed to Frank, certainly, her unflagging good spirits, her optimism, her eagerness to challenge parts and tasks unknown. She also gave him a sense of self-awareness, which no one in coaching can do without.

Frank started with early size, dexterous hands, and a quick mind. And, he said, luck. He always believed in his own good fortune.

"If I had been raised during the Depression, as my older brother Huck was, I probably would have been put to work with no time for sports," he said. "Dad had been in and out of the grocery business four or five times. Delivering on credit. That was tough, and he wasn't as hard as you have to be to collect. Things were better, though, when I started coming of age."

He cut grass for movie money and caddied on weekends for money he turned over to his mother. Mostly, he played games. The die was cast when he was 12 years old and his father caught him smoking a cigarette.

"I'm not sure whether it was tobacco or cornsilks, but it was the kind of thing all kids tried," he said. "Dad laid the law down. 'When I was your age I was helping my parents put food on the table. You're playing games. That's all right, but smoking and games don't mix. You can leave that smoking off and go on playing or you can go to work.'"

Young Frank knew a bargain when he heard one. After that he never touched a cigarette—nor did any work not at least indirectly connected to athletics.

Atlanta now surrounds Decatur, Georgia, but in the late 1930s, Decatur was a contiguous suburb. Frank played for Boys High. He lettered in and excelled at everything. There was never any question in his mind he would go across town to Georgia Tech, even though most people he knew were Georgia fans.

When Broyles was still an assistant coach, this was written about him by Harry Mehre, a former Notre Dame star and coach at Ole Miss and Georgia who wrote a syndicated football column: "No minister, priest, or rabbi is more devoted to his religion than Frank Broyles is to football."

It was not always so.

"In high school and college I started in basketball and baseball before I did in football," he said. "The first offer I had from Tech was from the basketball coach—a combined scholarship in basketball and baseball. I was offered a small bonus to sign with the Yankees as a pitcher before I enrolled at Tech. I laughed. I was going to college, even though my long-range dream at that time was to play big-league baseball."

Approaching the seasons of 1943 and 1944, his sophomore and junior years at Tech, he heard it all the time. "Football isn't his best sport."

"I felt insulted, infuriated every time I heard or read it," he said. "I was determined to overcome that, so I re-doubled my efforts in football."

Tech had had only two head coaches, both legendary figures: John Heisman, for whom the trophy is named, and Bill Alexander, "Coach Alec," up in years by the time Broyles enrolled. Frank played fullback, tailback, and wingback in Alexander's single wing. Dodd, the backfield coach at the time, was Coach Alec's obvious successor.

The lanky, red-haired Broyles showed many of the traits which had made Dodd a quarterbacking genius at Tennessee—shrewd play-caller, artful punter, and crafty passer. Broyles was heavier-footed. When Frank ran back a kick nearly 100 yards against Tulane in 1944, his teammates called it the longest punt return on record—in elapsed time.

He picked up a trophy as the Southeastern Conference's most valuable player for the 1944 season. In the 1945 Orange Bowl game he passed for 279 yards, a record for all bowl games that lasted 25 years. He could feel he had proved a point to his football skeptics.

Frank was studying civil engineering but was also enrolled in the Navy V-12 program. This took him to active duty in the Seabees for a year; he wound up briefly on Okinawa in 1945.

While in service he married his steady girl, Barbara Day, who worked in an aircraft plant in nearby Marietta (and kept his scrapbook, her wedding present to him). While Frank was away in the navy, Dodd became Georgia Tech's head coach and installed the T-formation.

"The old Chicago Bears' T," Broyles said. "Dodd told me this would be ideal for me, and I could fashion a career as a pro quarterback. I wouldn't have to run, just pass and hand off. We worked on it all spring and summer in 1946. You could do that then. Two weeks before our opener with Tennessee, my shoulder got separated. The doctors debated, but I knew I wasn't going to let them operate. They fixed a harness, braced up my shoulder, and I played the whole season. The shoulder never did go back in place; I still have a knot there."

Was it the injury that turned him to coaching?

"No. By then I think I knew what I would do. That summer I helped Sid Scarborough, an Atlanta high school coach, work with the Georgia high school all-stars. Just three days of it fascinated me. Baseball was out; all I had done for three years was warm up my roommate some week days and pitch for amateur teams on weekends. The Bears had drafted me, but I knew I was ready to get into coaching."

When Frank's sons entered their teen years and riffled through the scrapbooks and learned that he had a chance to play baseball for the Yankees or football for the Bears and did not do either, they could not believe it.

"Dodd's most frequent statement to the writers was that I was a 'coach on the field.' That stuck in my mind. I did go on and sign with the Bears. They would be needing a successor to Sid Luckman, but they had also drafted Johnny Lujack from Notre Dame and a few others."

Bob Woodruff, Dodd's line coach, had been hired as Baylor's head coach. Back in Atlanta, moving his family and saying his goodbyes around Tech, Woodruff ran into Broyles. He asked if Frank would like to visit Waco, Texas, during Easter break and do a little work with the Baylor kickers and passers.

It was then that Broyles told him flatly he did not intend to play any more football, college or pro, and asked for a job on the Baylor staff.

"Do you mean that?" Woodruff said. "I'll make you my backfield coach."

As Broyles related in his autobiography, published in 1979, he was dumbfounded. He had hoped for "freshman coach" or something like that, anything to get started.

But Woodruff had some concerns. Due to relaxed wartime regulations for athletes who served in campus military units, Broyles still had some Tech eligibility if he wanted to use it. Woodruff didn't want Dodd to think he had wooed away his quarterback to coach at Baylor.

So Woodruff suggested that Broyles go ahead and sign with the Bears. That would settle the issue of college eligibility.

Broyles played in the Southeastern Conference basketball tournament at Louisvillle—the SEC always made it convenient for fans of sure-winner Kentucky—early in March of 1947. After Tech was ousted, newspapers reported that Frank had signed with Chicago. Woodruff then called Dodd and told him he was interested in Broyles as a coach.

Dodd told Broyles, "Bob Woodruff wants you. That's what you ought to do. You know you're going to coach. The sooner you get started the better."

Broyles had just turned 22. Baylor announced his age as 25, since he might be coaching returning war veterans older than he was, which actually happened.

"The first thing Bob told me," Broyles said, "was that I'd better learn something about pass defense, because he didn't know anything about it and we were getting into a conference where they'd throw 50 passes a game and we could get fired awful fast.

"I coached the backs both ways. We evolved a 'defend' defense; the more passes they completed, the fewer people we rushed, the more we dropped back. If they couldn't run pretty good, they were out of luck. That defense drove teams out of the league's famous spread formations."

Baylor had won one game in 1946. The Bears started 4-1 for Woodruff and Broyles in 1947 and finished a creditable 5-5.

"Then we recruited Adrian Burk," Broyles said. "I've always said, but for that, Woodruff and I would be in the insurance business. We had to have a quarterback to execute the short passes in the T-formation. Hayden Fry was a good quarterback, but he wasn't a passer. Burk had played wingback and punted for Kilgore Junior College. He became their tailback in the Little Rose Bowl game when their regular got hurt, and he passed for over 200 yards. He was a tremendous kicker and passer.

"We worked on him all summer. We thought we had him. When practice was about to start, we heard he was at TCU. We found out his clothes were there but he wasn't. TCU wanted him to kick and play defense; we wanted him as a meal ticket. We found him at the home of his girlfriend's parents. He'd been so upset about what to do that he hadn't eaten in three days. Woodruff brought him to Waco, fed him steak about three hours, and Burk decided to stay.

"I think he finally got his clothes back from TCU.

"I'd told Adrian all summer that he could be a great pro quarterback if he'd come with us and run our offense. And he was, for many years. It took Joe Namath to break some of his records."

Woodruff coached the line, Broyles the backs, and the basketball and baseball coaches helped out. It was heady elixir to the youthful Broyles, a brilliant, brash tyro in a league dominated by crafty old sages.

At a time when the SWC was strong, Baylor advanced to 5-3-2 in 1948 and gained a rare chance to win it all in 1949. It came down to Baylor or Rice in the season's final game. The Bears took the opening kickoff down the field and scored, but Jess Neely's finest Rice team prevailed.

Woodruff then left for the University of Florida with a 10-year contract starting at $17,000, a princely sum in 1950. He left Broyles in Waco for an extra month to contend with unhappy Baylor fans and stand in on a cold December day at the groundbreaking ceremony for Baylor Stadium. (Both coaches had bought bonds to help finance the new facility.)

"Some of my Baylor friends urged me to apply for the job," Broyles said. "They thought I was 28. I'd just turned 25. I knew I wasn't ready."

At Florida, Woodruff used part of the newly-available wealth to expand his staff and divide it along platoon lines. He put Broyles in charge of the secondary, a blow to the young coach's pride, but a lesson he applied later on most of his bright backfield assistants at Arkansas. Football is won on defense, Broyles knew, and the winning view of it is acquired from the defensive backfield.

Broyles did also coach the Florida pass offense; one of the freshmen he directed was a tall, stringy quarterback named Doug Dickey who would become important to him later.

After the 1950 season, Tech's first below-par campaign since 1945 and its last until 1960, Frank was summoned back to Atlanta. Thus began the easiest, most triumphant and most frustrating six years of his life.

From 1951 through 1956 Georgia Tech won 59 games, lost only seven, and went to six bowls and won all six.

"When I went back," Broyles said, "Tech had about 100 kids who were some of the finest athletes in the South. They weren't very big, but they were all good prospects as two-way regulars.

"Dodd had decided to do what Woodruff did at Florida, play and coach by platoons. He called me in and said, 'You'll coach the offense. If everything is going all right, I don't expect to see you in my office. When things aren't going right, I'll be in your office. Get to work.' He gave Ray Graves the defense and told him the same."

It was then a radical system. "It jolted me," Broyles said, "But it made me a 40 percent better coach." When Tech became a trendsetter, as it promptly did, most head coaches delegated authority and organized along similar lines. Dodd's chairman-of-the-board approach was the wave of the future.

"I had to dig for everything and so I learned more," Broyles said. "I could tinker all I wanted to. Once Dodd approved something in a staff meeting, it was mine to go with."

Tech's light, quick athletes became the scourge of the region, swarming on defense, error-free and deceptive on offense. "Football for fun," Dodd preached. He never spoke the corollary, that football is fun only when you win, because Tech hardly ever lost. Graves's dazzling defenses concealed their true intent with last-second slants and stunts. Broyles devised the inside and outside belly series which many coaches came to prefer because the options were safer than those of the Oklahoma split-T. The Tech inside belly off-tackle play remains the No. 1 goal-line play in college football, as run out of most any formation.

Dodd traveled the lecture circuit with Broyles usually with him to fill in the offensive details. They coached the 1952–53 College All-Stars against the NFL champs. They told everybody how to win bowl games: treat 'em as a reward, have a good time, don't leave your game on the practice field.

"Trouble is," Bear Bryant said, "nobody but Dodd can coach that way." (Bryant, however, quietly adapted much from Dodd.)

Broyles learned the three E's: Enthusiasm, Encouragement, and Execution.

He also came to understand that "up and down will get you beat. The kind of emotionalism that gets you high just before a game won't sustain you. It'll wear out before halftime. It is far better to build on tradition, know your assignments, have confidence you're doing the right thing."

Someone described it as keeping the players cool and the fans inflamed.

Through most of the glory days at Tech, though, Broyles came no closer to his goal of becoming a head coach. The view from afar, he said, was that "Broyles won't ever leave Tech—he's Dodd's replacement. Wrong. I was crying to leave, begging to leave."

"December was always a trying month for us at Tech," Barbara Broyles said. "Frank would get his hopes up for this or that job, but never get it."

He saw coaches in his age bracket—Darrell Royal, Jack Mitchell, Paul Dietzel—moving ahead. He felt left at the station.

Broyles probably would have become Vanderbilt's coach except for ill feeling between the heads of the two schools. Chancellor Harvie Branscomb was too proud to request Tech's permission to talk to Frank and too honorable to approach him secretly. He was interviewed for only one job, at the University of Houston, which he declined. His name was frequently mentioned, but his still-tender years, his glib brightness, his association with specialized offense scared some schools. It was worse that he had no hobby (he did not take up golf until he reached Arkansas) and thus stayed absorbed in football and his career all the time.

Later he realized the good life at Tech made him too choosey. A whiz with the media, alumni, and business community, Dodd taught his chief aides how to make commercial attachments, and Broyles's fringe benefits put his earnings in the $15,000 range—bountiful for assistant coaches of the time. When he realized how cozy things had become, he verged on seeking an assistant's job on another staff—Oklahoma crossed his mind —for a fresh start and a change in perspective.

He was dismayed, too, when after the 1956 season Dodd was asked to investigate an opportunity at the University of Texas, declined to pursue the job (which Darrell Royal took), and did not think to recommend Broyles as an alternative. "The truth is, Bobby couldn't see why anyone would want to leave Tech," Broyles said, "and he was right. We had a lot going for us."

Dodd plainly did not wish to lose his offensive overseer.

Drawing on his own 10 years as an aide, Broyles was determined once he became a head coach to keep his assistants' ambitions in mind. (At Arkansas he actively pushed his best assistants as head-coaching prospects. He gave them up regularly, but in turn attracted able replacements who, knowing people called Broyles looking for head coaches, usually gave him the best three or four years of their lives.)

On the heels of the Texas disappointment came the invitation from Faurot. Broyles could not have been more flattered, because of Faurot's high standing in the profession as a man and a coach. His first and most important step was to locate a defensive coordinator. He went to Bear Bryant at Texas A&M and came back with Jerry Claiborne, who brought along young Jim Mackenzie.

Broyles had met Mackenzie, then graduating from Kentucky, at the College All-Star game in 1952. Jim had been coaching at a junior college near College Station. Claiborne would go back to Bryant (at Alabama) after a season; Broyles and Mackenzie would spend momentous years in close harness.

At Missouri Frank inherited good linemen, but the slow backs promised more of a challenge than this offensive innovator cared for. By dint of sturdy defense, an off-tackle play, and the quick-kick, the 1957 Tigers achieved a 5-1 start. At Dallas they held on at the end of the game when SMU, trailing 7-6, had second and inches near the goal line. Broyles's players carried him off the field on their shoulders, a spontaneous thing but one which he generally frowned on.

That August, Oklahoma's Bud Wilkinson spent his annual preseason session with the writers, worrying about which Big Seven team would end OU's 10-year league winning streak. This time, Wilkinson insisted, his concern was justified. He pointed to Missouri. This mystified reporters; Missouri had won only four games in 1956. Did Bud have inside information on the Tigers' personnel? "No," he said, "but I know their coach, Frank Broyles. In a few years you won't have to ask his name. He'll be a great one."

Frank did not hear of that until long afterward. What he remembered best was talking with Bryant while their teams warmed up before their game at Columbia. Bear studied a while and said casually, "Frank, I don't see a single damn athlete on your end of the field." Bryant's best A&M team, then No. 1 in the polls, won by 28-0.

John Barnhill finally offered Frank Broyles the job he'd always wanted.

THE RAZORBACKS

Still, when Missouri and OU met, each was 3-0 in the league, and an Orange Bowl bid was at stake.

"We didn't have a chance," Broyles said, "and I'm the only one who knew it. I don't guess Bud ever enjoyed such a psychological advantage. We were set up for the kill, and there was nothing I could do."

Oklahoma had just squeaked by Colorado and Kansas, and never in any recent two-week period had OU encountered such a critical home-state press, not to mention national news services predicting the downfall of the Wilkinson dynasty. At Columbia students held pep rallies every night. The Associated Press had Oklahoma ranked second and Missouri out of sight, and yet its forecaster predicted Missouri to win.

"We did right well for three quarters," Broyles said. "They had us 13-7 and then intercepted a pass and made it 20-7 entering the last quarter.

"Then Phil Snowden, my sophomore quarterback, hurt his shoulder, and we couldn't throw. They made three more, and it ended 39-14. They got the Orange Bowl, but I'm sure their effort left them a little short the next weekend. They lost to Notre Dame, and that ended their 47-game winning streak."

Missing Snowden, Missouri lost to Kansas State, 23-21, and Kansas, 9-7, on last-minute field goals.

"Still it was a very happy season, and people seemed pleased," Broyles said.

He had, however, suffered three closing defeats, an experience which, some felt, set him up for Barnhill's call. Little did he know that his personal losing streak would reach nine before he could right things at Arkansas.

— 24 —

THE LESSONS OF ADVERSITY

Bobby Dodd served as the speaker for his protégé, Frank Broyles, at Missouri's team banquet at the end of the 1957 season. Three weeks later Dodd concealed whatever he felt about Frank's move and gave this statement to an Arkansas writer:

"Frank is a high-type person who will bring credit to your school as its representative. He is a good recruiter, but he will not break any rules. There are some things he may not know, for they come to a head coach only through experience. But right now he is the equal of any college coach in America in his teaching of techniques."

Some of the things Broyles did not know, he learned quickly at Fayetteville. He had to complete the only course he had never had to take: facing, accepting, and surviving adversity. The experience of six straight Arkansas defeats humbled him—and braced his chin-up squad for better things.

Frank enjoyed a perfect honeymoon. The day he was hired— December 7, 1957—he added to his staff, on Barnhill's recommendation, Wilson Matthews, an Arkansas graduate whose Little Rock Central teams had powerfully, mercilessly dominated high school football in Arkansas and other states for 11 years. Matthews had coveted the job Broyles got and thus might have been suspect. The loyalty of Wilson Matthews to Arkansas, however, transcended anything else.

Matthews was exultant in victory, raging in defeat. He taught Razorback teams how to celebrate a victory over a Texas team. To the wobbly tune of "The Old Gray Mare," they sang, "We don't give a damn about the whole state of Texas, we're from Ark-in-saw."

Mackenzie had arrived with Broyles from Missouri as his defensive overseer. Matthews would coach the linebackers. Soon, Doug Dickey (known first to Broyles as a Florida quarterback) resigned an army commission and came as coach of the secondary. Dixie White and Steed White (not related) stayed on from Jack Mitchell's staff to coach the line. Merrill Green, once a hot Oklahoma halfback, came along from Missouri to handle the backs.

They recruited one of Arkansas's finest freshman teams ever, one that had everything and contributed over the long haul. "Everything was waiting for me when I came," Broyles often said. "The unified support, the desire to get moving."

Broyles added the final ingredient, the blue-chip athlete from outside Arkansas. In August of 1958 he signed Lance Alworth of Brookhaven, Mississippi, who had run afoul of Ole Miss coach Johnny Vaught's no-marrieds rule. One of the most gifted athletes of any time, any place, Alworth had signed early with Ole Miss and then married his high school sweetheart, Betty Allen. Vaught said he could come on a baseball scholarship and play football, but Alworth turned that down. So Lance was a free agent, so to speak, when he went to play in a high school all-star game held at Memphis.

Broyles had an edge or two. For the first time he involved his wife in recruiting. Barbara, who was pregnant, knitted baby things while visiting with Betty and the Allens; Frank golfed with Lance and his father. Shortly thereafter, Lance and Betty Alworth set up housekeeping in Fayetteville.

Lance and the other frosh were for the future, accurately promising a bright one.

Broyles startled his new staff by passing out copies of the Iowa-Delaware winged-T manual just published by Forest Evashevski, the Iowa coach whose team had gone to the Rose Bowl, and Dave Nelson, the innovative Delaware coach. They had taken a complex offense they played at Michigan under Fritz Crisler and adapted it to the T-formation. Broyles saw this mixture of the single wing and the T as the way to attack the 5-4-2 defenses that had cooled the once-rampant split-T down to a dull scene described as "three yards and a cloud of dust."

Arkansas, Broyles thought, had the quicksilver backs for the tricky crisscrosses and reverses. He even brought in Nelson and his line coach Milo Luke as technical advisors in the spring.

The fans spent six months hearing about the wonders of the winged-T. They were spellbound, delighted, agog over the prospect a seeing the new coach unleash the new offense in a league game with Baylor as an unusual season opener.

Never were so many high hopes so thoroughly doused as on September 20, 1958, a foggy night in Little Rock, before a sellout crowd. Baylor won, 12-0. That high-geared Arkansas attack malfunctioned, earning only three first downs.

When Broyles called for punts on second and third downs with his impotent team backed up, some fans booed. Years later, Frank vividly remembered one leather-lung's complaint in the second half: "Hell! We might as well have Barnhill back coaching!"

Baylor, headed for a last-place SWC finish, had surprised Arkansas with a defense no one thought would work against the winged-T; it had worked.

There was some consolation. The defense played well, and a coming star made his debut. Through Broyles's early organizational weeks at Fayetteville and between recruiting trips, he kept hearing about Wayne Harris, "The Thumper" from El Dorado, a freshman the previous fall. Frank believed what they preached at Georgia Tech, "Any size can play," but a 182-pound linebacker? Finally, he sat still long enough to see a piece of freshman game film and knew Harris could play. Harris could play anywhere. He made All-American as an Arkansas senior and became a Canadian Football League legend for Calgary.

Broyles could not fly to Little Rock on Sunday after the Baylor game to do his television show. He had to drive through fog and rain from Fayetteville. Dixie White accompanied him. What turned out to be an eight-hour offensive soul-searching session—four hours down, four hours back—had far-reaching effect.

They agreed their green, undersized linemen could not master the full winged-T's pulling and trapping blocking assignments. They decided to combine the simplest parts of the Georgia Tech belly series with straight-ahead scramble blocking, as Dixie had taught in the split-T, with some backfield features of the winged-T.

Somebody gave the new mixture a working title of "belly-wing." Wilson Matthews said it might be okay, "but it sounds like a piece of chicken."

James Monroe, broad-shouldered and tough, proved he could pass in the second game, but Tulsa won, 27-14, another indignity. At this point, fans wrung their hands over the awful possibility of 0-10. The first rays of hope that this team could get "bettah" (in Frank's familiar term) came the next week.

At Fort Worth, Arkansas led TCU, 7-6, with five minutes to play. The Porkers punted out to their 40 and recovered the safety's fumble—except that the turnover, obscured from the back judge's view, was not allowed. On the next play TCU fullback Jack Spikes popped on a trap play for 40 yards and TCU won, 12-7. Abe Martin, headed for his third Cotton Bowl bid in four years, informed the league that Wayne Harris was "a heckuva linebacker."

Normally a robust 6'2", 200-pounder with the appetite of a 17-year-old, Broyles watched his weight dip to 182 by the kickoff against Rice, which turned into a horror show on the order of the Baylor opener. The Owls won a sloppy game, 24-0. At the end of the first quarter, Mackenzie turned to Broyles and said, "I don't see how either team can win this game."

Against Texas in Austin, Broyles found his taw at halfback. Jim Mooty turned the corners for 77 yards, a goodly total in those days, while the Longhorns won a 24-6 game that did not foretell the auspiciousness of the first matchup of Darrell Royal and Frank Broyles.

A 165-pounder, Mooty did not need much room to cut in, and he had quick speed. He was "the fly man" Broyles had been looking for, the wingback who could start in motion back into the play and wind up with the ball. In another formation, he was the tailback who could run that stovepipe route off-tackle in the belly power play.

Broyles had any number of fast backs to choose from in 1958. Everybody on campus sensed that Mooty would be *the* one.

"Others were faster," Wilson Matthews said. "But Jim could be running, then flutter, then give you that quick burst and turn and wiggle after he was hit, and you'd have more yards than anyone was supposed to get. He saw the whole field as well as anyone we've had—like Dickey Morton later."

Things started poorly. Like on the first play of the opener against Baylor. Mooty and the other halfback, Don Horton, collided in the middle of the backfield on an attempted counter crisscross. That set the tone.

As disaster followed disaster in the early stages of the season, Mooty one day found himself on the sixth team, running plays against the varsity.

"You know how young coaches are," Broyles sighed years later, in an attempted explanation.

"What happened," Matthews said, "is that Jim was pacing himself, practicing the way he wanted to. It got to the point where we thought the team effort would be hurt if he didn't get in line. We convinced Frank that something had to be done. We thought Jim (Mackenzie) and I could make him go hard against our defense because we just wouldn't put up with a half-hearted effort. When we called his hand, he said, 'To hell with it.'"

His pride hurt deeply, Mooty headed home to El Dorado.

A phone call to the late O. C. Bailey, a shrewd and wealthy oil man and an original Barnhill booster, beat Jim to the El Dorado city limits. Bailey dispatched the junior halfback back to Fayetteville.

Matthews met him with an arm around the shoulder. "Hell, Jim, there's nothing wrong with quitting as long as you know you made a mistake."

Broyles, however, had a problem to face. You have rules, and you must abide by them. (Later he would dispense with all but the most necessary framework.) At that time the Razorbacks had permanent captains; when a man missed practice, the captains had to submit his punishment to a squad vote. Broyles gave the captains three options to put to the squad. Somehow they forgot to mention one of them.

"The way I heard it and the way it sounds now," Mooty said, "it was a little bit comical. They were voting on two punishments, and one of them was to drop me from the squad through spring training. I could come back the following fall. Barry Switzer, one of my best friends then and now, is supposed to have told 'em, 'Shoot, Mooty doesn't need any spring practice. Let's just bring him back next fall.'"

The squad voted that way.

The decision appalled Broyles. He had hoped they would put Mooty back where he had him, on the B team, and let him work himself back up with his effort, a level a day, maybe.

A day or two later, Broyles sat down with Mooty and his roommate, Jimmy Van Dover, as they were having lunch. Mooty remembered it this way: "Coach Broyles was asking me what I thought about the options, and Jimmy interrupted, 'Nobody told us he could come back and work his way from the bottom.' Coach Broyles just looked at me and said, 'Jim, report for practice this afternoon.'"

Mooty regained a regular's status against Texas, and no one looked back.

(Oh, he did pass up spring training because of what were described as "persistent headaches" and said he wouldn't play again, and his name was not listed in the pre-season roster for 1959, but Broyles said afterward, "There was no doubt in my mind he'd be our left halfback in the fall." An All-American halfback on a championship team, as it turned out.)

The Texas game in 1958 was the fifth straight loss. Broyles could see good things and so could fans, but the squad needed a victory. The next best thing came against typically undefeated Ole Miss before a packed house in Little Rock.

The Rebs jumped into a 14-0 lead before quarterback Bobby Franklin had to be carried from the field. By then Mooty had already taken over. Monroe established himself and the belly series, mixing Mooty's runs with short passes. Jim gained 120 yards against a salty defense, and the Razorbacks were not done until Monroe's two-point conversion pass fell just beyond Mooty's fingers. The Rebs held on, 14-12. When one team enters 5-0 and the other 0-5, that is what they call a moral victory.

Still it was the worst start in history for an Arkansas team. As Broyles went to Texas A&M, he had lost nine games in a row going back into his Missouri season.

"We were blue," Broyles said of himself and his staff. "I was standing on the field at A&M with Dixie before the game. He had been at Arkansas four years. I asked him if there was any way Arkansas could compete with the Texas teams and all their great athletes. And he said, 'Frank, at one time I thought we might be average or better and sneak in every once in a while and win. Now I don't see any way Arkansas can compete in the Southwest Conference.'"

A&M had a new coach, Jim Myers, and some leftovers from the 1954–57 Bryant era. Myers confronted Arkansas with Charley Milstead throwing from a spread-T. Milstead completed 21 of 42 passes for 278 yards. (Monroe completed two of three for 10 yards.) The Porkers dropped back eight and nine men and rushed only two and three and staved off the Aggies five times near or inside the 20.

At the outset the Hogs recovered an Aggie bobble at the A&M 16. From the eight Monroe went the wrong way. His backs headed right, he rolled left. And walked into the end zone. "Well, Dixie," Broyles said, spirits revived, "I don't see how we can lose this one."

A&M led 8-7 at halftime, but Joe Paul Alberty took the third-quarter kickoff. His blocking formed to the right; Alberty goofed and went left. The Aggies did not find him until he had reached the A&M 20. Broyles winked at Dixie White. And the Porkers won, 21-8, going away, a mile-stone victory for the Broyles regime.

The next weekend, the morning after Arkansas trampled Hardin-Simmons, Barbara presented Frank with twins. After four sons—Jack, Hank, Dan, and Tommy—they had hoped for a girl. They got two, Linda and Betsy.

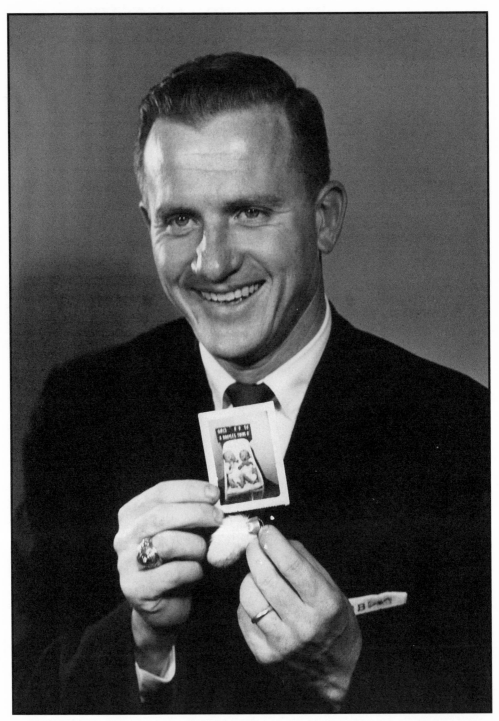

Frank Broyles displays a photo of newborn twins Linda and Betsey on November 9, 1958.

Elated, Frank showed the pictures from the hospital to the studio crew at his Sunday television show and said, "Just lucky."

Jim Mooty and Billy Kyser had kept the fans jumping in Little Rock the previous afternoon by each returning a kickoff from about six yards deep in the end zone, each getting credit for a 100-yarder. Sammy Baugh's Hardin-Simmons team twice worked hard and long to score, getting back in the game. Each time Mooty and Kyser deflated the Cowboys with a stirring runback. In a much-needed breather, the final score was a whoop-de-do 60-15.

This added interest to Broyles's first homecoming weekend at Arkansas.

SMU had Don Meredith and a gifted ensemble, and the Ponies thought they were headed for a championship—as had been predicted in August. Arkansas fell behind by 6-0 but kept scrapping. In the second quarter Broyles pulled his tackles and inserted two more ends, giving him four ends with which to rush Dandy Don, who could run almost as well as he could pass in his college days. Finally the fleet Kyser, a big-play man off the bench all his Arkansas career, streaked down a sideline for 37 yards to wrap it up, 13-6.

They closed by beating Texas Tech in a 14-8 struggle.

"Winning the last four gave us a lot of momentum," understated Broyles.

Arkansas was not to lose a game in November—Alumni Month—until Frank's fifth year at the helm.

— 25 —

LIKE WILD HOGS

Freddy Akers barely attained second team halfback status in his third varsity year at Arkansas. He was not big enough (164), not fast enough, and kicked only fair. Later to coach against Arkansas as Darrell Royal's Texas successor, he was smart, and he played with suicidal determination. What he will be remembered for in Arkansas annals is that he kicked a 29-yard field goal to provide the points in a 3-0 win over TCU that began to turn the Southwest Conference around.

Abe Martin's big, doughty, balanced TCU teams were a persistent force in the league, and they were to hang on strongly through 1959.

Arkansas had won six games in a row after losing the first six under Broyles when TCU went to Fayetteville for the 1959 league opener. Rain began to fall, a good omen for an Arkansas team outweighed 26 pounds to the man, a bad omen for TCU's passing game.

"We were lucky last year against A&M and SMU," Broyles told his squad. "Still, we've come a long way. Today is the day we decide whether we can play on equal terms with the league. If we can play with TCU, we'll be as good as the best."

The wild card rule of that time allowed a team to sub one player per down. Broyles used it to keep Wayne Harris in on defense for both the Big Red and Wild Hog units and to employ Barry Switzer at center for both units. Switzer's leadership, later to show in his coaching career, was particularly helpful to the alternate Wild Hog unit, which proved that it could hold its own.

The second team was in there for the field goal; Darrell Williams set it up with a 23-yard sweep. Late in the game TCU began to overpower the Porkers' slanting, slashing defenders with big backs Jack Spikes, Marshall

Harris, and Marvin Lasater. The Frogs reached first down at the 20, their deepest penetration. Abe Martin's offensive style was to run for first downs and pass for points. TCU's first-down pass from the 20 did not catch the Hogs unprepared. Linebacker Gerald Gardner tipped the ball, and Wayne Harris, also back, intercepted it.

Dutch Meyer, the TCU athletic director and former coach, wrote a post-game column for a Fort Worth paper. "Arkansas is a title contender," he proclaimed. "When we read that, our chests stuck out a little," Broyles said.

John Bridgers had gone to Baylor from the Baltimore Colts, bringing a pro-type offense, and the Bears pranced to a 7-0 lead at Waco. Arkansas's offense was not up to it (James Monroe had injured his shoulder making a tackle in the first quarter of the TCU game and could not throw), but the defense was. Jim Mooty showed his versatility. He set up a touchdown with a quick-kick out of bounds on the one and returned two punts and an interception for 128 yards. Arkansas won a crucial but not pretty 23-7 game.

A then-record War Memorial Stadium crowd of 40,038 assembled for the first of the Royal versus Broyles showdowns, each undefeated: a game to set the tone for many taut classics to come. The Razorbacks apparently took charge when, from the second-half kickoff, Monroe took his team 89 yards in 19 perfect little plays. No fumbles, no penalties, no incomplete passes, no plays out of bounds. Monroe shouldered his way over from the three, and the Hogs, having used up almost 10 minutes, led by 12-7.

But Lance Alworth fumbled the Steers' next punt as he was mobbed a moment after the ball touched his hands. Texas recovered on the Arkansas 31, and Bart Shirley threw a running left-handed pass to Jack Collins for the touchdown from three yards out. Texas won, 13-12.

Fans who watched Broyles and Royal spend several minutes together at midfield after the final gun witnessed an early manifestation of what was to become one of football's famed friendships. Darrell was telling Frank he had a good thing going, to stick with it, and he was asking Frank's advice as to how to better employ his talented but green backs.

The Razorbacks took their bitter medicine at Memphis, losing 28-0 to a superb Ole Miss team that was on a par, at least, with any in the country. The Hogs shrugged off the bruises and returned to league wars. What was to come will never be forgotten by players, coaches, and fans.

"In its own way, the finish of that season can never be topped," Broyles said.

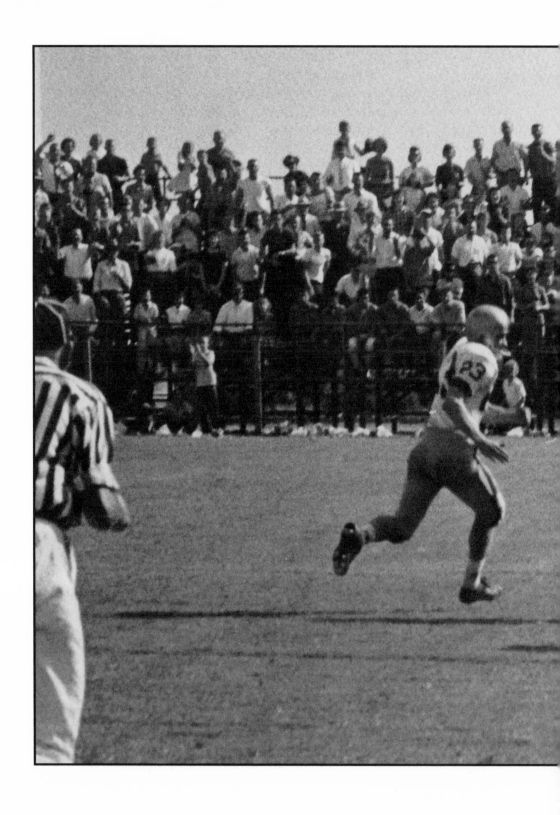

Jim Mooty (24) is about to score against Tulsa.

Texas A&M played a perfect game at Fayetteville; no turnovers. Arkansas fell behind, 7-0, in the third quarter. With Monroe idled again, George McKinney, the Wild Hogs' go-go quarterback, had to take over. Alworth returned the next kickoff 51 yards, and Mooty broke for 38 yards on the power sweep, the season's trademark play. A missed extra point and a missed field goal after another drive sent the pressure mounting, but Mooty came up with a storied six-yard run at the last to pull it out, 12-7.

Monroe and Mooty remained on the bench at Rice. Jess Neely's regulars dominated the game while they were in there. Each time Neely sent in his second team, Arkansas struck with McKinney, Alworth, Kyser, and Alberty operating behind the Wild Hogs' line.

After Rice took its 10-0 lead, Alworth sprinted 40 yards with the kickoff return, then threw a running halfback pass to Kyser at the one. McKinney sneaked across. Then the Porkers moved 80 yards in the third quarter, and Alworth's running pass to Kyser gained 27 yards and penetrated the Rice 20. Kyser scored from the six. The 14-10 win revived Arkansas's hopes.

The last big special football train Razorback fans ever used took thousands to Dallas for the final league game against SMU on a freezing afternoon in Cotton Bowl stadium. Alworth, who refused even to be taped at that stage of his career, shucked the long socks Broyles had ordered against the cold after only a few plays.

Some recall the game for one of the most thunderous hits of all time. Late in the game, Don Meredith backed up to pass. Wayne Harris backed up to defend. Meredith decided to run up the middle, and Harris came up to meet him. Harris met Meredith all over. The senior quarterback was knocked out of the game for a spell. "It's hard to see your receiver," Wilson Matthews said, "when your eyeballs are in the back of your head." Harris weighed 186, Meredith about 200.

Monroe was back and healthy, and he directed what Broyles always called the greatest running show he ever witnessed in one-platoon football. Alworth took over the injured Mooty's role and gained 131 yards to 99 for Alberty and 85 for Monroe. Arkansas amassed 400 yards on the ground, only three in the air.

It all boiled down to a two-point play after Arkansas had cut its deficit to 13-14. Alworth made it over right tackle, spinning off tacklers. When he looked at the run on film for the umpteenth time some 15 years later, Broyles still called it "one of the greatest runs anyone will ever make."

The moment Alworth's run made it 15-14, the news came from Austin that TCU had just upset Texas. If the Razorbacks could hold their edge, they would have a 5-1 record, a share of the title clinched. TCU and Texas would have to win three more games between them to tie with Arkansas (which they did).

"I've never seen a happier, more fired-up team," Broyles said. "We got the ball right back and used up all but 19 seconds in going 75 yards to the three-yard line."

Meredith gave up a deliberate safety, and it ended, 17-14.

"When I met SMU coach Bill Meek at midfield and he congratulated me, I had to tell him it was the happiest day of my career," Broyles said. "I'd dreamed since I'd come into the league in 1947 of winning a championship, and it had happened."

A 27-8 win over Texas Tech finished an 8-2 season and cinched an appealing bowl bid. Officials of the Gator Bowl cannily decided to match pupil Broyles with master Bobby Dodd, whose Georgia Tech team lost four games that year but had not been beaten in eight bowl trips under Dodd.

At least 10,000 Arkies trekked to Jacksonville, Florida, a totally new experience they reveled in. Thirty and more years later, those Razorbacks and fans said they never enjoyed a bowl trip more. It helped that Arkansas won the game.

Tech kept the ball for almost all the first quarter, and quarterback Marvin Tibbetts scored on a 51-yard cutback. Healthy again, Mooty took over with his sizzling power sweeps, abetted by Alworth and Monroe's shrewd direction.

The Harris-led defense cracked the Yellowjackets, and Arkansas prevailed, going away 14-7.

Two days before the game Dodd had confided to a friend, "If that rascal (Broyles) beats me, I'll never hear the end of it." However, Arkansas's ending of Tech's long-winning bowl ways created no personal waves. Dodd and Broyles were both too gracious to make an issue of it, much less prolong the matter.

The undercurrent that made Jacksonville headlines came from nearby Gainesville, where Broyles's one-time employer Bob Woodruff was first trying to save his job as head coach and then, as athletic director, looking for his successor. The *Houston Post*'s Jack Gallagher began his Gator Bowl story, "Coaching his last game at Arkansas, next to appear at the University of Florida, Frank Broyles . . ."

Woodruff *had* phoned Broyles daily, but the result was that Frank

James Monroe quarterbacked the first championship team of the Broyles era.

helped steer him to Ray Graves, Frank's former Tech confrere, who soon took the Florida job.

Arkansas had won nine games including the bowl, the most ever in one season, and other coaches marveled. They wanted the secrets of the Arkansas monster-slant defense, which soon became a sweeping trend, and of the power sweep as run by Mooty. They asked Dixie White about the scramble blocking techniques that let 190-pound linemen stop 225-pound defenders.

Dixie talked techniques with them, but waxed more enthusiastic when pointing out, "I don't think any group from any state will get with it and put out and hit the way these good old Arkansas boys will."

"When Monroe, our established quarterback, got hurt in the first quarter of the first league game, I never dreamed we'd win nine," Broyles said. "He's the only quarterback I'd had I never called plays for. I was afraid I'd mess him up. He blocked and tackled and ran with more determination than anyone else. On third down, he was going to get it himself and did. That's leadership.

"He was quiet and workmanlike, but when he walked onto the field the team did his bidding. He'd tell 'em, 'You get that end, I'll get five yards. I'll get that linebacker and you cut behind me.' And when that shoulder let him throw, he could kill a team with short passes."

To Harold Horton, a sophomore on that squad headed for a coaching career, "We played like wild hogs."

"You know," elaborated Wilson Matthews, "Lean, mean, and hungry, tusks out all the time, looking for something to hit."

And that is the definitive description of the Razorback team which ushered an occasional longshot into the arena of perennial big-timers.

– 26 –

MICKEY'S TOE

In February of 1960, Broyles advised everyone to "forget about the Gator Bowl and remember that Arkansas has only won from adversity, never in a time of prosperity." The Razorbacks' share of a three-way tie in 1959 had impressed few people or teams in Texas. But the Hogs were able to slip into an outright title in 1960.

George McKinney, who played with feverish intensity, would throw nine touchdown passes as Arkansas exploited the acrobatic catches and runs of Alworth and Jimmy Collier. However, a little dynamo of a quarter-back named Billy Moore, one of those 1958 freshmen who had been red-shirted, supplied the winning note against TCU after Alworth's punts and pass receptions had keynoted wins over Oklahoma State and Tulsa.

A determined TCU team took the opening kickoff at Fort Worth and smashed to the Arkansas 10-yard line. There, Wayne Harris met the Frogs' fullback in the hole on fourth and inches, and there was, of course, no gain. That defensive gem changed the complexion of the game.

Billy Moore entered in the third period, taking over at his 33. Joe Paul Alberty's darting runs up the middle on the fullback counter advanced the ball inside the TCU 30. In that area the Frogs, who had Bob Lilly, generally held. Moore bootlegged the ball 15 yards to the 14, then again nine to the three. Alberty squeezed over. Arkansas won, 7-0.

In John Bridgers's peak game at Baylor, the Bears destroyed the Hogs, 28-14, worse than the score reflects, running effectively with Ronnie Bull as the Hogs played back to guard against the pass and adjusted too late.

It was the year that Baylor's Bears should have, finally, reached the Cotton Bowl; defeats in their sixth and seventh games by small margins did in the Bears.

Bridgers had taught Broyles something: You *could* pass in the one-platoon era, if you went at it properly. McKinney spent the week of the Texas game coming out early for specialized passing drills.

Everything boded ill at Austin. Since the game would be on regional television, the kickoff had been advanced to the afternoon, when the damp heat seemed to envelop the visitors from the Ozarks, where there was already a nip in the air.

Sure enough, Texas exploited a James Saxton punt return and an Arkansas fumble to seize a 14-0 lead.

On the last play of the half McKinney found Collier in the end zone. George came back, passing to Collier for 37 yards, to Alworth for 14, and then to Jim Gaston on a little two-yard jump pass for a score.

Texas pulled back into a 23-14 lead. The Steers botched a two-point conversion play which seemed meaningless at the time, although Darrell Royal had sensed a need for it. Back came McKinney, finding halfback Jarrell Williams open for a little pass and a 19-yard run to the goal when Texas over-reacted to Alworth and Collier on the other side. It was 23-21.

Late in the fourth quarter the Hogs backed up Texas, and Harold Horton returned the punt 15 yards to midfield. McKinney and his team-mates hacked and slashed. On the sidelines Broyles readied Mickey Cissell, a reserve fullback who had wanted to drop out in September because he could see he would never play.

"If you leave, you'll have to whip me and walk over my body," Broyles had told him. "And the minute you leave town I'll have a police car after you. You're gonna stay here and kick for this football team. You're my only place kicker."

Broyles had more prolific ones later, but none ever won two games the way Mickey did.

On fourth and two at the 20, Alworth dived straight ahead to the 18, where an anguished measurement moved the stakes. McKinney passed incomplete for Collier, then called time-out with 30 seconds left.

Broyles pushed Cissell, but McKinney waved him back. "We've got one more time-out," he told Broyles. McKinney kept to the left, toward the posts, and cut inside and fought to the 12. Then he called time-out and signaled for Cissell.

Not a quarter hour previously, a front had moved through, shifting the wind. It was behind Cissell's back now. His wobbly kick cleared the post by inches, falling dead, straight down. If the wind had not changed, if McKinney had gained three yards instead of six putting the ball in place . . .

All-American Wayne Harris was respectfully known as "The Thumper."

The Broyles motto: "You gotta be lucky."

Arkansas got mileage from that 24-23 miracle for years, Broyles's first decision over Royal. One vital benefit was that Texas high school athletes noticed.

At the time, this victory over Texas quickly became overshadowed among Arkansas fans by an infamous 10-7 loss to Ole Miss at Little Rock. In the final seconds referee Tommy Bell, later of NFL renown, gave Mississippi's Allen Green two chances to kick a winning field goal. The first kick was good and should have been allowed, except that Bell called time-out as the ball was snapped because of what he thought was excessive crowd noise. Green's second kick hooked, probably wide of the posts. Bell signaled "good" immediately, however, and Arkies caricatured what they called Ole Miss goal posts as one crooked and one leaning.

As long as the Hogs played Ole Miss in the middle of their league schedule, they usually turned in lackluster games against Texas A&M, which they were now lucky to top, 7-3. Then came a showdown against Jess Neely's last contending team at Rice.

The Owls had a great pass receiver in Johnny Burrell, as Arkansas did in Collier, but defense ruled on a windy day in Little Rock. In the third quarter, when Rice had the wind, Harris leaped for an interception at the Arkansas three. Moore used up half the period chewing up yardage, always getting it on third down with his determined roll-outs inside the ends. That kept the ball from Rice when the Owls had wind and field position.

With time running out, Moore took the ball at his 20 and joined Billy Joe Moody and Alworth in banging it out to the Arkansas 46.

Then Moore sprinted right and at the last second—referee Burns McKinney threw his cap to mark the spot inches short of the line of scrimmage—lobbed a pass to Collier, who was five yards open between defenders, waiting at the boundary. Collier skipped past one man and reached the 18. Two downs later, with 30 seconds left, Cissell kicked a 26-yard field goal for the 3-0 win.

The Porkers then smashed SMU, 26-3, and Texas Tech, 34-6, to take the title with a 6-1 record, another 8-2 overall. Tech that year became an official member in the football standings.

The Cotton Bowl could not find Arkansas a high-ranked opponent. Though humiliated by UCLA on national television in its last, listless game, Duke (7-3) had to do. Thus unchallenged and uninspired, Arkansas wasted its chances with offensive mistakes, scoring only on Alworth's 49-yard punt return (after his punt on the run had gone out of bounds on the Duke two) and losing to the Blue Devils' sheer determination to redeem themselves. Duke's sophisticated short passing finally paid off, 7-6.

Wayne Harris capped his career by gaining All-American honors, as Mooty had done the year before. With Harris the defense had allowed 10 regular-season foes only 87 points, the fewest yielded by Arkansas since 1936.

Back-to-back championships, gloated Hog-wild Arkies. How about that?

— 27 —

THREE IN A ROW

When Arkansas and Mississippi began to clash regularly at Memphis in the late 1930s, neither side took prisoners. The 1938 match turned into such a dangerous brawl that a one-year cooling off period was observed before hostilities resumed. Their rivalry might have equaled the fierce Texas-Oklahoma vendetta except for one thing—Memphis stayed too long with Crump Stadium, which was easy to quit.

Oklahoma and Texas could not afford to move their fixture from the 75,000-seat Cotton Bowl, which produced immensely profitable sellouts. By the late 1940s each renewal of the four-year Arkansas-Mississippi contract required more negotiations than a Bosnian cease-fire, featured by mutual distrust if not dislike. They fussed over dates, sites, plus trivia.

John Barnhill did not like the game because, in the middle of the schedule, it proved for fans and players an emotional distraction from the No. 1 job at hand, trying to beat all those Texas teams. Too, while Ole Miss scheduled its home games at Oxford, Memphis, and Jackson, the Rebs refused to play at Fayetteville in Arkansas's year. It had to be Little Rock or nothing.

The continued expansion of War Memorial Stadium made it desirable to schedule a fourth game in Little Rock every year instead of Ole Miss every other year. Teams could be found which would come for modest guarantees, leaving a bowl-sized check for the U of A, which supplied all the fans through its pre-season ticket sale.

Mississippi had a suggestion: If Arkansas did not wish to play the Rebs between Texas and Texas A&M, why not play them first and get it over with? Barnhill agreed to that for 1961, but in the interim he let the contract run out. Ole Miss fans chided Broyles; they said he wanted out because he could not beat Johnny Vaught, something his predecessors had accomplished with gusto three times in four years. However, the decision to end the series was Barnhill's alone.

Broyles drew the best teams Vaught fielded, including two chance bowl meetings later on. Frank had reasoned, "Not playing them in the regular season makes it possible to play them in a bowl game," which it did.

The argumentative aftermath of the 1960 game and the teams' recent records and high hopes for 1961 led NBC to schedule the game for national television. Furthermore, they were to dedicate Mississippi Memorial Stadium in Jackson.

Arkansas trained in the coolest September in years and found the temperature above 100 degrees on the floor of the Jackson stadium. That was not the main trouble. Injuries to key people left the Razorbacks non-competitive for their two big early games with Mississippi and Texas. At other times in 1961 they were an outstanding team, even against the national championship team Alabama in the Sugar Bowl.

Billy Moore could not play at Jackson; George McKinney stuck it out for 60 minutes in searing heat. Nor did Arkansas have an established fullback. Ole Miss won with reckless abandon, 16-0. Turnovers gave the ball to the Hogs six times in Ole Miss territory; they did not really come close to scoring. Alworth gave his home-state friends a few thrills with a 72-yard quick kick and two scary punt returns.

Broyles found his fullback in a game against Tulsa played in a driving rain. Billy Joe Moody provided the needed inside runs in the 6-0 win. By the TCU game everything was in place.

The Horned Frogs had Sonny Gibbs, their ballyhooed 6'7" passer, and high expectations. But by now Arkansas had both McKinney and Moore as gifted two-way players; Alworth and Paul Dudley as the strongest, fastest halfbacks yet in the Broyles regime; both Moody and Jesse Branch at fullback; and Frank's best line yet with Jerry Mazzanti and John Childress at the tackles, Ray Trail and Dean Garrett at the guards, Jerry Lineberger at center, and Collier back as a dangerous receiver.

Hayden Fry, Frank's onetime Baylor pupil, had been hired away from Bridgers's staff as Arkansas backfield coach, and he injected true balance into the attack.

Shaken by a plane mishap on the way out of Fort Worth, TCU left Little Rock talking about an Arkansas jinx. The Frogs moved the ball, but only between the 20s, and McKinney and Moore directed two touchdown drives each, one in each quarter, a beautiful blend of running and passing for an impressive 28-3 triumph.

The always-risky-for-Arkansas trip to Waco produced a 23-13 win over a favored Baylor team. Cissell kicked a field goal, and Dudley, Alworth, and Collier caught touchdown passes.

Texas was on a tear, thanks to the innovative flip-flop winged-T which suited Royal's bevy of backs—Mike Cotten, James Saxton, Ray Poage, Jack Collins, Jerry Allen Cook, and a newcomer to keep an eye on, Tommy Ford. Arkansas had to confront that speed and power at Fayetteville with Tommy Brasher and Garrett, its linebackers, crippled and Mazzanti and others out of action. Texas won as it pleased, 33-7.

If there was one thing Arkansas had learned, it was that losing to Texas was not the end of its title hopes. If there was one thing Royal had learned, it was that he could not count the Razorbacks out. He began dropping remarks that he wished other SWC teams worried as much about Arkansas as he did. "Give me some help," he meant.

None was forthcoming. Texas A&M led Arkansas by 8-7 at Fayetteville. With time running out from the Hogs' 10-yard line, McKinney saw two of his passes dropped. Third and 10, 90 yards to go. McKinney pitched to Alworth, who handed to McKinney, who handed back to Alworth, who pulled up and hurled a pass to Dudley for 36 yards. McKinney completed the 90-yard drive with a minute to spare, arching a seven-yard touchdown pass to Jim John. It ended 15-8.

Rice was not allowed out of its end of the field in the mud at Houston, and Jesse Branch, gaining 93 yards, led Arkansas's inside game that proved decisive, 10-0.

And history repeated itself at Dallas and Austin. Hayden Fry lived out a dream, calling a first-play bomb that resulted in a McKinney-to-Alworth completion for 69 yards. The Hogs still had to hustle for the 21-7 win over SMU, which they finished on cloud nine. Sonny Gibbs had found Buddy Iles with a bomb at Austin, and TCU again upset Texas, this time by 6-0. Arkansas and Texas were to be the co-champions—at least they would after Arkansas finished beating Texas Tech the following week, 28-0, and Texas got through with A&M on Thanksgiving.

The Razorbacks tied A&M's 1939–41 record of winning or sharing the Southwest title three years in a row. They also fulfilled a longtime dream of their fans in earning a bid to the Sugar Bowl.

Bear Bryant had produced his first 10-0 team, his first national championship at Alabama. Alabama had given up only 22 points all year with a defense featuring Leroy Jordan and Billy Neighbors.

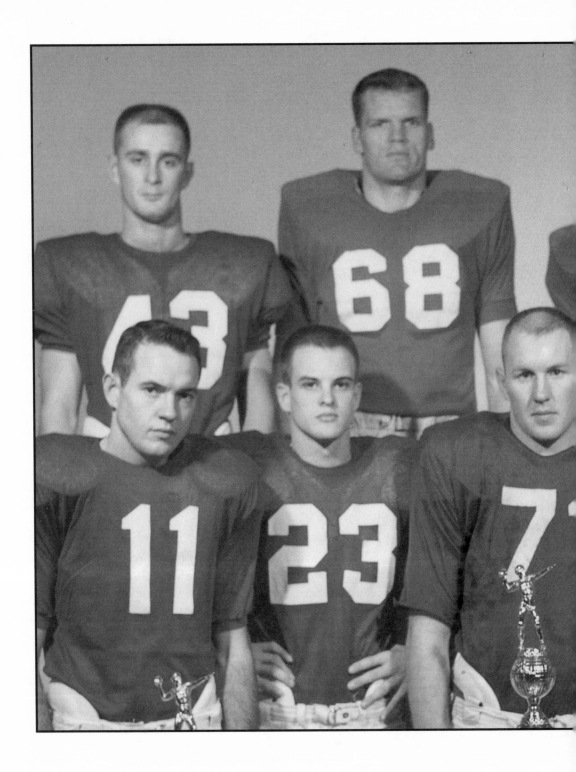

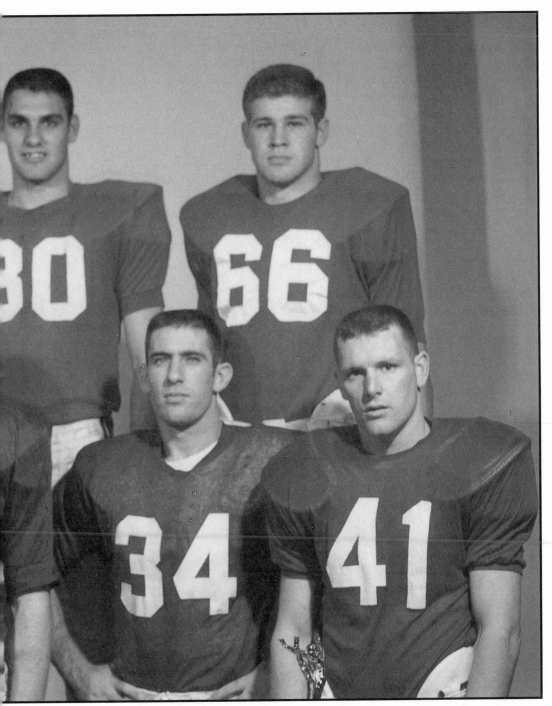

George McKinney (11), Lance Alworth (23), John Childress (71), Paul Dudley (34), Harold Horton (41), Darrell Williams (43), Charlie Moore (68), Jim Collier (80), and Dean Garrett (66) played for three straight title teams, 1959–61.

A heavy underdog, the Hogs did not get their bearings until after Mike Fracchia exploded for 43 yards and quarterback Pat Trammell squirmed over to give the Tide a 7-0 lead late in the first quarter.

The teams stymied each other the rest of the way. Tim Davis cashed in a pass interception with a second quarter field goal, 10-0. Alabama's Tommy Brooker halted Dudley's 38-yard run at the 10, and Cissell's field goal went wide. McKinney passed 24 yards to Alworth at the 22, and the drive reached the 10. Cissell got the Hogs on the board and within reach as the third quarter ended, 10-3.

Alabama used clutch defense and booming punts to stave off McKinney and his passes to Alworth and Dudley at the end. The Tide drew one pass interference call and escaped another at the goal. Then Butch Wilson intercepted at the one. Trammell kept it there, sneaking for no gains. Alabama refused to punt to All-American Alworth, the nation's runback leader.

On the field immediately after the game, Alworth signed a pro contract with Al Davis. He would be the premier pass-catcher of pro football in the 1960s, San Diego's celebrated Bambi.

– 28 –

THE SLIPPERY EDGE
OF GREATNESS

By 1962 Arkansans had come to expect something special out of a Frank Broyles team. On a gorgeous early October afternoon in Fayetteville, however, even the most optimistic Hog fans began to pinch themselves. Could this be true, could this finally be the Arkansas of their wildest dreams?

The Razorbacks had stomped Oklahoma State by 34-7, Tulsa by 42-14, TCU by 42-14. And now they led always-pesky Baylor by 28-0, and it wasn't even halftime.

In terms of yardage earned and yardage allowed, the Razorbacks had hit some all-time bests in 1961. From that squad, though, they lost eight familiar contributors: Lance Alworth, Paul Dudley, George McKinney, John Childress, Dean Garrett, Darrell Williams, Jimmy Collier, and Harold Horton (who often had wild-carded for Alworth and Dudley at defensive back).

Hayden Fry left to be head coach at SMU, and Dixie White took an assistant's job at LSU. Broyles rebuilt his offensive staff by moving Doug Dickey from the secondary, bringing Mervin Johnson back from Missouri (Johnson had captained Frank's 1957 Missouri team, come to Arkansas for two years, then spent two years back at Columbia with Dan Devine), and advancing Barry Switzer from the B-team staff. Bill Pace came from Kansas to coach the secondary, joining defensive veterans Mackenzie and Matthews.

Like all coaches, Broyles copied as much as he was copied. He borrowed from Royal the flip-flop winged-T which sacrificed the mirrored attack but let him utilize one fine runner all the time at tailback. And he sized up his large but inexperienced squad and decided he would do what LSU had done starting in 1958—beat the limited substitution rules with the use of a unique three-team system.

At that time a player could re-enter a game only once a quarter, except for one wild-card player per down. LSU was able to attain the needed depth with which to combat the heat at Baton Rouge by fielding one two-way team, one unit of defensive specialists, and a third unit of offensive specialists. The number-one unit would start every period, and the other two units would finish it. The number-one unit would always be available to come back in a pinch in each period. The morale factor would be no small gain; 33 to 35 players would see action each quarter.

Broyles and his staff had an inventive and productive spring. The last piece fell into place that fall during two-a-day practices.

In August of 1959 Jim Mackenzie had found Danny Brabham as a 6'4", 215-pound sleeper in Greensburg, Louisiana. A running back, among other things, he had led his litttle school to the Class B state championship. Danny's signature in hand, Mackenzie had only one thought on the long drive back to Fayetteville. "I hope he's a player."

Brabham turned out to be an exceptional student, a horn-rimmed intellectual almost, but he did not live up to his potential in his first two years as a linebacker, center, and offensive guard, where he played most of the time. In the spring of 1962, which Danny missed (and almost left school), Broyles had him pegged as a defensive tackle. That fall, in one of Frank's famous switches, Brabham was moved to fullback.

Broyles said his assistants were dubious when he ordered the experiment, but "the first time Danny ran the ball against our main defense, he left a trail of bodies."

"All elbows, knee bones, and shoe leather," was the way Wilson Matthews described the Brabham style.

Billy Moore was to become the first and last T-quarterback to lead the Southwest Conference in rushing, a not unexpected feat, so quick were his feet, so big was his heart. The addition of Brabham stomping up the middle kept defenders from waiting for Billy at the corners.

Jesse Branch moved from fullback to tailback, and a sophomore, George Rea Walker, emerged as the perfect wingback. On top of that, two sophisticated sophomores from Helena, quarterback Billy Gray and halfback Ken Hatfield, along with split end Jerry Lamb, gave the Tush Hogs, the green offensive specialists, aerial striking power. Coming in after Moore's unit had done its damage, Gray's crowd passed OSU and Tulsa into a state of demoralization.

Still nothing was underway at Arkansas until the TCU game. The

Horned Frogs had begun to chafe at having to start each league race 0-1 because of upstart Arkansas. Their showdown at Fort Worth brought out a full house, including Dan Jenkins, a TCU grad who would soon become for *Sports Illustrated*—which had sent him back to his hometown to cover the game—the nation's most readable sportswriter.

It was a rout, with Branch, Brabham, and Walker crashing or skipping through the Frogs for monstrous gains as TCU concentrated on Moore. By midway of the second quarter Jenkins slammed his hand on his notepad and exclaimed, "TCU will never beat Arkansas." It was a prophetic remark that held firm until 1981. "We were humiliated," said Abe Martin.

Baylor provided a scare. Passer Don Trull brought the Bears back from 28-0 to 28-21 as the Porkers faced and staved off their first adversity of the year. This brought on the biggest Arkansas versus Texas confrontation yet. The two teams had not only come to dominate the league; their meetings now assumed national importance.

Although generally outplayed, Texas blighted what otherwise could have been the Razorbacks' first crack at a national title. This is how Walter Bingham described it in *Sports Illustrated*:

> Football games last an hour, which is lucky for Texas. Only one minute short of that hour in its game against Arkansas in Austin last Saturday night, Texas was in jeopardy of losing a whole bundle—the game, its ranking as the nation's top team, and most probably the Southwest Conference title. But with only 36 seconds to play a bulldog of a tailback named Tommy Ford cracked into the Arkansas line for four precious yards and the touchdown that gave Texas the game, 7-3.
>
> Even as Ford lay in the end zone the whole world seemed to explode. Cannons went off. Cushions flew through the air. Bugles blared, horns honked and drums banged. People—and there were more than 64,000 of them in the stadium—screamed and yelled and slugged each other happily while a sad, few Arkansas rooters cried and silently cut their throats. Texas was the winner and still heavyweight champion of college football.

Arkansas had shut out Texas only once. This appeared to be the Steers' humbling fate, however, when they gained what would most likely be their last chance. They were at their 15. They had not threatened to score all night and had made just over 100 yards against a Porker defense led by Tommy Brasher and Ronnie Caveness, the linebackers. And on first down Dave Walston threw Duke Carlisle for a five-yard loss. With

In 1962, Bill Moore became the only T-formation quarterback to lead the SWC in rushing. As there is no longer an SWC, his record is safe.

that Arkansas loosened up. Carlisle hit Tommy Lucas and Bubba Sands for two passes that put the ball at midfield. Royal switched to Johnny Genung at quarterback.

Now it was a different battle; desperation was felt on every down. Texas won three vital measurements by inches and survived a pass which Arkansas's Stan Sparks intercepted—but on the out-of-bounds line, an official ruled. The Texas cannon reserved for touchdowns began to boom on first downs. And finally it was third and four, and Ford crashed over right guard on a special trap play seldom used on the goal line.

Texas had widened its ends, containing Moore, and Arkansas had played conservatively, hesitating to pass. Branch found holes off tackle, and in the second quarter Tom McKnelly kicked a 42-yard field goal.

The game's great might-have-been took place in the third period. Arkansas moved from its 49 on Moore's passes to Walker and Lamb, and finally Gray scrambled to a first down on the Texas five. On second down Brabham rumbled through, no one to keep him from entering the end zone. At that point Texas linebackers Pat Culpepper and Leon Treadwell converged on Danny. Out flew the football. Had he crossed the goal? Arkansas thought he had, but Texas had the football in the end zone. The Porkers wasted another chance on a Texas fumble near its 20, but never mind.

The game is perpetuated in the Texas Lettermen's Lounge by a huge photomural of Culpepper and Treadwell hitting Brabham.

The Razorbacks recovered from crushing disappointment to dominate the rest of the league as they had never done before, suffering a scare only at the hands of Hayden Fry's SMU team. Fry knew Moore well. Blessed with a wet field in Little Rock on which Billy's footing would betray him, the SMU coach decided to make Billy pass, which he was loathe to do when he thought he could see running room on pass-or-run sprintouts.

SMU led by 7-0 into the fourth period. Arkansas had fumbled at the two. Finally Billy Gray came in to open up the Ponies with his passing, and Branch burst over from 11 yards out. Moore was stopped on a two-point try.

Gray and Moore ran and passed the ball within range for McKnelly, who kicked a 31-yard field goal. But at the end SMU had a shot at a field goal. Guard Mike Hales blocked it, saving a 9-7 win.

Arkansas had set scoring records and hogged the all-league honors but Texas had won the Cotton Bowl host role. So it was back to New

Orleans, again to face an unbeaten SEC champion, this time Broyles's nemesis, Mississippi.

Late in a 34-0 romp over Texas Tech (that had been the halftime score), Broyles, at the behest of assistants and players, sent Moore back in on the goal line to make a try for a touchdown to break the school's scoring record. Billy went in half-hearted, interrupting a gabfest on the bench, and came back in pain. He had failed to score, which was not that important to him, but he had suffered a knee injury.

The knee went out on him again in the Hogs' pre-bowl camp at Biloxi, Mississippi, dooming the Hogs' offensive effort against Vaught's only perfect team (10-0 after the Sugar Bowl).

The pro-sized Rebs, typically fast and talented, won by 17-13. It should not have been that close, for Ole Miss quarterback Glynn Griffing broke Davey O'Brien's Sugar Bowl total offense record with over 300 yards, much of it on big sprintouts on third downs. Arkansas stayed in it on a few big passes from Gray to Lamb and McKnelly's two field goals. Moore had to leave twice when his knee went out on him on corner cuts.

The overall 9-2 record that had left the Razorbacks ecstatic in 1959 seemed terribly disappointing to what at times was an awesome team in 1962.

— 29 —

SIDETRACKED

Arkansas had finished 8-2, 8-2, 8-2 and 9-1 in the last four regular seasons; Broyles's teams had won 34 of their last 41 games, not counting bowls. They had ranked ninth, eighth, eighth, and sixth in the last four Associated Press polls. They had gone to four bowls in a row. Southwest Conference writers decided it was time to make the Razorbacks the pre-season favorite for 1963.

In truth, plenty of raw talent was on campus. Broyles had exploited the Razorbacks' expanding reputation by broadening his recruiting net. For the first time, Arkansas could pull blue-chippers out of Texas—Jerry Lamb and Ronnie Caveness being among the early prizes—and the 1962 freshmen, headed by Brinkley quarterback Jon Brittenum, showed extreme promise. The 1963 freshmen represented another bountiful haul in and out of state including Loyd Phillips, Harry Jones, and Ronny South.

The main hitch was that rules makers dealt Broyles a rude blow that wrecked his three-unit system.

The rules committee ordered flat-out one-platoon football in 1963, excepting the one wild-card player per down. This weakened Arkansas, loaded with potential specialists, and proved a boon to Texas, which had an ample supply of "complete" players and promptly won a national championship with them.

The bad news started on the first day of fall practice when George Rea Walker, the only returnee from what had been virtually an all-SWC backfield, reported with a knee injury that ended his career. The defense would prove respectable, thanks to such as end Jim Grizzle, one of the most colorful Razorbacks of all time, and linebackers Brasher and Caveness. The offense lacked punch.

Broyles tried several fullbacks before Bobby Nix settled into the role in mid-season. Sophomores Jim Lindsey and Jackie Brasuell made reasonably good wingbacks and tailbacks. For the first time as head coach, though, Broyles failed to settle on a No. 1 quarterback.

Billy Gray, who had excelled as a spot sophomore passer in 1962, had speed but was not a durable runner. Brittenum indicated his potential in the spring, but inexperience hampered him. Fred Marshall, in Moore's shadow so long, had not regained the fine passing touch he showed on the freshman team in 1960.

Gray's passing had been enough to beat Oklahoma State, 21-0. Then Missouri's huge, tough ends collapsed on him, and the Tigers rallied for a 7-6 win. Marshall was given the starting nod against TCU, usually the tipoff, and his 56-yard pass to Jerry Lamb in the second quarter led to a rousing 18-3 win. Gray came on late to cash in two touchdown opportunities gained by the defense.

Arkansas scrambled well at Waco, losing 14-10 on two touchdown passes from Don Trull to Lawrence Elkins. Baylor would surpass every team in the league except Texas, a 7-0 winner over the Bears.

Broyles started an all-sophomore backfield against Texas—Brittenum, Nix, Lindsey, and Brasuell. The week before, Texas had unleashed a mighty blow for SWC prestige. The Longhorns put a 28-6 whomping on Oklahoma, which was rated No. 1 after a conquest of Southern Cal, the previous year's consensus national champion. That Texas triumph ended the Bud Wilkinson era and shifted the focus on the Southwest Conference the rest of the 1960s.

This was Texas's Duke Carlisle Crowd, featuring Scott Appleton (plus sophomore Tommy Nobis) on defense, but a little-known fullback named Harold Phillip almost wrecked the Porkers on quick counter plays before Mackenzie's defense could make the corrections.

Texas scored on its first three possessions and led 17-0. Brasuell's 89-yard kickoff return ignited the Hogs and a big War Memorial Stadium crowd. Brittenum's short passing, chiefly to Lamb, took Arkansas 90 yards in 20 plays early in the fourth quarter, but Texas held on and won, 17-13. And for the first time since 1958 Arkansas was out of a league race.

The Porkers' string of November victories ended at 20 with a 7-0 loss to Rice, and they reached bottom in a 14-7 setback at SMU. By then Broyles had decided on Marshall, but Fred suffered a slight shoulder separation in the second quarter. He had taken the team to a 7-0 lead off the kickoff, but there had been a failure at the SMU one. "A miserable, miserable game," is the way it stuck in Broyles's mind. The Ponies won going away with fanatical effort.

On the plane ride home some juniors, mainly Marshall and Lamb, asked Broyles if they could scrimmage the following Monday. A Broyles team *never* scrimmaged in-season; he preferred to concentrate on assignments and keep his team fresh for Saturdays. This time he agreed.

That week the Razorbacks turned the corner. The contact work in pads probably left them vulnerable after they grabbed a 20-0 lead over Texas Tech, and Gray had to rescue Marshall again to nail down a 27-20 win. But a winning pattern, a state of mind if nothing else, had been re-established.

— 30 —

AT THE PINNACLE

The 5-5 season of 1963 had taught that year's juniors one paramount lesson. Once a winning tradition becomes established, losing is miserable. Any sacrifice paid to avert defeat becomes worth the price.

Those juniors who became the exemplary seniors of 1964 were quarterback Fred Marshall; linebackers Ronnie Caveness and Ronnie Mac Smith; offensive linemen Jerry Jones, Jerry Welch, Dick Hatfield, and Jerry Lamb; defensive backs Charles Daniel and Ken Hatfield (the nation's top punt returner of his time); defensive linemen Jim Finch and Jimmy Johnson; quarterback and defensive back Billy Gray; and sub wingback Gary Robinson and place kicker Tom McKnelly.

They began their leadership meetings in December when for the first time in five years there was no bowl trip. They applied themselves with crusader zeal to the January-to-March out-of-season conditioning, agility, and strength-building work. They christened it the Fourth Quarter Class. They began in the fall the U of A tradition of raising four fingers when the teams changed for the fourth period, conveying "The fourth quarter is ours."

Sacrifice? Glen Ray Hines, whose father was a 280-pound giant, stood 6'5" and tended to weigh 260. Broyles had never played a "big man" because none had either matured early enough or had the quickness required by his standards. Hines took on a diet of eschewing "everything white." That spring he had to have a new uniform to fit his new 232-pound frame. Jimmy Johnson, the play-wrecking nose guard, performed best at 200, but his weight tended to soar to 220 out of season. He lived on lettuce the last two weeks of August so he could meet Jim Mackenzie's specifications.

Jerry Lamb, maybe the best 185-pound end Arkansas ever had, had sacrificed his pass catching to become a fantastically quick defensive end in 1963. Now he relinquished some of the limelight at split end to a big, gifted receiver named Bobby Crockett. Lamb lined up next to tackle Hines at tight end. Their combined thrusts against defensive men were to help spring wingback Jim Lindsey around the weak side for six or seven yards on first down on several occasions against the Texas Longhorns, whose strategy was to give opponents minus plays on first downs, forcing them to the air.

Offensive coach Doug Dickey was lost to Tennessee, where he soon rebuilt the Vols. (John Barnhill exulted privately. He had once lost to his alma mater a head coach, Bowden Wyatt, whom he felt to be the son he had never had. Now Tennessee was coming back to his program for an assistant coach to spark its revival.) Broyles advanced Bill Pace to the offensive side and hired Johnny Majors, a former Tennessee All-American back, to handle the secondary.

Southern Cal had won the national title in 1962 by putting two wide receivers on the old experimental I-formation: the pro-I, they later called it. J. T. King of Texas Tech, whose offensive knack Broyles admired, had further modified the Southern Cal stuff as a vehicle for Donny Anderson and Dave Parks in 1963.

Frank produced his own touch, the wide slot-I, which Mackenzie called the ultimate offense of the 1960s. Nebraska kept it going toward 2000.

Actually, the rules committee provided the key that unlocked all the Razorbacks' immense potential for 1964. Taking note of the increasing popularity of pro football, where free substitution encouraged specialization of every kind, the committee decreed in January of 1964 a loosening of the rules which had forced a return to old-time two-way football the year before. Just a crack, mind you, but it was a crack the resourceful Broyles could see his way through.

The Broyles staff voted 6-0 in March to train players only one way in the spring, trusting they could use incomplete passes and time-outs to get their units switched properly.

Only two other SWC teams decided to take the risk that early; significantly, Texas was not one of them. Darrell Royal would continue to play his solid hosses both ways. His decision meant that, for the next two years, Texas would face Razorback players who had enjoyed twice as much practice time at their specialties as did the Longhorn regulars.

Thus Broyles was able to utilize the special abilities of players from the three strongest classes he had ever had on one squad at Arkansas. Harry Jones, who reminded the excited coaches of a larger Lance Alworth, could play safety for the time being and start as a sophomore. Jones would get his hands on the football three times that fall and score each time. Jerry Welch and Jerry Jones, enthusiastic Tush Hogs playing only offense in 1962, but limited when they had to play defense as well the next year, could come back and excel as offensive guards. And so on.

Under Broyles, Arkansas had played relatively error-free football. With the deep handoff in the I-formation and Pace's cure for fumble-itis, turnovers would become almost nonexistent.

Pace thought he had the makings of an ideal I-back in leggy Bobby Burnett, big and fast. He had seen him fumble, though. That spring Burnett was coached to keep two hands on the ball all the way to the safety on every carry, with Pace yelling, "Don't fumble." Chunky little Jackie Brasuell, who had come from Van Buren without a scholarship, remained the starter at tailback, but Burnett would play equal time or better. Nix became in essence a deep guard at fullback, hardly ever to touch the ball except when delivering his high, 40-yard punts. The wing-back or slotback had to be Lindsey, whose dedication became legendary even when he was a sophomore.

Jim's older brother, Elmer (B) Lindsey, had starred at Forrest City and became the first athlete to announce for Broyles in December 1957. However, he signed a $75,000 bonus baseball contract with the St. Louis Cardinals the next spring. After a few years in the minor leagues, B went home to manage the substantial Lindsey farm, and Jim, bigger at 195 with 10-flat speed and a hucklety-buck running style, became the athlete in the family.

Jack Davis, the freshman coach, called Lindsey "Twenty Questions" after the popular panel quiz show of the time. Jim's mind constantly worked ahead, analyzing himself and the team and gauging attitudes. In his own unobtrusive but insistent way, he served as the conscience of the 1964–65 Porkers.

Broyles knew all along that Marshall would be the quarterback. Fred had established in the spring the necessary rapport with Lamb, the Hogs' first split end. And Fred could run tough and effectively along Monroe and McKinney lines, if not quite so effectively as Billy Moore.

However, Broyles kept the useful Gray in the quarterback picture, even though defensive halfback was now his main job.

Marshall started against OSU. His first four passes sailed wildly off the mark. A shoulder injury he suffered 10 days previously obviously

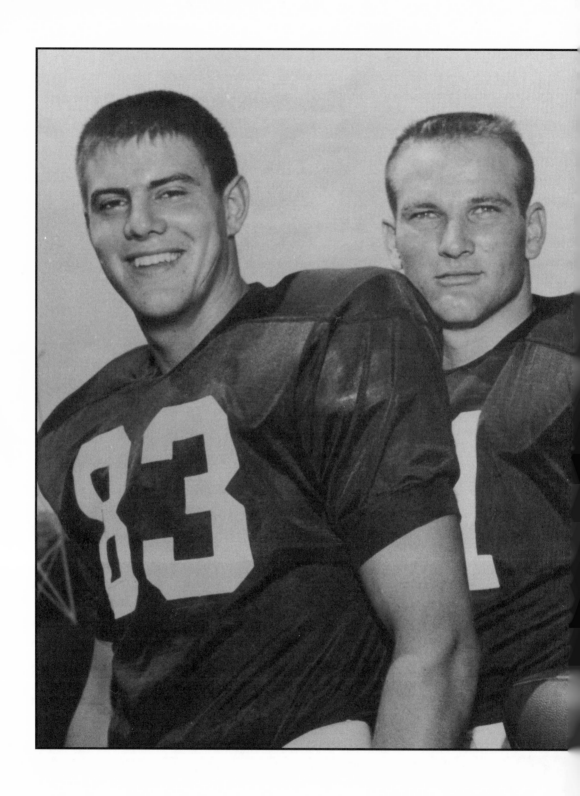

Bobby Crockett, Jim Lindsey, and Jerry Lamb, left to right, *caught the ball under the pressures of a perfect season.*

bothered him. Broyles benched Marshall immediately. Gray took over the reins and scrambled up a 14-10 win.

Marshall sat on the bench the next Saturday. Tulsa, the nation's best passing team, shot to a 14-0 lead. Some great plays by Ronnie Caveness turned the tide. He read a Jerry Rhome pass, stole it, and ran 12 yards for a touchdown. Then he caused and recovered a fumble at the Tulsa 30, setting up another score. Again Gray and the defense pulled it out, 31-22.

TCU did not know whether to expect Gray, Marshall, or Jon Brittenum (although Broyles had announced Brittenum would be red-shirted, as he was). Marshall stepped out, completed his first pass to Lamb, and went on to direct a 29-6 victory. Two interceptions by Gray, who became a brilliant defender, killed the last TCU hopes.

Fred Marshall had finally made it, and he ran and passed for 202 yards in a 17-6 win over Baylor before a roaring, overflow crowd of 41,000 at Little Rock. The razor-sharp defense held Lawrence Elkins, who shattered SWC receiving records the previous year, to four catches.

As in 1962 Texas was rated No. 1 in the polls. The Longhorns had not lost a regular-season game since a 6-0 upset by TCU in 1961. The setting was the same as 1962, a showdown of unbeatens in Austin, only more important. Every year Arkansas versus Texas loomed larger. Between them they had won or shared each SWC title for five years and were battling for the sixth.

"It wasn't many years ago that the hog call sounded hoarse, tears were in the eyes of Texas, and a game between Arkansas and Texas was just another line in the Sunday papers," commented a national magazine. "Then in 1957 Texas hired Darrell Royal, and a year later Arkansas hired Frank Broyles. Since then the two coaches have dominated the Southwest Conference with their energy, imagination, and keen sense of public relations.

"Broyles is 39, has reddish hair, was a star quarterback at Georgia Tech, has his own TV show, doesn't smoke, doesn't drink, plays golf in the mid-70s, not quite as well, he says, as Darrell Royal.

"Royal is 40, has reddish hair, was a star quarterback at Oklahoma, has his own TV show, doesn't smoke, drinks only a social Scotch and water, and plays golf in the mid-70s, not quite as well, he says, as Frank Broyles. There are some differences, of course. Royal thrives on a steady diet of pills during the season. Not Broyles, who winks and he's asleep. The pills on his desk are for hay fever."

Jim Mackenzie was the one who needed the sleeping pills. He had to direct the Arkansas defense. Any time Arkansas played Texas, he called it a "five-pack day." All Camels.

A 15-yard penalty gave Texas momentum from the opening kickoff, and the Steers barged to the 20. A five-yard penalty and a 10-yard loss suffered by Marv Kristynik on a Ronnie Mac Smith blitz forced a field-goal try that missed. With that it became a punting duel between Nix and Ernie Koy, who could really get his foot into it. Midway in the second quarter Koy launched a 47-yarder that Ken Hatfield gathered in at the 19. Men in orange clutched and missed as blockers hit them just in time. Hatfield found his alley for an electrifying 81-yard jaunt worth a 7-0 lead.

"That one went the way it was drawn up on the blackboard," Hatfield recalled a decade afterward. "Ernie Koy's kick was right straight at me and a little too far for them to be there when I got it. Texas is a good team, and none of their players were loafing. They were all just where they were supposed to be. I couldn't tell it at the time, you never can, but five Texas guys got blocked just as they reached out for me. In the film you can see their hands disappear as I go by. Harry Jones and Jim Lindsey turned me loose with the first blocks. I kinda juked Koy after he'd been screened by Lamb. Lamb in my three years made some of the greatest plays on punt returns you'll ever see. He'd never clip. Sometimes he'd just stand still and let the man run over him if he saw he couldn't throw a legal block." (Hatfield led the nation in punt returns his last two seasons and posted career totals of 70 runbacks worth 1,135 yards and five touchdown. Guess which run is best remembered.)

Koy sought to atone for what some thought had been his error in outkicking the coverage. The 195-pound tailback kept tearing into the Hogs' weak side, away from the Arkansas "monster" (roving defensive back) to make four, six, 11 yards a whack. Texas pushed the Hogs back. Finally wingback Phil Harris crossed from the two, ending a 12-play, 46-yard drive and tying it 7-7 with 12:05 to play.

Texas made a fatal error. A Longhorn was late in leaving the field as Arkansas punted; the penalty for the 12th man produced a first down. Bobby Crockett caught a must third-down pass at his shoe tops on the 36. The next Marshall-Crockett completion would be worth 34 yards and the winning touchdown.

"After we got our break (on the 12-man penalty), we faced a third and eight," Marshall said. "I sprinted right, and Crockett ran down and out. I threw it low. He caught it spread-eagled, two feet off the ground.

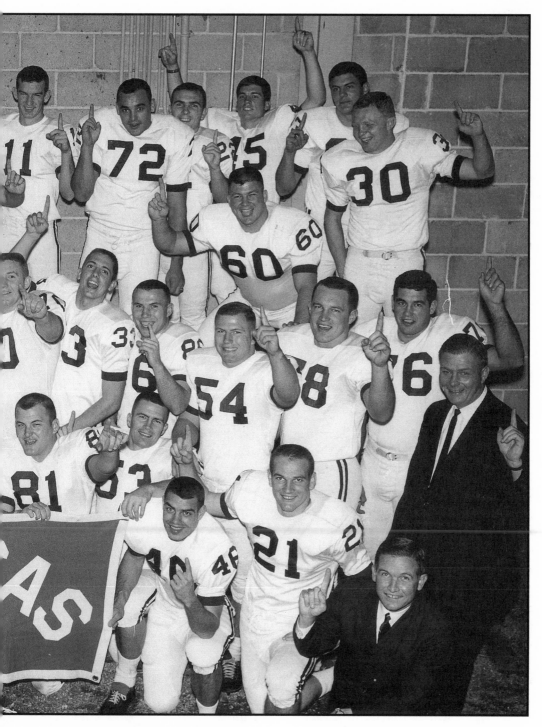

The 1964 national champions

"Two downs later we called the same play to the left. When it came time for Crockett to make his 90-degree turn to the boundary, the defensive back came up hard. Bobby saw it, and I saw it, and I knew he would switch to a fly pattern and he did. The excitement that came over me in the next second is indescribable. 'My god, six points,' I said to myself. 'All I've got to do is throw it.' I'd never had that feeling before. The rest seemed like an eternity. The play covered only 34 yards, but it seemed like I threw the ball 80 yards, most of it straight up. Knowing Crockett, he'd be under it. By the time the ball got there, a man was on his back, but he caught it and stepped on over."

Texas drove back inexorably with Koy and scored. Now Royal had to gamble; the No. 1 team could not kick for a tie, and that wasn't Darrell's nature anyway.

As the 66,000 fans clamored, Royal debated during a time-out. On their side of the field, Broyles and Mackenzie watched for a clue. Out came Koy. In went Hix Green, a good pass receiver but too light to be a power runner. Mackenzie sent in the word. Kristynik faked and backed up. Jim Finch got in his face. The UT quarterback threw frantically for Green. The ball fell on the turf, low and short.

The ball, in fact, landed near where Ford had taken off for the climactic points in 1962. A group of Arkansas fans walked toward the scoreboard, reading 14-13, and scooped up handfuls of turf from that spot as souvenirs.

Royal, always gracious in his rare defeats, quickly joined Broyles in Arkansas's rowdy dressing room. "You have a great team and earned the win," Darrell told the Razorbacks. "I hope you bring another national championship to the Southwest Conference, but—remember—we'll be right behind you to pick up anything you drop."

No one dropped a thing. There was to be no more scoring on this team. Wichita (17-0), Texas A&M (17-0), Rice (21-0), SMU (44-0), and Texas Tech (17-0) succumbed to the confident combination of error-free offense, perfect kicking, and swarming defense.

Only Texas Tech proved worrisome. It was 0-0 at the half. Then Bobby Burnett showed the Raiders his high-speed hurdling, and Lamb made a spectacular takeaway of a pass from a Tech defender in the end zone. The Hogs were free and clear at 10-0.

Notre Dame, in a revival year under Ara Parseghian, looked set to walk off with the national title until Southern Cal upset the Irish at the end. With Notre Dame knocked off the top, the final AP poll moved Alabama to No. 1 with 515 1/2 points and Arkansas to No. 2 with 486 1/2.

They were the only 10-0 teams among the majors. Notre Dame (9-1) would not yet go bowling and Michigan State (8-1) was bound to the Rose Bowl. Texas finished 9-1 with a No. 5 rating and headed to the Orange Bowl to meet Alabama in the first of the Miami extravaganzas to be played at night on prime-time television. Arkansas drew the best available Cotton Bowl opponent, Nebraska (9-1), rated No. 6, loser only to Oklahoma in a Thanksgiving Day upset.

Nebraska took the ball, and Arkansas accepted the wind. A short punt immediately gave the Razorbacks field position on the Cornhuskers' 46. Marshall hit Lamb for 10 yards, and Lindsey ran for seven to set up Tom McKnelly's 31-yard field goal.

Nebraska took a 7-3 lead in the second quarter after quarterback Bob Churchich flooded a zone and hit halfback Harry Wilson deep for 36 yards to the Arkansas 21. Wilson popped through for the last 10 yards.

The huge Huskers and quick Porkers sparred evenly until Wilson broke away for 45 yards to the Arkansas 35 in the middle of the last quarter. Jimmy Johnson, the nose guard, helped smear three plays, one of them a spill of the passer on third down. On fourth and 12 Nebraska punted over the goal.

"I knew then that Arkansas was a great team," Nebraska coach Bob Devaney said. "Wilson's run should have broken their backs. Instead they rose up and won the game."

Given that save with 9:21 to play, Marshall and his unit ripped and snorted 80 yards until they scored.

Bill Pace had spotted something. When Nebraska rotated its excellent secondary, the end on the weakened side continued to rush, leaving a hole. This let Burnett drift out from his tailback spot to the weak side and take a little throwback pass. That, plus a famed 11-yard scramble by Marshall up the middle and an equally famed over-the-shoulder grab by Lindsey of a pass he never saw, got the drive started. It ended in a hurry. Lindsey caught a throwback pass in the left flat and rambled 27 yards to the five. Burnett crashed over from the three with an option pitch from Marshall.

"There's no way to explain all the things that happened on that 80-yard drive," Marshall said. "One early passing down, both their big ends got through, and I couldn't begin to look for receivers. I ran up the middle. I was hit and jerked and turned this way and that way. Finally I was down, and a man had his thumb in my mouth trying to jerk my cheek off—and we had a first down.

"There was that pass to Lindsey. I had to throw quick, and they'd knocked him down at the line of scrimmage. I yelled; he couldn't hear me. He never did get turned around. He says he heard a blur, the ball approaching, and got his hands up, and the ball stuck in them. And he dragged some tacklers for a first down."

Arkansas threw two post-game parties at Holiday Inn Central in Dallas, one for teetotalers, one for all-out celebrants. Mackenzie was informal host for the latter shindig. "If I felt any better, I couldn't stand it," he said. And that was before Texas, ever the friend against outsiders, outlasted Alabama, 21-17, in Joe Namath's last college game.

Broyles watched that game from the other party. He and everyone else knew what it meant. Alabama already had its No. 1 trophies—the polls closed at the end of the regular season—but there would be others for Arkansas. Sure enough, a six-man committee of the Football Writers of America voted one-sidedly to award the Grantland Rice trophy representing the national championship for 1964 to the Razorbacks.

In the balloting for coach of the year honors at the American

The Football Writers Association gave Arkansas a No. 1 trophy after other polls closed too soon.

THE RAZORBACKS

Football Coaches Association convention a week later, Broyles and Ara Parseghian wound up in a tie. For the first time two plaques were presented.

Broyles departed Dallas eager to share the "emotionalism" of the pinnacle of success with his boss and preceptor, John Barnhill, who no longer traveled out of Fayetteville. Barnhill in 1946 had set in motion the program that produced a national title 18 years later.

As Frank told it, he virtually "floated" into Barnhill's office. The athletic director's deflating first words: "Frank, you've just screwed up the best coaching job in America.

"Eight, nine wins a year; you've been perfect. Now that you've won it all, they'll expect you to do it every year. You've ruined this job."

It was an opinion widely unshared.

At Tampa, Florida, where he had gone years before to establish a prosperous business, Arkansas expatriate Jim Wright said, "Now I tell everybody I'm from Arkansas."

A 30-year reunion of the 1964 national champions

STORYBOOK SATURDAYS

By shutting out their last five regular-season opponents, the Razorbacks of 1964 led the nation in defense against scoring, an average yield of 5.7 points for 10 games. They turned around in 1965 and led the nation in scoring by averaging 32.4 points per game. Once again they posted a 10-0 record, becoming the first SWC team to put perfect seasons back to back.

In seven years under Broyles, Arkansas had evolved from a light, scrambling team to a moderately big, quick, and fast powerhouse.

The only sophomore who played regularly in 1965 was defensive back Tommy Trantham. Frank suddenly had his most experienced team with the most depth and most size.

"All my life we looked for size," Broyles said. "We would not play a big man who couldn't move, but we kept looking for size. For a while every big man we recruited could not move. Then it seemed every big man we took could move and came through."

The 1965 squad featured Broyles's biggest and best group of linemen: Loyd Phillips (6'2", 220) and Jim Williams (6'2", 210) on defense; Glen Ray Hines (6'5", 240), Dick Cunningham (6'3", 220), and Mike Bender (6'3", 220) on offense. They were all tackles. "Other things being equal, the team with the best tackles will win," Broyles quoted Tennessee's General Neyland.

The backs, too, had more size than the 1960s norm as well as speed and niftiness: Bobby Burnett at 6'1", 195; Bobby Nix at 6'2", 200; Harry Jones at 6'2", 193; Jon Brittenum at just under six feet and 185. Split end Bobby Crockett ran like a halfback at 6'1", 195.

All but one of the players named signed pro contracts. Seven of them became regulars. Burnett earned American Football League Rookie of the Year honors at Buffalo.

The first of three sons of former high school coach Clell Burnett, Bobby carried 232 times for 947 yards in 1965, mostly in thick traffic between the ends, breaking Arkansas records, and did not lose a fumble. (The Porkers lost only six fumbles in 1964, only seven in 1965.)

Extending a 12-game winning streak hinged on establishing a replacement for Marshall and replacing the core of the 1964 defense, the nose guard, and both linebackers. Actually eight defensive starters had to be replaced. Wilson Matthews found two fifth-year men, Joe Black and Buddy Sims, who could give him canny if not stout linebacking. As we shall see, what this defense could do best was make big plays—and often score. The offense set them up, forcing the other teams into desperate situations and high-risk plays.

Brittenum had the quickness to run the option, but he was first and foremost the strongest-armed quarterback Broyles had had. So the Porkers could hammer inside with Burnett, sweep the ends with Jones (who had 9.7 100-yard speed and could swerve fluidly) and Lindsey, and throw to Crockett, Lindsey, and Jones, all superb receivers.

As a redshirt in 1964, Brittenum had not gained the needed confidence, and the following spring he was faced with competition from Jones and Ronny South. Broyles always said that if he had it to do over, he would have played Lance Alworth at quarterback. Now Harry Jones, who had been a high school quarterback at Enid, Oklahoma, excited him just as much with his tearing sprint-out runs. South, a natural all-around athlete but not a threatening runner, looked like a pro prospect as a passer.

Nothing was decided at the end of spring. Brittenum got away from football in the summer, at first in anger and disappointment. He returned with a devil-may-care attitude not typical of his nature.

"He came back brazen," Broyles said. "He told me he was our quarter-back, and I could tell immediately that he was."

Jones was moved to wingback, behind Lindsey, and South func-tioned as a kicking specialist and backup quarterback.

Despite their sweep of 1964 the Hogs were not favored going into the new season. Texas, which had lost only two regular-season games in four years, and those by the narrowest of margins, rated a slight edge and for sound reasons. It was to be the senior year for linebacker Tommy Nobis and several other Longhorns—Diron Talbert, John Elliott, Pete Lammons—destined to become outstanding pros.

Oklahoma State exposed the greenness of the new U of A defense, but not before the Razorbacks used their shattering offensive balance to take a 21-0 lead toward a 28-14 triumph.

Tulsa had linemen as big and good as Arkansas's, plus excellent passing. Tulsa led, 12-10, at halftime on the passing of Bill Anderson to Howard Twilley, later a Super Bowl hero with Miami. A fumble recovery at the Tulsa 42 let South turn it around with a 45-yard field goal, and Brittenum's passes to Crockett delivered the clinching touchdown in a 20-12 win. The Porkers were later to say that Tulsa, which finished 8-2, was their second strongest foe.

TCU's young team went down, 28-0; the last two touchdowns came on breakaways of 21 and 59 yards by Harry Jones, the early-season sensation.

Baylor had to play a sub quarterback, and six interceptions paved the way for a 38-7 romp. Trantham returned a theft 69 yards for a touchdown, and Jackie Brasuell, now at safety, returned a punt 72 yards to the Baylor four.

Thus Texas and Arkansas found themselves in the same old delightful spot, each 4-0 and everything riding. Once again Texas was No. 1 in the polls. Arkansas, No. 3, was listed as a three-point favorite, probably on the basis of playing at home. The man who did the play-by-play for NBC-TV, Lindsey Nelson, would later call it "the best college football game I've ever seen."

Royal had a manhandling front eight on defense, but any time Brittenum could get a pass away he might have a big gain—even a touchdown. Amazingly, the Razorbacks shot into a 20-0 lead, and two other touchdowns, on passes to Crockett and Jones, were called back.

The defense scored two of the three touchdowns that stuck on the scoreboard. Phil Harris tried to handle Nix's 58-yard punt near the Texas five. A lineman hit him as he bobbled it, and defensive back Martine Bercher covered the ball in the end zone for a touchdown. That seemed fitting, because Crockett's 58-yard catch-and-run, a twisting beauty, had just been wiped out by penalty.

Texas retaliated, using misdirection plays in the clever hands of stumpy, never-say-die Marv Kristynik, and was nearing the Arkansas 20 when Bobby Roper jostled the ball loose from Harris. Trantham caught it in midair and ran it back 77 yards to score.

The Hogs then added one with their offense. Brittenum's passes of 28 yards to Jones and 11 yards to Crockett wide open in the end zone made it 20-0.

Texas snarled back. Kristynik began faking option plays one way and throwing back quickly the other way to his wingback. The first of David Conway's three field goals and Kristynik's one-yard keeper cut it to 20-11 at halftime.

In the UT dressing room, Royal put "21-20" on the blackboard.

Texas came back with momentum. Arkansas had poor field position, could not run against the eight-man front, and passed rarely and cautiously. The Hogs did not make a first down from late in the second period until late in the final one. Conway added a 34-yard field goal, and Kristynik capped a short drive with a 14-yard run. Darrell's score is now 21-20. As the Porkers faltered again, Conway added a 34-yard field goal, 24-20.

Texas looked unstoppable. The Longhorns' raging comeback bespoke their determination to live up to their credo, "No one beats Texas two years in a row," which had stood up in Royal's time.

When Arkansas prepared for its last drive from its 20 against the wind in the gathering gloom of near darkness, with fans drained and almost resigned to defeat, Broyles was an emotional wreck, sickened by the fact he had blown a huge lead, the biggest anyone had known against a Texas team under Royal.

"Sometimes I hate myself because I won't throw deep in my own end of the field," Frank said. "They were making things happen; we weren't. But we could have, I think. We were all concentrating on defense on the sidelines because they had us so confused. Jim Lindsey is who rallied our team. Not me. I was a babbling idiot."

The combination of Jones's fresh brilliance and an injury had relegated Lindsey to a supporting role at times. Now on the sidelines he huddled the offensive unit together. Almost tearfully he reminded them that Texas was not double-covering Crockett, that he was wide open, that Brittenum could hit Crockett if they blocked, that if the coverage doubled up, Jones could run outside, and that this was the last chance.

"If I did anything useful," Lindsey said later, "I just put everybody's gut feelings into words."

The 80-yard drive began with Lindsey in there, ostensibly to block. On first down Lindsey did what the Hogs had not done all day. He fought through the left side for seven yards, taking some pressure off. Then down the field they went, nine men blocking, Crockett the only man out. First Brittenum found his crazy-legged battery mate for 22 yards. In his dreams Jon may still be yelling "Crockett" for fear Bobby would not turn around in time; he had had to throw early.

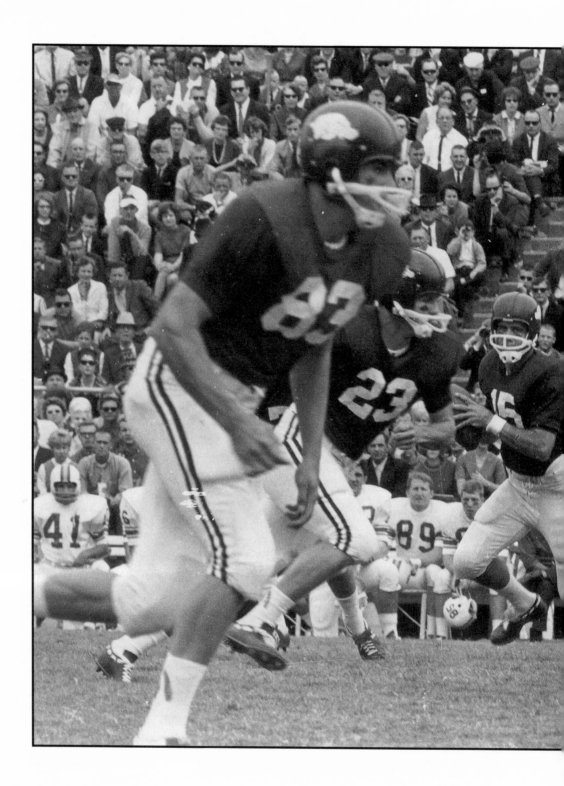

THE RAZORBACKS

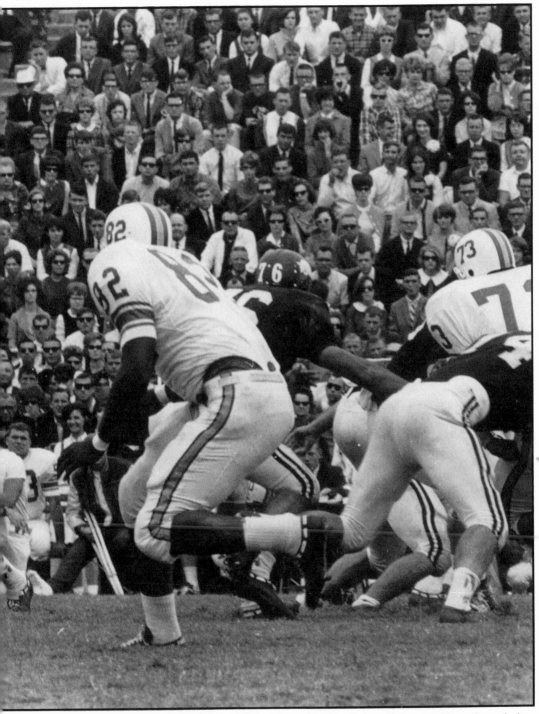

A scary sight for 1965 foes: John Brittenum (15) sprints out as Harry Jones (23) and Bobby Crockett (83) break open.

Royal had alternated his two-way halfbacks on Crockett, but neither had hindered him or slowed him. Now, on third and four at the 15, Royal moved an end out to put in Crockett's face. The end was told to force Crockett to the inside, where the halfback and the inside help would have a better chance. Bobby got by the end (a flag fell) and quickly cut outside. He was open. The halfback could not catch up. Brittenum's roll-out lob was high. Crockett leaped for it and caught it as he fell head first and onto the coffin-corner flag.

Razorback Stadium went into orbit, but not until after the official retrieved his flag. He had called the Texas end for holding in his futile effort to deflect Crockett from his route.

Brittenum sneaked the last yard. "I didn't want to risk any exchange," Jon said. "And I told myself that if I fumbled, I'd just run right out the end of the stadium and disappear forever."

"Now in those last four minutes of the splendid, excruciating game that everybody knew it would be," wrote Dan Jenkins for *Sports Illustrated*, "Jon Brittenum did his best, all right. He completed six passes and drove Arkansas 80 yards to the winning touchdown while Frank Broyles's shirttail came out . . . and 42,000 people made noises that sounded like an attack from another planet, or Cecil Buffalo and the Prophets playing and singing 'Jon Brittenum, Quarterbackin' Man.' When Brittenum, an unemotional and heretofore unpredictable junior, punched into the Texas end zone with just 1:32 to play, a national television audience as well as all of Arkansas saw helmets sail into the air almost as high as Broyles jumped, and red-sheathed Razorbacks on the field and sideline hugging, kissing, and weeping like soldiers who had been rescued."

Early the next week, for the first time ever, the Razorbacks found themselves rated No. 1 in the nation by a wire-service poll. This was to last just a week, even though their 17-game winning streak was the best thing going. While they were beating North Texas State, 55-20, Michigan State was knocking off Purdue, which had upset Ohio State. Superior voting strength from the Big 10 sector put Michigan State on top.

Still, Arkansas had arrived as an accepted national power.

One at a time, Broyles preached, and the Razorbacks complied. They went out in a seeming state of unconcern, ran their simple potent repertoire, and polished off Texas A&M, 31-0; Rice, 31-0; SMU, 24-3; and rallied to whip Texas Tech's talented offensive team, 42-24.

Texas never recovered from the Fayetteville crusher and lost four of its last six games.

"It was boring, almost," Brittenum said of the final month. "We knew what we had to do, we went out and did it. There was no big thrill at winning, just relief that we could keep the streak going."

Few teams had ever so demolished the rest of what was normally a balanced league.

Crockett, Hines, Jones, Burnett, and Brittenum made the all-SWC offensive unit; Phillips, Roper, Williams, Brasuell, and Trantham made the defensive unit. Phillips and Hines made most of the All-American teams; Crockett made one.

This time the Associated Press would not take its final football poll until after the bowl games, a decision reached after Arkansas survived the games of the previous January 1 as the only 11-0 team but went unrewarded by the AP. Michigan State, Arkansas, and Nebraska survived the 1965 season with 10-0 records. All went bowling, and all lost.

The Razorbacks, as in 1960, had the misfortune of drawing a capable but down-graded Cotton Bowl opponent. LSU, 7-3, had lost three games due to fumbles and injuries to quarterbacks. The Tigers, however, were a typically sound, strong Charley McClendon team. Uncelebrated by their own fans, they licked their wounds in Baton Rouge, staying at home to prepare five weeks for the challenge of their lives, a shot at a team with a 22-game winning streak.

The Razorbacks, mostly fourth and fifth year men, spent a week at Brownsville, Texas, and Padre Island and another week at San Antonio, where the chief topic was whether Jim Mackenzie would get a head-coaching job. He did. While he was being interviewed by Maryland, Oklahoma called. Jim hurried on to Norman to accept that plum of an opportunity, then returned to his pre-bowl duties.

Some Arkansas fans believe to this day that the Razorbacks left their game on the beaches of Padre Island. Certainly they enjoyed the training junket, but the truth is, LSU got its quarterbacks well and played not only an inspired game but a perfect one, with no fumbles, interceptions, or kicking-game mistakes. That usually wins against anyone. And Arkansas, slightly impaired because old-timer Joe Black, the defensive signal-caller, had to watch hurt from the bench, also lost its offensive mainspring in the second period—or at least lost his effectiveness.

Arkansas scored quickly on an 87-yard drive from the kickoff, capped by Crockett's 19-yard pass reception. LSU began ganging him, but that opened running lanes for Jones, who averaged seven yards a carry.

The game seemed to turn, though, when a Pat Screen pass sailed out

Darrell Royal and Frank Broyles shook hands before the 1965 Arkansas-Texas game, but probably didn't wish each other good luck.

of the hands of an Arkansas linebacker and into an LSU receiver's grasp, giving life to a drive that tied it 7-7. Moments later, blocking on a Jones sweep that gained 15 yards, Brittenum came down on the point of his shoulder, dislocating it.

Two plays later Jon's replacement, Ronny South, could not get the ball back from his fullback on an attempted belly play, and a fumble resulted. LSU covered the 32 yards in seven plays for a 14-7 lead, mostly on stubborn runs by stumpy tailback Joe Labruzzo, who had also plugged through in the late stages of the Tigers' previous drive.

His shoulder deadened, Brittenum returned for the last half, but the teams played each other to a standstill. Four men were on Crockett for the last desperation pass; one of them intercepted it.

"We should have run more inside, to gain consistency," Broyles said. "It looked like we might score every time we went outside, but we didn't."

Michigan State lost to UCLA, and Nebraska went under to Alabama, which was then voted, with a 9-1-1 record, the AP's national champion. Bear Bryant's team had it both ways in two years.

In the resulting slough, Broyles received a note from Ara Parseghian. "You'll still be remembered for that 22-game winning streak," wrote the Notre Dame coach. "That's quite an accomplishment in this day and age."

It was slight consolation.

— 32 —

AN ERA ENDS SADLY

After a two-year blitz of the Southwest Conference, Arkansas became impossible to ignore, even by Texas-based football experts who made careers of trying. So finally the Razorbacks found themselves the pre-season target in 1966, the choice of 14 of 21 writers participating in *Texas Football* magazine's summer poll.

Even so, such an astute observer as Blackie Sherrod, then of the *Dallas Times-Herald*, pegged Arkansas fourth; Texas could come back, he figured, with eagerly-awaited sophomore quarterback "Super" Bill Bradley.

The Longhorns had sunk to 6-4 in 1965. Their second loss to Arkansas —the only league team to beat them from late in 1961 halfway into 1965—left them shattered and disenchanted. After Texas lost its next two games, to Rice and SMU, Broyles consoled Royal during one of their frequent telephone visits. "This may turn out for the best," Frank said. "Our 5-5 season in 1963 cleared the way for better things."

"Okay," Darrell said doubtfully. After TCU handed Texas its fourth loss, he said, "Frank, you think maybe I'm over-doing it?"

Arkansas entered the 1966 season with some fine leftovers from 1964–65 but not much new help. The Razorbacks stood out for three main reasons: senior All-American candidates Jon Brittenum, a proven winner at quarterback; breakaway marvel Harry Jones; and tackle Loyd Phillips, whose fierce pride, burning desire to get to the ball carrier in an angry mood, and ability to chase from sideline to sideline made him the best defensive lineman of Broyles's coaching time at Arkansas.

It turned into a most unusual season. The Razorbacks struggled offensively in the early stages, then high-balled the second half, except for a tragic 10th week. They convincingly whipped the three other contending teams, SMU by 22-0, Texas A&M by 34-0, and Texas by 12-7. But SMU wound up on top of the standings with a 6-1 record.

Uncharacteristic of Broyles's Hogs, they lost to two low finishers, Baylor by 7-0 and Texas Tech by 21-16.

At the time of the Baylor game, however, John Bridgers's Bears seemed a serious challenger. On a long, dreary afternoon in Fayetteville, the Razorbacks made over 300 yards and failed to score. Terry Southall, the Baylor quarterback, kept kicking the Hogs back with high boots that could not be returned. Brittenum would take Arkansas 40, 50, or 60 yards, but the drives would stall or there would be a fumble.

Finally, with fourth and three at the Baylor 29, Broyles opted for a "pooch kick." It was the only time he ever elected to punt so near the other team's goal. He hoped to bottle up Baylor inside its 10 and force either a turnover or a prompt return punt. He was dealing from pure Tennessee field position theory.

"When I saw them line up to kick, I knew we'd had it," Southall said later. "We'd have to try to throw the ball from in front of our goal line and against the percentages, and they'd wind up with at least a field goal."

The snap sailed over punter Martine Bercher's head. Baylor recovered at midfield. Southall completed two sideline passes and one down the middle to Bobby Green for 27 yards and a 7-0 win.

"Pooch kick," though this kick never had a chance to be pooched, became a taboo phrase in the U of A lexicon. The high snap from center led to the end of the Hogs' then-record 16-game win streak in SWC games.

The gloss was off the Arkansas-Texas rematch in Austin. Texas had lost twice, Arkansas once. Bradley and Chris Gilbert bedeviled Arkansas, but they fumbled. The Hogs won a hitting match going away after Bercher returned a punt 59 yards to the Texas 16, from where split end Tommy Burnett took a short pass and scored.

Texas A&M's young, talented team had a 3-0 league record, representing the first challenge the Hogs had known so late in a season in some time. Brittenum and Jones put on a marvelous show. After Arkansas scored the first three times it had the ball, tight end Richard Trail went back to the huddle and told his teammates, "That'll teach 'em that sophomores can't keep up with us vet-runs." This was the game where Brittenum, trapped against a sideline, switched over and completed a pass with his left hand.

Phillips went out with a bad ankle as Rice was put down, 31-20, despite Arkansas native Chuck Latourette running the Hogs crazy with his punt returns. Limited November action would not prevent Phillips from winning the Outland Trophy or becoming the U of A's first two-time All-American, but it was quite a blow to a team beginning to feel the squeeze of attrition.

The SMU game loomed as the season's championship showdown. Arkansas had a solution for an SMU defense aimed at stopping Brittenum's sprint-outs. Sophomore tailback David Dickey carried 38 times and let Arkansas control the ball all day.

But even as the Razorbacks racked up the Mustangs, whose sophomore star Jerry Levias had integrated the SWC in dazzling fashion, a cloud hung over their camp.

Claud Smithey, a fifth-year sub tackle from Searcy, lay in a coma in a Houston hospital. He had collapsed in the midst of the dressing room celebration at Texas A&M. Smithey had been ruled out of football by U of A doctors because his history included a head injury. He obtained clearance from his own doctor. A knee injury sidelined him early in the year; by mid-season he begged to be allowed to return to the squad. He went in for a few plays after the A&M game was put away. The films showed nothing that could have caused a new injury.

Smithey died as practice began for Texas Tech. An autopsy indicated that even an emotional outburst could have caused his death, so thin were the walls of blood vessels in his brain.

"I knew he was taking a big risk trying football again," his widow said. "So did he. What could you do in face of that?"

"It was the Lord's will," his mother said. "He had to play football; it was what he lived for."

Two days later the Razorback seniors served as pallbearers in a country churchyard in White County. Broyles spoke at the memorial service. A trust fund was set up for the education of Smithey's infant daughter.

When word of Smithey's death reached Fayetteville, some assistant coaches suggested a "Win One for Claud" campaign.

"No," Broyles said emphatically. He would not look for slogans and gimmicks in a tragedy that obviously shook him. Arkansas would do its best to prepare for Texas Tech in conventional ways and go play the game.

Tech had not beaten Arkansas in nine previous tries and would pit a 3-6 squad against the Hogs this time. The way to Lubbock was marked by several ominous signs unrelated to the Smithey tragedy, but few people would notice them except in retrospect.

A half-dozen Arkansas players, including Jones and Phillips, were either definitely out of the Tech game or would be no better than half-speed. And early in the week, Tech coach J. T. King gave a controversial interview in which he said, in effect, that game officials tended to protect highly ranked, bowl-bound teams toward the end of a season, with conference prestige at stake. Broyles responded with "No comment," while privately resenting an unsubtle psychological ploy aimed at officials working the Tech-Arkansas game.

On form, the Razorbacks seized a 10-7 lead and believed they scored again in the middle of the second quarter. On third and fourth down from the one, Brittenum aimed himself toward the end zone on sneaks. He and his teammates thought he made it each time. However, neither official on the ends of the formation recognized his forward progress.

Those two officials happened to be men who had played under Broyles at Baylor and remained his good friends. Had they subconsciously leaned over backward to be fair? Broyles said years later, "We thought we scored, but you have to get it in there far enough for officials to see it, I guess." (At any rate, three of the five officials never worked another league game, and the SWC immediately restructured its entire officiating setup.)

Tech seemed as flat as Arkansas when the game started. After their goal-line stand, the Raiders fired themselves up and won.

Cotton Bowl executive Field Scovell made the trip to Lubbock to issue what would have been the Hogs' third straight invitation. Instead, he watched with mixed emotions as his son, long-legged quarterback John Scovell, rode the Raiders' gathering momentum in the second half to a 21-16 upset. Brittenum tried to pull it out, but a 20-yard run with a stolen pass by Tech lineman Gene Darr did him in.

Then the Hogs clustered in a stadium ramp, listening on radios to learn if Baylor could finish its upset of SMU and send Arkansas to Dallas after all. SMU pulled out another of its patented harum-scarum wins, blocking a Terry Southall punt in the final few seconds.

"It was like we were put out of the Cotton Bowl twice the same afternoon," Broyles said. "You talk about feeling drained."

On the way home, the team's upperclassmen conveyed to Broyles they did not want to go to a bowl game if it couldn't be the Cotton. He understood; he had no heart for any bowl trip, either. He talked his way out of two bids.

It was a sad ending for what had been a 29-3 era at Arkansas.

Broyles was to grieve at two more funerals in the next few months. Late in May of 1967, Jim Mackenzie died of a heart attack. In his first year

Tackle Loyd Phillips, the U of A's first two-time All-American pick

at Oklahoma he had won the hearts of Sooner fans with his rough-edged, folksy charm—and his team's conquests of Texas and Nebraska. The last staff meeting of Frank's original 1958 Arkansas group was held over the bier at Norman; everyone who ever coached with Jim at Arkansas was there.

And in September leukemia finally took Bill (Ground Hog or Groundy) Ferrell, a sweet son of Virginia who had served as father confessor and motivator in his role as trainer to Razorbacks in all sports from the time he arrived with Otis Douglas in 1950.

Charley Coffey, a captain for Bowden Wyatt back at Tennessee, had succeeded Mackenzie on Broyles's staff in 1966. A man driven with a quest for perfection, Coffey cultivated small, agile linemen, the kind of player he had been, and he preferred more conventional defenses. The Porkers were slipping away from the stunting monster-slant to the pro 4-3-4.

Bill Pace left to become head coach at Vanderbilt, and Johnny Majors advanced from the secondary to offensive coach. Hootie Ingram of Georgia came to coach the defensive backs.

Finally it was Ronny South's turn as a fifth-year quarterback. He had kicked for 61 points and backed up Brittenum in 1965, and he had watched entirely from the bench in 1966, with Bob White coming on as a place-kicker.

An ankle started bothering South during two-a-day practices, and it was soon apparent that a time of difficulty was on hand. If it had not been a rebuilding year, with untried starters throughout the offensive unit, South might have had a better chance to get established. He was no running threat, and this imposed limitations on the offense, which failed on third and one and fourth and one while leading both Oklahoma State and Tulsa early by 6-0.

Oklahoma State took heart and won, 7-6, and Tulsa came back to prevail, 14-12, on the running of Glen Stripling, one of the region's pioneering black quarterbacks.

John Eichler, a supercharged redhead from Stuttgart, took over late against Tulsa and then fired Arkansas to a 26-0 jolting of TCU, which forever saw the Hogs rising to heights not hinted at in their first two games. The *coup de grace* turned out to be Eichler's 76-yard touchdown run on a routine quarterback sneak.

Arkansas was lucky to salvage a 10-10 tie at Baylor. White's closing field goal went under the arms of leaping rushers, but inches over the post.

Texas was to go 6-4 for the third straight year, but the Longhorns survived five fumbles by Bill Bradley and Chris Gilbert to edge Arkansas on national television at Little Rock, 21-12. John Eichler did well until a blocked punt and a blocked extra point ruined the Hogs' early momentum. Also, Eichler threw four interceptions in the middle of the game. South came in and rallied the team with his passing, narrowing it to 14-12. An on-side kick failed, and Texas punched the ball over to settle the issue.

Though hurting at tackles and in the kicking game, the Razorbacks had an excellent secondary in Gary Adams, Tommy Trantham, and Terry Stewart, plus three promising sophomore linebackers, Cliff Powell, Lynn Garner, and Guy Parker. The Hogs also had the league's best defensive end, senior Hartford Hamilton. All their useful weapons, it appeared, were purely defensive.

Then the offense came somewhat alive. Eichler went out with a serious ankle injury in a 28-7 romp over Kansas State. South finished that game impressively, and Broyles decided to stress South's specialty, the passing game. Arkansas passed for 11 touchdowns in November, when David Dickey, who resembled Jim Lindsey in many ways, would catch as a wingback in midfield and become the dependable I-back in scoring territory.

Still, Arkansas could only break even in the final month. South completed 18 of 21 passes against Texas A&M, but the Aggies had superior troops (12 of them would go into the pros), and scrambling Edd Hargett passed them to a 33-21 win, their first over Arkansas in 10 years. A&M earned a Cotton Bowl trip with a series of late-season wins, all thrillers.

Arkansas dumped Rice, 23-9, and rallied past SMU, 35-17, on South's four touchdown passes against Pony defenses massed to stop the run. If Arkansas could beat Texas Tech and go 5-4-1, it could have a Liberty Bowl bid.

The previous year, an 8-2 Arkansas team shrugged off the Liberty Bowl and stayed home. Now a trip to Memphis was viewed as a prize. Football outlooks can change, and quickly.

Texas Tech scuttled Hog bowl hopes with a 31-27 win in Little Rock. The Raiders took a 24-0 lead, partly because of Arkansas's kicking errors, and then intercepted a South pass to blunt a rally built on South-to-Dickey completions.

The 4-5-1 season was Arkansas's first losing campaign since 1958. Broyles saw it as an interim year from the start. If there was a positive aspect, November served as a dress rehearsal for what he had in mind for 1968, pro-type passing featuring the precocious Bill Montgomery.

— 33 —

PASSING,
FOR FUN AND PROFIT

Bill Montgomery's first play as a Razorback was an incomplete pass, but it brought roars from the capacity opening crowd in War Memorial Stadium. The ball carried about 70 yards, just beyond the speeding Max Peacock.

The very idea of starting a game with a bomb attempt thrilled fans accustomed to climax passing but habituated to conservative running, especially to start with. Well, the Razorbacks did have to resort to running to win that game, but the gauntlet had been thrown.

Broyles began 1968 with his first seniors in 10 years who had not shared in a title or gone to a bowl game. He had been busy, however, as in the aftermath of the disappointing 1963 season, plotting changes that would effect a quick comeback.

Johnny Majors left to become head coach at Iowa State and took offensive end coach Gordon Smith with him. Broyles hired offensive backfield coach Don Breaux, a former pro quarterback, from Florida State, which had developed a mixture of pro-type passing and collegiate option running that Alabama and others adopted. From Alabama, Frank wooed Richard Williamson, Bear Bryant's first split end, who had tutored Alabama All-American wide receivers Ray Perkins and Dennis Homan.

Harold Horton came up from Forrest City High School, replacing Wilson Matthews, who was in charge of the linebackers. Matthews moved into administrative duties, meanwhile coaching the freshmen as a form of gradual withdrawal from the field.

The Porkers would use the pro-I, known in the trade as the Florida State offense, and the pro 4-3-4 defense.

Montgomery, studious and nimble and almost cocky, grew up

Bill Montgomery

steeped in a Dallas football environment. He could do a little of everything, just whatever a coach wanted done. And he had boundless poise for a sophomore. Across town at Dallas, Chuck Dicus functioned as a waterbug of a running quarterback. Arkansas recruited him, too, and Williamson immediately turned him into a flanked receiver.

And then there was Bill Burnett, the last and smallest of the Burnetts. He looked least like a football player than anyone else on the squad, but by the time he finished his redshirt year in 1967, he probably knew more about running the football than anyone else his age in America. "He's the only back I ever saw who could change directions in mid-air," said one coach. Like his older brother Bobby, Bill was as nearly fumble-proof as a running back can be. David Dickey survived knee problems long enough to set an Arkansas career record of 28 touchdowns, but Bill would come behind him and break a national record with 49.

Conventional wisdom said you could not win with three sophomores handling the ball, but these three were different. Besides, they were to be surrounded by solid players developed in the previous seasons: Bruce Maxwell, who came back from a year of military duty bigger (215 pounds) and more mature and rarely making a mistake, ready to be Broyles's best and most versatile fullback of the platoon age; offensive guards Jerry Dossey and Jim Barnes, who could pull and lead the Green Bay sweep; center Rodney Brand, a crunching blocker; tall, big tackles Webb Hubbell and Bob Stankovich; and good ends Peacock and Mike Sigman.

Coffey's defense looked most suspect. He eventually broke in a new front four of "old man" Gordon McNulty, a Pine Bluff boy who transferred from Vanderbilt, with Bruce James, Dick Bumpas, and Rick Kersey, sophomores who could fight their way to the football in a flash. This might have been, in fact, the most ball-conscious Arkansas defensive unit yet. Defensive backs Terry Stewart, Gary Adams, and Jerry Moore had been quarterbacks in high school, as had Bobby Field, a new monster man.

In a year when collegiate offense took off in all directions and scores mounted, teams began taking more risks. The 1968 defensive unit lived on making those other teams pay the price; they grabbed fumbles and interceptions in record numbers, scoring or setting up 28 of the team's 49 touchdowns.

"If the good things happen to us," Broyles told the writers in September, "we can have a good team. I do know this is the most confident *young* team I've ever been around. They're far more optimistic than the coaches."

Chuck Dicus

The opener against Oklahoma State demonstrated that (1) the Hogs would come ready to throw; (2) they would use the passing threat to open up what they had rather do, which is *run;* and (3) in some manner or another, they would win.

Montgomery threw 25 passes in the first half, and the Porkers trailed, 15-3. They came back in the third period with a new plan and, as was the case generally that year, took over the game from the second-half kickoff. With OSU players backing off the line to defend, Burnett and Maxwell ran them out of the park. Still, it took Dossey's recovery of a fumbled punt in the fourth quarter to set up the 32-15 rout.

Montgomery threw bombs of 60 yards to Dicus and 61 yards to Peacock in the first quarter of a 56-13 laugher against Tulsa. TCU rushed Montgomery vigorously and led 7-3 into the fourth quarter. A pass inter-ference penalty started to turn the tide, and Montgomery's squirming runs on key downs set up Burnett's scores in a 17-7 win. Montgomery

Fullback Bruce Maxwell, on a typical jaunt, plows through SMU tacklers.

THE RAZORBACKS

completed 22 of 35 passes in a 35-19 victory over Baylor that wasn't as easy as it sounds. The typically persistent Bears narrowed it to 21-19 late.

So the Razorbacks found themselves 4-0 at Austin again. Texas was only 2-1-1, since the Horns had started with a tie against Houston and a loss to Texas Tech. At that point Darrell Royal moved quarterback Bill Bradley to defense and switched to James Street, who was never to lose as a UT starter.

Texas was having the same kind of offensive success as Arkansas, but with the triple option out of something called the wishbone. Before anyone else, Broyles said Royal's new toy was "the best offense ever devised for getting outside, for hitting from sideline to sideline with almost one play."

Parker and Kersey collaborated on recovering a fumble, and Bob White kicked a field goal, 3-0. Texas intercepted a pass, and Happy Feller kicked a field goal, 3-3. Montgomery began hitting Maxwell, Sigman, and Peacock, and Burnett ran the last eight yards. White missed his first extra point in 31 tries, 9-3.

Street began mixing sprint-out keepers with the wishbone carries of Ted Koy, Chris Gilbert, and Steve Worster. Gilbert scored from the five, and Happy Feller kicked it, 10-9. Montgomery threw 14 passes on an 80-yard drive, hitting Dicus for the last six yards. Montgomery was smothered trying for two, leaving it 15-10. Texas thundered back, and Worster bulled over from 16 yards out. Street ran over on a pass option for two points, 18-15. So far, the game was tit for tat except for conversions.

Then Freddie Steinmark intercepted Montgomery at midfield, and Street lofted a bomb that Cotton Spreyer ran under and took off Stewart's fingertips at the goal, a 51-yard touchdown play worth 25-15 at halftime.

No one had ever seen the likes of it at an Arkansas-Texas game. It more resembled a track meet or tennis match.

Its triple option unfathomed, as executed by four exceptional runners, Texas scored the next two times as well, 39-15. Arkansas switched to option running and claimed two more touchdowns on long drives, but to no avail, 39-29.

The Longhorns had run up 36 points in five straight possessions, forecasting the awesome clout of the wishbone against an unsuspecting team. Royal had found his quarterback and his offensive *modus vivendi*. A burnt orange dynasty was underway and would produce 30 straight wins, two national titles, and six straight Cotton Bowl bids before running its course.

The Porkers managed to beat North Texas State, 17-15, as Broyles withheld some bruised regulars against the Eagles' best team ever (Mean Joe Greene, most notably).

The Texas Aggies, defending champions and pre-season favorites who returned some of the league's best players, were not yet out of things when they faced Arkansas. Montgomery out-dueled Edd Hargett in a perfectly played offensive game. Neither side suffered a turnover.

Completing 20 of 29 passes for 258 yards, many of them on third down, Montgomery took the Hogs to touchdowns on their first three possessions after halftime, and the defense hung on to preserve a 25-22 win. It was Montgomery's finest game until he was a senior.

All members of the passing game broke school records in a 46-21 win over Rice. Hayden Fry had his best team at SMU, but the Ponies cracked in the critical early stages against Arkansas. Maxwell had an outstanding day as the Hogs rolled up a 35-0 lead on regional television. Then SMU's Chuck Hixon, a pure passer, got in a groove and threw for four late touchdowns. Arkansas had to cover an on-side kick with 56 seconds left to save a 35-29 decision.

That swift turn-around was cited as justification by many coaches in the next few years for running up scores. If Arkansas with a 35-0 lead was not a safe winner, who would be? The sensational comeback earned SMU a Bluebonnet Bowl bid.

Montgomery had not yet passed in a high wind; his introduction came at Lubbock. He threw cautiously, completing only three of 12, but Tech did not throw cautiously and saw seven passes stolen by the Porkers. Those, with a big scramble by Montgomery in the third quarter and Burnett's incessant gains on the pro sweep, created an eventual 42-7 romp.

So it was back to the throne room, a title tie with Texas at 6-1 each, and another trip to the Sugar Bowl. "That ain't bad," said David Dickey, who "preached" to the youngsters on the squad every Thursday, joining other seniors in promoting a level, winning attitude in the minds of the squad's newcomers.

For the third time at New Orleans, Arkansas drew an unbeaten Southeastern Conference champion, which usually meant a defensive powerhouse. The link between the Sugar Bowl and the SEC was still informal in those days, but SEC champs regarded New Orleans as their natural destination.

The Georgia Bulldogs (8-0-2) were proclaimed by Bear Bryant as "probably the best team in the country by the end of the season." Going to this Sugar Bowl, the Razorbacks faced odds at least as long as they had against Alabama and Mississippi. Everybody had moved the ball on their defense; only turnovers had saved them. And Arkansas's versatile offense would be going against what was, and may still be, the strongest defensive unit Arkansas ever faced.

A few things helped. Hootie Ingram knew Georgia's personnel, especially Mike Cavan, the sophomore quarterback who was a good scrambler. Arkansas's little buzz saws might get some bad plays out of him. On the other side of the coin, Jake Scott, the Bulldogs' daredevil All-American safety, might have too much to handle in Dicus. Georgia's ends helped some in pass defense, as did the linebackers, but in a normal situation the three deep backs divided the field three ways and came up awfully fast. Arkansas geared its offense so that Scott would have to cover the middle "half" of the field and cover Dicus. Scott's swift aggressiveness, Arkansas coaches hoped, would backfire a time or two.

On the first play of the second quarter Dicus broke behind Scott and with a large lunge caught Montgomery's soft strike as he reached the end zone. It was the game's only touchdown.

The teams started out exchanging fumbles. Arkansas settled down, but Cavan and his successor did not. The Porkers picked off three passes and recovered five fumbles. The most spectacular was that of Brad Johnson, the fullback, who was taking off from the Arkansas three-yard line when a helmet hit the ball. Popping as high as the goal-post crossbar, the ball skittered past scrambling players and out of the end zone for a touchback.

"Georgia's defense was even better than I expected," said Broyles. Bill Stanfill, the tackle who along with Scott later played brilliantly for Miami's 17-0 Super Bowl team, threw Montgomery to the ground in the second quarter, so injuring Bill's shoulder that off-season surgery was required. Burnett was tossed in the end zone for a safety; no one had ever thought to see that.

"Our defense surprised us, too," said Broyles. "Georgia had field position a lot of times but couldn't do anything."

After the safety, Cary Stockdell, the 6'5" punter from Virginia whose hits and misses kept fans nervous all season, blooped his free kick from the 20, not even to midfield. But Coffey's scrambling kids held.

Throughout, Dicus caught a Sugar Bowl record 12 passes for 169 yards, and Bob White kept kicking field goals, three of them. At the end, by 16-2, Vince Dooley's proud troops were beaten and bedraggled.

To Broyles, to this new breed of Razorbacks, and to newly-enthused fans, it was like 1959 all over again. For the third time, the Porkers won

10 games overall and were solidly back in the Top 10. The Southwest's three bowl teams enjoyed a clean sweep. In addition to the Arkansas achievement, Texas manhandled Tennessee 36-13 in the Cotton Bowl, and SMU beat Oklahoma 28-27 in the Bluebonnet.

The collective SWC triumph was to influence ABC-TV's scheduling ideas heavily for the next two years. Texas and Arkansas would cooperate. Momentous things lay ahead.

— 34 —

THE DAY
THE NATION WATCHED

Until the press of administrative duties came to bind him to his desk, forcing him to commute by air in late afternoon to appearances around the state, Frank Broyles operated out of Little Rock during "speaking season."

He would visit supporters and play golf, then ride a short distance to each town on the Razorback Club circuit. One day in mid-March of 1969 he found a call from New York waiting for him in the pro shop after he finished 18 holes at a country club in Little Rock.

ABC's college football expert, the brash and knowledgeable Beano Cook, had consulted his sources and checked the schedules. He decided if one game would decide the national championship in the 100th year of college football, it would be Arkansas versus Texas.

Therefore, said ABC's Roone Arledge on the phone, how would Frank like to move his game with Darrell to December 6, with the chance they might wind up in a collegiate Super Bowl?

It took Broyles and Royal about 30 seconds each to agree to the switch, although in the end, they coaxed concessions out of ABC that would bring Southwest Conference schools about $1,500,000 in television revenue. SMU was granted the national television opener, against Air Force, on September 13. Arkansas and Texas each bagged a national game in addition to their own match and a regional game.

Thus began the ballyhoo leading up to Big Shootout I or, as it was hailed briefly and mostly regionally, The Game of the Century.

John Barnhill cautioned Broyles, "By December, you could be playing for the championship of Washington County," but if the network wanted to take the risk, the schools could do no less.

The very arrogance of the proposal caused muttering around the SWC, softened only by the fact the other six members would share almost equally in the television loot. After a two-year hiatus in which SMU and Texas A&M won titles by a series of eyelash decisions—years in which Arkansas and Texas clearly defaulted—the monsters had returned in 1968, more awesome than ever, with sophomores and juniors at the throttles. The remainder of the league was clearly whipped down.

Royal and Broyles mouthed words that gave due respect to their regular opponents, but in all candor they were feeling their oats. They knew what they had.

Broyles had what promised to be his best defense ever or, for those unwilling to burn bridges, at least on a par with 1964. And the key skill people of the 1968 offense, which had scored 350 points, a new U of A record, returned as juniors. He needed only two or three offensive linemen, plus a split end. They would be found.

What Arkansas arranged first was a guarantee that its offense would have decent footing in Razorback Stadium on December 6. No game had ever been played that late in Fayetteville, where freezing and thawing begins as early as mid-November. Broyles had to have Astroturf, which Monsanto Chemical Company developed for the Astrodome in Houston in 1965 and was promoting as the universal playing surface of the future. Astroturf was obtained at an outlay of $291,000, representing the athletic department's cash reserves at the time. Broyles saw this as a long-term investment, a recruiting aid of incalculable value as well as a saving on land usage, grass maintenance, and equipment. (If Arkansas can do it, said other Southwest Conference schools, we can, too. For recruiting purposes, they had to. When TCU ordered its turf in the spring of 1973, the SWC became the first league in the country with artificial grass on every home field. By the 1990s, the cycle was running the other way across the country, and Arkansas returned to the real stuff.)

For the longest time in 1969 Arkansas had, as one man said, "a predicted world-beater playing Guam every week." Oklahoma State and Tulsa were trying to rebuild under new coaches. TCU had a fine sophomore quarterback in Steve Judy but went down early, 62-0, at Ohio State. Baylor was headed for 0-10 under Billy Beall. Then came an open date; then came Wichita State.

There was nobody to play to prove anything. Worse, Burnett had delicate surgery on his big toe in January, following a dislocation against Texas A&M, and he missed all the spring and early fall work—not that he was affected. But Montgomery's shoulder surgery, following his brush with Stanfill in New Orleans, did hamper the peerless leader. He missed spring practice and did not throw well until late in the season. Also, his ribs were injured painfully in the Tulsa game and again against TCU. He played in great pain against Baylor, an astonishingly close call. Luckily, he could be held out for three weeks because of the open date and the Wichita breather.

With Texas running roughshod over everyone at the time, it was clear the schedule switch had worked in the Hogs' favor.

OSU went down, 39-0. Terry Stewart returned the first punt to the Cowpokes' 40, and while the offense was not sharp, the defense kept blitzing the OSU passer and providing close-up opportunities. The defense also plundered Tulsa, 55-0.

As the TCU kickoff approached, Arkansas assistant Mervin Johnson voiced one of his incessant truisms: "This is a game that will please neither the coaches, players, nor the fans."

Steve Judy had his greatest day for TCU as a sprint-out runner-passer, but the Arkansas defense claimed three fumbles from Marty Whelan, stopping three long drives. And the hard-pressed Montgomery broke the game open when, on third and three, he faked to Burnett and lofted a pass that Chuck Dicus gathered in behind the secondary for a 73-yard touchdown play. Dicus also caught a 23-yard scoring pass in the 24-6 win, which impressed few people.

At Waco they played in a high wind on a gloomy night, and Baylor fought fiercely to stop the run and harassed Montgomery badly. It was 7-7 as the fourth quarter turned. From midfield Bill scrambled out of the pocket and heaved to Dicus, who caught the ball just short of the goal, falling on his shoulder. Chuck had to leave the game, but the Hogs took the ball in and also collected an insurance touchdown, 21-7.

Montgomery had won 14 of 15 games as an Arkansas starter, but had spoiled the fans. They would look at the boxcar figures being posted by Texas and ask, "What's wrong with the Razorbacks?"

John Eichler, who limped off the field but not on, and who had developed passing accuracy, riddled Wichita, 52-14, as the Porkers completed 26 of 47 passes. Meanwhile Montgomery got well.

Texas A&M had given up only five touchdowns in its last five games. Broyles turned his offense over, stressing Maxwell outside and reversing previous tendencies. The defense set up two easy touchdowns, and the offense rambled for three. Between A&M's touchdowns, Arkansas scored on five straight possessions in a 35-13 win. More like it, said the fans.

Still, beating Rice by 30-6 was not impressive. Rice switched Stahle

Vincent, its first black athlete, to quarterback, and he ran the Razorbacks ragged at the ends. It was only 10-6 at halftime, then Burnett got going and it was soon safely in hand. After the game, waiting reporters heard Broyles tongue-lash the players for 15 minutes before opening the dressing room door.

SMU again had Chuck Hixson throwing to five receivers in Hayden Fry's "ABC Offense," and this sophisticated attack troubled Coffey's defenders. They came on with big plays late, though, and Burnett's inspired running and pass-catching accounted for three touchdowns. A punt out of bounds on the SMU one by Stockdell, followed by Bobby Field's theft, clinched the 28-15 win.

The Texas Tech game had been rescheduled for Thanksgiving at Little Rock, fitting television's needs. On a cold, rainy, and windy day in War Memorial Stadium, the Razorbacks produced magnificent defense and superb work by Bill McClard and the kickoff unit, which kept Tech starting from well inside its 20. Montgomery's passing effectiveness was finally all the way back. Burnett scored twice, giving him a school-record 19 touchdowns for the season. The 33-0 victory was the 100th of Broyles's career, a span of only 13 seasons.

Front-running Ohio State lost two days later to Michigan. The Monday Associated Press poll showed Texas No. 1, Arkansas No. 2.

The *game* was now safely on.

There would be two weeks for the build-up, a fortnight for the nation's top football writers to realize there was just one game left, the only game that counted, and that they had to be there. No two college teams had ever taken 9-0 records into a season-ending television shootout. That was for the national guys; in Arkansas and Texas, it was just Frank and Darrell at it again. Incredibly, in the years in which both had been in the league, their teams going into this game had posted identical conference won-lost-tied records of 62-18-1.

Notre Dame ended its long, self-imposed bowl ban and agreed to go to the Cotton Bowl and play the Texas-Arkansas winner in what would amount to a second national championship game on New Year's Day. The loser would go to the Sugar Bowl against Ole Miss.

Here is how *Sports Illustrated*'s Dan Jenkins set the scene:

> All week long in Texas the people had said the Hogs ain't nuthin'
> but groceries and on Saturday, in the thundering zoo of Fayetteville,
> the No. 1 Horns would eat—to quote the most horrendous pun ever
> thought of by some Lone Star wit—"Hog meat with Worster-Speyrer
> sauce."

Texas fans, buoyed by the knowledge that their team had buried all six common opponents by much fatter scores than the Razorbacks had, and flaunting dozens of those wonderful statistics, had forgotten what this game always is, close and psychotic. They strolled around muttering absurdities like "42 to 7 and bring on Notre Dame." Terrific, just terrific.

"We're beginning to develop some difficult fans," said Royal. "They don't understand there's no such person as King Kong, and that when you start thinking that there is, you can get ready to wipe your bloody nose."

"They're gonna come after us with their eyes pulled up like BBs," said Darrell. "And they'll be defending every foot as if Frank Broyles has told 'em there's a 350-foot drop just behind 'em into a pile of rocks. If you BELIEVE that, you're pretty hard to move around."

Richard Nixon, of course, was coming and little old Fayetteville was agog at its first presidential visit in history . . . Every hour there was some new rumor about who was coming. For sure, Billy Graham was coming to say the invocation. He'd have brunch with Barbara Broyles. "What does a coach's wife say to Billy Graham?" she worried.

As early as the morning before the game, on Friday, as marvelous Indian summer weather lingered impossibly into early December, instant traffic jams developed around the campus and along the drags with students just driving around, honking and hollering. They waved beer cans and Confederate flags, their roadsters painted red and white, their hands uplifted in signs.

Royal himself was totally amazed at the excitement around his own campus. The University of Texas is a vast place with an enrollment of more than 35,000 and it is becoming sort of a Berkeley in a lot of ways. But more than half the student body turned out for a Wednesday pep rally in Memorial Stadium at which the squad members and coaches were loaded into convertibles and driven around the track while the crowd roared for its No. 1 team and the big band played "The Eyes of Texas" over and over.

Compounding the madness, of course, was the President's visit. This meant among other things that Arkansas would have to scare up some room in its picturesque stadium that would sway with only 40,000. Fifty White House press corps members would have to have seats, each supplied with a telephone. No luck there. The world's most crowded little press box could not contain the 100 or so writers and TV men. But the President and his aides and the Arkansas politicians got their 50-yard-line seats.

The distinguished guests from Washington missed the 12:20 P.M. kickoff. Fog delayed them; their helicopters landed in a miserably cold rain on the adjacent practice field, in full view of the crowd, and as they passed the scoreboard they could see it was already Arkansas, 7-0.

Royal's fears proved justified. Coffey had arrayed his men in the old Tennessee 6-2-3: Bruce James, Rick Kersey, Dick Bumpas, and Roger Harnish as the interior linemen; monster Bobby Field and outside linebacker Mike Boschetti serving the same function as defensive ends; All-American Cliff Powell and Lynn Garner as the linebackers; Jerry Moore, Terry Stewart, and Dennis Berner in a three-deep zone secondary.

Quick beyond belief, they got underneath the Texas muscle, as Coffey put it, and burst off the blocks to limit backs who had been averaging seven yards a play to 4, 1, 0, 6, 2, 1—and causing fumbles. Field recovered Ted Koy's bobble on the second play at the Texas 22. On third down, split end John Rees caught Montgomery's pass tumbling out of bounds at the two, and Burnett wormed over.

Arkansas's plan was to try to run with option plays and to get big things out of Montgomery's passing, mostly to Dicus, who caught nine for 146 yards. Dicus would line up frequently in a slot. He would have to get by Mike Campbell, the Steers' able, roving linebacker, and then go one-on-one against safety Freddie Steinmark, playing his last game before cancerous tissue was discovered in his thigh.

Texas was to throw Montgomery for 59 yards in losses, but Bill was to scramble for that much, often eluding 250-pound end Bill Atessis. On Arkansas's second possession he took the Hogs from their eight into the end zone—except that a 26-yard touchdown pass to Dicus was called back. Rees had not heard an audible because of the crowd noise; he had thrown a block at a defensive halfback.

When threatened by Oklahoma in mid-year, Texas had defeated a 9-2 defense by throwing deep to Cotton Speyrer, a wonderfully elusive speedster. When James Street tried for Speyrer deep against Arkansas, first Stewart and then Berner intercepted. Speyrer fumbled the second-half kickoff and lost a pass reception at the Arkansas 47 on UT's next try.

Montgomery scrambled for 18 yards and then hurled 29 yards to Dicus for a 14-0 lead.

Texas had won 18 games in a row with Street (compared to Arkansas's 15 in a row) and for good reason. Handsome, happy-go-lucky Street stayed lit up like a pinball machine on his own effervescent juices. His team was down, beaten, but he was not.

On the first play of the fourth quarter, he called a pass to tight end

Randy Peschel, could not see him, and lit out through the Arkansas rush. One defender slipped on the wet Astroturf, and some Arkansans still insist another got clipped. Looking trapped, Street cut left, then right, and out-ran everybody 42 yards for a touchdown. Then he whirled over the goal on a counter-play option for a two-point conversion.

Montgomery brought Arkansas right back, once completing the same 20-yard pass to Dicus down the middle a second time after a penalty wiped out the first one. Campbell was caught holding Dicus up, and Texas drew a 15-yard penalty. On third down from the eight, Montgomery sprinted left behind Maxwell and Burnett. Dicus had Danny Lester isolated, and Chuck's cut for the flag left him wide open. It would either be a touchdown, or the ball would sail out of bounds past the flag and McClard could try a field goal from close-up. Instead the throw came behind Dicus. Lester broke on the ball and intercepted, and Arkansas had committed its first error since the penalty that cost an early touchdown.

Texas fumbled at the Arkansas 42, then got one more chance.

On fourth and three at the Texas 43, Royal pulled a play out of his hat, a pass to tight end Peschel, who would be the only receiver out. Street's fake brought Moore up just enough; Peschel got behind him. Moore and Berner recovered, but the long spiral just eluded their hands. Peschel grasped it and tumbled to the turf, 44 yards to the 11. Koy cracked to the two, and Jim Bertelsen followed Steve Worster through on the inside belly play. Happy Feller kicked Texas to a 15-14 lead.

Still, Montgomery came back. With 3:58 left, he passed the Hogs to the Texas 39. One more completion and McClard might be in range. But Tom Campbell wrestled the ball away from Rees for an interception at the Texas 33.

The Texans could not stop cheering. Tears flowed unashamedly on the Arkansas side.

"Sometimes you just have to suck it up and pick a number," Royal said of the fourth down pass to Peschel. With the wishbone stifled, he knew Texas could not grind out a late comeback running the ball.

Nixon went to the Longhorns' dressing room and congratulated them as national champs. He went to the Razorbacks' dressing room and congratulated them for fighting the good fight. He told Chuck Dicus he reminded him of "that fellow Alworth."

By this time, the nation's most highly-placed football fan was catching heat from Pennsylvania for putting the presidential seal of approval on Big Shootout I. What about Penn State? Nixon said he would give Penn State an award for having the longest current winning streak. Royal grinned and shrugged to writers: "What else could he say?"

It was traditional that anywhere from three or four to a dozen sportswriters would have dinner at the Broyles home following a Fayetteville game. Crushing disappointment or not, Broyles kept the amenities in place that evening. "I think eventually what everybody will remember about this day is that Arkansas and Texas played a great game, and the President came," he said. A veteran Texas-based reporter said 25 years later, "I never had so much respect for Frank as I did that night. He had just lost the crowning game of his career after coming so close, and he was willing to sit there and make small talk. It must have been excruciating for him and Barbara."

All the accolades you could imagine fell on both teams, but nothing could change the fact that Texas was going to the Cotton Bowl to play

President Nixon visited Fayetteville for Big Shootout I.

THE RAZORBACKS

Notre Dame for the final No. 1 prize and Arkansas was going to the Sugar Bowl to play Ole Miss for nothing, compared to what had just been lost.

Texas beat Notre Dame, 21-17. At that point, the wishbone had a string of 20 straight wins.

Montgomery, Maxwell, Dicus, and teammates made 537 yards in New Orleans and lost by 27-22. The only sophomorish day of McClard's career cost the Hogs heavily—he missed field goals and extra points—but mainly Arkansas could not find a handle on Archie Manning, the best pass-run operator Ole Miss ever had, until it was 24-6 at halftime.

Dicus finally just collapsed from exhaustion. He had run deep routes the whole game. When safety Glen Cannon hit him for the last time after his sixth catch (for 171 yards) at the Ole Miss 29 with just over a minute to play, Chuck fumbled. Archie snuck out the clock.

Ole Miss finished 8-3 and toppled some giants—Tennessee, Georgia, LSU, and Arkansas—along the way.

Montgomery had thrown one less pass than Archie, 34 to 35, but outgained him 338 yards to 273. Everybody wondered what Bill might have done against Notre Dame's huge, slow team if Slick Street had not saved Texas up in the hills.

A moot question, of course.

A ROYAL ROUT

Facing mandatory retirement at the age of 67 on July 1, 1970, John Barnhill had already told Frank Broyles to take over the schedule making. Early in January members of the NCAA surprised even themselves by doing away with the 10-game regular-season limit, approving an 11th one.

All the way back to Barnhill's early years there had been criticism of the U of A schedule, one modeled on the philosophy of General Neyland at Tennessee. Neyland's idea was to bring a team along slowly and schedule breathers around big games, a policy still followed to a certain extent by many powers. Barnie justified this at Arkansas because the Razorbacks usually started over-matched against the Texas teams. When he achieved his goal of concentrating entirely on league teams, the Razorbacks came to dominate every SWC school with the conspicuous exception of Texas.

The so-called one-game seasons of 1968 and 1969, however, left fans feeling short-changed. The Porkers' ability to handle in an error-free manner the complex multiple offense Don Breaux had devised shot them far ahead of most opponents. It appeared Tulsa, Oklahoma State, and teams such as Wichita did not deserve to be on the schedule— although Tulsa and OSU were Arkansas's nearest and (except for Texas) oldest traditional rivals.

Given an opening by the NCAA, Broyles in one stroke traded an easy schedule for a more demanding one and provided his senior specialists a needed attention-getter for 1970. He scheduled Stanford for an opening game in Little Rock, and ABC snapped it up for the national television opener. It was necessary to raise $500,000 to provide Astroturf and color-television caliber lights for War Memorial Stadium. This was done by Little Rock businessmen and through the resourcefulness of Howard Pearce, who succeeded the late Allan Berry as stadium manager and secretary of the Razorback Club organization.

The game caught the fancy of the state; prestigious Stanford, Harvard of the West, against little ole Arkansas. It would match two of several Heisman Trophy candidates, Jim Plunkett of Stanford and Bill Montgomery. Since the Hogs retained prestige from their gallant showing against Texas, and since Stanford had the makings of its best team in ages, the winner would soar in the rankings.

Broyles had some patching to do. Richard Williamson returned to Alabama; Raymond Berry, the Baltimore Colts' all-time receiving hero, was the surprising, dramatic replacement, hired away from the Dallas Cowboys. Hootie Ingram took the head-coaching job at Clemson, and Billy Kinard came from Georgia to take over the secondary.

Offensively Bruce Maxwell had to be replaced, but Russ Garber and sophomore Scott Binnion looked like they could do it. Defensively there was no way to replace that cohesive, sure-striking unit of 1969.

Broyles's teams had been slow starters; even the 10-0 teams did not fall into place until the TCU games. Frank was determined to dispel that image. So was his squad. Montgomery toured the Far East military hospitals with Plunkett that summer; Bill came back with a Stanford T-shirt he wore in two-a-day practices.

Stanford shot into a 27-0 lead in the first 20 minutes. And yet, with less than a minute left in the game, it was 34-28, and Arkansas faced third and one on Stanford's four-yard line. Stanford had three great linebackers, each of whom became an immediate regular in the pros. For Arkansas, the impossible happened. Bill Burnett got stood up in the hole. At first it appeared left linebacker Jeff Siemon did the job single-handedly. No one man ever got that clean a hit on Burnett, though. The films showed it was a simultaneous tackle; Bill tried to make his miss-me move on Siemon, and a safety plastered him.

After a time-out Chuck Dicus was isolated to the left, one-on-one, and Montgomery faked and rolled left on an option run-or-pass. Bill was going to get it himself. He never looked for Dicus. He made one linebacker miss him, but the next one collared him. The measurement showed he was a foot short.

It had been a deeply traumatic game. Although the defense suffered, permitting Plunkett to complete 13 passes to his backs, Montgomery could not get the passing game going against Stanford's blitzing, unorthodox defense. Behind, 27-0, you have to throw. So Broyles called on Joe Ferguson, the sophomore he had recruited with so much fanfare from Woodlawn High in Shreveport, the finest high school passer anyone had ever seen.

Joe whipped his first pass complete to Jim Hodge, his high school teammate. Although Stanford came back and flattened Joe, the Porkers reached the Stanford five on their next possession, thanks mainly to Hodge's end-around sprint that caught Stanford defenders out of place, as they often were against the run due to their pell-mell pass rush.

Broyles sent Montgomery back in to handle the goal-line offense. Fans booed. They were, of course, objecting to Broyles's decision to withdraw the rookie who had perked things up, a manifestation of the old American cry for fair play. Montgomery felt the fans who had cheered him so for two years had turned on him.

Nonetheless, Bill's expertise at running some new veer options, mixed with short passes, was needed to bring Arkansas back, which he did magnificently. The defense began to pick the tiring Plunkett's pocket, but, critically, Stanford marched 69 yards late in the third quarter with ground power massed against the 'Hogs' weak side, collecting with Hillary Shockley what proved to be the deciding touchdown.

Stanford went on to a Rose Bowl victory. Plunkett got the Heisman Trophy. Arkansas came back strong with nine straight wins only to collapse completely in Big Shootout II. ABC had pressed for another Arkansas-Texas December match and landed it.

The day before the Stanford game, Broyles confided to a friend, "We are lining up on defense with youngsters of good character who are only average athletes." Later he described the early troubles of the season:

> We would have demoralized our seniors if I publicly spelled it out going into the Stanford game. All I said was, "We haven't replaced some of last year's seniors." Well, you never do, but we didn't have anyone comparable in ability. We were sitting on a powder keg. We were huddling on the sidelines (against Stanford) and when you see that, you know we're starting all over. We had an open date, and Charley Coffey, Harold Horton and Billy Kinard worked every night for two weeks until 1 A.M. They did the greatest patch-up job in a defense I'd ever seen. We became a good team by TCU. It was all uphill until Burnett got hurt against A&M. Then everybody started getting hurt.

The Hogs downed OSU by 23-7 and Tulsa by 49-7. They flowered awesomely, 42-14, against TCU, which struggled to contain Burnett and

Tailback Bill Burnett earned the SEC's Kern Tips Award despite an injury-plagued senior year.

Garber on the veer runs and got burnt by the deep passes of Montgomery and then Ferguson to Dicus and Jim Hodge. Broyles used his second unit extensively, the pattern in runaways to come, and the offensive gains of 658 yards set a new team high (excepting one old game against Pittsburg Teachers).

With such leads the defense came on and intercepted 32 passes. Jerry Moore, Guy Parker, Mike Boschetti, Ronnie Jones, and Bobby Field led the ball-hawking perimeter. The line's upper-class stability came from Bruce James, Rick Kersey, and Dick Bumpas.

Montgomery's versatility enabled play-caller Breaux to pick apart teams with every type of short pass and sophisticated running. The senior specialists could handle everything. They bopped Baylor, 41-7; Wichita (coming back after much of its squad had been killed in a plane crash) by 62-0 with the regulars retiring after a few plays; and A&M by 45-6 (the score was 38-0 early in the second quarter, thanks to a series of errors).

"Despite what anyone might think," Montgomery said after his career ended, "I know I was a far better quarterback as a senior. The defenses were catching up with our passing game, and we had to do more things."

Burnett suffered a shoulder separation against A&M; only the fact that the Texas game would again be played in December gave him a chance to recoup from the surgery.

Already Montgomery and Dicus had broken school records at their specialties. And they were playing only half the games. Leading the nation in scoring through the first 10 games, the Razorbacks were to finish with a school-record 402 points.

Sophomore Jon Richardson, Arkansas's first black football recruit, had played right along, winningly, but when he was thrust into the big role he fumbled twice as Rice took a 14-3 halftime lead. The Hogs came back with Garber and Mike Saint running straight at the pass-minded Owls. Arkansas scored on five straight tries and won, 34-18. Montgomery's nimble running really killed the Owls.

Eight interceptions, three by David Hogue, wrecked SMU, 36-3. Texas Tech was stubborn on the goal line, but Montgomery's passes to tight end Pat Morrison broke things open, 24-10.

Now Texas had won 29 straight, avalanching its league foes off the field. Arkansas looked about as good on paper. No one outside the UT family could guess, however, how much thought, time, dedication, energy, and emotion Royal and his staff and squad put into correcting things that went wrong in the 1969 squeaker at Fayetteville.

Halfback Jon Richardson became the Razorbacks' first black football recruit.

Broyles heard a warning in mid-season. Barry Switzer, his former team captain and assistant coach, had gone to Oklahoma with Jim Mackenzie and remained there with Chuck Fairbanks. The Sooners tried the Arkansas 6-2 scheme against the Texas wishbone in 1970 and were handed their heads, 41-9. "Coach, if you line up in that defense again, they'll eat you alive, just like they did us," Switzer told Broyles. "It came as a surprise to 'em last year. They've worked on it all spring and fall."

Coffey wanted to use the same defense. He and Broyles had some severe disagreements about it. Coffey became head coach at Virginia Tech soon after the season ended.

After Texas took care of A&M by 52-14, Royal announced a long list of injuries, an old ploy. Arkansas had the real injuries, the heart of its offense (Burnett, Garber, and the two offensive guards) plus a defender or two. A visitor from Arkansas learned the worst on Friday in Austin. Royal's "cripples" bounced about with ease in a 15-minute workout that was little more than a squad pep rally with cheerful calisthenics.

That night it became plain that Arkansas was up against the full force of the mighty Texas establishment.

Some 39,000 rooters packed themselves elbow to elbow in one side of Memorial Stadium in a cleverly programmed pep rally which resembled a Roman pageant. ABC's Chris Schenkel was there to broadcast the game. He said during the rally, with Royal and his squad seated on the same stage: "If I've told [Ohio State coach] Woody Hayes once, I've told him a thousand times, Texas is No. 1 [thunderous roars]. Tomorrow, in this arena, I am fully confident that the Texas Longhorns will maintain their rightful place as champions of college football."

James (Slick) Street and his star-kissed intangibles were gone, but in Street's place at quarterback the 1970 Horns installed Eddie Phillips, a wishbone technician smoother and swifter than Street.

Texas was ready. The Steers blockers had failed to make or sustain contact at Fayetteville. They got body on body at Austin. Royal described it later: "If you can put the fingers of both hands together, you can force one hand back. If they miss, you've got nothing but confusion."

Arkansas's weak side was especially vulnerable; it had to withstand Jim Bertelsen coming around on the inside belly power play behind Steve Worster, stumpy Terry Collins, and tight end Deryl Comer, 6'3" and 230 pounds. It was a blitzkrieg. Yet, behind 14-0, Arkansas rallied. Richardson had some zip as a runner and receiver, and Montgomery scrambled. Two long passes and two pass interference penalties cut it to 14-7, and Arkansas had a first down on the three.

Before the game, tough-minded defensive coach Mike Campbell, who had been with Royal since their Mississippi State days in the 1950s, told why Arkansas differed from those SWC passing teams that Texas seldom feared and usually wiped out. "You knew those other teams would die inside the 20, no matter how fast and easy they'd go up and down the field," Campbell said. "Arkansas is different. When they get to the goal line, they know what to do and can get it."

This time, no. Richardson put it on the one in two tries. Burnett, though he had not practiced, was sent in. The Texas linebackers caught him in mid-air, as they had done Richardson once. On fourth down Montgomery went left on the option. He was supposed to look for Richardson who was open going wide, but he wanted to get it himself. And when he turned inside, he was stopped inches short, although he thought he had slid off and gotten over.

That did it. Only Ronnie Jones kept Bertelsen from going 99 yards on the next play; Jones made a saving ankle tackle at the 13. The Steers drove 99 yards anyway for 21-7 and stole the show after halftime, 42-7, treating Arkansas no different from any other SWC patsy, making sure the pollsters took notice.

Big Shootout II, a joker said, came off as the Cap Pistol Follies.

"We were in a precarious position psychologically," Broyles said. "We had been soothed and petted for a year on how well we played against Texas at Fayetteville, and Texas had been hearing for a year how lucky they were, and they were sick and tired of it."

The Cotton Bowl put Texas in with Notre Dame again, but this proved one rematch too many. The Irish ended UT's 30-game winning streak, 24-11.

Broyles and his seniors had already decided it would be Cotton Bowl or nothing. It was nothing. They did not want another meaningless Sugar Bowl game, nor did the New Orleans sponsors.

The Montgomery-Dicus-Burnett era was over. For all the unprecedented excitement and high stakes, this team, 28-5 in three years, was fated to be remembered more for the five losses than any of the victories.

"You want to win everything, but we didn't have anything to apologize for," said Dicus in 1994, as president of the Razorback Foundation, a fund-raising support arm of the U of A athletic program. "We lost three times to Texas—the best teams Texas ever had and the best in the country at the time, since they were winning 30 in a row. We lost to Ole Miss and Archie Manning. We lost to Stanford and Jim Plunkett. Did you know we never lost to a team that finished lower than eighth in the country?"

Three of the losses were consecutive heartbreakers on national television from December 1969 to September 1970: Texas, 15-14; Ole Miss, 27-22; Stanford, 34-28.

Years after the fact, Bill Montgomery still craved to have one pass back, the one intended for Dicus that could have made it 21-8 over Texas late in the national title game of 1969. The one that missed its mark and wound up in the hands of UT's Danny Lester.

"That play never ends in my dreams," he said. "If I could change one thing, that would be it."

Bill could do everything, but he was brilliant only in the sum of his skills, not in any one thing. The pros didn't even draft him; they looked for a bigger body and a stronger arm.

"All the pressure winds up on the head coach and the quarterback," Broyles often said. "You can protect the quarterback just so much. Ultimately it's all on his shoulders."

Speaking of pressure, the time had come for Joe Ferguson to try his hand.

— 36 —

LIBERTY, NOT COTTON

Since he was in the 10th grade, Joe Ferguson had hardly let a day go by without practicing throwing the football the way Shreveport Woodlawn coach A. L. Williams told him to—the way Terry Bradshaw had at Woodlawn before Ferguson. Ferguson's goal was to be as good as Bradshaw. He could already zip it almost as well, though he lacked Terry's robust body. Joe stood 6'1" and just could not gain weight. However, he had the natural athlete's quickness and winning instincts.

Before he got out of high school he was a near-legendary athletic figure in Louisiana and a blue-chip recruit of national stature. Everybody wanted Joe; he opted for Arkansas almost from the start and for one reason—the Razorbacks had the closest winning program stressing prototype passing techniques.

The day Ferguson signed, Frank Broyles seemed to imply that his presence guaranteed Arkansas a national title. What Broyles actually said, and never retracted, was that a team with a quarterback of Ferguson's ability *should have a chance* to win a national championship before he graduated.

Joe differed from Bill Montgomery in that he was almost a loner and that he was almost painfully intense, a perfectionist. Montgomery commanded with an outgoing personality; Ferguson led with his sometimes matchless deeds.

As with Montgomery, Broyles recruited Ferguson and then found it easy to round up the super specialists to go with him; Jim Hodge, Mike Reppond, Jon Richardson, Jack Ettinger. Frank thought the emphasis on drop-back passing would also attract the needed pro-sized linemen, but he was to be disappointed. What good linemen who came in the 1970 group soon disappeared—injuries, academic failures, and the malaise of the counter-culture growing out of the draft and the Vietnam War were factors.

Only insiders knew what a burden would fall on Joe Ferguson's group.

As he did after every disaster, and the 42-7 loss to Texas had been all of that, Broyles analyzed the situation and took a fresh approach. Charley Coffey left for Virginia Tech. Tennessee had been strangling foes with a new twist on defense, a 4-3-4 with a standup nose guard. Broyles hired Buddy Bennett, who coached the Tennessee secondary, and moved Mervin Johnson to the defensive front. "If they've got a tough job they want done up here, they give it to Coach Johnson," place-kicker Bill McClard once observed.

Joe Gibbs, a future NFL sage with the Washington Redskins, was hired from Southern Cal to coach the offensive line—to keep folks off Ferguson.

Johnson had worked with All-American offensive linemen Glen Ray Hines (1965), Jim Barnes (1968), and center Rodney Brand (1969). There were no defensive linemen of that caliber in sight in the spring of 1971. The defense got whipped every day by Breaux's most promising scheme yet, a mixture of the wishbone with its triple option and the pro-I with passing. Dickey Morton had arrived as something special in the backfield.

So many fullbacks were running wild in the spring, Broyles gave Scott Binnion, one of the squad's best leaders, to the defense, where he would at least bring some game experience to linebacking. It was Broyles's youngest squad since 1958, but it had enthusiasm and dedication.

Broyles realized one thing. After four losses in a row, he *had* to beat Texas. The defense practiced against the wishbone every day as it was run by the offense on the goal line. And the offense spent the remainder of the time without a tight end; Reppond would line up in a slot inside Hodge and Ettinger, both wide, as a deep threat against the Texas 4-4-3, a defense to be used by as many as six Arkansas opponents.

When fall began, the freshman team sacrificed its own record by using only Texas plays; the Hog squad did not have enough depth for a presentable B-team which normally functioned as a scout unit.

Gibbs's linemen tended to be big but slow. They protected Ferguson so well, Breaux dubbed them the Clean Machine. Few teams dared rush Joe with anything but their front four. If they did, they could get killed by Richardson or Morton on the sprint-draws or the screens, and any secondary needed all the help it could get against Joe's arm.

California proved the perfect opening foil. Ray Willsey, soon forced to resign with other Cal-Berkeley administrators, had a big, gifted, but unhappy squad. Cal had violated some NCAA rules and refused to declare Issac Curtis, a halfback and track star, ineligible. Cal competed well in front of a War Memorial Stadium sellout of 54,176 until its quarterback left the game, hurt. A pass interception at the eight by Jim Benton gave the Hogs' defense new confidence. Down 13-7 with 2:27 to go in the half, Ferguson hit Ettinger twice and Mike Hollingsworth for five yards and a touchdown. Cal fumbled on the kickoff, and with four seconds left in the half McClard kicked a 52-yard field goal. Arkansas had gone from 7-13 to 17-13 in a twinkling and would win overwhelmingly, 51-20.

It was the same story against a hard-hitting, motivated OSU team before another absolute capacity Little Rock crowd. The score was 10-10 inside the last three minutes of the first half. Ferguson worked the ball 80 yards in a hurry with two big passes to Reppond setting up Richardson's four-yard scoring run. Arkansas won, 31-10.

The Cal and OSU coaches said they had never seen teams so deflated by one man's passing brilliance as theirs had been. Many Arkansas fans genuinely thought they were seeing the best Razorback team of all time.

The other side of the coin turned up the next week at Fayetteville. Arkansas cruised to a 20-0 lead against Tulsa. Suddenly fullbacks Skipper DeBorde and Russ Garber were out of the game. Richardson limped off, too, and Ferguson was out there without running strength, passing into a 3-8 defense. The green U of A defense lost its poise, and Tulsa rallied to win, 21-20.

And that is when two years of rumors began sprouting. (Coaches and players don't get along; players and players don't get along, etc.) How could a team look out of this world for two weeks and then lose to Tulsa? Actually that is par for a passing team when its running support goes; the result is monumental highs and lows.

The high returned quickly with a 49-14 breeze over a disorganized, slow TCU team against which Ferguson executed the offense to textbook perfection, running as well as he passed. Baylor went down, 35-7, when Ferguson found Reppond for two long strikes early in the game. It was encouraging that Garber could come back and play a little at fullback despite "Astro-toe," a new term for a painful and lingering foot injury. Garber had size and quickness and knew what to do, but he re-injured his foot—an ominous final blow to the running game.

Broyles had refused to consider switching the Texas game to December for television this time, so they headed for a normal national television test at Little Rock in the regular October slot. Not really normal. Arkansas had lost to Tulsa, of all things, and Texas had been hoisted by its own petard, a 49-27 victim of the wishbone as run in hyperactive fashion by Oklahoma's great athletes. The Longhorns also had been hit by injuries, including one to Eddie Phillips, their superb playmaker. His sub, Donnie Wiggington, was not too fit, either, and several other players were bruised. Arkansas did not buy all of that, but the Texas injury list was, this time, pretty much genuine—not that you could tell it for a while. Reppond thought Dean Campbell was going to fair-catch a punt; instead the 5-5 return specialist darted away for 56 yards, and Jim Bertelsen barged over, 7-0. The Arkansas defense, helped by penalties and fumbles, began to stymie the Texas wishbone, held to 140 yards on the ground for the day, a new low for Texas.

Ferguson went into action.

Joe mixed in Morton on the sprint-draws with his rollout passes to Reppond, who ignited a drive with a great catch. Finally Joe passed out of the wishbone to tight end Bobby Nichols for five yards and a touchdown on fourth down. Texas kicked the Hogs back to their six; Ferguson came out throwing and eventually scored on a 10-yard wishbone keeper. The pre-halftime humiliation was a 37-yard lob to Reppond, who was all alone when he caught it on the 16 after a mix-up between UT defensive backs. At intermission it was 20-7 and Texas had not threatened offensively.

Rain began to fall in sheets. McClard kicked a field goal, and Ferguson threw another little touchdown pass to Nichols, and Broyles let the clock and the rain and the Longhorn fumbles take care of a 31-7 win.

Just a few months after the blow-out loss in Austin, Arkansas's 451 yards in offense—202 on the ground and 249 by air—set a school record for gains against Texas. Ferguson won national player-of-the-week honors, and Broyles labeled it the best big-game performance by any quarterback he had ever coached. Royal bid the Razorbacks good luck in the Cotton Bowl. All this was enough to spur Arkansas fans into ordering Cotton Bowl seats.

Two weeks later on the same field the fans saw why *not* to order tickets. For the first and last time with Ferguson, the Hogs had played a perfect game against Texas. No fumbles, no interceptions. This team would set a school record for turnovers, 25 fumbles lost and 16 interceptions, all of which blighted record gains of 4,898 yards. The fumble-free players of the past had come off the B-team after a redshirt year; now inexperienced backs were jumping into high-pressure situations running a high-risk offense.

The lack of a solid fullback had not been noticed against Texas, so rattled were the Steers. It was a different story against Texas A&M, which kept kicking Arkansas back, giving Ferguson the short ones (31 of 51 for 345 yards but no touchdowns) and then held on third and one and fourth and one at crucial times. Gene Stallings's Aggies did not make a single drive of consequence, but they cashed in two fumbles and an interception for all their points in a classic 17-9 upset.

Arkansas fumbled on its first two plays at Rice, falling behind, 10-0. Ferguson played one of his greatest games, ripping deep curl routes to Reppond and scrambling. But the patched-up secondary gave up two long scoring passes. Ferguson was knocked loose from the ball a step before he would have scored the winning touchdown. That should have settled it, but a Rice goof let McClard close enough to kick a tying field goal as time ran out. It was a very interesting 24-24 tie, but the result knocked Arkansas out of the Cotton Bowl. More precisely, the Rice tie combined with the A&M loss knocked out Arkansas. Texas got its players well, fixed its defense, and won its fourth straight title, 6-1 to Arkansas's 5-1-1.

Out since Tulsa because of a leg injury, Richardson returned for SMU, and Mike Saint became the fullback. But it was Morton who streaked off the bench to break open an 18-13 win. Ferguson was injured slightly in that game and had to leave in the first quarter against Texas Tech. Walter Nelson stepped in and ran the options, and the defense stole four passes. Arkansas beat the listless Red Raiders, 15-0.

Circumstances combined to provide the Liberty Bowl at Memphis with its best match ever, Tennessee (9-2) vs. Arkansas (8-2-1). Tennessee, winning with a raging defense, had pillaged Penn State unmercifully in a national television game in early December. Some thought the Vols were in a spot to be beaten; the Hogs figured to be more hungry. Too, Tennessee's offense had struggled because its fifth-year quarterback, pulled off the B-team in mid-year, could throw but not run.

Jim Maxwell's long pass set up tailback Bill Rudder's two-yard run for a 7-0 Vol lead midway through the first quarter. Arkansas soon started taking over, though, and on a long-yardage down just before halftime Jim Hodge found All-American safety Bobby Majors out of position. Ferguson stepped out of the pocket to find Hodge on a 47-yard scoring strike.

Arkansas threatened to break the halftime tie right away, with Ferguson's screens to Richardson and Morton's outside runs, but Joe misfired a pitchout on the Vols' seven. Three straight Louis Campbell thefts stopped the Vols at midfield, and McClard kicked two field goals. Then he kicked a third one for 48 yards. The scoreboard read 16-7,

Arkansas. But an official called tight end Bobby Nichols for holding on the kick; the scoreboard went back to 13-7.

Still, Tennessee could not move, and Arkansas was using up the clock when Richardson fumbled after catching a screen pass. Razorback Tom Reed came out of the pile with the ball, but the official who had also called the holding penalty, Preston Watts of Memphis, insisted to referee Burns McKinney that it was UT's ball.

Tennessee scored in three plays. Coach Bill Battle sent in Curt Watson, his fine fullback who had been held out with an injury to that point, and Watson followed crisp blocking into the end zone from 17 yards out with 1:36 left. Tennessee won, 14-13. Arkansas players almost literally chased the officials out of the park, an unseemly display, but no one would ever convince them that Watts did not err grievously on his two late decisions.

Ferguson broke a Liberty Bowl passing record. When he received the most valuable player trophy at midfield before the television cameras, he wiped away tears and told viewers that Arkansas would go on to better things in 1972, a feeling with which most everyone concurred.

The day in 1970 the NCAA voted in the 11th game, Broyles had rushed to book a home-and-home series with Southern Cal. John McKay placed Frank second in line, right behind McKay's close friend and business associate, Alabama's Bear Bryant. So Arkansas settled on Stanford for 1970 and California for 1971.

Within weeks, though, Broyles had worked out a three-game series with the Trojans, 1972–74, the first and third games at Little Rock, the second at Los Angeles. (How times had changed. John Barnhill in the beginning could not find good teams willing to play in Little Rock; now Broyles could persuade one of the most glamorous to appear twice in War Memorial Stadium.)

Broyles knew USC would field the finest troops in the land; he also knew they sometimes played lackadaisically. What only a few knew was that McKay, saved from serious alumni pressure only by victories over Notre Dame in two otherwise ordinary seasons, had done everything possible to sharpen the focus for 1972.

The changes included the Trojans' first out-of-season conditioning program; grouping of fourth and fifth-year players on offense; assignment of the quickest, fastest young athletes (including sophomore linebacker Richard Wood) to defense; and unprecedented (for USC) year-round dedication. The Trojans even joined the Fellowship of Christian Athletes, whose national president was then Frank Broyles.

Joe Ferguson spent 18 years as a premier passer in the NFL.

The combatants knew that the winner of the Arkansas-USC game would probably jump to No. 1 in the polls. And in fact this happened. Southern Cal never looked back, murdering a row of difficult foes to go 12-0 and gain a stamp as one of the great college teams of all time, maybe *the* greatest.

And Arkansas dropped to 6-5.

"You ruined a good coaching job," Barnhill told Broyles when he learned of the head coach's first ventures into schedule-making. "You got rabbit-eared, that's what happened. People run your schedule down, so you want to take on the world."

"We'll never know how much losing to Southern Cal took away from us," Broyles said in retrospect.

The scoreboard read 3-3 in the third quarter, and Arkansas had driven inside the USC 20-yard line on straight-ahead runs by Dickey Morton and Mike Saint against a pass-conscious defense. A penalty and the USC linebacker blitz stopped the drive. Minutes later Ferguson went the wrong way on an option play, turned up field for three yards, and had his helmet bar smashed against the bridge of his nose. He came up bloodied and was led from the field. As he passed the USC defensive huddle, the Trojans cheered to each other, "He's out, he's out!" Joe paused and told them, "I'll be back."

Before he got back Mike Rae had completed a bomb to fleet Edsel Garrison to the Arkansas 16, and Rae had carried over the tie-breaking touchdown. An interception set up another USC score. Reppond dropped Ferguson's perfect home run pass in the end zone, and a 31-10 runaway was on.

Even casual fans could judge Arkansas's shortcomings against so much USC physical excellence on the field. Arkansas had the skill people but lacked muscle, a void that was to show up all season, putting intolerable pressure on Ferguson. From the beginning Broyles had foreseen and tried to forestall this.

Don Breaux had left the staff to take an assistant's post with the Houston Oilers under his old Florida State boss, Bill Peterson. Richard Williamson returned from Alabama to take his place. Ferguson and the receivers missed Breaux, but no matter who coached the offense, conditions had changed from the cherry-picking days of 1968 when Montgomery and Dicus often faced three-deep defenses playing man-to-man.

To all passing teams in 1972, the story went like this: "If they are expecting the pass, there will be no place to throw. You'd better be able to run, to set up an occasional clutch pass."

Williamson understood it, of course. He had seen Alabama go down in flames with a passing quarterback and come back with a running quarterback. His goals in the spring were to develop a fullback and to polish Ferguson as an option runner.

Of maybe 10 fullbacks tried, all either got hurt or failed to step forward. For several days in the spring, Joe ran without that hated yellow caution shirt on his back and loved it, but he failed to excite anyone as an option threat. A tall, fast sophomore named Mark Miller seemed to be emerging as an option runner. He would definitely play and maybe even on the goal line. But on the last day of spring practice Miller suffered a serious knee injury.

In desperation Williamson tried sophomore quarterback Scott Bull at fullback as the Porkers pulled out 24-23 and 21-20 wins over OSU and Tulsa. Against TCU they junked the option runs altogether and committed to the pass with Morton and Richardson at split backs.

A fired-up TCU team led 13-0 until late in the third quarter; Arkansas had moved the ball well but stopped itself with typical mistakes. Then Ferguson scrambled for 21 yards, was hit late at the end for 15 more, and on the next play found Ettinger open deep for a bomb. TCU decided it had to blitz Ferguson, and he began to read the blitzes, with uncanny results. When the Frogs put on the big rush, Reppond, Hodge, and Ettinger would have a chance to get deep with only two defenders. By rolling out, Ferguson could avoid the rush and pick out the open man.

On four straight possessions he passed for 283 yards in 17 plays over a clock span of 8:45, completing drives of 70, 74, 83 and 56 yards for the 27-13 win. Wow!

Unfortunately no other team tried to defend Arkansas with a combined blitz and man-to-man coverage.

The Hogs beat Baylor, 30-21, with Baylor contributing seven turnovers. They played Texas in a televised night game at Austin in the rain, asserted some ball control with their own wishbone, and reached the half with a 9-7 lead. A high snap on a punt undid them, and Texas had it by 35-15 at the end. Roosevelt Leaks and Alan Lowery each rushed for more than 150 yards once the Steers quit fumbling.

Texas A&M, starting a rebuilding job under Emory Bellard and heading for 3-8, showed a pro-type defense that cried for a running quarterback. And the option offense was working with sophomore Marsh White making his second debut at fullback—he had bowed out in despair early against USC—until a Ferguson pitchout to Morton went wild. Joe never pitched as well as he passed. So Arkansas went back to the air. A&M read everything, had people clogging the zones, and—the final indignity—stole six of Ferguson's passes to win, 10-7.

So it was back to the wishbone against Rice. The Owls capitalized on a fourth down pass at the very end to win, 23-20. As in 1963 the Hogs hit a new low against SMU, which had to travel less than 100 yards for all its points in a 22-7 win. The NCAA made freshmen eligible for varsity play in 1972, and by the SMU game, three Arkansas freshmen were defensive regulars.

Ferguson, who would play 18 years in the NFL and complete several miles' worth of pro passes, spent his last college game sitting forlornly on the bench at Lubbock, along with main receiver Mike Reppond.

Broyles sent out Scott Bull at quarterback, with Morton, White, and Reggie Craig in the slot-I arrangement he had pioneered in 1964.

The 6'5", 200-pound Bull ran the unsuspecting Red Raiders ragged. Arkansas hogged the ball. Morton, completing a fantastic season in which he broke all Arkansas ground-gaining records with 1,188 yards, carried 33 times for 135 yards. White added 72, and Bull netted 65.

Bull threw only five passes, one of which led to a pass interference penalty that set up the tie-breaking score. Sophomore linebacker Billy Burns caused a fumble that led to a 21-7 lead. Mike Kirkland capped a long ball control drive at the end with a strong field goal into the wind.

The 24-14 victory over an 8-2 Tech team gave Broyles his first closing victory since the 1968 season and ended his longest league losing streak—four games—since 1958.

Clearly Frank had switched back to the basics that established his program in the first place.

He always regretted, though, that he had not been able to put a better team around a once-in-a-lifetime passer. No telling what might have happened.

— 37 —

FRANK
AT THE CROSSROADS

As early as 1970, Frank Broyles pondered his retirement from coaching.

He might have quit, he said, if Arkansas had won Big Shootout II with Texas at Austin. Nobody knew that at the time except his wife, and Barbara kept telling him, "You're not ready." Then it became purely academic.

"All of a sudden, our program went down," Broyles said. "We were so far behind in facilities by 1972 that our recruiting suffered tremendously. We knew I couldn't retire until the program was restored. For one thing, we couldn't hire the kind of replacement we'd want, with everything at such a low ebb. Who'd want to step into that situation? This was the practical consideration, but there was another. My pride demanded that we get things rolling again before I quit."

Broyles was preparing his 1970 team for Big Shootout II when he received his first scary signal. Word came from Stillwater, Oklahoma, that his freshman team lost by 56-0 to the OSU freshmen. Only two members of that Arkansas freshmen squad, Dickey Morton and Danny Rhodes, would contribute as seniors in 1973.

On homecoming weekend in November of 1972, which produced a snowy 22-7 upset loss to SMU, Broyles met with the athletic committee of the U of A Board of Trustees. He was blunt.

Things would get worse before they got better, he told them. After assessing the personnel on campus, he said it would be 1975 before he would be coaching a squad with four strong classes, providing that recruiting gains could be made. To improve recruiting, he would have to have new facilities. None had been built since 1955. He proposed to raise the necessary money with a new form of subsidy that might prove unpopular since it was tied to ticket priorities.

"I don't want to sound like a prophet of doom," he told the trustees and U of A president David Mullins. "But unless we can make improvements, we can never again be competitive in the Southwest Conference. And there are no guarantees. The entire foundation of college football is undergoing change after change. We might not make it back."

Proceed, he was told.

Broyles would become athletic director in July of 1973 with the retirement of George Cole. His contract, drawn by his friend Pete Raney and approved by the board a couple of years earlier, specified that when a vacancy in the athletic director's position occurred he would have the option of serving as head football coach and athletic director, or as athletic director alone, more or less into infinity. It was, as all coaches and athletic directors who knew of it readily agreed, the best contract in the profession.

So Frank's job was never in jeopardy, and his abilities were never questioned by anyone in position to influence U of A athletic policy. He developed some loud critics, responsible and otherwise, regarding the ticket priority plan and the fact the Razorbacks were no longer winning at their accustomed rate. He expected it. "Any time you don't win big, you have to expect some heat," he said. "The worst thing is if fans don't care."

In 1973 Broyles had the youngest and least experienced Arkansas squad since 1945. The Porkers had to settle for 5-5-1 and hopes of a brighter future. It was a team with only two important seniors, Morton and linebacker Danny Rhodes. At least 16 freshmen played at times, and 10 lettered.

The Razorbacks played Southern Cal's Trojans off their feet through most of a 17-0 loss at Los Angeles, then got clobbered at Little Rock by Oklahoma State, 38-6, sweet retribution for the long-suffering Cowboys. Then they won five of their next six games, the exception being Texas (34-6). At times they were starting seven or eight freshmen and about as many sophomores, but they appeared to mature in a 14-10 win over Texas A&M. At 5-3, Arkansas had three bowls paying attention.

The turning point came on the opening series against Rice. Arkansas reached a first and goal at the Rice four-yard line on a 25-yard screen pass from Mike Kirkland to fullback Marvin Daily. But Daily came down on his shoulder and had to leave the game. The next play was a pass, and a Rice defender intercepted in the end zone and returned 60-odd yards. That led to a touchdown. Hardly moving the ball on its own the rest of the day, Rice won 17-7 with field position, pass interceptions, and the kicking game.

Dickey Morton (33) never missed a game and hardly a series in three seasons as a great runner for ordinary squads.

The next week SMU scored with moments left to salvage a 7-7 tie. And the final week Texas Tech (11-1 after a bowl game) broke a tie in the fourth quarter and beat the Razorbacks 24-17.

After the 0-2 start Broyles junked a primitive version of the wishbone and went to the slot-I. He had to get the ball to Morton, and he found in Alan Watson a long-needed blocker. Though running behind a young line in an offense directed by sophomore quarterback Mike Kirkland, who took over after Scott Bull suffered a knee injury in August, Morton excelled all year as a one-man gang. He gained 1,298 yards for the season and set Southwest Conference career marks (soon broken) for carries (595) and total gains (3,317 yards). He set the Arkansas one-game rushing record at 271 yards against Baylor, breaking the Muscles Campbell standard of 236.

Though banged about constantly, the thick-necked 180-pounder danced every dance. He played in all 34 games in his three years. Some backs lose speed when they cut; Morton actually accelerated.

Broyles beefed up his staff in 1973 with the addition of Bill Lewis, Frank Falks, and Jimmy Johnson. The nose guard on the Hogs' all-winning 1964 team, Johnson moved from Oklahoma, where Barry Switzer had just been appointed head coach. Jimmy was esteemed as a bright, salty comer, although his future success with the University of Miami and the Dallas Cowboys was still unimagined—even by him, probably.

The revamped staff followed up by recruiting for 1974 the most blue-chippers Broyles ever signed in one year. Among them were a junior college running back, Ike Forte, and an all-everything freshman from Brinkley, Jerry Eckwood.

Going with the wishbone, the Hogs excited their fans at the start by dominating a Southern Cal team that would not lose again and would salvage three versions of the national title. The momentum from that 22-7 upset win in War Memorial Stadium evaporated the next weekend at the same site. Oklahoma State, talented and still vengeful, made Arkansas look bad in a 26-7 thumping. The pattern of a 6-4-1 season was set. The Razorbacks would be good in spots but were not settled enough for consistency.

They could have beaten Baylor, but a fumble turned that one around late, 21-17, and opened the way for the Bears' "miracle" drive to the Cotton Bowl after a 50-year championship drought.

By the end of the season Broyles was convinced the veer was the best option offense for his purposes, so he hired Robert (Bo) Rein off a flourishing veer team at North Carolina State. It did not mean much to

Ike Forte, an impact runner from a junior college, led the Hogs in rushing in 1974 and 1975.

Arkansas fans at the time that Rein's head coach at NC State was named Lou Holtz.

Everything finally fell into place as the 1975 season approached. The squad would include not only four good classes but a handful of key fifth-year men. For the first time since 1970, the offense would show both ability and experience in good numbers. The offensive side would also have three aggressive new coaches; Don Boyce from Oklahoma State and Jesse Branch of Kansas State joined up with Rein. Branch had been one of Frank's favorite Razorback players of the 1960s.

The defensive staff would have a tougher job. The defense looked inadequate in a painful 20-13 loss to Oklahoma State at Stillwater, but it came along and swarmed like the Red Ants of Jimmy Johnson's playing heyday.

At the end of the spring work, it was obvious Arkansas should be competitive every Saturday. The questions concerned "intangibles." Namely, no members of the squad had ever won big or gone to a bowl game.

The Razorbacks of 1975 were the first team to work out of the North End Zone Facility (later renamed for Broyles), a new multipurpose plant that Broyles considered essential to the program's resurgence. Money from the priority contribution plan made it possible, and recruiting became easier when U of A coaches were able to show prospects the plans and drawings for the structure.

It proved to be a long, tense, frustrating, and anxious season with the happiest of endings. For the first time in 10 years, Arkansas won the right, with a little help, of course, from Texas A&M and television, to represent the Southwest Conference as the host team in the Cotton Bowl.

"That was the key to it all," Broyles told the media on December 7, the day after the Razorbacks' 31-6 thrashing of the previously 10-0 Aggies.

"For this team to reach its potential, to be motivated and improving at the end, it had to retain its goals through November. If we had had to play A&M on November 1 [the normal time] . . . well, I won't speculate because I wouldn't change a thing.

"Moving either the A&M or Texas game would give us a chance. When ABC called, I was very eager to see this done. It helped the entire league financially; we couldn't have turned it down. And it helped us gain a great deal of momentum by the time we actually got to A&M in December."

The early loss to Oklahoma State prompted fans to write off the Hogs as another struggling team in the .500 range—shades of the past three dismal years. The Razorbacks came roaring right back, fanning their partisans' hopes for the Texas game. They suffered eight turnovers and lost to the Longhorns at Fayetteville, 24-18. Now that *really* dashed expectations, but the players kept working grimly on a script they believed in 100 percent. By winning the rest of their games they could go to the Cotton Bowl.

Much was made of the role of Scott Bull, the quarterback who "wired it all together" after coming off the bench in the third game. Much was made of the fact the Razorbacks kept grinding as if nothing happened despite the loss (either temporary or permanent) of their entire starting backfield. Not just three backs but three gifted types: quarterback Mike Kirkland and running backs Ike Forte (who graded higher than any previous back ever at Arkansas) and sophomore Jerry Eckwood, who started the year with five straight 100-yard rushing games (and could also block, throw the halfback pass, catch passes, and return punts). Much was made of the way the defense rallied and solidified as the season went along.

Much should have been made of all these things. It was quite a story.

Broyles never doubted Scott Bull; his leadership, his amazing stamina and toughness, his knack of getting the job done regardless.

"Few people knew how good Scott looked in the spring and early fall of 1973, before he had the knee injury a week before the Southern Cal game," Broyles said. "He had every reason to give up during his long recovery; I knew he wouldn't."

With three senior quarterbacks on hand in the spring of 1975, Broyles decided the veer-T best suited the running and passing skills of Kirkland, who had halfback speed. He would be the quarterback. With the ability to play another position, Mark Miller would go to the defensive secondary. As for Bull and the knowledge he could step into any emergency and take charge, Frank figured he had the best No. 2 quarterback in America.

A knee injury in the third game, against Tulsa, put Kirkland out for the season. A knee injury in the seventh game, against Utah State, finished Eckwood for the season. Forte had to watch all the Texas Tech game from the sideline because of a foot injury. Roland Fuchs served as the key runner who took up the slack for Eckwood and Forte.

Bull shook off the adversity of the Texas game and all the criticism that fell on him for that defeat and led Arkansas to the Cotton Bowl.

The veer was thunderously effective. Kirkland, Forte, and Eckwood all made more than 100 yards rushing in the 35-0 opener with Air Force. These Razorbacks gobbled up ground yardage like the Texas Longhorns

Scott Bull was one of those hardy winners who defies easy classification.

at their wishbone summit. The Hogs' greatest show came in a 41-3 crusher of defending champion Baylor at Waco. Arkansas rushed for 460 yards that evening, and Bull, Forte, and Eckwood made more than 100 each.

After the fumble-filled loss to Texas, the Hogs had one chance for the Cotton Bowl. They had to finish in a three-way tie with A&M and Texas. For that to come about, the Aggies had to beat Texas (they did), and Arkansas had to handle the Aggies in their national television show-down on December 6. Then the bid would go to the tri-champion that had been absent longest from the Cotton Bowl. In this case, it would be Arkansas.

When they met the Razorbacks in War Memorial Stadium, the 10-0 Aggies were rated No. 2 in the nation and considered one of the SWC's strongest defensive teams ever.

The weather was cold, damp, and dreary when the kickoff came shortly after 3 P.M. Arkansas caught A&M unprepared on a halfback pass, but it sailed long and incomplete. The first big break went to the Aggies. Lester Hayes covered a fumble at the Arkansas 29. The Aggs smashed to the seven with Bubba Bean. They stalled on the five, and Tony Franklin missed a field goal.

A&M fumbled away another chance as the second quarter started. The game was settling into a hard, scrambling standoff. With less than two minutes remaining in the first half, A&M had to kick from its 26. The punt went high, short, and out on the Aggies' 41.

Scott Bull spotted Teddy Barnes ("the immortal Teddy Barnes," Broyles was to say the next day) in the corner of the end zone. Bull threw a bomb. Two defenders were there—crowding, leaping—but Barnes came down with the ball. With 34 seconds left in the half, Arkansas led, 7-0. And that, really, was enough.

Arkansas grew surer and stronger with every minute of the second half, and the Aggies grew more despondent and disorganized. The 31-6 stunner trapped the Aggies in the Liberty Bowl, Texas in the Bluebonnet, and sent Arkansas to the Cotton against Georgia. "Our defense out-Aggied the Aggies," Broyles said in the madhouse Razorback dressing room.

This was not a Georgia team of the caliber the Hogs demolished in the Sugar Bowl seven years earlier, but it was good enough to grab a 10-0 lead. Arkansas needed less than two minutes to swing that to a 10-10 tie just before halftime, and Vince Dooley's Bulldogs went downhill to a final defeat of 31-10.

Linebacker Hal McAfee, a leader in the rebuilt defense, covered a fumble on the Bulldogs' 15, and Steve Little ultimately kicked a 39-yard

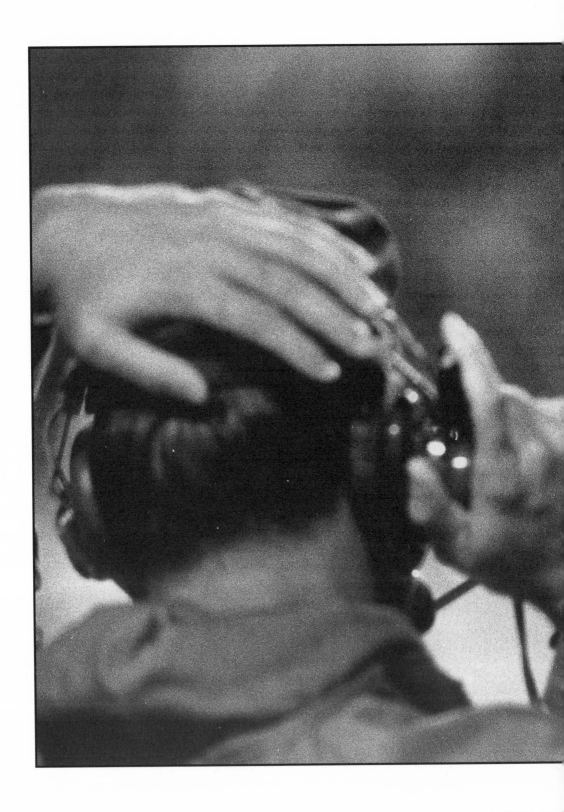

Information from upstairs appears to startle the head coach.

FRANK AT THE CROSSROADS

field goal. The Bulldogs then tried a trick play, "the shoestring," but it misfired spectacularly. Tommy Harris forced a fumble that McAfee recovered, and Ike Forte scored two plays later for the 10-all tie at the half. After a scoreless third quarter, Arkansas iced it with a 21-point flurry. From the second quarter until late in the fourth, the Hogs' defense held Georgia to one first down.

So Arkansas was all the way back. Why didn't Broyles quit then, on top of the world at 10-2?

"Well, I thought about it," he said, "but things were going so good then, it just didn't seem the thing to do. I wasn't sure I wanted to quit at that time."

By the following October, he made his decision. After a 14-7 victory in the first league meeting with new SWC member Houston, Broyles told U of A faculty representative Al Witte and president Dr. Charles Bishop, and a few old and trusted friends, that this was to be his last season as head coach.

"At that time, I thought we'd win it again," he said. "We had just beaten Houston, which wound up in the Cotton Bowl, and we looked to be the best team in the league at that time."

In preparation for the 1976 season, he had to make staff adjustments around the departure of Bo Rein, who was replacing his former boss, Lou Holtz, as head coach of North Carolina State. Holtz went to the New York Jets. Although all the potential offensive problems of the Hogs were unmasked in a 9-3 loss to Tulsa, they reached mid season as contenders with a 5-1 record. They finished 5-5-1.

"Our sophomore quarterback, Ron Calcagni, got hurt, and everything changed," Broyles said. "We didn't have any offense after that, and our defensive players finally lost their morale when they saw we couldn't score."

In Frank's 19 years as Arkansas coach, his Razorbacks failed to win eight or more games only in those seasons where they lacked a running quarterback or—due to inexperience or injuries—failed to get a No. 1 quarterback established.

"If you have a strong runner at quarterback, you don't have to be as strong elsewhere," Broyles said. "There is no offense that can't be handled by a running quarterback. You are severely limited in your choice of offenses if your quarterback is primarily a passer."

And yet during the late 1960s and early 1970s Arkansas became known as a passing team.

"That was our image, and it was created for a purpose," Broyles said.

The "immortal" Teddy Barnes

"In 1966–67, we could not find quarterbacks. Nor could we recruit great runners. I'd watched John Bridgers compete for quarterbacks in Texas. Because he was using the Baltimore Colts offense, he'd have first choice. He'd also get the wide-outs and one or two runners who liked the idea of playing in a pro offense.

"We hadn't had a top quarterback in our state for some time. I couldn't go to Texas and get a top running quarterback; they'd go to Texas or Oklahoma. For us to compete, we had to have another Brittenum, and I couldn't see any.

"So I went to Bill Montgomery. I told him I was going to switch to the pro offense, which would give him a chance to become a pro quarterback. There were at least eight truly outstanding quarterbacks in Texas that year. I thought Bill was the best suited for our purposes. The biggest reason I wanted him was that I realized he was a winner.

"Everybody said we were going to the pro offense. We didn't deny that, but we weren't using the pro offense. We were using a pro set some and throwing drop-back passes with pro techniques, but our running game consisted of the veer option, the counter option, the down-the-line (split-T) option, roll-outs, sprint-outs, and keepers.

"Montgomery had quickness, and he was great throwing the football. We actually threw fewer passes per number of plays per game in 1968–69 than 1966–67.

"It makes a big difference in recruiting as to what your image is.

"Once Montgomery became established, and what a great job he did in his sophomore year, we had our pick of quarterbacks and skill people all around. Joe Ferguson would not have come if we had not been using two wide-outs and throwing to them.

"The decision made us highly competitive again after a lull. We were telling everybody we were using the pro offense in order to establish an image with which to recruit. Finally we did really get into the pro offense because we couldn't run, and that was our downfall.

"Joe Ferguson could run, but he couldn't. He had the speed but not the knack, and there's a difference. Fred Marshall, for instance, didn't have the speed Ferguson had, but Fred was a so much better runner. Brittenum had real quickness, but he wasn't a strong runner. We could run with him, however, because he passed off roll-outs and sprint-outs. He was so accurate throwing on the run, 40 yards and like a bullet.

"Monroe, McKinney, and Moore would get it themselves, running. The more they played, the better they got as passers, which is typical of running quarterbacks.

"Montgomery came so close to gaining recognition as one of the fine college quarterbacks of all time. Bill wasn't big, but he was so strong, so tough mentally, and so smart in his knowledge of everything it took to win.

"Even though Ferguson didn't win consistently for us, it wasn't his fault. We didn't have the material to complement him. We ran into two bad years recruiting.

"Scott Bull was one of those winners who defy easy classification. I can't explain it, but under some quarterbacks each man on the team plays 15 percent better. And Scott could run."

The Arkansas-Texas game of 1976 was switched to December for television, but instead of one of the traditional shoot-outs it marked the official end of the Royal-Broyles era in the Southwest Conference.

Darrell was one of the few friends Broyles had told of his impending retirement plans. This was during a mid-season telephone chat about a film exchange. Darrell startled Frank with confidential news of his own. "I'm quitting, too. This is my last year."

The word was out on both men's decisions before their teams played at Austin on the night of December 4. The television show was saved by nostalgia. Two .500 football teams floundered to a 29-12 decision in favor of Texas while everybody talked of Frank and Darrell and their better days.

"You try to imagine Arkansas without Broyles or Texas without Royal, and it's like trying to imagine 'White Christmas' sung by anyone other than Bing Crosby," wrote Mickey Herskowitz of the *Houston Post*. "You are not sure it can be done. How fitting that they should go out together. But how wrong the stage, how strange the setting, in a game that meant nothing. No unbeaten season. No championship. No bowl invitation. Nothing except remembrance of glories past. Yet, what a special game, because it was their last. And it told you a great deal about their sense of self, their security, that they could step down without the need of a big finish, a socko closing act. A winning season would have been nice, but it certainly would not have been new."

In Broyles's early years at Arkansas, fans assumed he would eventually answer his alma mater's call, like Bear Bryant with Alabama or Bowden Wyatt with Tennessee. The call from Georgia Tech came twice, in December of 1966 when Bobby Dodd retired and in December of 1971 when Bud Carson was released. Frank and Barbara were not interested, although the 1971 package may have been the most lucrative dangled before a college coach to that point in time.

A 31-6 upset of Texas A&M put Arkansas in the Cotton Bowl and gave Frank Broyles his seventh and last SWC title.

As full-time Arkansas athletic director, Broyles remained locked in on improvement; he simply widened the scope and excised negatives from the University of Arkansas's total athletic program. A person who left the country in, say, 1973 and came back in the 1990s would have been flabbergasted at the surges in basketball under first Eddie Sutton and then Nolan Richardson, track under John McDonnell, baseball under Norm DeBriyn, et cetera, and to find seething interest in Razorback athletic teams from September to June. That sort of stuff used to die down from the day after the bowl game until the start of spring practice.

When it came time to lead Arkansas out of the dying Southwest Conference to the dynamic Southeastern, Broyles didn't hesitate and thus jumped out ahead of a major realignment movement in college athletics. He always had a knack for reading trends.

John Barnhill, who picked him, died in October of 1973 after 25 years of almost constant pain.

By the early 1960s Barnhill was going to his office for only three hours a morning. His progressive multiple sclerosis had already robbed him of most of the use of his right side (eye, arm, leg). His balance had long been affected. You did not, however, lend him a hand, nor did you help him insert a key into the lock of his office door, even into 1973. The pride remained.

After 1961 he did not travel. Others did the legwork, and Barnie made the decisions until George Cole became athletic director in 1970. Barnhill's life followed a carefully prescribed regimen, adhered to rigidly. He had ulcers and other problems. He did not talk of them. He was usually cheerful in his own way. His mind remained sharp to the last.

His maxims should be well remembered.

"You can't pay a good coach too much, or a bad one too little.

"A team isn't remembered in December so much for its record as from what was expected of it in August.

"Heat and fatigue make cowards of us all. That's why Arkansas never did much good until they put those lights in at TCU, Baylor, and Texas.

"The success of your team depends at least 50 percent on the strength of the people you're playing.

"There's one good thing about losing a bowl game. You're sure to have a good spring practice."

"John Barnhill was the most courageous man I've ever met," Broyles said, "and one of the wisest."

"I guess," Barnhill said a few months before his death, "that bringing Frank to Arkansas was about the best thing I ever did. He's sure been a

THE RAZORBACKS

Frank Broyles and Darrell Royal ended their coaching careers together on December 4, 1976.

comfort to me. Just knowing you wouldn't have to be hunting another coach some cold December, if nothing else.

"It was obvious to me when he came that our budget was going up. He was used to the finer things, and we were cutting corners. And the way he coaches, with organization, he has to have top assistants. It has all paid off so well. You couldn't buy our reputation for a million dollars. We've got at Arkansas what everybody is looking for, if we just don't ruin it ourselves.

"It's difficult to stay on top and please a great number of people year after year. Frank has come closer to doing that than most coaches ever do.

"I told him the other day he's trying to win, and I'm trying to stay alive. They're both hard to do."

— 38 —

MIAMI HONEYMOON

Thick fog enveloped Fayetteville on December 11, 1976. The temperature did not rise above nor fall below 32 degrees all day, a treacherous situation, what with the mist in the air.

Some members of the University of Arkansas Board of Trustees had difficulty reaching the campus for the first hiring of a new football coach any of them would have experienced. The coach had been delayed by the need for his private plane to land 30 miles north of the city. Once on site, he balked until he could try to reach his former employer, the ailing—dying—owner of the New York Jets pro football team. He wanted to apologize for walking off after just 13 games on the job. He never did reach the owner, Phil Iselin.

The parties sat down to the routine chore at about 5 P.M. and completed it in minutes.

Two hours later, athletic director Frank Broyles introduced his hand-picked successor to the typical jam-packed basketball crowd in Barnhill Arena.

Looking more like a student manager than a big-time coach, the yellow-haired newcomer took the microphone and said, hoarsely, "I stand 5'10", weigh 150 pounds soaking wet, speak with a lisp, and look like I have beri-beri. I'm not Frank Broyles. I am Lou Holtz and that's all I can be. For the last 19 years, Frank Broyles did the most fantastic job of anyone in coaching. I didn't come here to maintain what he did. I came to build on it."

Thus did the football reins of Arkansas pass from the hands of a tall, robust Methodist with roots in the Deep South football and into the custody of a short, mercurial Catholic from a little backwater town in Ohio and an off-the-football-main-line college where he scarcely played.

Broyles stepped completely aside, but not before telling close friends, "Lou Holtz will take this state by storm."

That's exactly what Louis Leo Holtz did. His Hogs started 11-1, 9-2-1, and 10-2, the most wins (30) in so short a time ever at Arkansas. And his bowl foes were Oklahoma, UCLA, and Alabama, the latter a two-year national champion.

A couple of years later, *Los Angeles Times* reporter Bob Oates was to remark on Broyles's astuteness—and courage—in this delicate, critical matter. He noted how few successful coaches, picking their successors, jealous of their own records, dare to tap such a dazzler who likely would win big. Furthermore, Broyles passed up any number of his former players and aides, including Jimmy Johnson and Fred Akers, the latter soon to be hired by Texas.

Frank explained, "The Arkansas job is a special one. As athletic director, running a big business, I could operate and be happy only if the football program were very successful. I knew Lou was a great promoter. Arkansas has to have a coach who will sell his program all the time. Lou was also known as a fundamentalist as well as a disciplinarian.

"And Lou's teams could always score. It takes good defense to win, but scorers win championships.

"I'd known about Lou for some time. We were lucky he became available."

Broyles had learned the most about Holtz from Robert (Bo) Rein, whom he had hired off Lou's North Carolina State staff to put in Lou's offense at Arkansas in 1975.

"Lou coached option running from the split-backs veer-T plus drop-back passing and did it all without turning the ball over," Broyles said.

Arkansas had gone 10-2 and to the Cotton Bowl by setting school ground-gaining records in that attack in 1975. But for fumbles against Oklahoma State and Texas, the record might have been 12-0.

Rein once told a reporter, "To understand what drives Lou Holtz, you need to go to his hometown, to see what he came from."

East Liverpool, Ohio, is a small, falling-down place on the Ohio River below Pittsburgh and across the river from West Virginia. Its pottery factories closed years ago. The steel mills up river aren't what they used to be.

Lou needed to get out of East Liverpool, Ohio, the way Bear Bryant needed to leave Moro Bottom, Arkansas.

Lou's father, son of German-Irish immigrants, was a bus driver. His mother, Mrs. Anne Holtz, from a Russian background, was a practical nurse.

Growing up, Lou became attached to his uncle and namesake, Lou Tychonievich, who, among other things, was a hearty sports follower with an active sense of humor. Before he'd finished high school, Lou had begun making his mark exploiting Uncle Lou's knacks as a jokester, an entertainer. Indeed, he early augmented his coaching salary by speaking for fees. Before he left Arkansas, he commanded $15,000 or so for special speaking assignments, many for giant corporations.

Other than playing games and amusing his friends, Lou says he grew up doting on "working in the steel mills across the river, getting a car, and driving my girl to the Dairy Queen."

Younger than his teammates in high school, he was also much smaller and showed no signs of getting bigger. His coach, however, told him that he should go to college to gain credentials as a coach, his natural field. His family was so informed. Lou says he had subconsciously fought this so hard, he finished 234th in his class.

His parents remained adamant; Lou would be the first in the family ever to go to college. Kent State accepted him on a basketball grant. An injury stopped that. He caught on in football as a blocking back (the play caller in the single wing). Basically, he was a pepper-pot second-stringer limited by a bad knee.

When his summer job after his freshman year turned out to be a steel mills chore that he gave up after two weeks, the die was cast. He would coach.

During his senior year at Kent State, sidelined by that knee, Lou helped coach the junior varsity and hitchhiked to a nearby high school to assist there.

No beginner ever worked harder or longer to set his course so solidly on achieving his goal, that of becoming a thorough, brilliant, big-time coach. He had the required drive, ego, and ambition.

Indeed, Lou would privately admit to feeling crushed when Jimmy Johnson, not himself, became the one to follow Tom Landry as coach of the Dallas Cowboys, even though Lou already held what he had called the only job he'd always aspired to, that at Notre Dame.

"Hi, I'm Lou Holtz," the little guy with the long, quick stride greeted everyone as he worked his way from low-paying underlings jobs at Iowa, William and Mary, Connecticut, and South Carolina to, finally, Ohio State. There he handled a great secondary and became a Woody Hayes man in the Buckeyes' undefeated national title season of 1968.

(Lou still uses a banquet yarn from the Buckeyes' Rose Bowl win. Lou says his boss grabbed him by the throat in the tunnel going to the halftime locker room. Woody said, "How could O. J. Simpson go 80 yards on us?" Lou says he replied, "Why, that's all he needed.")

With prestigious Ohio State on his resume, Holtz was given a shot as head man at weak William and Mary. There, he was able to acquire some offensive philosophy (mainly from Bill Yeoman at Houston) and took his team to a bowl game—always his number-one criterion for success.

Lou moved on to North Carolina State. Usually underdogs, and frequently major upsetters (twice of Penn State), his Wolfpacks went 8-3-1, 9-3, 9-2-1, and 7-4-1, losing just once at home.

At Raleigh, the quick-witted, quick-triggered, hyper-sensitive Holtz thrived on the kind of controversy peculiar to the 20-mile triangle where fans of North Carolina, Duke, Wake Forest, and North Carolina State read the same papers and rub shoulders daily.

Late in the 1975 season, Lou got involved in a squabble with a professor who insisted on running the circling track during closed practices. This on top of nettlesome relations with the administration led Lou to quietly tender his resignation.

He accepted the head coaching position of the Jets. He soon recognized his mistake.

He could not take the bone-chilling winds of practices on Long Island. Ironically, he would spend many years dreaming of coaching in, even at, Florida, and vacationing in the warmth around a second home at Orlando, while practicing and coaching his teams in the blustery, frigid climes of Fayetteville and, worse, Minneapolis and South Bend.

He realized that his talents were best-suited to college athletes and college environments, although he has since wished that he could prove he would not be a failure in the NFL.

The truth was, he had really not made a commitment to the lowly Jets.

When, in October 1976, Broyles heard this, he telephoned Holtz. His words were, "If you knew that a very good college coaching job would open up in a couple of months, would you be interested?"

Holtz said, "Is this job as good as the one I think it is?"

Broyles said, "I think it is."

Holtz said, "You've found your man."

They kept the secret until the week after Broyles's retirement became known in the first days of December.

Holtz wavered only one day. On a Thursday, he allowed himself to be persuaded by the bed-ridden Iselin to issue a pledge to stay with the Jets. He reneged on a Friday. He signed at Arkansas on Saturday.

Lou remained moody, often miserable, for his first eight months at Arkansas.

He did not mind the fact that he was tackling a no-no, succeeding a legend. He relished such challenges.

He just did not like what he called the surprises. He thought he would retain Broyles's staff intact, part of the promise. Instead, key men like Jimmy Johnson and Bill Lewis, each of whom wanted to succeed Broyles, fled.

He was able to hire the mysteriously masterful Monte Kiffin from Nebraska for his main requirement, that of defensive coordinator. He would be reunited with his longtime offensive line coach, the esteemed Larry Beightol. Don Breaux, a former Broyles's aide on offense, would return after a spell at Texas. Lou, of course, would be his own offensive coordinator, the daily handler of quarterbacks.

He found that he would have to contend with what he called racial, academic, and discipline problems.

On top of all that, he could not sell his house in New York. Until midsummer, he was making two large mortgage payments (although Broyles arranged to assist him there, undoubtedly through the Razorback Foundation).

Following his usual dawn-till-exhaustion schedule, Lou attacked the obstacles on all fronts, flew over the state nightly to wow fans with his one-liners and magic tricks, and conducted what he called later, "survivor" spring practice.

So, picked to finish sixth in the SWC, Lou's first team of Razorbacks finished sixth in the country through December and bamboozled Oklahoma in the Orange Bowl to peak at No. 3 on the day after the bowls.

To that time, no Arkansas football team had ever had such an impact on the nation. Well, for four quarters. The Hogs had everybody's attention with a 14-0 lead after three periods in 1969, but Texas's turn-around to 15-14 negated that.

What few knew in 1977 was that Arkansas was probably just as good as Barry Switzer's OU team that had featured his best recruiting crop ever, the freshmen of 1975.

The Hogs' defense figured to be quick with Jimmy Walker, Dale White, and Dan Hampton returning in the interior and William Hampton and Larry Jackson back at linebacker. It became devastating when little Bob Cope groomed a great secondary with Larry White, Howard Sampson, Vaughn Lusby, Patrick Martin, and Brad Shoup.

Holtz had doubted that Ron Calcagni, recovering from the injuries that left the 1976 team impotent, could be his type of quarterback. The junior from Youngstown, Ohio, erased those feelings in the fall. There had been no doubts about the running backs, Ben Cowins, Cowboy Forrest, and Roland Sales.

As he was to do routinely, Beightol succeeded in rebuilding the offensive line.

Then there was Steve Little. For the one year, he kicked off, punted, quick-kicked, and kicked field goals as well as anyone ever has.

(Holtz had told the phenom from Kansas City that he'd heard he had a drug problem. If he saw any manifestation of that, he'd said, he'd so inform all NFL teams. Little's total 1977 performance so awed Bud Wilkinson, the old Oklahoma master turned St. Louis Cardinals coach, he drafted Steve No. 1—the last kicker taken high in an NFL draft. Little, unfortunately, went sour for St. Louis. Late at night on the day in 1979 he was cut, he suffered almost total paralysis when his car planed on wet pavement in a rainstorm and crashed.)

In that 11-1 year, Arkansas mostly just wiped out the other team in the first half and then coasted. Terrific as a game planner, Lou liked it that way. By halftime, the other team had usually experienced his whole bag of tricks.

When it came time to play Texas, unbeaten with wondrous senior Earl Campbell healthy again for new coach Fred Akers, ABC had to television the old classic when it hadn't planned to—and was delighted with the result.

Earlier in the year, Texas hotshot Russell Erxleben went in against Rice when UT led by more than 50 points and, instead of punting as was expected, kicked an NCAA record 67-yard field goal.

With Texas ahead 6-3 just before halftime at Fayetteville, and a wet norther at his back, Little lined up, pressure on, and equaled the 67-yard record.

Arkansas blocked a try by Erxleben, and Little kicked a third field goal for a 9-6 lead.

With time running out, Texas barely made a first down from its 20, shades of 1969, and went the distance. Campbell took a screen pass 29 yards to the lip, and Ham Jones scored going wide.

Holtz took the loss hard, blaming himself for a third and three failure on the Hogs' last try, but when wouldn't he?

The Hogs resumed their winning ways. When Calcagni hit Robert Farrell for 58 yards and a touchdown for a 26-20 win at Texas A&M, Orange Bowl scouts inked in Arkansas instead of Penn State as the foe for Oklahoma, the automatic host because of its Big Eight championship.

Arkansas clinched the bid with a 49-7 thrashing of SMU at Fayetteville.

The events of Thanksgiving week cast long shadows.

Holtz couldn't have written a script more to his liking. First, ABC asked Arkansas to move its game against Texas Tech at Lubbock to Thursday, five days after the SMU game. Granted. Arkansas, drained by recent events, found itself behind by 14-3 at halftime. Though Tech was hard to pass on, Calcagni rallied the Hogs to a 17-14 win with touchdown flings to Donny Bobo and Bobby Duckworth. The win was, however, hurtful in the polls, not helpful.

The next day, Oklahoma, which had lost only to Texas, 13-6, also finished 10-1, but by shattering its regular closing foe, Nebraska, in a manner which, the critics thought, restored the Sooners to national title contention.

Barry Switzer, a 1959 captain and a favorite assistant to Frank Broyles until he went with Jim Mackenzie to OU in 1966, and the "Arkansas Mafia" on his staff did not seem concerned about their next matchup.

Oddsmakers reflected that by making OU an 11-point favorite.

Privately, Holtz felt Arkansas would win—and big.

The grass at Miami, he felt, would inhibit the wishbone cuts of a team that played every game on artificial turf. Arkansas would keep its quickness on defense.

More important, he had developed a scheme that would use Calcagni on sprintouts and options to make OU's fast linebackers run with the flow and away from the middle, and an "influence block" inside to clear the way for the fullback to run straight ahead on simple handoffs.

At Notre Dame years later, Holtz was still doing unusual things with blocking schemes to confound such as Florida State, Michigan, Southern Cal, Florida, and Texas A&M.

Never, however, did it all succeed so well as in that 1978 Orange Bowl.

OU entered that game lulled to sleep, irreparably unprepared.

Lou maximized something he hadn't planned.

On the day after the Razorbacks completed an excellent week of preparations, the day that they would break camp for Christmas, Holtz made these announcements: Leotis Harris, his All-American offensive guard, would make the trip to Miami but would not play because of a knee injury suffered in the day's scrimmage. And Cowins, Forrest, and Bobo—everybody but Calcagni in the starting backfield—would not go to Miami.

This is what had happened: Following the scrimmage, a coed who had entered the room in the athletic dorm of a freshman running back soon found herself being, at best, intimidated by football players. She had previously been intimate with a veteran running back who now was intruding and threatening to resume his place in her affections—by force. This later was described as a "playful act," but the woman felt otherwise.

Lou Holtz gets up close and personal with quarterback Ron Calcagni.

THE RAZORBACKS

The freshman running back in whose room this was taking place summoned campus police.

No charges were ever filed.

It was said that the woman, daughter of frequently moved military parents then living in New Orleans, agreed privately not to press charges if the athletic department would somehow punish the players she named —and if they would keep her name out of it.

Ever since Bear Bryant held Joe Namath out of a Sugar Bowl game as punishment for a late-season campus violation, coaches have found that a bowl-game suspension is the easiest penalty they can administer, but a telling one. No action is required by any other campus authority. The athlete doesn't even miss a class. His eligibility resumes unimpaired the day after the game.

The existence of an agreement with the woman was never made known, if indeed an agreement was even made. The entire affair became, as far as the public was concerned, a rumor-strewn whirl around a void. This was a time before tell-all tabloid journalism, of course.

Lou's announcement prompted second thoughts by the three players and their hometown lawyers. Black players more or less organized in Little Rock and threatened an Orange Bowl boycott. This appeared likely, but private dialogues between black leaders (some for it, some against it) and Broyles, Holtz, and others quieted that over the weekend.

The next day, the day of departure for Miami, lawyers for Cowins, Bobo, and Forrest appeared in federal court in Little Rock asking for an injunction to force Holtz to return them to the squad for the game. (So far, no court has ruled that a coach must use this or that player in a game.)

The suit proceeded quickly. With the woman in the wings should her name be introduced, Cowins was asked to discuss what happened and to identify the complainant. His lawyer immediately interrupted to ask that the suit be dropped. It was.

Holtz received the good news in Miami.

He was hailed nationwide for standing up for discipline and what he called his "Do-Right Rule," however vague and unwritten.

This was a ripple compared to what happened after the night of January 2.

Lou had concentrated at Miami on rebuilding morale and confidence.

He begged for "respect," citing the fact that the bookies in Las Vegas had let the point spread jump to 17, 18 points, then had taken the game off the boards for a while.

THE RAZORBACKS

The Razorbacks' 31-6 stunner of Oklahoma was one of the great upsets in bowl history.

They were reflecting fans' doubts that a team could make a decent showing against the sensational Sooners with 4 of 11 offensive starters suddenly sidelined and replaced by who knew what.

Holtz's biggest daily task was in trying to change Cowins's replacement from a tabby to a tiger.

Roland Sales, handsome and gentle, had always been a decent back, neither more nor less. He had, however, been Holtz's unfortunate choice to get it on that fateful third and three against Texas, and had not.

Against OU, Sales "got it." And then some.

Arkansas was so ready for the kickoff, Holtz had to lighten things with players, standing up to tell jokes—"The worst I've ever heard," he said later. When the kickoff did come, late, and in a light shower appreciated by Lou, Little kicked OU deep.

Aroused Arkansas swarmed the Sooners, who lost 11 yards and then the ball on a Billy Sims fumble covered by Jimmy Walker at the OU nine. Calcagni, stronger and quicker than any quarterback OU had faced, faked to Sales and followed him through for seven. Sales scored from the two.

Lou got what he had to have—quick success.

Oklahoma tried to rally. Elvis Peacock got away but, after 41 yards, Vaughn Lusby tackled him. OU botched the field-goal attempt.

By now, the Hogs and Sooners both knew that one team was totally prepared, the other one wasn't prepared at all.

Arkansas roared to a 14-0 halftime lead on a three-yard keeper by Calcagni after a Dan Hampton recovery of a Kenny King fumble at the Arkansas 42 and a 38-yard run by Sales.

After Little suckered the Sooners with a booming quick kick out of the end zone, he kicked a 32-yard field goal. A four-yard run by Sales let the Hogs frolic into the fourth period with a 24-0 lead. The 31-6 final was almost merciful.

Holtz calls his own plays. He wound up having Calcagni feign sprintouts and passes and hand off 22 times to Sales on quick-hitters straight ahead. What a dream—in a big game, to run straight ahead and find huge holes achieved with only one block.

Sales made 205 yards, an Orange Bowl record, and caught four passes for 52 yards. Arkansas gained 407 yards.

Larry Lacewell, the legendary defensive coordinator for OU, said that he had "forced" Switzer to look at Arkansas films for the first time only two days before the game and that his boss had emerged pale-faced.

"No matter what adjustment I called, we wound up wrong," Lacewell said. "It was the first time I ever came to fear a coach."

They had wired Lou for sound.

At the end, the television picture and the sound told it all when William Hampton, one of the athletes who had been for a time a part of the boycott threat, said, "Coach, we love you."

So did Arkansas—and the football world.

─ 39 ─

CHRISTMAS IN PHOENIX

"You sure know how to kill a controversy," a man laughed at Lou Holtz in the wake of NBC's hit television show the night of January 2 in Miami.

Winning an Orange Bowl game Arkansas had only dreamed of appearing in did settle a lot of things.

For instance, Cowins, Bobo, and Forrest reenrolled in January on schedule, the so-called "sexual incident in the athletic dorm" forgotten.

Lou found himself with 14,000 letters to answer (he finished in April) and more speaking invitations than he could fill in years.

He picked up every "Coach of the Year" award that hadn't already been awarded (some to Fred Akers, who was 11-0 until Notre Dame ambushed Texas in the Cotton Bowl).

But Lou lost his beloved underdog's role.

For 1978, with Calcagni and most of the others returning, Arkansas would be favored for 12 straight games, picked to win the SWC, and chosen No. 1 nationally in several pre-season ratings, including that of *Sports Illustrated* (which put Lou—and Cowins and Calcagni—on the cover for his first time).

"Now we'll find what real pressure is like," said Holtz after a spring practice which he described as "no more difficult than your average death march," his typical statement for out-of-season exercises.

At times in 1978, Arkansas looked far and away like the best team in the league, maybe as good as anyone in the country. The final record, 9-2-1, was taken as disappointing.

Arkansas, of course, had never won the SWC title when it was picked. Lou was never to beat Texas and Houston back to back, and he beat neither this time.

Obviously, the Longhorns and Cougars had viewed the Orange Bowl game, as had most of the country. They had, as Tommy Nobis once said, been thinking about the Razorbacks "a little bit each day." Both played their best games of the year back-to-back against the Hogs.

Holtz never got his passing game quite right, nor that gorgeous secondary of 1977 rebuilt.

Still, he had his Hogs fired up for both big tests.

After four blah games, but four wins, Cowins and Jerry Eckwood, redshirted with an injury in 1977, ran wild on the Steers to begin each half. Arkansas had never quite started each half against UT with a powerful touchdown drive.

Holtz erred just before halftime, when a Texas interception of an ill-advised pass let the 'Horns score right on top of a previous touchdown for a 20-7 lead.

Still, Arkansas led 21-20 entering the final quarter.

Two years in a row, the Hogs' defense never got a handle on Randy

Ron Calcagni prepares to fire a pass against Baylor.

THE RAZORBACKS

Ben Cowins (28) rushed for more than 1,000 yards three straight years.

Gary Anderson, who ran with the best, thanks Steve Korte (66), who blocked with the best.

McEachern, the not gifted but doughty UT quarterback. When they did, it wasn't always good. Dan Hampton got in McEachern's face once when Arkansas had momentum, and Jim Howard intercepted the pass near midfield. That was wiped out, and Arkansas was penalized 15 for roughing the passer, the key play for Texas in the first half.

Arkansas wasn't lucky. Vaughn Lusby, key man in the secondary, was knocked out with a broken cheekbone when he was clipped at the sidelines in the second period. Texas put its 6'6" tight end, Lawrence Sampleton, on O. C. Jackson, Lusby's 5'6" replacement, on one-on-one routes. Sampleton caught 4 for 102 yards.

McEachern hit Olympics sprinter Lam Jones for two touchdowns.

Lou loved to retaliate. His offense gained over 200 yards in the first quarter the next week in the Astrodome. Houston bided its time as Ish Ordonez kicked three field goals.

The Hogs' secondary suffered again, this time to UH's famed option running. Kevin Evans, Lusby's replacement that week, was clipped and knocked out of the game, also at the sidelines.

Artful Danny Davis led the Coogs on their first error-free game that coach Bill Yeoman could remember. They harvested a touchdown in each of the last three periods and won, 21-9.

Holtz quipped, "Three touchdowns beats three field goals every time."

After that, the Razorbacks walloped Rice, Baylor, A&M, SMU, and Tech routinely.

Tech had won six in a row entering Razorback Stadium, including an upset of Houston. Holtz had the Hogs on a tear. They led by 42-0 just before halftime and won by 49-7.

"It's all right to run up a score," Lou liked to say, "if you do it in the first half."

Cowins needed just a little over a half to get 148 yards on 19 carries, Eckwood blocking, to give him 1,006 for the year, his third 1,000-yard season, and a four-year total of 3,570 yards. This passed Dickey Morton and left Cowins second only to Earl Campbell on the SWC rushing list of the times. (Writers later named Campbell and Morton to the all-decade SWC backfield, but not Cowins.)

Lou desperately wanted a January 1 bowl game for the seniors who had gone 20-3 for him. This was not to be. He settled for "the best trip," to Phoenix for a Fiesta Bowl game against UCLA on Christmas Day.

Arkansas had the better overall team, but UCLA had more great athletes and an enormous psychological advantage. UCLA had five

Roland Sales (21) ripped the bewildered Oklahoma Sooners for 205 yards.

weeks to get ready and no classes to attend. The Bruins put in a running quarterback, fifth-year man Rudy Bukich, to surprise and take advantage of the Hogs' tendencies.

Arkansas's season had gone into December, and exams extended to December 21.

Once again, a "sexual incident in the dorm" hit as the Hogs left Fayetteville. Forrest, Bobo, and Duckworth stayed home. The first two were charged by a female visitor. Months later, Forrest and Bobo were cleared in court.

Arkansas seized a 10-0 halftime lead at Phoenix, but UCLA took advantage of both its closing opportunities to salvage a 10-10 tie.

Bukich's 15-yard run on a keeper when the Hogs' expected pass tied the game. Arkansas couldn't get field position against a bristling UCLA defense the last half.

The night that Woody Hayes slugged a Clemson player in the Gator Bowl, Lou was in Hawaii to coach in the Hula Bowl. He was everybody's pick to succeed Hayes as Ohio State's coach. But the man who hadn't hesitated to follow a legend at Arkansas allowed that he didn't want to be the one to pick up the pieces after Woody. Earle Bruce did, and Ohio State enjoyed an 11-0 season in 1979 before losing in the Rose Bowl.

However, Lou knew something others didn't. The final week of the season, the president of the University of Florida had come to Fayetteville hoping to satisfy Lou's dream of coaching out of the cold and in the balmy breezes at Gainesville. He could supply for Florida something it had never had, an SEC championship.

Lou sent the UF president home empty-handed. He had a new clause in his contract saying that, should the athletic director's position open up at Arkansas, he would enjoy first refusal.

Popular basketball coach Eddie Sutton did not care for that development, but Frank Broyles had no choice.

It was Lou's price plus his reward for a 20-3-1 start, unprecedented at Arkansas.

Thus ended two tempestuous, triumphant (but not totally satisfying) years for Lou Holtz at Arkansas. He had battled everybody to the hilt—even the Southwest Conference on its refusal to use any officials but Texans in Arkansas games—and jumped readily into other controversies. He had finished second in the league twice, but, however close he'd come, he had not beaten Texas.

That bugged him more than fans would ever know.

─ 40 ─

A SOUR TASTE OF SUGAR

Early in 1979, Lou Holtz pondered stopping his watch and not starting it again until 1980.

"We ought to redshirt everybody," he said.

The key men from his first 24 games were gone, from Ron Calcagni through Dan Hampton, who had blossomed as a playmaker (he had always played good techniques) about mid-season of his senior year and would become a Chicago Bears all-timer on defense and as a leader, no small honor.

Lou said, "The only place they're holding graduation in the Southwest Conference this year is Arkansas."

"We'll be so young, five guys I signed out of Little Rock may be starting."

That was scarcely an exaggeration.

As in 1977, the Hogs would be picked to finish fifth or sixth in the league. This made sense. The SWC would be its strongest ever, top to bottom, with experience abounding. Arkansas would go to war with two quarterbacks not gifted as runners—and runners usually won in the SWC —and a defense that would lack strength and size, not to mention savvy, and could be weak against the run, a factor that does not promote winning.

But, on December 1, 1979, Lou and his aides spent a rollicking afternoon watching on television and listening on the radio to learn whether, as Southwest co-champions with a 7-1 record in league play and 10-1 overall, they would face Nebraska in the Cotton Bowl or go against 11-0 Alabama in the Sugar Bowl.

Texas A&M upset Texas, knocking the Longhorns out of what had long been a three-way tie for the league lead.

The result was that Houston went to Dallas and Arkansas to the Sugar Bowl—as was the Hogs' hoped-for destination. It never occurred to Lou that he might have just missed his best chance for a trip to the Cotton Bowl while at Arkansas.

Over the 11 games, Lou had penciled in the names of 47 starters at the 22 positions. Despite that, the Razorbacks lost an undefeated regular season only by the margin of the first field-goal miss of the year by Ish Ordonez, after an NCAA record 16 in a row, on the final play against Houston.

Except for Ordonez and punter Steve Cox, the Razorbacks put only four players on the all-league team: quarterback Kevin Scanlon, receiver Robert Farrell, tackle Greg Kolenda, and free safety Kevin Evans. While Evans held the Hogs' defense together, Texas had a future all-pro, Johnnie Johnson, at that post. Evans was the only Arkansas player who started every game.

Unquestionably, Arkansas won because of all the league's quarterbacks, only Scanlon could do almost everything right.

Everybody knew how bright, how handsome Scanlon was, but the son of a Beaver Falls, Pennsylvania, manufacturer had not really played much football since he broke Joe Namath's records in high school.

Scanlon played one game for Holtz at North Carolina State, played a little in a running scheme for Bo Rein there in 1976, sat out 1977 at Arkansas, and played little (but not well, because of a back problem) behind Calcagni in 1978.

The staff consensus was that redshirted freshman Tom Jones, Bert's brother from Ruston, Louisiana, who had had a good spring, would have to do it in 1979.

Instead, Scanlon became the most "perfect" passer in Arkansas history. Running only north and south, he also showed his toughness. Whatever, he protected the football, the number-one concern at Arkansas under any coach.

Scanlon had no rivals for the league's passing title, posting 152.2 points in the new NCAA rating system, 37 points ahead of the number-two man. He completed 66.2 percent of his passes, a new league record, breaking Don Meredith's, and led Arkansas to a 63.9 percentage, also a new SWC record.

Above all, his mental agility and football awareness let Holtz use all his playbook when he needed to. By the end of October, Holtz was the envy of his rival coaches, who voted Scanlon all-SWC unanimously.

Scanlon provided the glue.

Kevin Scanlon's precision passing and senior expertise served as the catalyst for a Sugar Bowl bid.

Frank Broyles said at the end, "Lou is the greatest at masking his own weaknesses and maximizing his strengths. This season, he had a veteran quarterback and offensive line and some receivers and they carried the load and bought time for the defense until it matured a little."

The defense had to mature. It had let Colorado State make 363 yards on the ground alone (although Arkansas won, 36-3, with field position).

In a year when Arkansas beat Texas, to the relief of all Razorback fans, the true crisis came against, of all teams, TCU.

Scanlon had come out of two-a-days with a deep bruise under his throwing arm. Holtz had decided that he would hold Scanlon out of the final pre-season test against Tulsa. Jones would be prepared to play, and Scanlon would do nothing but jog for a week.

On the fourth play against Tulsa, Jones lofted a 38-yard scoring pass to Bobby Duckworth, triggering a 38-8 romp.

On Monday, Scanlon knew fear for the only time of the year. He picked up a football for the first time in nine days. After he followed through on his first throw, he relaxed. There was no pain.

Five TCU coaches had come and gone (one via death on the sidelines) since the Frogs notched their last win over Arkansas in 1958. TCU had hired F. A. Dry because, at Tulsa in 1976, he had showed he could beat the Hogs.

Now, with 7:45 to play, TCU appeared to have ended a 20-year hex. The Frogs led by 13-6. Dry's offensive game plan, involving a running quarterback and two tight ends and misdirection plays right at the middle, had provided TCU ball control against the Hogs' green defense.

On Thursday, Arkansas had changed its pass-protection scheme, a mistake Lou later admitted. Scanlon's blockers couldn't pick up TCU's blitzes.

TCU quarterback Kevin Haney then made a crucial mistake. He was supposed to scramble rather than throw when under pressure. With Hogs on him, he flipped out toward a running back. Arkansas linebacker Mike Massey intercepted and romped 33 yards alone for the touchdown. With a tie score, the Hogs got the ball back 80 yards away with two minutes left.

Still blitzing, TCU was fooled when Scanlon faked a short dump pass to tight end Darryl Mason, then uncorked to him deep for a 48-yard gain. With the clock running, and to 0:07, Ordonez hit a perfect 44-yard field goal to end it, 16-13.

The real season began.

The contracts called for an open date the next week but Holtz and

Rex Dockery, Tech's coach, had agreed to move the game from the end of the schedule, December 2, where it would have messed up bowl bids and recruiting.

The Hogs made the most out of little and won 20-6 on two Ordonez field goals, a 74-yard pass from Scanlon to Duckworth, and a closing 67-yard punt return by Gary Anderson, who, one of six superb freshmen, began showing Lance Alworth potential in an open field.

Lo and behold, Arkansas and Texas again would be meeting as unbeatens.

Using its stifling veteran defense, Texas had throttled Missouri, Iowa State, Rice, and Oklahoma, gaining a No. 4 national rating. Arkansas had given up few points (playing field position) but had made only one touchdown with its offense in two weeks.

All year, Lou Holtz had felt good about the Texas game. He liked playing it in Little Rock, where he felt invincible, having never lost there. Arkansas had not beaten Texas since Joe Ferguson passed for three touchdowns in the rain for that 31-7 win in War Memorial Stadium in 1971.

By now, everybody had a book on Holtz. They knew of his first-play ploys. So, when he had Scanlon throw deep from his end of the field to Duckworth on the first play, Johnnie Johnson was waiting on the pass as two men covered Duckworth. Arkansas held and got out of an anxious first quarter behind by only 7-0 on A. J. Jones's 37-yard sweep.

With the wind in the second period, Arkansas cashed in on UT's mistakes.

Evans intercepted, and Anderson scored from 28 yards around Farrell's block. Jeff Goff covered a fumble at the UT 28, and Scanlon threw 12 yards to Mason in the end zone.

The Hogs then got a winning cushion by driving from their 20 into the heart of the 'Horns proud defense. From the 14, Ordonez hit his 15th straight field goal for a 17-7 lead.

Three Holtz teams had led Texas into the fourth quarter. This one maintained its edge, even though Lawrence Sampleton caught a tipped pass from the ill-starred Donnie Little for a touchdown at the end.

The 17-14 win gave Lou his best start yet, 6-0.

"It certainly feels good to win this one," he said, understating his reaction to Arkies' feelings about Texas.

For months, at various forums, he had teased Arkansas fans, "Why don't you people get emotional about playing New Hampshire or somebody? All I hear is Texas."

ABC had rescheduled that Arkansas-Texas match of unbeatens for national television. Now it had no choice but to do the same for the match of two more SWC unbeatens at Fayetteville the following week.

Although the Cougars dominated the game, they were fortunate to win, 13-10.

Lou said in his typically weary post-game way, "We achieved none of our goals and therefore didn't deserve to win, but we still had a chance at the end."

When it was 10-10 in the fourth quarter, Scanlon made his only such mistake of the season. He threw into a crowd down the middle. A linebacker intercepted, and UH collected the decisive field goal from Kenny Hatfield.

On the last scrimmage play of the game, Farrell leaped at the sidelines and caught a bomb at the UH 25, stopping the clock.

After all the timeouts television could find ads for, Ordonez failed to get the kick airborne immediately, and it glanced off the helmet of UH tackle Hosea Taylor. The Coogs prevailed.

For the third straight year, Holtz would lose only in October, never in November, reminiscent of Broyles's early years. Houston was Lou's nemesis, just as then-mighty Mississippi was for Broyles.

Baylor and A&M both had two weeks to get ready for the Hogs, a schedule break each had chosen after the slate was re-done with the addition of UH in 1976.

Baylor led by 14-0 at the half—and it could have been 28-0—and then by 17-0 in the third period. The defense began ravaging Baylor's offense and finally Scanlon's 60-yard bomb over reckless BU defenders broke open the 29-20 victory.

The defense played its best game of the year at Kyle Field. Despite the presence of six freshmen as starters for Arkansas, A&M could not solve Monte Kiffin's cockeyed defenses against two great backs, Curtis Dickey and George Woodard. Darryl Bowles dominated A&M's defense as Arkansas led, 22-3, before the Aggies scored a touchdown at the end.

That led to a Sugar Bowl bid which a 31-7 win over SMU cinched. As usual, with the Cotton Bowl involved, it took Texas's closing loss to A&M to decide the Hogs' destination.

If Arkansas had a chance to win in New Orleans against a veteran Alabama team vying for its second unbeaten season in a row, it was for Alabama to become complacent. This chance disappeared when Alabama slipped by a mere point and a half to No. 2 in the Associated Press poll early in December.

Given a cause, Alabama would not be deterred.

As is his nature ("Always prepare for the unexpected") Bryant collected film on every big game Lou Holtz had ever coached in. He catalogued the common denominators of all the major upsets—including the quick kicks. He booked the huge old Roosevelt Hotel on Canal Street for his team. Chefs were moved there from the campus to cook the Tide's usual meals.

Arkansas's players were given meal money. They could eat where and as they liked—or not.

Lou attended press conferences in his New York suits; Bryant, in coaching clothes.

Alabama came totally prepared for an impressive, inexorable 24-9 conquest of the Hogs sealed by an 82-yard drive at the end.

How big was that last drive? Well, down by just 17-9, the Hogs kicked the opponent back to his two-yard line and before the Hogs could get the ball again, it's over. That was wishbone power in the hands of fifth-year players rolling up the lightweight, youthful Hogs at the end.

The Razorbacks did compete. They scored first, but only a field goal after a fumble recovery on the opening kickoff, the only Tide turnover. They scored first in the third period when Scanlon completed a fourth-down pass to Farrell from the one-yard line to climax an 80-yard drive featuring short passes. Scanlon completed 22 of 39 passes for 245 yards against one of Bryant's best defenses ever.

But Alabama executed a superb, dominating game plan against the Hogs' vulnerable defense.

Bryant, who was doing it before Lou was born, twice quick-kicked from his own end zone, escaping traps each time, regaining momentum.

A notoriously hard loser, Holtz could not quibble.

He said, "The job facing us is obvious. We've got to get bigger and stronger, the way Alabama was."

That lofty goal proved unattainable.

— 41 —

DOWN TO EARTH

Beginning with the 1980s, Lou Holtz's one-liners suddenly lacked some of their snap and most of their humor.

His Arkansas teams had lost only five games in his first three years, two each to Texas and Houston at near their best and one to Alabama at its pinnacle.

His 1980 team lost five games, once by 17-16 to a Rice team that had trailed by 0-16 after three quarters in an arena at Little Rock where Holtz had cruised in all his 12 previous games.

For his four years of the eighties at Arkansas, his Hogs went 30-16-1 and finally in 1983 didn't even rate a bowl appearance.

Here are his five one-liners published in the *Arkansas Gazette* after the 23-17 loss to Texas on Labor Day evening in 1980, a special opening-the-decade offering arranged by Arkansas's old friends at ABC:

IRRETRIEVABLE
    "A loss is always disappointing. One to Texas is unbearable. So
    very many people are involved who don't have any control over
    the game. It's like someone gives you their money to hold and
    you lose it and can't give it back."

IN A NUTSHELL
    "You can't win, especially away from home, if you don't play great
    defense. We didn't. We couldn't get the football. If you want to get
    the football, you knock the other fellow down. We didn't."

INEXPERIENCE
    "Youth is not an 'out.' The people who played for us were on our
    practice field. When someone fails to learn, we fail to teach."

"This is really a poorly coached team. It hurts me to say that, but it's a fact."

WHAT'S AHEAD

"I don't know where this team is going. It may go right down the chute. But if they do, they're going to be one unhappy team doing it."

• • •

Later, at the end of the spring of 1983, Lou Holtz could do a better job of reading what he had. Then, he had said, "We are looking at a difficult time next fall, because our people can't control the line of scrimmage on either offense or defense."

That proved to be the truth. In Lou's final game at Arkansas, only Brad Taylor's determination swung the issue between two lack-luster teams playing let's-get-it-over-with on a dreary day at Lubbock. The

Billy Ray Smith jolts Texas passer Rick McIvor in the Hogs' 42-11 rout of the Longhorns in 1981.

THE RAZORBACKS

Quarterback Brad Taylor hurries through the fog of the 1981 Gator Bowl.

Hogs' 16-13 win over Texas Tech let them go 6-5 and avoid their first losing season since 1967 (4-5-1).

A man close to Lou had suggested to him in the preceding months, "You've stayed too long. In fact, you ought to move every three years, giving a lot of different people a chance to enjoy your flashdance before you get bored."

Lou Holtz was an ingenious, often absolutely brilliant coach at Arkansas—and probably everywhere else.

He had no equal in preparing a capable team for one major performance, especially when his team was the underdog.

There is a flip side to that.

He lost nine games in the final period at Arkansas. His tendency then was to use his team up early. He would be just as drained at the end, as well.

Of course, a team that loses in the last quarter was at least in the game all the way.

His team of 1982 took a 7-0 record (only the fifth such start at Arkansas to that time) to Waco. Baylor had lost four games in a row. Lou switched his quarterback rotation for that game, a fatal error. Baylor won, 24-17. What might have been his best team with his own players limped in 9-2-1.

Lou was not a highly successful recruiter at Arkansas. He had little to do with the wooing of his two greatest players, Billy Ray Smith (Dallas-reared but born in Fayetteville, son of the renowned first Billy Ray Smith) and Gary Anderson (who, after Jesse Branch brought him to Arkansas for a visit, declined to get into another airplane to look at Oklahoma or any other school that wanted him).

Holtz thrived later at Notre Dame because the Irish mystique and its system suck in pre-NFL players just naturally from everywhere.

The consensus was that he won big at Arkansas until he ran out of players left by Broyles—players who had been rounded up to a great extent by Leroy Montgomery, who decided to retire when Broyles did.

Recruiting was hard for Lou at Arkansas because he couldn't stand rejection, which is the nature of that game. If you don't want to hear a no, you don't chance one.

As a motivational specialist, as a coach who believes in coaching ("I'll take yours and you take mine and I'll still win"), Lou also tended, consciously or not, to under-value the importance of talent. Bud Wilkinson, winner of 47 games in a row over one stretch at Oklahoma, called recruiting 93 percent of the job. That may be high, but Wilkinson obviously practiced what he preached. He plucked his share of the best from Texas steadily.

It was also thought that Lou came to neglect Arkansas and its grateful but sensitive people.

Some took him very seriously when he said, "Fayetteville may not be the end of the world, but you can see it from there."

Others felt that his concurrent career as a speechmaker took him away from the state entirely too much.

Lou was born poor. He ached to be rich, but on his own merits.

The fame he gained at Arkansas opened all doors to him, from Johnny Carson's "Tonight Show" to the White House to the office of Wendy's Dave Thomas. At one time, Lou had two distant agents booking speeches for him. He would travel all night on redeye flights to meet dates. He would speak morning, noon, and night and anywhere, for any price.

He spoke on behalf of religious leaders involved in far-right politics. He became a hit speaker for President Ronald Reagan and Lou's long-time friend, Sen. Jesse Helms of North Carolina. His last public act at Arkansas was to make two television commercials endorsing Helms's senatorial candidacy, each filmed in his Fayetteville office adorned with Razorback logos. A furor resulted, and the ads were never shown, but he had violated University of Arkansas rules.

He would protest, "Aren't I a citizen?" Well, his wife had registered to vote in Arkansas, but he had not.

Lou would land in Fayetteville exhausted and ill-tempered. His staff often felt his irritability. He never would admit to the harm done as he pushed himself too hard physically and into dire emotional straits.

He constantly berated and lost assistant coaches and had trouble finding capable new ones. He would hire old cronies, as many head coaches do, but his would be just that, and not qualified to coach in a top-ten program.

He'd try to pick up the slack himself.

This is the way 1980 began: On the bus from the Superdome to the hotel after the loss to Alabama, the Arkansas coach said the Hogs would return in 1980 in the I-formation so that they could overpower defenses like Alabama's, that they would begin to recruit big, strong linemen and backs like Alabama's, that they would quit enrolling "brother-in-law athletes" that anybody could sign, that Bob Cope, the smallest man on his staff, would become the defensive coordinator to succeed the departing Monte Kiffin (whose touch wasn't replaced until Joe Kines arrived for Jack Crowe in 1991).

After the defense allowed Texas 400-plus yards the following Labor Day and exacted not one turnover, Holtz in effect fired Cope and took it over himself for the 19 days before the next game on the schedule.

That merely frustrated him, the defensive players, and the offense that usually claimed all his attention.

The defense—and everything else—hit bottom in a 42-15 loss at Baylor in November.

Which brings us to Lou's worst handicap.

Texas, Texas A&M, and Texas Tech remained decent during Lou's time in the league. Houston, Baylor, and SMU peaked, each winning championships, and Rice and TCU came back.

In fact, Lou Holtz hit Arkansas just in time to face the best athletes and the most top teams the Southwest Conference had ever known. It was the SWC's last hurrah before the cheating scandals and the NCAA penalties led to its downfall.

"The speed in this league is unreal," he said when he arrived. That had not changed when he left.

He set a new curve for Arkansas coaches through his time with a seven-year record of 60-21-2.

Ironically, although he snared one co-championship, Holtz never took his Razorbacks to the Cotton Bowl. And against Texas he fared about the same as all the other Arkansas coaches, 2-5.

– 42 –

PRECOCIOUS NEWCOMERS

Little did Arkansas's fine freshmen of 1979 realize that what was facing them in their four years would all but wind up the Lou Holtz regime.

Six newcomers started in the game at Texas A&M in 1979, dazzling a veteran Aggie team that had expected what Arkansas eventually got, a co-championship with Houston.

Kim Dameron, a little walk-on thrust into the Kyle Field fray at cornerback, pitched A&M split end Gerald Carter for a five-yard loss on the first play of the game—and made the next two as well.

Ron Matheney made his first start at the other corner. Darryl Bowles and Gary Anderson started as the two halfbacks. Billy Ray Smith and Ricky Richardson started in the defensive front, as they would for four years, and Phillip Boren relieved an injured regular at tackle during the game.

Other 1979 freshmen who would figure big in their time: Keith Burns in the secondary, Steve Douglas at linebacker, Jay Bequette at center, Derek Holloway as a receiver and kick returner, Earl Buckingham as a defensive end, Mark Douglas as a running back, and, through a quarterback's ups and downs, Tom Jones.

Lou Holtz didn't pick Tom Jones.

One spring day in 1978, Tom's father and his brother, the strapping, talented, and hard-nosed Bert Jones (of LSU and Colts fame) informed the Arkansas coach that they had picked him to coach Bert's brother at Arkansas. If necessary, Tom would walk on, without a scholarship.

They couldn't have made a better choice. Where Bert was hard and physical, Tom was soft and cerebral. Lou Holtz insists on cerebral. He *will* get into the heads of the people who play quarterback for him.

Tall and poised, Tom Jones didn't have the legs for running or the arm to rifle passes with. However, he could execute a Lou Holtz game plan, one that would lead him into special running situations and put receivers where he could lay soft passes into their hands.

Thus, he could put points on the board.

He could *not* stand up to the physical toll of playing every down against these SWC powerhouses.

And there were times when Lou's game plan, which would try to stretch the defense horizontally with options as well as vertically with passes of every length, might require a stronger, faster quarterback, hopefully with a stronger arm.

Thus, in 1981 and 1982, Arkansas put on some fantastic offensive exhibitions with Tom Jones *and* Brad Taylor, who, while hardly cerebral, rated tops as one heckuva country football player.

Plus, with Gary Anderson.

After Anderson's freshman season, Holtz had him pegged for Heisman candidacy down the line. That was a possibility until the 1982 season blew up late on the road, at Baylor, SMU (the famed, controversial 17-17 tie), and Texas. Actually, Anderson, like Lance Alworth in his time at Arkansas, never quite had the numbers. The guy who can do everything but is mostly spotted in special situations stars in the late-night bull sessions; the back who slogs down the field 27 times a game for 1,200 yards a year is the one who sways Heisman voters.

Anderson, pass receiver and punt returner as well as speedy runner with dipsy-do moves, did win MVP trophies in each of his last three bowl games, and he did give Texas fits all four times he played against the 'Horns.

As for Taylor, the home-state loyalty of the son of a Danville farmer and banker was used once to explain to Holtz why he was so lucky to be coaching at Arkansas. Taylor, just a regular kid who could run, pass, and punt and competed with reckless abandon, skipped the recruiting season and its folderol, even to ignoring Barry Switzer's invitation for a visit to OU. Taylor moved his act straight from Danville to the U of A, which was spared all the time and trouble.

Jones got little help from two freshmen, however, in what became the 7-5 disaster season of 1980.

The I-formation attack didn't fool Texas in the early opener (Jones threw for 178 yards and the Hogs ran for 151, mostly in chunks). The same offense scored just one touchdown in a scary 13-10 win over Tulsa 19 days later, even with the aid of five recovered fumbles.

Still, Arkansas was 4-1 going to Houston at the end of October. For four straight years, 1979-82, Bill Yeoman's Cougars came from behind in the fourth quarter to knock Holtz's Arkansas teams out of the Cotton Bowl. The tally in 1980 was 24-17.

Out of the race, the Razorbacks clearly blew that one to Rice in Little Rock, 17-16, and then got run over by Baylor and SMU. Only A&M's typically dismal play in Fayetteville and a fortunate 22-16 victory over Tech achieved a bowl bid. It wasn't much of one, to the Hall of Fame in Birmingham, where Tulane was clearly out-matched.

The final 7-5 record could have been worse.

Things picked up in 1981, a year of monumental highs and lows. The defense acquired a dynamic approach with Lou's hiring of Don Lindsey, an Arkie who had been John Robinson's right hand man at Southern Cal. The offense found a power back in Jessie Clark, a Crossett product who transferred after growing up some at Louisiana Tech, plus a blocking crew of Jay Bequette, Steve Korte, and Alfred Mohammed— plus freshman quarterback Taylor, late.

About 25,000 Arkansas fans helped form a Mississippi record crowd of 63,552 for the resumption of a storied series that had lapsed after 1961. Holtz had asked for the return of the Rebs to the schedule as a possible antidote to the fans' obsession with the Texas Longhorns. Frank Broyles readily agreed. For one thing, Ole Miss had long lost its status as a national power that whipped some of his best Arkansas teams.

With 5:46 to play, and Arkansas ahead by 20-13, Ole Miss quarterback John Fourcade threw a pass from the left hash mark all the way to the right boundary, a no-no even in the pros. Danny Walters read the pass easily and sped through Mark Harmon's route and stole it. The 87-yard runback sealed the 27-13 victory.

The next week, Holtz felt the sting of what probably had been inevitable—some year. Arkansas hadn't lost to TCU for 22 years, not since 1958. It happened, but did it have to be like this? Ahead by 24-13 with 5:13 to play, and TCU facing a third down at its three-yard line, the Frogs got away, 28-24.

In the delirious denouement, Steve Stamp passed 22 yards to Stanley Washington to complete that drive, then to Washington for 15 yards and the winning points after Jessie Clark lost a fumble on the previous play.

Two weeks later, Texas came to Arkansas fresh from a stomping of Oklahoma and rated No. 1.

The Razorbacks won, 42-11. Their fans even today can show pictures of the scoreboard in the fourth quarter, 42-3, a report card beyond their wildest dreams.

Holtz entered the game with a manila folder full of special scoring plays for Jones and Anderson. He spent three quarters sending them in, watching them work.

The story was, Texas had staked its hopes on passing quarterback Rick McIvor, who could and would fumble and throw poorly at times, and a kick returner who would make bad decisions.

Harassed by the Smith-led swarm, Texas made so many mistakes from in front of its goal, it had an average of 88 yards to go and Arkansas, only 44. In effect, Texas played the game from the bottom of a well—and drowned.

A tornado had been forecast for the kickoff. It was mere rain and wind—but the Hogs took an 18-0 lead against it. Smith recovered McIvor's fumble at the Texas 21, Jones hit Anderson with a screen pass for 14, and Jones scored from a yard out. Stopped at its own 6, Texas snapped the ball over the punter's head for a safety. Jeff Goff recovered Jam Jones's fumble at his 5 on the next play and Anderson romped in on the play after that. After Anderson returned a punt 16 yards to the Texas 45, Bruce Lahay kicked a 47-yard field goal. Kim Dameron intercepted a McIvor pass and Jones beat the clock with a 19-yard touchdown pass to Anderson for a 25-3 halftime lead. So it went.

Fred Akers's team started from its own 21, 6, 5, 2, 15, 15, 3, 20, and 20 in the first half and lost two fumbles, gave up a safety, and threw an interception.

The scoreboard constantly flashed, "Fantastic," an understatement.

The next week, Tom Jones, with a beat-up arm and a sore knee, played on only two possessions against Houston at Little Rock. He passed for two touchdowns. When it was 17-10, Arkansas freshman Bill Pierce forced two passes, and Houston intercepted and cashed in both for the 10 decisive points, 20-17. That hurt.

While freshman Brad Taylor emerged to star against Rice and play key roles in three wins in a row—including a 41-39 defeat of Baylor in which Clark scored five touchdowns—upping the Hogs to 8-2, the Coogs in the final analysis had done it to Lou again.

The Hogs could not overcome SMU's great team that rallied late for a 32-18 win at Fayetteville on an Eric Dickerson breakaway.

Finally, in the Gator Bowl, three North Carolina I-backs ran right at the Hogs, confounding Lindsey's blitzing schemes, building up a lead that even Taylor's flinging deep to little Derek Holloway in the late fog could not overcome. The Tar Heels held, 31-28.

Some fans wondered. Some just accepted the excitement. Some thought this cast might return for better things in 1982. It did, to a point.

— 43 —

FIT TO BE TIED

The tipoff that something huge might be possible in 1982 came in the opener, a 38-0 thumping of Tulsa.

John Cooper's Hurricane had held the Razorbacks to cloudy 13-10 and 14-0 wins in the previous seasons.

Coming on in the second period, Brad Taylor reprised his Gator Bowl doings with the 5'7" Derek Holloway, who had caught bombs of 66, 44, and 43 yards at Jacksonville. They broke Tulsa's back with a 67-yarder that made it 10-0 and teamed for five receptions worth 169 yards.

Some fans applauded the end of yields of 31, 32, and 39 points in the team's previous three games. Billy Ray Smith certainly did, noting with pride that this was the first "0" he'd seen on a scoreboard in his four seasons. Indeed, against a minimum of stunting by Lindsey's men, Tulsa didn't threaten to score.

From there, the Hogs breezed to 7-0, and to top five status, slowing just once—in a 14-12 win over Ole Miss.

Holtz enjoyed the luxury of a 38-3 win at Houston.

Actually, he and the fans could see all the way to a November 20 showdown against SMU, at its modern best, in Texas Stadium. The Ponies had already defeated Texas, which Arkansas would meet at Austin in another of those games moved to December for television.

Thus, the Razorbacks, and everybody else, overlooked Baylor.

Two years before, the veteran Grant Teaff's team had swept the SWC, 8-0. Rebuilding in 1982, they stood 2-5-1 with four humiliating losses in a row.

However, Teaff always had a good book on Arkansas. The Bears knew that, in a normal year, the timing was such that a win over the Hogs meant a bowl game. Out of season, they devoted as much time to preparing for Arkansas as they did on Texas.

They groomed a cagey fifth-year quarterback, Mike Brannan, to operate a special mixture of I-formation and veer-T offenses, each featuring power running and play-action passes plus options.

They would have to be patient, because the Arkansas defense had not yielded even a 20-yard run all year.

However, by its nature, Arkansas's defense could be set up for what are called "crack-flag" passes—essentially passes down the middle after fakes to the fullback or tailback. "Up" for the challenges posed by the Hogs, Baylor, though behind immediately by 14-0, found it could stay and compete and slowly established a tenacious ground game that set up deadly little passes—and the occasional down-the-middle longer ones.

Offensively, Holtz did not start Tom Jones, who, though not physical, had been valuable in setting up the other team for Taylor.

Baylor knew this about Taylor: The excitable young man did not like to stay in the pocket. He preferred to throw on the run. He did this well, but Holtz's game plan would use the whole field, whereas a sprintout pass play thrown on the run from near the boundary uses only half of it.

Just as tenacious on defense, Baylor got into a mode that stopped Taylor and his offense six times near the Baylor 30, usually against the wind and out of field-goal range. Brannan doggedly held the Bears together. They got better every period. Against the wind in the final period, Brannan won the game with one gritty play after another—and some faltering by the Razorbacks.

With 7:19 to play, Arkansas apparently had stopped the Bears at the 16, after one of those play-action passes over the fooled Arkansas safety netted 60 yards. A barefooted, left-footed kicker named Ken Perry came in and hit a low, ugly 33-yard field goal to tie it at 17-all.

Holtz at that stage of his career liked quick retaliation tries with trick plays.

With Gary Anderson sidelined by a toe injury and Jessie Clark knocked out with a hip-pointer and two smashed teeth, Holtz decided to go for it all with two lesser lights. Mark Mistler came around from the Hogs' 20 on a flanker reverse. Tailback Thomas Brown went into the right flat and turned up field. Mistler, a onetime quarterback, threw it. What was a botched play wound up as an interception by Preston Davis at the Arkansas 47. Baylor powered it in, mostly with the powerful Alfred Anderson right up the middle, in 10 plays.

The 24-17 loss shocked what had been the nation's No. 4 team. Its four previous SWC foes had scored 0, 3, 3, and 6 points.

Years together, Holtz and Larry Beightol, the feisty, prized offensive line coach, parted company bitterly over the recriminations from that loss. Beightol found a home in the NFL.

To Lou's credit, he and his Hogs recovered fully.

They blitzed Texas A&M, 35-0, and headed all business for Texas Stadium and the Ponies, whose illegally assembled greats were enjoying their third year in a five-year run toward the NCAA death penalty.

Seen for just one series at Baylor, Tom Jones started and executed beautifully in the rout of A&M, both running and passing. He obviously felt a lift.

Thanks in part to Arkansas fans, who always loved to travel to Dallas, SMU had its first sellout crowd since the days of Doak Walker after they enlarged the Cotton Bowl for him in the late 1940s.

One of the two or three best-played Arkansas games under Holtz resulted only in a 17-17 tie that pleased SMU, which finished the game 10-0-1 and repeat SWC champion with its first Cotton Bowl host role since 1966—and distressed and deflated Arkansas beyond belief.

Said Holtz: "At the six-minute mark (when the Hogs led by 17-10), I thought it was a perfect football game for us. We moved the football, did not turn the ball over, did not give up a cheap touchdown, and had them on third and long at their 20."

Then came the flag. Here's the background: Arkansas's defense was a fit for SMU's attack featuring the fabled Eric Dickerson and Craig James as alternating I-backs and Lance McIlhenny running an option attack. McIlhenny wasn't an artful passer, and the running game could be crowded, which was the Hogs' style under Don Lindsey.

McIlhenny, nonetheless, had a stunning game.

So did Tom Jones. He converted 9 of 20 third downs and 4 of 4 fourth downs.

When SMU took a 10-7 lead, though, Holtz inserted Taylor. Punted back to his 8, Taylor hurled a bootleg pass to Holloway for 45 to the SMU 41. That set up a 27-yard field goal by Martin Smith, the swimmer from England Holtz had drafted to kick placements, tying it.

Jones took the Hogs 83 yards on their next possession. His 24-yard pass to Anderson, caught leaping on a crossing route, put the ball on the 5. Anderson hurdled people with an option pitch from Jones for the last three yards.

From his 20, McIlhenny did not pass; he made five on the option.

Tackle Bobby Shantz, rushing the passer, cut down Dickerson for a loss of four on a draw play. On third and eight, McIlhenny sent Bobby Leach against cornerback Nate Jones. Leach caught it against tight coverage for 21.

From the SMU 43, McIlhenny decided to pick on Jones again with a rare deep pass, this time to Jackie Wilson deep down the left boundary.

The consensus was that Wilson pushed Jones from behind, offensive interference. But veteran official Horton Nesrsta, once a famed Rice punt returner, called the foul against Jones.

The resulting 40-yard penalty to the Arkansas 17, 4:25 left, set up McIlhenny's touchdown on a third and two and Don Harrell's tying kick. (SMU coach Bobby Collins wasn't greedy. He'd take the luckily attained tie—and the title—on a day when the other team might have played better.)

That was that, but what came out of the reporters' visits to the locker rooms made big headlines the next day—and changed the game of college football.

No player on either side thought Jones was guilty, and SMU's Wilson claimed credit for yelling at Jones, doing anything to make Nesrsta think that the Arkansas player, not him, was the guilty party. He rolled the dice, Wilson said, with nothing to lose, and won.

Nesrsta was dropped from the SWC officiating rolls. The NCAA Football Rules Committee, listening to Holtz, changed the rules to reduce pass interference penalties to 15 yards and ordered that penalties be ignored on un-catchable balls. This negated the effect of fouls on late-game Hail Mary passes.

The major shock was that the SWC, listening to an Arkansas coach after all these years, voted to institute officiating by set crews created on merit ratings—with nothing to keep a qualified Arkansas graduate from working an Arkansas game or a qualified Texas graduate out of a 'Horns game.

This lasted seven years, until a (correct) decision by ex-Razorback Ron Underwood resulted in pass interference against Texas A&M that led to a 23-22 Arkansas win in the SWC championship game of 1989.

The league quickly agreed that it wasn't right for one Arkie to see what five Texas officials wouldn't—and caved in to the Aggies before another season arrived. Old grads again were barred from working their schools' games, even if they were the top-rated callers at their positions.

Unfortunately, the SMU tie didn't end the season. Rested and hungry, Texas was waiting at Austin to avenge that 42-11 thing of 1981, and did. Arkansas, not mentally sharp, limited the 'Horns to just four first downs on the ground, but Fred Akers didn't mind. They'd honed all kinds of things to create big plays off fakes that sucked in the Hogs' ground swarm and won, 33-7.

Lou's best class of his own went out with a 9-2-1 finish and a happy Bluebonnet Bowl game. At the Astrodome, Holtz had Anderson running 26 times as an I-back behind Jessie Clark. Gary netted 161 yards and two touchdowns in the final period as the Hogs beat back Florida, 28-24. But it was too late for the Heisman.

— 44 —

"AM I FIRED?"

To get Don Lindsey, both brilliant and unorthodox, Lou Holtz had agreed to give the Camden native the same arrangement the latter had with John Robinson at Southern Cal. Lindsey would run the defense without interference from the head coach.

This became a source of constant pain to Holtz in 1983, when he found himself without the kind of players required to run Lindsey's gambling scheme. It takes a talented secondary to back up a front seven or eight committed to forcing tactics mostly against the run. By 1983, Arkansas had only two defensive players of great ability, safety Greg Lasker and Ravin Caldwell, and they were both sophomores not ready for much risk taking.

The truth was that schemes weren't the problem. This was a squad without a single standout down lineman or running back, which is where natural ability prevails.

Holtz's philosophy mandated doing whatever it took to avoid giving up big plays, to win by making the other team go long distances and pay for every yard. You needed to do this even more so when the other team had the better players. However, he had ceded decisions in that area to Lindsey.

Lou watched tight-lipped in 1983 as Texas again plundered Lindsey's scheme for over 200 yards on five big plays in a 31-3 rout. Brad Taylor at his best could not overcome such as that. With a big lead, Texas teed off on him.

Baylor rolled up whopping stars in a 24-21 win. Late against Texas A&M, Arkansas switched to man-to-man coverage all over the field. A&M hit big plays on every possession and won, 36-23.

Now 5-4, Arkansas needed an upset of mighty SMU in Little Rock to hope for any kind of a bowl bid. The Ponies defeated teams with their running and their defensive talent. Lou knew that his only chance to win would be to limit the length of the SMU runs. He inserted this into the Hogs' concise, two-page official game plan: On short yardage, no defense would be used that put an excessive number of players on the line of scrimmage.

Arkansas got a break. Rain fell in torrents on War Memorial Stadium. Bobby Collins wisely threw out risky options and passes. The Ponies would not gamble against the elements and a fired-up underdog.

It was 0-0 in the second period when SMU faced a third and short at its own 34-yard line. Lance McIlhenny handed to his I-back, Reggie Dupard, an All-American type. With nine Razorbacks on the line, everybody crashed and slanted, and nobody touched Dupard. He went 66 yards right down the sprinkler heads. SMU won, 17-0.

The enraged Holtz scarcely did any on-the-field coaching that final week, but his 5-5 team rallied to a wet and raggedy 16-13 win at Lubbock. There, at the end, the game Taylor reverted back to Danville, doing whatever to win, which he did.

No bowl game called, not that Lou cared.

In a few days, he fired the three defensive aides under Lindsey. He never formally fired Lindsey, but the latter assumed as much in a press conference he called the next day.

If necessary, Lou had the SMU game plan handy, the one which Lindsey had, in Lou's mind, ignored.

Such things take place. Charley Coffey's version of the old Tennessee wide-tackle-six defense stopped the Texas vaunted wishbone unthinkably dead in the Big Shootout of 1969. Throughout the 1970 season he insisted that it would work again in the rematch at Austin. Frank Broyles told him that Texas would defeat such a defense the second time. When Coffey remained adamant, he was told that his job was at stake. The day after the 42-7 loss, Coffey was on his way to a head job Broyles had helped find for him at Virginia Tech.

Frank Broyles never wanted to fire Holtz, never intended to until he felt he had no choice. Although totally different, and sometimes at odds on how certain things should be done, Broyles and Holtz had a common ground in the offensive game plan.

Luckily for Lou, his athletic director seldom attended an Arkansas game. Broyles for nine years, through 1985, was usually gone from Thursday until sometime Sunday working under Keith Jackson as the coach-analyst for NCAA Football on ABC-TV.

As succeeding coaches learned, Broyles watched Arkansas games not as athletic director or former coach or fan, but as all three.

He was instantly, severely critical, usually of inside things gone wrong that, as an alert, lifelong technician, he spotted immediately.

Frank and Lou had their best times on Sunday evenings. Lou would have finished the game plan for the up-coming week. Frank would have returned from his game and worked out. He would sit in the steam room and listen to Lou tell what he was preparing for the next foe. Coaches win all their games in their game plans, but Lou's kept his boss fascinated and intrigued.

Coaching the games wasn't Lou's problem at Arkansas. And it didn't bother Frank so much that Holtz upset the faculty by making television commercials for Sen. Jesse Helms of North Carolina, a man so repugnant to women and blacks, among others. Lou's old friend Jesse was conducting a one-man filibuster against the establishment of Martin Luther King Day while the Arkansas staff was calling black mothers trying to recruit their sons.

Lou wasn't that political. He just liked being invited to the White House and knowing powerful friends.

Broyles didn't object to the mass firings of the defensive staff, either. What tore everything was the telephone calls he had made around the state concerning a bumper crop of athletes. Not only Keith Jackson of Little Rock Parkview, but almost all of the blue-chippers planned to leave the state, many for Oklahoma.

Broyles knew that Holtz's inability to maintain a strong squad and a staff of effective coaches had put the program in great jeopardy. He doubted that Holtz, who had never stayed anywhere past four years, retained the enthusiasm needed to win Arkansas people and athletes all over again.

When Lou returned from a recruiting trip (making a speech?) shortly after noon on a Sunday in December, he answered a phone call from Broyles.

He blurted out immediately, "Am I fired?"

Broyles, who abhors confrontations, let that slide. He said, "Lou, you need to come over here as soon as you can."

Holtz hit Broyles's office talking, saying, "Coach, help me find another job. I'll take anything, the lowest one. I'm going to prove that I can coach."

Hardly anyone bought the official version, that Lou had resigned because of "burnout."

He soon signed on at Minnesota, which was, indeed, the "lowest" place there was at the time. And he did, indeed, prove again that he could coach.

His further deal with Broyles was that Frank would do and say nothing that would keep him from getting the one job he still wanted, the one at Notre Dame. That worked out well. They remained friends and admirers.

Before his 11 A.M. Monday meeting with the media, Lou Holtz had cleaned out his office and settled completely with the University of Arkansas.

Fred Vorsanger, the university's chief finance officer, described Lou as "a real pro."

"He was due two checks, for about $125,000 each, one for what was left in his contract, one from the incentive fund we set up to influence him to stay. I asked if he needed any help on deferring any of the money. He said he'd just take it all in one check."

If Holtz didn't get rich at Arkansas, he came close. He left with direct payments of about $250,000 from the Razorback Foundation, up to $100,000 in a profit on the sale of his house (which the purchasers said they intended to be a boon for the ex-coach), and around $600,000 from the sweetheart Little Rock cable television deal that Jackson T. Stephens had arranged for him.

The figure Lou quoted to a close coaching friend was, "Over $800,000."

Most fans felt that Lou had stayed his time, but some felt like the Wolfpack booster who said after Lou's departure from North Carolina State, "He was crazy, of course, but I wish we had him back."

Crazy, of course, like a fox.

– 45 –

THE MAN OF THE MOMENT

Ken Hatfield proved that you *can* go home. You just can't stay.

He had a choice toward enhancing his popularity, one man had told him.

He could either beat Texas, or, with his 10-2 records, drop in at the men's grill of the Country Club of Little Rock and have a few drinks and, for a spell, make a pleasant fool out of himself.

Ken shrugged wryly.

Ken Hatfield returned to his alma mater to coach football and make them the Fightin' Razorbacks the way they were when he was the nation's best punt returner in the 1960s.

He didn't come back to cultivate a role as conquering hero or to cater to his old coach's high-toned friends and millionaire acquaintances or to anyone else.

When he returned to the campus after a 19-year career elsewhere, one that prepared him pretty much perfectly for the job, coaching-wise, he perhaps expected to remain forever. Frank Broyles, now his boss, certainly thought he would.

Ken Hatfield stayed one month over six years. On the day in 1990 when he had said he would sign a solid longterm contract, a reward for two 10-2 seasons, two SWC championships, and two Cotton Bowl trips in a row, all in 1988 and 1989, and after posting the best winning percentage in the school's history, .760 on 55-17-1, Hatfield got a surprise call offering him the job at Clemson. Sight unseen, he accepted it.

The call came, it is said, right after Ken and his wife, Sandy, had read that Broyles, then freshly 65 (and with tenure not affected by the school's age limit of 70), had just accepted a new five-year contract.

To begin with, Broyles had considered himself fortunate to have found such a paragon for this position from one of his own.

To replace Lou Holtz, he announced in December, 1983, he would consider only former Razorbacks, mainly Barry Switzer of Oklahoma, Fred Akers of Texas, Jimmy Johnson of Oklahoma State, and Ken Hatfield of Air Force.

Switzer and Akers each wanted to be romanced, as all coaches do, thus enhancing their value where they are, but there wasn't time for that. Besides, Broyles knew that no coach willingly separates himself from positions like those at OU and UT.

However talented, Jimmy Johnson was well known to Broyles as a former aide and as a man sometimes too hot to handle, certainly at an avowedly simon-pure place like Arkansas. Johnson was even then on the verge of problems with the NCAA, which would hit OSU hard after he left the following June for Miami (and a blazing ascent to the peak of his profession).

Ken Hatfield prepares to sign something, but it wasn't a contract extension.

Hatfield proved to be the man of the moment. Coaching-wise, he had everything anybody could be looking for. In 1986, at the height of the reform waves in the presidents' takeover of the NCAA, Alabama wanted Hatfield, who demurred, and UCLA was ready to bid for him if their coach took a certain pro job, which he didn't.

As an undergraduate at Arkansas, Ken Hatfield had the leadership, the dedication, the discipline, the competitive, never-say-die spirit, and the smarts it took to be football hero, academic All-American with a degree in accounting, ROTC brigade commander, and student body president.

He fulfilled his military commitment coaching freshmen at West Point, where he battled coaches such as Bobby Knight and Bill Parcells endlessly at racquetball while his teams stayed unbeaten.

He coached under Doug Dickey, Broyles's former top aide, at Tennessee (when the Vols had the best record in college for one five-year period) and Florida. He went to Air Force to call plays for Parcells in

Ken Hatfield found a meal-ticket receiver in James Shibest to build around.

1978, then became head coach a year later when Parcells left for the New York Giants, which he took to a Super Bowl championship.

After a first typically miserable year at Air Force, 2-9, Hatfield developed a five-point plan which the Academy superintendent accepted, albeit dubiously. Against the advice of "everybody," Hatfield vowed that the wishbone formation and its triple option attack could work where it never had, at a have-not instead of Texas, Oklahoma, Alabama, et cetera.

Late in the 1983 season, Air Force's jazzed-up "flexbone" beat Notre Dame for the second straight year, this time at South Bend, to cap a 10-2 season. The small, quick Falcons out-foxed the Irish behemoths with passing and options and ran them ragged so that, at the finish, Hatfield's fullbacks repeatedly netted big gains at the middle.

Broyles noted all that while helping describe the game for ABC's national telecast. It was that sudden, refreshing eye-opener, coming after almost nineteen years in which he and Hatfield had had almost no contact.

Hatfield had a good thing at Air Force, just one man to please, and he had lifted the spirits in the uniforms there by whipping Army and Navy regularly. He was not on his hands and knees pleading for the Arkansas job. He was, however, amenable to returning to the University and the state that he loved, once and for always.

Some high-placed fans in Little Rock wanted Johnson; so what if it took a hickey from the NCAA to get the program rebuilt. They launched a mini-campaign for Johnson, who was trying for the job he had also coveted in December, 1976.

Broyles hastily hired Hatfield.

— 46 —

MORE "BONE" THAN "FLEX"

From the start, Ken Hatfield stayed home and tended to business, allowing for recruiting trips, a refreshing change to many at Arkansas.

"We've traded nonsense for sense," one man said.

Wilson Matthews, winding up his career as a popular fund-raiser, again heard the practice field words of his coaching career: "Quick, quick, quick. Stay low. Do your best this play."

Broyles liked it that not once did Hatfield or his aides complain about the lack of talent. Heck, they'd had worse at Air Force.

They'd win at Arkansas with over-achievers, the school's tradition. They'd run an offense other teams hated to play against, blockers scrambling after the defenders' knees. They'd play a gap-control defense which, almost an eight-man front, made running gains hard to come by and long runs almost impossible. They would *not* turn the ball over. Using all four downs a lot, they would seem, on some Saturdays, to keep the ball forever.

Auburn coach Pat Dye said at the Liberty Bowl after Hatfield's first year, "It's a pleasure watching Arkansas's films. They play football the way it ought to be played, the way it used to be played."

Still, talent prevailed. Held to nothing until a late handoff, future Heisman trophy winner Bo Jackson broke outside on a busted play and sped 40 yards to clinch Auburn's 21-15 victory.

That had been the story of the 7-4-1 campaign. It was a success.

Brad Taylor gave Hatfield a commitment. He took the hits, finishing up as a down-the-line option runner so he could set up the passing and the running by Ken's ever-present alternating fullbacks, Marshall Foreman and Derrick Thomas, one of them always fresh and dangerous.

Taylor finished with well-earned school career total offense and passing records.

A one-year transfer, Danny Nutt came off the bench hitting receivers, which included James Shibest, slow but sure, and a future record-setter, and Bobby Joe Edmonds, out of the backfield, deadly (like Shibest) on Hatfield's favorite crossing routes.

Tony Cherico, a freshman flake Hatfield had tried to recruit for Air Force, came off a redshirt year to become so much a pest at nose guard, he had to be double- and triple-teamed.

They won plaudits opening night by playing Ole Miss to a 14-14 tie after yielding two easy touchdowns to the Rebs right out of the gate.

For six weeks in the middle of the season, they went 5-1 in SWC play, losing only to Texas. At Austin, Taylor had thrown one interception after another. He was 0 for 10 and the 'Horns led, 24-3. Hatfield counseled his quarterback, "Wouldn't it feel great to win this one? It's not too late." Using mostly those crossing routes, Taylor passed for over 200 yards in the last period and had it inside the Texas five-yard line when the clock ran out. Texas survived, 24-18.

The same thing happened at SMU. Despite Shibest's greatest game, SMU held on, 31-28.

What hurt the most had taken place in Fayetteville on October 6. In Hatfield's first game as a SWC head coach, his team had TCU down by 31-14 late in the third period and was kicking at a likely field goal. The kick missed and TCU won on a two-point play as time ran out, 32-31.

That loss hung over the Hogs all year.

Hatfield played that season largely with what Holtz left him.

He redshirted virtually all of his 1984 recruiting class, mainly because he had not been able to change the decisions of impact players like Keith Jackson and Mark Hutson, who both kept their pledges to Oklahoma.

A freshman who did play in 1984, if only a little, proved a key man in the next three years. Unable to sign a renowned quarterback, Hatfield had come across Greg Thomas in San Angelo, Texas, Central. Thomas had committed to Baylor as a defensive back. When Hatfield recruited him late as a quarterback, he switched.

Thomas wasn't very fast, and he wasn't a strong-armed passer, but he carried the load in three seasons that produced 28 wins.

Hatfield's 1985 crop was also mostly redshirted, but halfback James Rouse, offensive guard Fred Childress, and kicker Kendall Trainor made a difference.

So did Mark Calcagni, the younger brother, a senior who in many games served as a spot passer in the place of Thomas.

When this group started 1985 going 5-0 with Texas next at Fayetteville, fans stirred again.

By now, Hatfield's offense was more "bone" than "flex." They had never had a runner at Air Force like Rouse, nor a guard like Childress. Against Texas, the Hogs stressed Rouse running left from right halfback over Childress, the 300-pound left guard.

That day, though, the difference was in the kicking. Texas's Jeff Ward kept hitting majestic field goals. A not-great Texas team went home a 15-13 winner. It was the first UT team Arkansas had held without a touchdown since that 6-0 win in 1936.

In Hatfield's stay, or the start of it, the strength of the league was not at Texas or Houston (which he always beat, as he did Rice, Ole Miss, Tulsa, and the other nonconference foe) but at Baylor, Texas A&M, and SMU, which Arkansas faced in a row in November. The way their schedules fell, each had an open date before they played the Hogs. On paper, this negated some of the Arkansas advantage in using the wishbone and the seldom-seen gap-control defense.

Winning two of those three was good. The Hogs lost a 10-6 bloodletting at A&M to Jackie Sherrill's first powerful Aggies' array, but Luther Franklin caught a sucker pass to beat Baylor, 20-14, at Little Rock, and SMU played in lack-luster style at Fayetteville and went down, 15-9.

With that, Arkansas went to San Diego for a Holiday Bowl game against Arizona State that Calcagni (to Shibest and Edmonds) saved and Trainor won, 18-17, with a last-minute field goal.

The 10-2 season indicated the squad's growing strength. Fans began looking for something awesome. The start in 1986, wallopings of Ole Miss, Tulsa, New Mexico State, and TCU, whetted appetites.

For the third year in a row, Arkansas lost a win-able game in Razorback Stadium. David McWilliams's Texas Tech team, in his first and only year there, played a perfect game and the Hogs didn't and lost, 17-7.

The next week, in an ugly one, new halfback Joe Johnson kept running right at Texas in Austin, and Arkansas prevailed, 21-14. (That one probably cost Fred Akers his job—and the result the previous week at Fayetteville probably designated his successor, McWilliams.)

So the Hogs went 7-1 into the crunch-filled finish. Beat up, they couldn't hold off a brilliant Cody Carlson, who rallied Baylor for a 29-14 win. But Thomas played his finest game as a Razorback against Texas

A&M at Little Rock, executing a special game plan of short passes that Hatfield had saved since spring, and the Hogs won, 14-10. Odis Lloyd tipped away the final pass at the A&M goal line. It was a sweet win; the Aggies obviously were loaded with pre-NFL talent.

That netted an Orange Bowl bid. The next week in Texas Stadium, SMU, beset by all the problems that led to the NCAA death penalty, just showed up and yielded, 41-0. That produced a second straight 9-2 regular season.

The Orange Bowl opponent would be Oklahoma.

Hatfield's Hogs, it seemed, had reached the bigtime.

Just not yet. Barry Switzer, a coach at Arkansas in Hatfield's last year as a player, made Ken pay for what Holtz had done to him in the 1978 Orange Bowl.

All night, Arkansas's little wishbone made one little play after another, moving the stakes, controlling the clock. From the second quarter on, when Spencer Tillmon streaked down the sidelines to cover big distances twice with late option play pitches, Oklahoma's big league wishbone fed the scoreboard. The Sooners won, 42-8.

Heaven for the Hogs would have to wait a little longer.

— 47 —

A TERRIBLE SILENCE

By returning practically everybody and exhibiting new stars like safety Steve Atwater, defensive tackle Wayne Martin, and fullback Barry Foster, and after beating the Aggies, the likely team of the decade, in the last two of three, Arkansas was picked to win the SWC in 1987.

One day in August, a man told Ken Hatfield, "You know this is going to be the worst year of your life, don't you?"

Hatfield nodded.

No Arkansas team had ever won when it was picked. Actually, except for Texas, only 12 percent of the SWC favorites ever won titles. The chosen team gets fat-headed; the other teams gear for them; bad things happen to the favorite.

Worse, he would be risking a whipping by mighty Miami early and right in his own front yard.

After Miami beat Oklahoma a second time in a row, and in Norman, Switzer told Jimmy Johnson, "You and your players are too good for us. Someone else can play you."

Given the schedule, and mindful of fans' criticism of the Hogs' traditional soft non-league opponents, Hatfield opted to take OU's place on the Miami slate.

Jimmy Johnson saw him coming. He scheduled a weak opener, then left two open dates leading up to his vengeful return to Little Rock.

Meanwhile, Hatfield was playing Ole Miss and Tulsa, two blood rivals of a sort.

At Ole Miss, Hatfield could see the makings of his good team. He also noticed when, with the score 31-10, passer Greg Thomas took a lick that separated his shoulder.

This wasn't publicized until late in the year, but Thomas did not throw in practice the rest of the year, nor did he practice at all at times. He played as best he could, or else yielded to Quinn Grovey, a redshirted freshman who was obviously the star of the future but needed time to master the passing. Grovey also got banged up immediately.

There hadn't been a non-SWC game in Little Rock so big since 1974, when the Southern Cal series ended with an Arkansas upset, 22-7.

It was practically a tossup in the betting line. Miami won, 51-7.

The Hogs threatened early, but Trainor missed a field goal. The rout was on. Miami looked like the Dallas Cowboys of a few years later—and that was partly the case.

Switzer observed, "The man who scheduled that game must be trying to get Kenny fired."

A devout fundamentalist, Hatfield freely offered that, "Everything is in the Bible. The flexbone is in there somewhere."

He read his book daily, put a message from it on the players' training room wall every day.

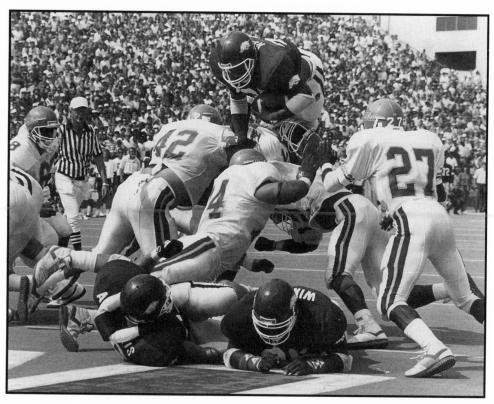

James Rouse soars over the top for one of his 17 touchdowns in 1987.

It was also his custom to start his Sunday television show with a biblical quote. After the massacre by Miami, as terrible a defeat as Arkansas had ever suffered in a match of Top 10 teams, Hatfield quoted John 11:35, "Jesus wept."

He tried to explain it later by saying, "It seemed appropriate."

Both secular and religious leaders fumed at the very idea.

Two weeks later, after Grovey picked Tech and TCU apart on the road, the Razorbacks returned to Little Rock to play what was yet another beatable Texas team.

John Bland, the Hogs' third-string quarterback, described the end of the game, which few UT fans attended.

"A terrible silence," he called it. "I could see the Texas players jumping up and down but I couldn't hear a thing. It was like watching a TV set with the sound off."

Well aware of Thomas's lame arm, Texas covered every receiver closely man-for-man, with 10 men almost on the line of scrimmage to smother the 'bone. Early, Thomas tried a bomb to his great-to-be freshman receiver, Derek Russell, but it became a dud at the goal line. He tried to beat middle linebacker John Hagy with a pass to his tight end over the middle. Hagy intercepted and returned it for a touchdown.

Barry Foster pops clean against TCU, as he did against many other teams.

THE RAZORBACKS

Hatfield had seen enough. He would call not one pass over the last three periods.

The strategy seemed to be working. Arkansas ran for over 200 yards in the second period alone, and Thomas carried the ball in twice for a 14-7 halftime lead. Thomas re-injured his shoulder, and Grovey re-injured a groin pull, and the Arkansas offense did not threaten the last half.

Again and again, the defense swarmed Eric Metcalf, the terrific little 'Horns halfback who took hits as a runner or receiver on almost every play.

Late, Texas hit a field goal, 14-10.

With 1:40 to play, a Texas receiver dropped a pass near midfield. The officials let it be a fumble. Steve Atwater seemed to have the ball, but officials waited as the players wrestled for it. Referee Frank Shepard unpiled them and awarded Texas the ball.

Later, Hatfield would say, "I thought that was the killer. It will be remembered like the crooked field goal by Ole Miss in 1960."

Wrong. Only one play is remembered from the game that day. With fourth and goal at the Arkansas 18 and four seconds on the clock, after the previous play went out of bounds and after Arkansas's Fred Goldsmith called a timeout "to set my linebackers" when Texas had no

Barry Switzer and Ken Hatfield share a laugh before the Arkansas-Oklahoma Orange Bowl rematch of January 1, 1987. Switzer did all the laughing afterward.

Quinn Grovey became the first quarterback to lead Arkansas to consecutive Cotton Bowl bids.

timeout left, Bret Stafford threw down field and into the end zone. Arkansas had three men there. One thought he'd tipped the ball, but it went into the supposedly bad hands of the shortest man on the field, 5'7" Tony Jones.

Texas didn't bother to kick the extra point in "the awful silence" of all those Razorback fans sitting there stunned . . . and bitter . . . and hateful.

Leaving the field, going up the ramp (which is uncovered where the home team exits), Hatfield heard the hoots and taunts, felt something liquid.

He told the writers asking his reaction to all that, "I've got the hide of an alligator," but he didn't.

Before long, as questioning intensified, he said quietly, firmly, in his Old Testament manner, "Nothing is forgotten. Nothing is forgiven," and left the interview room.

Arkansas fans, noting that, came to exercise the same options.

Hatfield knew then, and repeated again and again, that he had followed a strategy that Bear Bryant, Frank Broyles, and many others had used when they were leading in a big game and, crippled offensively, opted to play safe, not give away points with offensive mistakes, depend on kicking and defense to maintain the margin. No one listened.

Fans fumed on. Pundits on both sides of the notorious Little Rock newspaper war jumped in as critics. There had been a terrific traffic jam all the way to Russellville after one game, John Brummett wrote, because, "Hatfield wouldn't pass."

The coach had much work left, and his team responded. They lost just once in the final six games on the schedule, by only 14-0 at Texas A&M when none of four quarterbacks could function.

It was back to the Liberty Bowl, where the Hogs blew a 17-14 lead late to a Georgia team they had on the run. On two third and threes (a punt would have backed the Dogs up each time), Hatfield called for Thomas to pass. What irony. Each pass was tipped, Georgia intercepted both times, and Georgia kicked two field goals to win, 20-17.

The longest, worst year of Hatfield's life, including a 12th regular-season game at Hawaii, where he and his aides worried that, even with a 9-4 record, they'd be fired when they landed in Arkansas, was over.

— 48 —

BARGAINING STALEMATE

The best thing about Ken Hatfield at Arkansas was that he knew the ins and outs of college football and that he could coach.

Said Frank Broyles, "He was a 10 in a lot of areas. I do also believe he was as stubborn as anyone I've ever known."

Wilson Matthews, who recruited Hatfield from Helena Central in 1961 and who one September later picked him off the sixth team as a starting defensive back who could make a difference, said in Ken's second season as a head coach, "He's straightening out a lot of things. It's just a shame that he won't let us promote him or help him in his public relations." Ken never set out to be rich or famous.

Still, he came to work in a good humor, kept his staff happy, and made friends with the janitors, faculty, and the little old ladies, many of whom he corresponded with even after he left Arkansas.

Ken loves the people of Arkansas, and probably always will, but not "the beer drinkers—beer is the source of almost all of young people's troubles," and not many of the movers and shakers.

He started out earning the easy admiration of fans for the way his teams won on grit and heart. Then he became a victim of rising expectations.

His teams went to six bowl games—and lost five times. That's five chilly winters out of six for the head coach. His first four teams missed the Cotton Bowl by virtually a field goal a year—because they lost a game they could have won on a home field in Arkansas in October—32-31 to TCU, 17-7 to Tech, and 15-13 and 16-14 to Texas.

He beat Texas A&M, the league's strongest team of the late 1980s, four of six, but he lost four of six to arch-enemy Texas, then on the decline, and which Arkansas could have beaten six times.

Fans did not much remember the hair-breadth triumphs over SMU, Baylor, and A&M in November when they had wipeouts at the hands of Oklahoma and Miami to recall.

All this welled up after the seasons of 1986 and 1987.

Things would get better, much better, but that wasn't the fans' perception. Fewer fans were watching Hatfield's television program and listening to him on the radio, and fewer fans were buying tickets and contributing to the Razorback Foundation, which had to raise about $5 million a year to keep the program solvent.

Year by year in the 1980s, Frank Broyles strengthened the overall athletic teams, which, by 1988, would achieve the unthinkable. They would win or tie for the championship in eight of the nine sports fostered by the SWC. This reflected the ominous decline of SWC programs that had lost face and financially by NCAA sanctions—as well as Broyles's determination to win. He did hate to lose.

When Broyles met Hatfield for their annual evaluation session after the 1987 season, he asked for the heads of certain lightweight staff members (all "family" to Ken, and untouchable), a defense that would line up better to contain passers, a change in the offense that would appeal more to fans, a different format for his television show, et cetera.

Hatfield agreed to some of the changes, but he would fire no aides, which was his prerogative.

They argued over the television deal—and Ken's nonexistent contract.

Hatfield is a private person and a brooder. His lifelong friend, Bill Gray, who at first helped Ken as recruiting coordinator, then became an associate athletic director under Broyles, said, "When Ken first came back, he was a happier person, fun-loving like his mother, a practical joker. Now he's more like his father, who is reclusive."

His parents were divorced when he was in grade school at Texarkana. His mother returned to her family home in Helena. Her father was J. F. Wahl, an idol of Ken's who had been a fine athlete and Helena's superintendent of schools for decades. Ken's father, Chick Hatfield, a superb athlete in the 1930s at what is now Central Arkansas, remained close to Ken but never made a public "appearance" during Ken's years as head coach.

Brooding over his difficulties with Broyles and others, and ill at ease in his contacts with other people involved, Hatfield took a step that had seemed natural to many of his friends, including Bill Parcells of the Giants and Bill Curry of Alabama (and Orel Hershiser of the Dodgers).

He hired an agent. He turned over his contract and television show to Robert Fraley and, for a time, Kirk Wood, both of Leader Enterprises, Inc., of Orlando, Florida.

"That was his major mistake as head coach of the Razorbacks," according to Dale Nicholson, whose Little Rock television station, KATV, Channel 7, had handled the coaches' shows at Arkansas since the 1960s. "That tore it overnight for a lot of people."

Jack Stephens, the immensely wealthy and influential Little Rock investment banker who became chairman of Augusta National Golf Club and of the Masters, pioneered this show for Broyles in 1958. He saw the show as a way for the commercial leaders of the state to reward the head coaches of the Razorbacks. He would call on his own businesses and others to pay far more than the normal television show warranted so that the coach would earn money that would make his job competitive with other major ones across the nation.

Hatfield used KATV for three years, taping the show from Fayetteville (instead of Little Rock) on Sundays.

Broyles watched and told Hatfield, "That show won't work. You need to pitch the program to the fans."

Hatfield said, "I can't be you."

After a year or two, Nicholson found it almost impossible to sell sponsors. Stephens called Hatfield's biblical quotation lead-in "divisive." (Hatfield did not give that up until the administration told him to before the 1988 season.) Hatfield himself tried to sell the shows. When he found this took up his time all the way into August and yielded far less revenue, he knew he had to have outside help.

Early in 1987, Nicholson and previous sponsors received a letter from Kirk Wood, identified as Hatfield's agent, laying down terms and conditions for Hatfield's future television and radio shows. Nicholson threw in the towel. All the potential sponsors declined to participate.

For the rest of his time at Arkansas, Hatfield's television and radio shows operated on off-brand stations with minimal coverage and advertising. Within one year, his packager went broke.

The matter of his contract became a sore point with him and the administration his last three years.

To start with, Hatfield signed the standard university faculty appointment slip, a 4 x 5 piece of paper that provided not one detail.

Faculty are appointed for one year. Two extra words were scrawled on his slip, words that Hatfield interpreted as guaranteeing what he thought to be part of the widely heralded deal, an automatic five-year rollover.

However, the rollover was a vocal agreement not backed up by a contract with the Razorback Foundation, which has to approve and pay anything beyond the state's one-year limit on contracts.

Broyles contended that the agreement with Hatfield wasn't rolled over after 1986 and wouldn't be rolled over after 1987. Hatfield claimed that he had five years again in January 1987 and again in January 1988.

Fraley put on a power play, similar to what takes place in negotiations between a professional athlete and a pro team. To get what he can, the agent first asks for everything he or anyone else has ever thought of. Fraley met just one time with the financial officer of the university, the financial officer of the Razorback Foundation, Broyles, and various others.

Fraley began, "Coach Broyles, I understand you don't approve of agents."

Broyles agreed with that.

Fraley said, "You had better get used to the idea. I am Coach Hatfield's agent, and I plan to be around a long time."

Fraley passed around a thick proposed contract of thirty pages or so. The number of the specific extras appalled the University of Arkansas contingent. They gagged the most on just one little item. Fraley was asking that Hatfield and his wife be allowed to fill their automobile gas tanks free at any time at the pump at the Building and Grounds Station south of Razorback Stadium.

Eventually, Fraley gave up. Hatfield went the rest of his time at the university without a contract. Well, he'd never had one.

Broyles said, "We were close to getting it done several times. I just doubt that the University of Arkansas or the people of Arkansas were of a mind to do their business with the Razorbacks' head football coach through an agent from Orlando, Florida."

This was happening at Alabama, Clemson, and other places, but not at Arkansas, and not through Broyles for Hatfield.

— 49 —

NO ANSWERS FOR AIKMAN

Jim Lindsey, a Razorback hero of 1964–65, a seven-year Minnesota Viking, and lastly a real estate empire builder in northwest Arkansas, knew Ken Hatfield reasonably well.

"We weren't that close in 1964," Lindsey recalls. "You'd see if Ken wanted to go to a movie, and he'd politely beg off. He had to study, go to the library, do some Sigma Chi business, attend a ROTC thing or campus leadership deal. He used everything available at the University.

"He was a Christian, but he was also a little bit mean, just enough to meet his needs as athlete and coach.

"You should have played against him when they were winning the state basketball championship at Helena. If they were behind near the end, he just got busier, quicker, tougher. He couldn't stand for them to lose and you had to practically get him tied down before you could beat them."

Feeling similarly cornered, Ken Hatfield and his staff got the maximum out of everything in 1988 and 1989.

Losing to Texas on the last play in 1987 may have torn it for Ken with the fans and may have distracted the staff from recruiting, but it sure made better coaches of them. They told themselves, whether it was true or not, that it was either go to the Cotton Bowl—or get fired.

Actually, their time had come.

Like the fans, Hatfield wanted his team to be dominating someday, the way Miami and Oklahoma had been, but he had expected only that he could build up to Texas A&M and Texas. This he did. Thanks largely to his one superb class of 1985, his program came of age in 1988 and 1989.

The Hogs had reasonable size, strength, depth, and some speed at every position.

The pro scouts who had skipped Fayetteville from 1983 through 1986 were now getting eyefuls of Steve Atwater, Wayne Martin, LaSalle Harper, Derek Russell, Elbert Crawford, Freddie Childress, James Rouse, and Barry Foster, mostly early rounders.

And other coaches looked at Quinn Grovey and Kendall Trainor, two who didn't eventually fit in the NFL, and shuddered.

Everybody knows how Barry Switzer "gave" passer Troy Aikman to UCLA, because he was running option football at Oklahoma, not passing, and he had the world's greatest option quarterback, Jamelle Holieway.

Well, Switzer also presented Quinn Grovey to his alma mater. He had watched Grovey grow up as a winner at everything at Duncan, down the road from his campus in Norman. He'd had Quinn as a guest on his sidelines at OU. But one day, Barry pulled the little magician into a huddle with Holieway, Charles Thompson, and Eric Mitchel and asked him, "Would you rather battle these guys for three years or go to Arkansas and play now?" Or words to that effect. Grovey took the advice. He signed with Arkansas.

Over four years, Grovey out-executed every defense in the SWC each time he stepped onto the field. They couldn't tackle him, and, more and more as he played, he could find the receivers wide open against defenses weakened by trying to keep up with the triple option.

Fred Goldsmith coached defense for Hatfield until he went to Rice (with Broyles's help) as head coach after the 1988 season.

He seldom had the great speed or the great players needed to stuff the other offenses. He did have (and did credit) a head coach who called plays for an offense that kept the ball, didn't turn it over where the other team could get a cheap touchdown, and could score, thus taking the pressure off the defense.

Hatfield was smart and lucky. He got the most out of four indestructible offensive tackles in his six years, Dale Williams and David McGee, and in the two Cotton Bowl years, Jim Mabry and Rick Apolskis. He capitalized on fullbacks Marshall Foreman and Derrick Thomas for three years, then Foster and Juju Harshaw for the next three.

They frustrated opponents, who, used to penetrating to defend one-back sets and passers, had to play this one game against Arkansas by chasing laterally against a quick tackle like Mabry scrambling at, horrors, their knees.

SWC coaches dreaded a fourth quarter in which Foster or Harshaw, whoever was fresher, would ravage their weary middles.

Ultimately in 1988, though, Trainor did it.

First, the offense needed a late save from the defense to preserve a 30-26 win over Tulsa. T. J. Rubley had completed seven straight passes to give the Hurricane a first down on the Arkansas 8 with a minute remaining. Kerry Owens, an outside backer, teamed on a stunt with Wayne Martin. Owens caused Rubley to fumble; Martin recovered.

Then came Trainor.

Arkansas led Ole Miss 12-0 but fell behind, 13-12, in the third period. In 10 quarters, the big, strong-legged Trainor, senior from Fredonia, Kansas, had hit one little 21-yard field goal and had missed a 25-yarder just before halftime against the Rebs. Hatfield debated un-redshirting Todd Wright.

Challenged, Trainor succeeded from 31, 38, and 43 yards for a 21-13 victory. The die was cast.

Trainor added five against TCU the next week and wound up with 24 field goals, one short of an NCAA record, and 23 in a row. (A 24th straight in the Cotton Bowl didn't count against the record of Chuck Nelson of Washington set in 1982.)

Wayne Martin, headed for a smashing career with the New Orleans Saints, had four sacks against Ole Miss and became one of those rare Arkansas linemen to make All-American. Furthermore, Steve Atwater, 6'4" and 215 pounds, so polished his unorthodox style—from his safety position he came up and tackled like a linebacker—he became the Denver Broncos' first-round choice and qualified for NFL honors.

The Hogs paraded to 9-0 with one lopsided win after another.

Texas came back from a 24-3 deficit by knocking Grovey out of the game, but John Bland contributed there with a throw on which Tim Horton made a gallant catch and Atwater intercepted the final Texas pass to cement the 27-24 win.

The Hogs kept the ball 42 minutes at Houston, where John Jenkins's explosive if short-lived run-and-shoot offense was coming on. Atwater recovered the on-sides kick with 15 seconds left after UH scored to cut it to 26-21.

Foster (16 for 78 with two touchdowns) and Harshaw (20-105) joined with Grovey (6 of 8 for 157 yards) and the rampaging defense for the unusual 33-3 rout of Baylor at Waco.

That brought on the showdown game with Texas A&M at Fayetteville.

This was a powerful A&M team but two factors militated against it.

Arkansas always felt comfortable about playing the Aggies who, conversely, seldom played well against the Razorbacks in Arkansas. Secondly, A&M's style of defense, featuring crashing and chasing linebackers and cornerbacks headed for the pros, had to stay put, read, take on blockers, and chase laterally in playing Hatfield's wishbone. Linebackers looking for sacks of the passer would get nothing against Arkansas except bruised knees.

Eventually, A&M gained 414 yards that wild day in the hills, mostly on land, but Arkansas feasted on erratic Aggie passing. Its four turnovers included a theft by Patrick Williams for a touchdown and one in the end zone for a touchback by Anthoney Cooney.

Aggie defenders bragged truculently that they had held the Arkansas attack without a touchdown, which was true, but who cared?

By then Hatfield was showing no hesitation in exploiting Trainor's leg. Field goals of 29 and 49 yards to begin with followed drives to the A&M 12 and 32. Defensive pressure forced a wild pass that Williams returned 47 yards for what would be the Razorbacks' only touchdown. Joe Johnson ran in a two-pointer for a sudden 14-0 lead.

Here A&M stopped the unstoppable Grovey by knocking him out of the game, literally. Ducking one tackler 10 yards down field, he was blind-sided by another. John Bland, again, saved the day. He ran for 60 yards, including 36 on a quarterback sneak. The Hogs stayed ahead on Kerry Owens's tackle of an Aggie back in the end zone and three more field goals by Trainor—the clincher a mere 18-yarder to make it 25-14 near the end. The lead had been 22-7 entering the last round.

Hatfield's biggest win left Arkansas with a chance to notch its first-ever 11-0 regular season.

With an extra week to prepare, and vengeance on their minds, the Razorbacks went into the Orange Bowl stadium and led another of Jimmy Johnson's powerful teams by 16-15 in the final period.

Grovey entered the game to start the second period. Miami's players went after him so recklessly, his option "read" handoff to Foster resulted in an 80-yard romp by the fullback on the first play. Later in the period, the 'Canes chased Grovey all over the place. He escaped long enough to dump the ball to Foster for another touchdown scamper.

The Hogs made Miami fight for every yard and appeared to have stopped the big favorites on their last drive. After Atwater dropped what would have been an interception, however, Carlos Huerta kicked the winning field goal, a 20-yarder, 18-16.

This did not tarnish the team, but a 17-3 loss to UCLA in the Cotton Bowl did.

Hatfield had hopes when his team practiced that first day in Dallas in a cold mist. UCLA traditionally played poorly in bad weather. Each day the weather got better. By game time, UCLA had its day, as lovely as if it had been the Rose Bowl, plus Troy Aikman keyed to peak for the Dallas Cowboys, who already knew they would draft him. Arkansas's Quinn Grovey was sick with the flu and the two best linemen, Wayne Martin and Freddie Childress, were left home by Hatfield for undisclosed reasons.

Aikman picked the scrambling Arkansas defense to pieces with his short passes. Arkansas fielded what the wags called a balanced attack, 21 yards running, 21 passing. Trainor's 40-yard field goal ending the half, the result of a UCLA fumble, wasn't enough, but that's all their was.

Maybe 50,000 of the 70,000 fans at the game wore red. They had a great time until the game, which stuck the Hogs with an 0-2 finish to only the third 10-0 start in the school's history.

– 50 –

GETTING IT DONE
WITH OFFENSE

Hatfield blamed Grovey ("he had receivers open") for the embarrassing impotence of the Hogs against UCLA. Still, as fans resumed railing at him, the head coach, he agreed to Broyles's suggestion that he hire a coordinator who could jazz things up and, also, call plays, freeing Hatfield for other head coaching duties.

The Arkansas coach brought in Jack Crowe, who had done those things, or almost, at Auburn and Clemson.

No newcomer to the program ever found so much to work with offensively or achieved so much with it.

Everybody returned from 1988 offensively, it seemed, and James Rouse lined up for his fifth season trimmer and better in all ways. He was backed by two promising freshmen, E. D. Jackson and Ron Dickerson Jr. If Grovey had been terrific, now he became sensational and more durable. The veteran offensive cast set a school record with 4,926 yards in 1989.

If he hadn't learned the hard way about Arkansas's Texas game problem, and Arkansas's Cotton Bowl problem, Crowe would have enjoyed a career-high picnic.

However, as Hatfield knew better than anyone, the loss of eight regulars on defense, most of them three-year starters, could not be overcome. Opponents noticed the dropoff in the secondary and linebacking corps, especially.

Hatfield was to sigh all season, "We get it done most of the time, but we are obviously not dominating on defense."

Derek Russell launched things in a 16-7 win over Tulsa with a 30-yard touchdown on a receiver reverse. He was to make big plays all year—but who didn't? E. D. Jackson scored two touchdowns in a hurry at Ole Miss; James Rouse did the same against UT, El Paso; Barry Foster and Juju Harshaw pulverized TCU; Foster barreled through Tech, and Todd Wright came in kicking accurately.

The Hogs, 5-0, were going home against Texas. Good? In the Hatfield era (or in the time of almost any Arkansas coach), what could be worse?

They started strangely flatfooted against a UT offense directed smartly by freshman Peter Gardere, who completed 16 of 20 passes for 247 yards.

Grovey rallied a sputtering offense to a 14-13 halftime lead, but it could have been by more. Texas returned to take a 24-14 lead, but a rare fumble ended Arkansas's promising comeback attempt.

Texas won, 24-20. In the six Hatfield tenure games against the 'Horns, UT won by 6, 4, 2, and 2 points; Arkansas by 7 and 3, both at Austin.

Blamed by some for the loss to Texas, Grovey came back with what many called his best game, with what others called as good a game as they'd ever seen.

En route to his Heisman Trophy season, Houston's Andre Ware passed for 412 yards, 35 of 47, but Grovey directed the Razorbacks to 391 yards on the ground, 256 in the air, a total of 647, most ever given up by the Cougars, most ever made by the Hogs in "a big game."

Kirk Collins, a veteran in the Arkansas secondary, came out a hero. Playing "defensive end" in Hatfield's special scheme against the run-and-shoot, Collins sacked Ware when UH was leading 21-17 and driving, and the Hogs drove back 78 yards with Grovey scoring from the two.

Later, after Arkansas went 78 yards, Rouse scored from the two, to break a 31-31 tie, and Houston blinked. You couldn't falter in a game in which one team, Arkansas, made 27 first downs and the other made 26, but the Cougars did. A receiver dropped a third and eight pass. Houston had to punt. Grovey took the Hogs to a 45-31 edge, and Ware's scrambling for eight points with 0:00 showing proved meaningless.

That left only Texas A&M capable of keeping the Razorbacks from a repeat Cotton Bowl performance.

In a showdown for all the marbles at Kyle Field (where only 57,876 spectators showed up), Grovey reversed his field for 25 yards and a touchdown, and Mick Thomas returned a theft 23 yards and for an immediate 14-0 lead. But the Aggies rallied to go ahead, 20-17 in the last period.

Hatfield called on a fresh pair of players, E. D. Jackson at tailback and Foster at fullback, to hammer the middle. On a fourth and three at the A&M 19, however, it took a famous interference call on a pass to Billy Winston to prolong the drive. Foster banged in from two yards out.

Blitzes by Ty Mason and Thomas disrupted A&M quarterback Lance Pavlas when the Aggies had a chance at the end. Anthony Cooney intercepted in the end zone, as he'd done at the end at Ole Miss, to stop that. Rather than punt, Arkansas took an intentional safety for the 23-22 verdict.

The victory was the first by the visiting team in the six-year series that decided the championship five times. The Cotton Bowl matched two high-scoring teams with suspect defenses.

Atoning for the 42-yard net of a year ago, Grovey directed an attack that broke the Cotton Bowl highs with 31 first downs and 568 total yards. However, another huge outpouring of Arkansas fans saw the Razorbacks waste their first half chances. A fumble at the Tennessee 10 stopped a drive and, with Tennessee massed against the run, Grovey tried a pass to Russell from the two-yard line but let the ball hang and get picked off.

The Vols used the deep passing of Andy Kelly plus the sensational running of Chuck Webb (26-205, two touchdowns) to lead by 31-10 before the Hogs rallied desperately to a 31-27 loss.

It was another somewhat unhappy Arkansas camp at Dallas. Grovey again was ill, especially for the game, with a virus. All at the same hotel, University of Arkansas Board of Trustees members worried about getting Hatfield to sign a contract, and Hatfield dabbled with a vacancy at Georgia, where Vince Dooley had retired after a long reign. The excited talk among Ken's coaches was that they would all be at Athens on January 2.

Hatfield did not get a clear picture, however, from Georgia. While he was looking to move his aides to safety, Dooley, who stayed as athletic director, wanted a coach who would retain his UGA aides. On December 31, Dooley sought to do that by elevating one of them, Ray Goff. That, and the 31-27 defeat, left Hatfield dispirited for his normal visit with the Arkansas media on the morning after the bowl game. He didn't say that he had shaken hands with Broyles on the terms of a contract, which he had, but he volunteered, "I will definitely sign my contract."

The contract would be a virtual carbon copy of an everything-spelled-out, five-year rollover agreement that had been worked up in December 1988 for Nolan Richardson by his agent, Kevin Scanlon (yes, Holtz's 1979 quarterback) of Stephens Sports Management in Little Rock. The university and the Razorback Foundation accepted the conditions and terms of the contract as standard for the athletic director and the coaches of the two revenue-producing sports, football and basketball.

Hatfield was on the verge of signing the document until he read in it a reference to the basketball coach, not him. A secretary had erred in making the copy for him. Hatfield, chagrined, sent the copy back to be fixed. He had planned to sign the corrected version on the day that he got the call from Clemson. He accepted the job before even visiting the campus. The man who greeted him at Clemson and posed with him at the press conference was Robert Fraley, his agent.

The day Hatfield departed Arkansas, it was written that, not being a "people person," such as was Danny Ford, the man he was succeeding, he would encounter the same problems as he had at Arkansas. That proved to be precisely correct. Although Ken's teams proved mostly successful at Clemson, he alienated supporters, and this led to sharp dropoffs in attendance and contributions. After four years, Clemson bought up his contract for $600,000.

Hatfield happily found a new home at Rice, where there had been no real success for about 30 years and which had not hired a winning, big-time head coach from someone else since 1940—that being the now deceased Jess Neely, from Clemson.

— 51 —

HELLO, JACK; GOODBYE, JACK

Just before Jack Crowe was to get on the Clemson plane with Hatfield at the Fayetteville airport, Broyles's aide Terry Don Phillips rushed out and intercepted him.

As Hatfield spotted Phillips, he said to Crowe, "I thought they'd want you."

That wasn't quite right. Broyles did not want anyone who had never proved himself as a head coach at the top level.

For years, Broyles had brokered coaches, hiring aides and then placing them as head coaches; remaining current on prospective coaches at all times; advising other schools' presidents and athletic directors' and helping them find head coaches to fit their situations. He had been pre-eminent with his expertise in this area for many years. What he knew when he got the word from Clemson was that there was no sitting head coach out there who was both fit for Arkansas and readily available at that moment—two weeks before the date for signing recruits.

He was up to date on that. He had researched the field in working closely with his former aide, Alabama athletic director Hootie Ingram, when Hootie had taken a chance (and won handsomely) in hiring Gene Stallings off a losing NFL team.

A tipoff on Broyles's shaky feelings about Crowe was provided moments before the hiring ceremony the day after Hatfield departed.

Crowe said, with a bemused smile, while waiting in the wings, "I still haven't been asked if I want the job or told that it's mine."

Nor did any of that ever happen. With the usual fanfare, of course, Broyles merely introduced him as the new head coach.

Jack Crowe majored in chemistry at the University of Alabama at Birmingham. While others his age were playing college football, he was helping coach at West End High School, where he had played quarterback. He became head coach at Livingston State while in his twenties. Then he coached offense for Pat Dye at Auburn and for Danny Ford at Clemson.

Crowe came across more like a charming young professor and a highly social person than he did a football coach. He was a change from Hatfield as a mixer, which Broyles and his old friends liked, and he had proved that he could call the plays offensively (although, for that team, who couldn't have?).

Broyles liked his connections with Clemson and Auburn, established Southern powers.

He feared that Crowe's lack of experience as a college player, but more so his untested status as a head coach, could prove costly. Furthermore, Crowe was sure to have early problems assembling a strong staff, and did.

In the crunch, Crowe could not command, could not motivate. The man you'd love to spend time with wasn't the man you wanted in charge in the critical, powerfully important moments when it was just the coach and his team.

He had his best success in recruiting, such as in signing Barry Lunney and Mike Cherry, the best two Arkansas high school quarterbacks, on the same day. He went after top talent—but also took academic risks who didn't pan out.

That was a momentous first year, good and bad.

Crowe would have Grovey and Russell to build around—but without Foster, who opted to leave a year early for the NFL, which he proved he was ready for, and Harshaw, who just left. His best lineman, Tony Ollison, got hurt early and sat out his senior season.

Most important, when the Southeastern Conference voted in late May to expand so as to form a 12-team league, Arkansas almost immediately opted to leave the Southwest Conference, of which it had been a charter member since 1914, and easily obtained and accepted an invitation.

Jack Crowe, aware that the SWC was getting softer each year, may have been the only man in Arkansas to shudder. He knew what he might be in for, especially if he didn't begin immediately to recruit SEC-type defensive and offensive linemen, most especially the latter.

The truth was, if the SEC had asked Arkansas in 1933, when it formed a league from 12 break-aways from the old Southern Conference,

Arkansas would have accepted then. The Razorbacks' staunchest fans always had more feeling for games against Ole Miss and LSU than they did the rivalries with Texas teams.

Broyles had regrets early. He'd been associated with the SWC mostly since he went to Baylor as a 22-year-old aide in 1947. He didn't like much how he and Arkansas had been ignored or punished in league meetings, but by now he had moved the Razorbacks to the very top in almost all sports.

He recognized immediately that Razorback fans did not want to look back. They wanted Arkansas to step up in class right now, take on all those teams they used to see only in bowl games.

This meant, as Broyles knew only too well, the raising of $35, maybe $50 million to update Arkansas facilities to SEC standards. Doing this and overseeing the construction projects (he had become almost architect, builder, and contractor through 25 years of expansions and remodelings) would occupy his time, affect all his decisions.

Disaster gripped Crowe's first team in the second game, a 21-17 loss to Ole Miss at Little Rock.

Grovey led the team up and down the field. Arkansas led in first downs, 24-8; yards rushing, 157-52; yards passing, 270-59, but came away empty five times from the 10-yard line or better. Ron Dickerson was knocked down at the two-yard line on the last try.

Jack Crowe's finest hour: A win in Little Rock to end the Arkansas-Texas series on a high note in 1991.

Further, Ole Miss exploited something that all the run-and-shoot teams in Texas noticed. The Hogs' linebackers lacked the speed or ability to cover inside receivers going deep.

TCU (54-26), Tech (49-44), Texas (49-7), and Houston (62-28) passed Arkansas silly.

The 3-8 season looked just like the 2-8 one of 1952, which was the worst previous showing of modern times.

Joe Kines came in from his NFL and Alabama and Florida backgrounds to stabilize the defense in 1991, the last SWC year.

Redshirted freshman Jason Allen contributed leadership in a 4-0 run that included a 14-13 victory over Texas at Little Rock in their "last game ever." An injury against Baylor knocked out Allen. However, a 6-5 record brought an Independence Bowl bid. The Hogs could run there on a so-so Georgia defense, but the Bulldogs still prevailed, 24-15.

The start of SEC play in his third year had Crowe transfixed. Key men sat on the bench for the season opener against a Division IAA team, The Citadel. Neither team could get anything going until Todd Wright kicked a field goal. The defense held The Citadel and the reliable E. D. Jackson began pounding the middle towards a touchdown that would put the game away. He fumbled. The new NCAA rule permitted the return of fumbles behind the line of scrimmage. The Citadel returned that one to trigger a 10-3 upset.

The next day, Broyles fired Crowe. It was Sunday before Labor Day.

Perhaps the country's most astute athletic director, he was nonetheless widely censured for an act so "not politically correct."

The people of Arkansas generally objected to just one thing. Broyles had twice announced extensions of Crowe's contract. Why do that, then fire him?

Broyles merely followed his book. A coach without a winning record must be able to tell recruits his job is safe. That's why he would publicly roll it over at the start of each recruiting season. Besides, he knew that Crowe's contract included a mitigation clause. If he got another job, Arkansas would have to pay him only the difference in the two salaries for the five years. As it turned out, the Razorback Foundation ignored that and eventually paid him $500,000, on top of what he earned when, months later, he became an offensive aide at Baylor.

Broyles had been offered proof by The Citadel of what he already suspected, that Crowe was not the forceful man Arkansas had to have to compete in the SEC. After naming Joe Kines the interim coach, Broyles, quite by luck, found that man in Danny Ford.

Jack Crowe was fired on Labor Day weekend of 1992 after his team lost to The Citadel.

Frank Broyles discovered "change" early. Dramatic change became his key to success in coaching as well as in running a blue-ribbon collegiate athletic program for more than four decades.

If you're losing, or you're not winning big enough, or if the natives get restless, then you must do something to lift the players, intrigue the recruits, buoy the fans, enliven the script for the newspaper, television, and magazine guys.

So, do you fire the coach after one game, after an unspeakable loss to such as The Citadel? Yes, you do. The more dramatic the change, the better. Maybe.

During the 1992 campaign, the longest of his life, J. Franklin Broyles, almost 68, everything getting late, doing his darndest to get his football team back on a par with the basketball, the track, the baseball, the golf—everything—tried it all.

Eventually, he (the Razorback Foundation) was paying head coaches' salaries to Jack Crowe, Joe Kines, and Danny Ford, and something close to that to the play-caller, Tulane's fired head coach of the previous four years, Greg Davis.

Joe Kines's interim hitch started with this victory ride against South Carolina.

That's as expensive as it is dramatic.

The result was only a 3-7-1 season, although the SEC debut (3-4-1, including the school's first win over Tennessee, when UT was 5-0) wasn't half bad.

In the end, Frank Broyles somehow wiggled and watched and smooth-talked his way through the maze of Saturday after Saturday ups and downs and got lucky.

The patriarch of the Razorbacks wound up with what he—and many others—saw as a setup that augured well for the future of Arkansas football.

Two things necessary to Broyles's longtime formula took place at the end. The Razorbacks won their final game of 1992 by 30-6 over LSU, which they hadn't beaten since 1929. They hit on all cylinders, just like an old-time Arkansas team would.

And they then stepped into the euphoria of having not only their beloved Kines, the man for uncanny defense and kicking and other good things, but also the leadership and positive, rock-solid offensive foundations of head coach Ford to take into the off-season, to rely on, it would appear, for years ahead.

Arkansas players, fans, and, yes, men of the media who stayed down, down, and down for three years, with only a glimmer of relief now and then, faced 1993 thinking up, up, and up.

That's how Frank Broyles wanted it. When he became athletic director, he dared to choose a quirky, solid, surprise-a-minute man named Lou Holtz as his successor.

When Holtz lost interest (he stayed seven years, about three or four too many), Broyles went for a man who should have been a conquering, returning hero, Ken Hatfield.

Hatfield left for Clemson after six high-percentage but not sensational years. He finished 10-2 twice, in the Cotton Bowl twice, but something had gone wrong; maybe lots of things had.

One thing that didn't go right was that Ken kept losing his last game, usually in a bowl. That goes against the grain in the Broyles Plan.

"What counts is what you do in November," he said. Or, what counts is what happens in the last game.

Broyles's teams won their first 21 November games, 1958 into 1963.

What with bowl games and all, they did not fare as well at winning their last game of each season.

Broyles lost bowl games to Duke, Alabama, and Ole Miss, 1961–63.

South Carolina's Gamecocks forlornly chase Orlando Watters (3).

His boss, John Barnhill, never worried about losing bowl games. He'd tell Frank, "Aw, you had a good year and the kids who come back from the bowl game will lead you to having a good spring practice because they lost."

Frank came to know better, especially when bowls began to count toward national titles in 1965. He lost in the Cotton Bowl to LSU when, if the Hogs had won, they'd have been 11-0 and 11-0 two years in a row, winners of 23 in a row, national champions two years in a row.

He had some hidden horrors gaining a 27-20 victory in the season closer against Texas Tech to attain 5-5 in 1963.

He benched Joe Ferguson, headed for a long NFL career, and used Scott Bull to salvage a 24-14 win at Lubbock and a 6-5 record in 1972.

He had Ike Forte carry the ball the last 21 times of the game to win at Lubbock, 21-13, for a 6-4-1 finish in 1974.

This type of win often triggers something the next season.

Arkansas and Texas Tech were in a 13-13 tossup at Lubbock in 1983 in what became Lou Holtz's last game at Arkansas. Brad Taylor went back

Joe Kines introduces Danny Ford as a "consultant" four games into the chaotic 1992 season. Ford was hired as head coach at the end of the schedule.

to his Danville High Littlejohns instincts. He took over the game and set up a winning field goal. That kept Lou a winner with a 6-5 finish.

Hatfield's teams went to bowl games all six years.

They lost to Auburn, 21-15; to Oklahoma, 42-8; to Georgia, 20-17; to UCLA, 17-3; and to Tennessee, 31-27.

Kendall Trainor kicked a field goal in the last minute at San Diego to beat Arizona State, 18-17.

Hatfield held the best won-lost record of any Arkansas coach, but he was 1-5 in his final games of the seasons.

That can make for testy winters.

Presidential candidate Bill Clinton, who went on to a winning season, watches the 1992 Arkansas-Alabama game at Little Rock.

Jason Allen, the holder, jumps up and becomes the first to bear hug Todd Wright for the field goal that beat Tennessee.

Holtz went 4-3 in final games; Broyles, 7-12; Jack Mitchell, 1-2; Bowden Wyatt, 1-1; Otis Douglas, 1-2; John Barnhill, 3-1; Glen Rose, 1-1; John Tomlin, 0-1; George Cole, 0-1; and Fred C. (Tommy) Thomsen, 8-1-4.

How else could Thomsen have lasted 13 seasons? That was easily the longevity record until Broyles came along.

As for Danny Ford, he lost his last *three* games of his third campaign. However, his storybook Razorbacks of 1995 had played the best long enough to win the SEC-West title and make it to the championship game against Florida. That's what fans couldn't forget, ever.

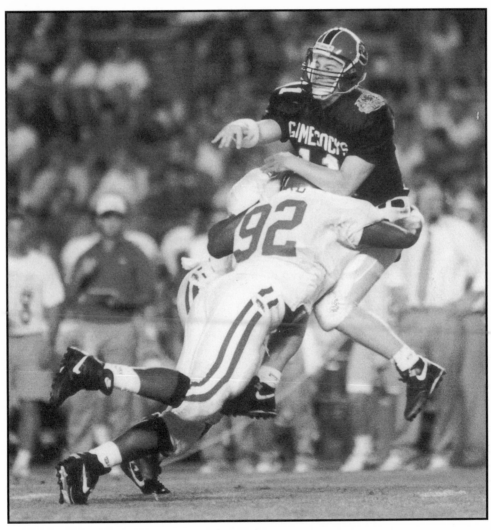

Sack specialist Henry Ford at work

A NEW (AND USED) FORD

Danny Ford and Arkansas? Unlikely, some people said.

Even in the summer of 1995, Jack Crowe, passing through Arkansas while delivering a son to a summer camp, expressed this private comment on a two-year Ford record that was still below .500: "Danny is not a fit for Arkansas. He ought to be at Oklahoma, where they win on talent. Arkansas has always done it on coaching and over-achieving."

Partly true, but Broyles had in mind what he'd done with the signing of Nolan Richardson. He saw in Ford a man who could win with coaching (the Xs and Os in the hands of proved aides) and also attract talent better than Arkansas was used to.

Looking back, Ford said, "I thought I had too many things against me. Clemson had been on probation twice while I was the head coach there. I'd gotten fired because I wanted us to build a new athletic dormitory and the president wanted to use the money for a new academic building. I made an issue out of that and lost. People would say that I was anti-administration, that I would buck the system. Sure enough, one of the first things Dr. Ferritor asked me was, 'Why should I hire you?'"

Dan Ferritor, chancellor of the University of Arkansas's main campus at Fayetteville, got honest answers to his questions at the end of the 1992 season, and the next day, Ford became the 27th head coach of the Razorbacks.

Frank Broyles had spent that year, the first on the field for Arkansas in the SEC, trying to heed his gut feelings.

He had become convinced that Jack Crowe could not lead the Hogs out of a deepening wilderness. At his first opportunity, after the weakest

Ford became the 27th head coach of the Razorbacks.

of showings against a division I-AA team before a smaller-than-usual opening crowd, he fired Crowe.

For the next three months, he nursed the other gut feeling, that the only man who might be available who could lead the Razorbacks to championships once again was Crowe's former boss, Danny Ford. This feeling became almost agonizing when, through a fluke, Ford spent most of the season on the Arkansas campus, and quite possibly unavailable.

Broyles almost never gives up on his gut feelings.

From the beginning: Moments after the axe fell on September 6, Crowe telephoned Ford at Danny and Deborah's lakeside home at Pendleton, South Carolina, near Clemson. Crowe needed someone to commiserate with. He also had an idea that Ford, idle for two years while accepting $190,000 a season in a five-year Clemson payoff, might be interested in the vacancy.

Ford returned the call when he got home from church, then scratched his head and got into his pickup and drove the 100 miles to the office of his lawyer in Columbia. It was there that the first call from Broyles reached him.

Ford told the Arkansas athletic director what he'd just learned, that if he took a head job before the following November 14, he would forfeit the last two years of his settlement from Clemson. No way.

Ford said three years later, "I came to be grateful to Coach Broyles. It is good to work for a man who was a top football coach, who knows the answers to the questions before you ask them. At the time, though, I didn't know what he might think about me. This is a little thing, but in about 1982, he was at our place doing a TV game and I called him by the name of Paul Dietzel, the former coach at South Carolina he reminded me of. And we never visited. He did his pre-game work with a man on my staff, not me. It was the only contact we'd ever had."

Ford stayed with his cows and his South Carolina friends who remembered him every day in some way.

Broyles chose popular defensive coordinator Joe Kines as interim head coach.

Kines, a veteran of the Dixie grid wars from Virginia Tech to Clemson to Florida to Alabama to Arkansas (and later, Georgia), became famous for his pre-season warning to his Razorback defenders, "You'd better get ready. In the SEC, if you're not, they'll slit your throat and drink your blood."

That's what the Razorbacks did at Columbia to South Carolina, 45-7, in the first SEC game ever for each team. It was the last hurrah for Jason

Allen, the game quarterback, and the first for Orlando Watters, return man deluxe, and for Kines. The old (50-ish) warhorse never forgot what it felt like to be carried off the field after his first game as a head coach.

Then Alabama's soon-to-be national champions blistered the Hogs at Little Rock, 38-11, and the next week, Memphis State blocked four punts and humiliated the Hogs at Memphis, 22-6.

Kines needed some help. With the headaches of the number-one job added to his defensive coordinator's work, he needed someone to fix the paper-thin, impotent offensive line and the woeful kicking game. He was entitled to a replacement who would complete a full staff. Could he have someone to replace himself?

Certainly, said Broyles.

Kines talked it over with Terry Don Phillips, Broyles's assistant athletic director, who had been with Ford and Kines at his own coaching stops.

"Danny Ford was the best offensive line coach I'd ever been around," Phillips recalled. "Joe felt the same way. And Danny was available, we thought."

Years ago, at Clemson, Kines had helped Ford when the latter was a young aide. Ford had said, "Joe, if I can ever repay the favor, call me, no matter where I am."

Thus apprised, Broyles thought that Joe ought to call the man, right that minute, even if he had to get him out of church. So, on September 27, 1992, Joe Kines called Danny Ford.

The next day, Ford boarded the private plane to, for him, uncharted waters. He knew next to nothing about Arkansas, where he had never set foot. His thought when he saw the mighty, muddy Mississippi was, "How will I ever get my cows across that river?"

Eliminating the blocked punts was not that hard. You put the stopwatch against the snapper and punter and tighten the alignment so that people didn't barrel through the middle, where the damage was coming from.

Finding a kicker would be harder. Fixing the offensive line, it turned out, quite predictably, would take three years, maybe four.

Mostly, Ford stayed out of the way. He hadn't been an assistant coach in 14 years and as a head coach, he'd usually watched from a distance except during teamwork. Even so, however unobtrusive he made himself, Kines's "advising consultant" looked like the imposing (6-3 and 230) head coach Arkansas hadn't had since the 1970s.

It wasn't until Broyles had seen Ford working his little ways on the practice field—totally within the framework of his role as "consultant," mind you—that the thought began to overcome him.

Of all the people he had heard of in his conversations with others around the country, none could compare with Ford as a likely answer for Arkansas's situation: the established coach, a proven winner, the man of his dreams, there for the asking, maybe.

When a writer suspected this much after a few days, Broyles smiled and shrugged and said, "Danny's going to South Carolina."

We soon learned that Sparky Woods, whose team had quit on him once in an 0-5 start, then rallied, wasn't going to be leaving his reborn Gamecocks (until 1993).

Two or three weeks later, Frank showed no interest in some names (some totally implausible) and bragged on Kines and then blurted out, "What would be perfect is to have Joe and Danny as co-head coaches."

He didn't mean that.

What he meant was, the ideal would be for Ford to run the team and the offense and for Joe to do his incomparable stuff with the defense.

Some couldn't yet envision Ford wanting the Arkansas job, which would mean jerking loose all his roots from his beloved South Carolina. He heard from Clemson fans daily.

"After the LSU game, I'm outta here," Ford would say.

John McDonnell, the track coach with 17 NCAA titles at that point, and more to come, twice took Ford to his farm east of Fayetteville, just to give him a feel for the countryside and let him ease the homesickness with looks at John's pasture. Danny acted as if he were hooked on cattle, which he raised and dealt in back home.

"I don't think Danny has his mind on moving here," was McDonnell's considered opinion.

Who could even imagine Joe Kines, a magnificent man, finding a rival in a friend he had turned to for a long-owed favor?

Ford said many times that he came to Arkansas to help Kines get the "interim" removed from his job description and that he would feel unsuccessful if he didn't achieve that.

"How could I come here and cut Joe's throat?" he'd say.

Then, like a lot of coaches before him, Ford could not help falling in love with the look and feel of Arkansas football. It could also be that, like many others, he might not be able to resist Broyles's salesmanship.

"The best coaching job in America," Broyles had proclaimed since the 1950s, although that wasn't always true.

Besides, how could a coach with Ford's background, a man at the peak of his powers, not want to get back into his life's work?

In 11 years at Clemson, Ford's teams finished first six times in the Atlantic Coast Conference. They went 12-0 in 1981, when he was 33, the youngest anyone has ever been while winning a national title.

His Tigers beat 18 teams ranked in the Top 20; they went 41 straight polls ranked there themselves.

They were 6-2 in bowl games with wins over Oklahoma, Penn State, Ohio State, and Nebraska (in the Orange Bowl for the 1981 crown).

"We need a proven head coach," Broyles convinced the selection committee, his department "cabinet," and all who approached him on the subject.

"We need someone who will rally the fans and bring 'em back."

Danny Ford, 44, who played to 41,000 fans when he arrived at Clemson, before almost 80,000 when he left.

Did he cheat doing all that? Al Witte, the Arkansas law professor who headed the selection committee, a Broyles confidant, was president of the NCAA when Clemson was handed a one-year probation. He says Ford wasn't named then or in a previous rap against Clemson.

Ford's school was one of the first hit for what were called "humanitarian violations," like, in its case, supplying money (by an assistant coach) for one poor player to take a bus trip home for a family emergency, for another to get his "rotten teeth" repaired. The NCAA has since sanctioned the use of special funds to be used for such purposes.

As for Kines, the players' choice, he could leave (who could blame him?) or he could stay (he'd be loved as long as he was at Arkansas).

That was a masterpiece of a statement an exhausted Kines made at his final press conference. He expressed his feelings appropriately on every subject, but he burned no bridges at Arkansas. He said of the selection committee's work, "It was a business decision."

Ford would sell tickets and bring in the funds Clemson and Arkansas must raise in the absence of tax money.

Kines's team might have won but three games, but his defense gave up fewer yards and fewer points to tougher SEC foes than Hatfield's 1989 team (10-2) that won its second straight SWC title.

All this seemed at the time to be the last blessing that Frank Broyles wanted and needed to complete his decades of building at Arkansas.

The 1995 season indicated that Broyles retained his great good luck, a euphemism, perhaps, for the product of gut wisdom.

He was a happy man, certainly, when he decided early in 1996 to take steps toward retirement.

— 53 —

FRAGILE TIMES

The experience of Earl Scott sums up the Razorbacks' rise from rags to riches in their first four seasons among the football powers of the Southeastern Conference.

Scott was the last person taken in Jack Crowe's February roundup of 1991.

"We knew Earl was out there," Harold Horton, the recruiting coordinator, explains it. "We had seen him when we were recruiting Kotto Cotton at North Little Rock. He was a defensive lineman. We had picked someone else to sign at his position. At the last minute, that person changed his mind. We got a call from another school in our state asking us to recruit Scott. Earl was about to sign with someone else, and they didn't want to have to play against him.

"A group of us gathered around a video, looking at what we had on Earl. He had quickness. He had a good attitude. He wanted to come, a whole bunch. We signed him."

Crowe had planned from 1990 on to recruit what he thought would be an adequate offensive line for SEC play in 1992.

He foresaw Chris Oliver and Bryan Cornish at the tackles, Ray Straschinske and Isaac Davis at the guards, and Tommy Jones at center. Oliver panned out, but of the others, three struggled constantly with injuries and Davis took hold only late in his final season, when he earned a high NFL draft choice.

Jones, originally a blue-chip from Dallas, had suffered a knee injury but agreed in the middle of the summer of 1992 to return for his senior season. Jones played virtually every snap into the open date before the game at Auburn. Then he didn't come to practice. Joe Kines sent for him. He was found at his girlfriend's apartment, enjoying a few drinks while trimming pumpkins for Halloween.

Kines dropped Jones and installed his backup as starter.

"That was me," Scott recalls. "I had been moved to center after my redshirt year, but I had never played a down at that position, anywhere, anytime. I looked at the game plan. I would be going against No. 94, a middle linebacker they called Darth Vader, a sure first-round draft pick. I thought I was going to explode out there."

Scott survived at Auburn, which was not going anywhere in Pat Dye's lame-duck season but rallied to tie the Hogs, 24-24.

Three years later, before his senior season, Scott sat down with Danny Ford for the traditional one-on-one with the head coach before the break for summer.

For all his courage and spunk, he had not been a dominant center in a line which could not control the exchange areas on the goal lines, among other things. The quarterback could expect to be hit about the time he needed to make a fake or hand off.

So, how did Scott feel about his job performances? He told Ford, "In my three years here, I've always played against people who are bigger, faster, and more experienced than I am. I've made every snap in almost every game. Under the circumstances, I think I've done as well as could be expected. I think I could do better if we could rest me for a series now and then."

Ford wanted to do that in 1995, but the backup line wasn't yet ready.

Against Auburn, however, after another open date, Scott found himself going against a true freshman. When the score reached 30-7, Earl got a chance to come out. He declined. He said he was having too much fun.

Earl Scott became one of the inspirational leaders of the Razorbacks through their rise to that SEC-West championship.

As such, he was duly appreciated by his coaches.

However, nothing in Danny Ford's experience had prepared himself for his first look at the Arkansas squads of the 1990s.

"I was surprised," he said. "The numbers you need to run a big-time football program just weren't there. Nor the quality. The Arkansas teams I'd known about all my life won championships and went to major bowls. This team obviously wasn't close to that."

How come? After the 1993 season, a man reviewed the results of recruiting from 1988 and 1989, Ken Hatfield's last two seasons. Those were the ones that followed the disastrous last-play loss to Texas in 1987. The reaction to that by Frank Broyles and fans prompted fears on the part of Hatfield and his aides about their security.

Of the 21 signees in 1988, only six came from Arkansas and only three of those earned even participation letters. Of them all, only place-kicker Todd Wright (from Stillwater, Oklahoma) earned any honor.

Of the 23 signees in 1989, 13 were from Arkansas, but only seven ever lettered. Of them all, only tight-end Kirk Botkin of Baytown, Texas, earned all-SEC honors (along with Minnesota product Pete Raether, an original baseball recruit who was chosen the punter on the 1992 all-SEC team).

It is true that an unusual number of Arkansas athletes at the end of the 1980s found the new NCAA academic requirements too much. Two such players, defensive lineman Cortez Kennedy (junior college, Miami, Seattle) of Wilson and offensive lineman William Roaf (Louisiana Tech, Saints) of Pine Bluff became all-NFL players.

One of the traits that made Danny Ford desirable as a head coach was that he had always been around and always could identify and recruit players with NFL potential.

He grew up in Gadsden, Alabama, a town of 10,000 with competitive high school teams, worshiping Auburn and Alabama—and the Baltimore Colts.

"You played games all week," he recalled, "and on Sunday, you watched a pro game, the 'Bear Bryant Show' [Alabama] at 4, the 'Shug Jordan Show' [Auburn] at 5, and 'Lassie' at 6. And then you'd play in the backyard until dark, imagining yourself as Alan Ameche carrying the ball into the end zone."

He grew into a 6'3", 195-pound tight end and offensive tackle, mostly the latter.

"I thought I'd be going to Auburn. An Auburn man took me to the Auburn-Alabama game when I was a senior. It was a hard choice then, still is. I wasn't sure I was going to be recruited. I'd gotten hurt after a good junior year and I took a blow on the head playing basketball. I didn't believe I was at my best as a 12th grader. But Alabama wanted me. They had taken a whole bunch from Gadsden the previous year. That kinda carried me. And once I got there, practicing as a freshman was such a chore I forgot all about the problem I brought with me."

Alabama, under Bear Bryant, had won versions of the national championship in 1961, 1964, and 1965 but had fallen into mediocrity at the end of the decade while relying too much on the passing game.

"We didn't win nothing in my time at Alabama," Ford says. "No championships, no bowl game wins from 1968 to 1970."

He graduated on time (bachelor of arts degree) while earning academic honors. He was invited to be a graduate assistant as he stayed in 1971 to obtain a master's degree in special education.

It was an anxious time. Already married, and living with his wife at the dorm, he could see others around him leaving for other coaching jobs, some in fear that they would get caught should Bryant give up and retire. That was a disturbing notion which ended with the success Bryant had when, just before the 1971 season, he adopted the Texas wishbone run-run-run attack. That led to three national championships for Alabama in the 1970s.

Ford worked up enough courage to tell Bryant that he needed a real paying job, not just a graduate-assistant assignment (a glorified athletic scholarship). He asked for help in finding one.

Says Ford, "He made a call and got me one at Eastern Kentucky. I didn't like what I found. So I went back to Alabama for less money. To understand that, you had to know Coach Bryant. I finally told him that I'd better call Eastern Kentucky and tell them I wasn't coming. He said he'd already called them and that I was now working for him."

When Jimmy Sharpe left the Alabama staff to become head coach at Virginia Tech before the 1974 season, Ford quickly volunteered for and gained a job coaching the offensive line for him.

Three years later, he left to do the same thing at Clemson for Charley Pell, a Bryant player and aide of the 1960s. When Pell left for Florida in December 1978, the 31-year-old Ford had become so popular with the Clemson fans, mostly down-home types like him, they handed him the number-one job immediately.

He handled Clemson's Gator Bowl game against Ohio State and came out with a historic win. Late in a see-saw game, Clemson leading, Ohio State's passer threw an interception. The man who stole the pass went out of bounds practically into the lap of the legendary OSU coach, Woody Hayes. Irate because the pass had been thrown at all, Hayes threw what looked like a punch that landed on the Clemson player. ABC-TV cameras caught the incident. Three days later, Hayes resigned. And Danny Ford had his first of many bowl wins over storied greats.

In 1981, Ford's third full year, his Tigers went 12-0, making him, at 33, the youngest man ever to win a national championship (gained with a victory over Nebraska in the Orange Bowl).

His record at Clemson was 96-29-4 when he completed a negotiated resignation with the president at Clemson after the 1989 season. Ford had wanted an athletic dorm with some funds his program had raised; the president wanted an academic facility. The president won (as Ford concedes now that he should have), but the president later gave up his post.

Ford went into dabbling with cattle and many other things out of a lakeside home at nearby Anderson, South Carolina, that his wife, Deborah, had built for the family (three grown daughters and young Danny Lee).

He remained one of the most popular figures in South Carolina. His fans never got used to his successor, ironically a man from Arkansas, Ken Hatfield, who eventually was paid off and dismissed.

As Arkansas fans were to learn, Danny has a way with people and with kids. He's down-home direct, willing to take time to talk, never at a loss for something to say.

And he might say an "ain't" or two.

Under analysis, you could tell that he had more in common with Frank Broyles, his new athletic director with the sharp track record, than one might suspect; that is, Frank being a city boy from Atlanta, Danny a country boy from rural Alabama.

Broyles was in on the start of the school of chairman-of-the-board coaching under Bobby Dodd at Georgia Tech. Ford picked it up from Bear Bryant.

Unlike Broyles in his time, Ford affects to disdain doting on Xs and Os, which he tends to leave to his aides.

"I can hire people to do that," he said.

What he likes, and what he says he achieved in 1995, is to assemble a staff so accomplished, so compatible, "All I need to do is stay out of their way."

This he did, except on Saturdays, when he tended to be in the thick of everything with players, coaches, and, yes, officials.

Danny Ford is best, though, going one-on-one with players.

He is regarded as A-1 in his profession at recognizing talent and the personalities to go with it and in recruiting it.

Broyles said, "I've talked to lots and lots of prospects, and I've heard lots and lots of talks to prospects. I've never been around any coach better than Danny at sustaining a telephone conversation with a young man he has yet to meet face to face. They can go on for half an hour, and Danny will still be relaxed, and funny at times, and never at a loss for words the kid can understand and regard as important."

Broyles also said in Danny's third year, "He looks the part, acts the part, and lives the part of a very good head coach. His leadership qualities are such that you know he's going to be successful."

During his first three springs in Arkansas, Ford toured the state during the months of May. He had little to talk about, since his program had yet to show real results, but the thousands of fans from all the cities and towns who came liked what they heard—and liked the man.

Former Razorbacks took a liking to him.

Carole Burns, often-reelected treasurer of Hot Spring County (home of Madre Hill), wife of 1954–56 Razorback Olan Burns, and homecoming queen in 1956, said early, "Danny is the first people person we've had up there. If anyone wants to get rid of him, I'll lead the fight to keep him."

The Hogs began to fill their home stadiums again—and to win at home again in 1995.

Terry Don Phillips, who left the Arkansas administrative staff in 1994 to be athletic director at Oklahoma State, knew Ford from the time they were the two coordinators under Jimmy Sharpe at Virginia Tech in the early 1970s.

Phillips said late in 1995, "Danny Ford as a coach is as close to Wilson Matthews as any man I've ever known. He gets with kids. He is a player's coach. He may have to jump a young man at some point, but he'll never let that youngster leave that day without hugging his neck."

Even in emeritus status, Wilson Matthews is the keeper of the flame for the Razorbacks.

And he became Ford's main man. As often as not in the fall of 1995, after the death of Matthews's wife of 50 years, Ford would leave the early staff meeting and have his secretary summon Matthews from his nearby home. And they'd look at a piece of film on a high school prospect, or maybe not; watch a fishing or a cooking show on television, or maybe not; try to bake a loaf of bread on a new machine (just to make the place smell real good); and deal with people on the phone or as drop-ins.

Neither one cared for golf.

In retrospect, quarterbacking was never *the* problem in the Razorbacks' trying, often embarrassing 1992–95 battle to respectability in the Southeastern Conference. Everything else was.

First there was Jason Allen, Jack Crowe's surprisingly effective import from Edmond, Oklahoma, with the knack for leadership to go with his average speed, average arm—a winner.

The severe knee injury suffered by Allen against Baylor in 1991 eventually turned him into a cheerleader-coach on the sidelines.

Barry Lunney was coming, anyway. When Arkansas lost to national champ-to-be Alabama at Little Rock in 1992 by 38-11, the last eight points of the game came via the accurate arm of the poised left-handed freshman from Fort Smith Southside. There, young Lunney had won championships with his father, Barry Lunney Sr. (son of a 1946–49 U of A tackle who could *really* run, John Lunney).

Soon, play-caller Greg Davis nodded at Kines and Lunney was given the start at Tennessee—before 95,000 people. Knocked down repeatedly, chased again and again, the limber, agile, and resourceful Lunney set up Todd Wright for must field goals at the end of each half. Wright hit both for a landmark Arkansas upset, 25-24.

Ironically, kicking game failures would thereafter doom Arkansas's hopes again and again until Todd Latourette, from a renowned Jonesboro family but now out of Panama City, Florida, took over in 1995. His kicks made the scoreboard difference over Alabama and Auburn, a prize parlay.

If anyone could make plays with the Hogs' ragtag offensive unit, Lunney could. That's where he maintained an edge over two good-looking prospects who'd gain ground on him with the coaches in spring football while he was playing baseball. When Lunney had a chance, he put on textbook demonstrations on how to move the ball, 60, 70, and 80 yards, little bits of this and that, occasionally an ingenious pass play. It was just hard to get the points on the board against the other team's massed defense inside the red zone, what with weak fullback and offensive guards play and dubious place-kicking.

In turn, both Mike Cherry, the tall, strong passer with the impressive arm, and Robert Reed, with light feet and a powerful arm, transferred out as Lunney eventually started 38 games, a Razorback record.

It was everything around him that limited Lunney until his senior campaign. Then, the best of the old guys girded themselves for great things and the first of Ford's acquisitions, especially Madre Hill and Anthony Lucas, began to pay off.

Ford had been "consulting" only a few weeks in 1992 when he looked ahead and said, "Things could get better next year (1993) but worse in the second year (1994)." And that happened, a 4-7 in 1994 after a shaky 5-5-1.

Products of Alabama, Tennessee, and Arkansas could turn once-established programs around in one or two years. Of course, in their heydays, they could bring in 50 to 100 players in one year for what amounted to one-semester tryouts.

By the 1990s, the limit was 25 per year, 85 all totaled.

Todd Wright

Bear Bryant gained renown of sorts for what he did at Texas A&M in 1954, his first year there. The legend and the truth coincided: He took two busloads of candidates to a pre-season camp at a hot, drab, and dusty A&M outpost at Junction, Texas, and two weeks later, needed just one bus for the return.

"It was the worst thing I ever did," Bryant said many times. Those Aggies went 1-9. They did establish Bryant's standards, but the notoriety of that widely told story ended all hopes of appealing to quality kids the rest of the time. The Aggies won three years there with their first freshmen (not eligible in 1954), but every other class was mediocre. When Alabama ("mother," as Bryant put it) called in December 1957, he hurried home.

Ford accepted his fate.

It takes well over 100 (counting walk-on) athletes to keep a good college program going. Arkansas's recruiting had sagged so since 1987, the numbers dipped to poverty levels. Ford could not run off fat fullbacks or weak players or malcontents. That is not his nature, anyway. He counseled, gave second and third chances, cited the advantages of degrees—anything to preserve the numbers as well as the futures of young men who had to be convinced of what was at stake, what could be done.

Leading into the 1995 season, Ford could and did say all over the state, "We don't have a lot to talk about, but we can show you a squad of student athletes who will go to school, will make their grades, will represent their state in a positive manner, will stay out of the newspapers."

Two of his starting seniors had once had brief flings as hot-check artists. Some had been rescued from alcohol or alleged sex offenses.

Ford had a five-man staff working overtime to encourage and counsel. That, of course, is a process almost all rebuilding coaches must sponsor—well, nowadays, all coaches.

And he spoke the truth. Although half of them weren't yet ready to play, he had remade the Razorbacks into a group anyone would be proud of. Confidence and morale can grow from that, too.

There are almost always enough athletes and fighters at Arkansas to make up a decent defense, if the coaching is there, and Kines was there with a good staff. They made the most of pass rusher deluxe Henry Ford, Crowe's best recruit, a first-round draft choice from Fort Worth; Orlando Watters, a sleeper from Alabama who made big plays from the secondary for four years; Ray Lee Johnson, a smiling assassin from Fordyce; and Junior Soli, a Samoan from a military family at Fort Benning, Georgia.

Offensively, the Hogs could not knock anyone off the ball in front of the two goal lines. They couldn't catch the ball properly, and their kicking game was a disaster. In three years, they had one big-hearted running back, Oscar Malone (hurt in 1994, held out in 1995), and no other fullback worth his salt.

Some of that was a lack of spirit.

"It is hard to build confidence when you've had it and lost it," Ford said. Many of the athletes had been recruited with the idea that they'd always go to Cotton Bowls, as in 1988–89. Some thought many squadmen never recovered from the nature of and the impact of the loss to Mississippi in 1990.

Henry Ford

Worse than that, when Ford brought in not one but two of his former Clemson aides to restore the offensive line in 1993, they looked around in shock. They had never seen such unlikely prospects at Clemson. The two veteran coaches seemed to remain deflated through their departures two years later.

"Fragile," is a word Ford often used to describe the Hogs' backbones. Indeed, in 1994, they lost seven games in which they still had a chance in the fourth quarters.

The previous year, they fell back repeatedly because of missed field goals, poor snaps, blocked kicks.

And they fumbled—and didn't post many recovered fumbles or intercept many passes. Lunney could count on looking at 80 yards or so almost every time he took the field.

For three years in the SEC, Arkansas could win only with exceptional effort, only if the other team seemed to be looking the other way, only if the other team did not prepare properly for the only edge the Hogs had. That was the true triple-option series on offense—with judicious passing; that is, if a fullback, the first threat in the triple, was available that day.

In Ford's first two games, they never led two weak teams until the final seconds but beat SMU, 10-6, and South Carolina, 18-17.

When ESPN commentator and ex-coach Mike Gottfried saw that 2-0 start roll by, he said, "Obviously, Danny Ford has gotten his new program going."

Hardly. Nothing worked, but then Georgia decided the way to beat Arkansas was to have passer Eric Zeier hand off and to play scared against the triple, back off. Arkansas won, 20-10. A 72-yard bomb from Lunney to J. J. Meadors, the tiny young receiver, got things going. Option running did the rest. Lunney was the leading ground gainer with 60 yards.

That was just about it until the season closer at Baton Rouge. For the second year in a row, the Tigers took the triple option so lightly, the Hogs ran for 412 yards (123 by fullback Carlton Calvin). And Orlando Watters returned a pass theft 99 yards in the 42-24 win.

They had wanted a bowl game and could have had it except for a 13-13 tie with Mississippi State at Little Rock. Arkansas led near the end after Watters returned a theft 42 yards for a score, and Marius Johnson ran 13 yards for another, but the extra point was missed. MSU kicked a field goal in the last minute for the stalemate that denied the Hogs what could have been their needed sixth win to meet NCAA standards for bowl teams.

Still, they avoided what would have been Ford's first losing season ever.

Arkansas began 1994 well with a 521-yard, 34-14 assault against SMU. Things were never the same, though, after a star-crossed 14-0 loss at South Carolina. The fans there made it a crusade against Ford, their old Clemson tormentor. The Razorbacks failed on numerous chances to score and succumbed to that bugaboo, the blocked punt. The Gamecocks used one to gain a 7-0 lead and control of the game, even while moving the stakes just four times.

Fans saw a difference the next week when the Hogs played Alabama to 3-3 for 44 minutes before a packed house at Fayetteville. The pain came with seconds left in the third period. Jay Barker got out of trouble, and Sherman Williams turned a short pass into a 73-yard touchdown run for what became a 13-6 victory.

The next week, Memphis deserved to win, again, but an offensive penalty against the Razorbacks on a two-point conversion attempt with 1:38 left made the 16-15 loss harder for Arkansas to take.

After that, the only high point was a 31-7 rout of Ole Miss at Fayetteville. Lunney threw early touchdown passes to the speedy Meadors and Oscar Malone, and the defense set up a runaway in the third period with the pass rush by Marcus Adair and Steve Conley.

The bleak November ended with a 21-point fourth period by LSU at Little Rock, leading to a 30-12 loss.

Madre Hill, later to return a kickoff 100 yards, put Arkansas ahead by 6-0 early, but Tory James blocked the extra-point attempt and returned it 66 yards for a two-pointer. That boomerang changed momentum and let LSU lead 9-6 (which could have been 7-7) all the way to the final period. Typical.

Things had gotten extra serious for Danny Ford, who had never experienced something like 4-7, much less all the silly things that had gone into it.

Ford called it, "A terrible, terrible year that I didn't enjoy much at all, the worst one I've ever been through. Once in a lifetime is enough for something like that. I don't think we want to witness that kind of a year again."

He'd feared as much. Late in July, he'd spotted Oscar Gray and Carlton Calvin, the two fullbacks he needed to tote and block and be senior leaders, grossly overweight. They'd planned on "getting into shape" the miracle way, with an 11th-hour water-loss cure.

With their graduation, or end of eligibility, that type of thinking came to an end.

And in 1995, the Razorbacks found out what, after true conditioning, a true miracle looks like.

However, that was on the come. Coaches' contracts cover January 1 to December 31. In December 1994, while Broyles, the athletic director, and basketball coach Nolan Richardson accepted routine raises from a base of $99,680 to $107,862, Ford declined a similar one, told Broyles not to "roll over" his five-year contract, and canceled raises for his assistants.

He knew how to define the seriousness of things.

By midsummer, at a stop in Dumas, he said, "I hope this is the year to turn the corner and that Arkansas will be like it used to be. Not always with the best players, but man, they played with pride and determination and they cared about being Razorbacks."

He added, "If we can beat someone we aren't supposed to beat, we can accomplish something."

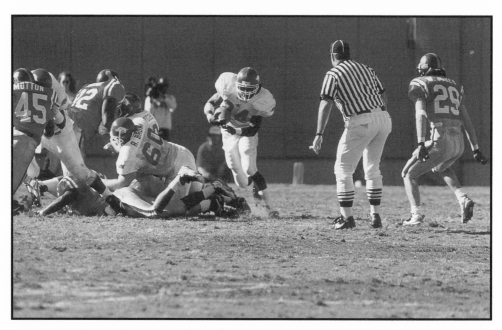

Openings like this for Madre Hill usually mean points.

– 54 –

THE WINNING OF THE SEC-WEST

"We need some heroes," Harold Horton, the recruiting coordinator, said the week of the 1995 opener at SMU.

Initially, they got goats.

With Arkansas ahead, 14-10, and SMU struggling, the defenders in one of Joe Lee Dunn's seemingly arcane schemes all went one way chasing receivers and SMU's pee-wee single back, Donte Womack, ran 37 yards alone the other way to put the Ponies on top. He would gain 137 yards on 21 carries.

In the final seconds, Madre Hill (22-89) was stopped in full flight just a foot from the goal. On the next play, needing six inches, senior quarterback Barry Lunney "dropped" the football. It was recovered behind him by the Ponies, sealing their 17-14 win.

SMU was to lose its next 10 games, many to poor teams.

Arkansas was to win eight of its next nine games and, to the amazement of all, tuck away the championship of the powerful SEC-West.

The Razorbacks, happily, wound up with enough heroes to satisfy Horton and everybody else. But . . . what had happened between 0-1 and 8-2?

Well, a lot of people jumped to the obvious. The day after the loss at SMU, Robert Reed had quit.

Danny Ford demurred. "There's no way it helps to lose a player," he said. "Robert Reed was here to try to help us win. Now, it did remove any question about who would play quarterback for us."

Barry Lunney was "it" from the moment that Reed left. And Ford no longer had any differences with him.

Any new coach coming in wants to see *all* his players out for football any time there is any football activity.

At the time he signed with Arkansas, Lunney was still switching sports every three months at Fort Smith. He won big as a football quarterback, as a basketball point guard, and as a pitcher in baseball. He had a left-hander's guile, and he threw hard enough, about 90 mph, to prompt the Montreal Expos to draft him as a high school senior and offer him $250,000 to sign.

That was in June 1992. The preceding February, Lunney had signed with Jack Crowe to play football for Arkansas. It was something he had always intended to do. And it was something he always put on the front burner. However, Crowe had promised that, after his first year, Lunney would be excused from spring football so he could play baseball.

Ford inherited that agreement and honored it. That doesn't mean he was happy about it. While playing both sports, Lunney would work out indoors for football, getting stronger and somewhat bigger, and then go to baseball, for which he would become leaner and lighter.

In baseball, which he played but two months a year, if that, the masterful control he'd had with his breaking pitches steadily eroded, putting more pressure on his fastball, which got slower, leading batters to wait on it and belt it hard. In the June after his junior year, when he was eligible again for the pro baseball draft, he wasn't named, although he could have signed then with a team or two, leaving Razorback football before his senior year. That he wouldn't think of doing.

In high school, Lunney had never truly had time to lift weights for football. This put him at a disadvantage on the gridiron.

He had the great ability to relax and perform; he could have used more body and arm strength.

Nowadays, it is simple. Athletes who truly "double up" do not achieve their potential in either sport. Most are forced by competition to make a choice by the 10th grade.

When Ford agreed, as with track athletes, they had to be able to contribute (score points) in the second sport, and they had to be available for spring football (now, just 15 days) if called upon.

Like any head coach in his position, Ford applied pressure to Lunney —the guy who started in the fall but wasn't there in the spring. In turn, he listed Cherry and then Reed as his number-one quarterbacks entering spring and again the fall during Lunney's last two years. Each fall, Lunney would demonstrate playmaking, gamesmanship that neither of the other two could match.

However, for 1995, a time of greater pressure, Ford decided to make sure that Reed could say that he was being rewarded for his labors of the spring. He and Lunney were told two days in advance that Reed, and not the three-year starter, would go out for the kickoff at SMU.

Reed played the first two possessions at SMU. He moved the team for two first downs, but looked tight and hesitant. Arkansas trailed, 3-0. Actually, after knocking out SMU's run-pass threat, Ramon Flanigan, on the very first play, the Hogs' new defense, showed little recognition of the run-and-shoot as operated by the number-two man, a senior and a passer. SMU kept the ball for a 10-0 lead before Lunney took over.

The change was dramatic. Lunney looked stronger and sharper than ever, thanks to the fact that he had worked on his football muscles (arms, legs, shoulders) and his speed and quickness at home at Fort Smith all summer.

In the breach at SMU, he packaged big plays (a 28-yard pass to Anthony Eubanks just before the half, a 38-yarder to Carl Johnson just afterward) and Arkansas had a 14-10 edge just three minutes into the second half.

Momentum changed in the fourth quarter when SMU stopped Hill at its 33 on a fourth and 1. The Ponies then sprung Womack for the go-ahead touchdown.

Lunney and Hill performed like demons on the final drive, covering 79 yards in 17 plays. Hill seemed sure to score on a first-down sweep from the five. He was jerked down at the one with a hard face-mask tackle. The penalty put the ball on the six-inch line, first down. Lunney tried what a lot of NFL quarterbacks do. He stuck the ball out in front of him. It may have broken the goal-line plane.

"Who knows?" he said weeks later. "I finally looked at the tape. It shows one of my linemen being knocked back into the ball, which bounced behind me."

After the game, with the stunned Razorbacks sitting motionless against the four walls of the Cotton Bowl dressing room, Lunney turned his back to the arc of writers, showing his teary embarrassment only to his locker. No matter what the question was, he answered over and over, "Earl (Scott) got me the ball. I dropped it."

On the bench next to him, Robert Reed, who had isolated himself from his mates on the sidelines, sat smiling. The next day, Reed bowed out. By week's end, he had transferred to a junior college in his home state of Mississippi, en route to Ole Miss.

The Razorbacks had already rallied around Lunney, their leader of longest standing. The truth was, they had invested too much, from January on, to be quitters as a team.

No one ranted at them, neither Ford nor Dunn, whose defense had spent the game trying to put out one fire after another. When the plane landed just after midnight Saturday, Dunn went to his office. He stayed there. When his aides reported before 7 A.M. Sunday, he handed them the South Carolina game plan and explained the SMU debacle, "We were doing the right things. We just need to do them a lot better."

That set well with a squad that had come to believe in itself and knew it could do better.

Danny Ford had launched his plans for 1995 this way: He said he'd been raised to give credit for victories to his coaches and players, to take the blame for losses himself. No more, he said. "I win, you lose." That was aimed mostly at his aides.

Joe Kines had switched to Georgia, in his home state, after just missing out on becoming head coach at Oklahoma State.

Ford rebuilt his staff and turned over the Xs and Os to his extremely experienced staffers. To direct the defense (and the kicking game), he hired Joe Lee Dunn. The legendary blitz-master had given terrible trouble to the offensively inept Hogs when he was at Memphis and Mississippi, where he had just been let out as interim head coach.

Maybe it was a good idea, Ford said, to give the other teams moving targets to try to block. Dunn, meantime, promised an end to the fourth-quarter losses; he'd get everybody in shape to play 60 minutes, he said.

Indoor conditioning had begun early under Virgil Knight, whose background included Clarksville, Arkansas, the University of Florida, and mostly, the Green Bay Packers. A new NCAA rule permitted most of the squad to spend the summer on campus and follow strength-building exercises laid down by such as Knight.

Then came the hundreds of daily ups-and-downs at the behest of Dunn during two-a-days. These onetime layabouts and avid newcomers began to feel like Razorbacks—paying the price.

At the end of two-a-days, Dunn picked his 11 best defenders and went with them for the year. That's his style. They started with him, finished with him.

Jim Washburn, who'd coached here and there with Ford and his aides, took over the defensive line with a lot of enthusiasm. Louis Campbell turned four senior defensive backs into an aggressive, big-play secondary. Mark Smith lived up to his reputation as a far-ranging line-backer to go with speedy Vincent Bradford. Junior Soli and Geno Bell took the heat inside as Marcus Adair and Steven Conley, a favorite of NFL scouts, harassed the passers from the outside.

Offensively, Ford hired two more enthusiasts, Mike Bender, one of those 11-0 Hogs of 1964, and Charley North, who had (under longtime Broyles aide Mervin Johnson) coached offensive linemen (and recruited really well) for 19 years at Oklahoma. They switched to a simpler zone blocking scheme that fit the Arkansas situation better—and they began telling their blockers how good they were getting to be.

It's Ford's nature to want to beat the other team physically, with body slams in a running attack, and maybe pass for touchdowns. A team that can run the football is just naturally tougher, more aggressive, he says.

He likes a fullback lined up in front of the tailback every time, blocking. Trouble was, no strong fullbacks had emerged in spring or fall. Rockey Felker, the coordinator, appeased his boss. He put a fullback in there after every opening kickoff, then switched to a pro set.

The only time Ford really and truly liked that pro-type concept was in the middle of the third quarter against Auburn, when Arkansas led, 30-7.

Felker had staked his career on his belief that the Hogs would do best while running (and passing) with two or three wideouts (Eubanks and the bigger Anthony Lucas added to the tiny hero, Meadors) and one or two tight ends, with Madre Hill, the all-the-way type, as a single back well behind Lunney.

Scott at center would be surrounded by guards Russell Brown, a stubby rassler from Bristow, Oklahoma, a redshirt freshman, and Verl Mitchell, a senior who would earn a second team all-SEC honor, and returnees Carlos Showers and Winston Alderson at the tackles. Three tight ends contributed: freshmen Al Heringer and Mark Baker and senior Carl Johnson.

The tipoff, the smash dress rehearsal, came during Hall of Honors weekend (for Eddie Sutton, Ken Hatfield, and others) at Fayetteville in a 51-21 smashing of South Carolina.

Lunney ran for 92 yards on 11 carries (the only day the option was really big) and passed for 179 on 13-18.

Madre Hill scored six touchdowns, a new school record, announcing his arrival as a premier SEC back. His touchdowns measured 3, 1, 2, 1, 12, and 68 yards on a 31-179 day.

Bill Burnett, also an honoree, told Hill on the sidelines that he was expecting his career record of 49 touchdowns to fall, "But, Madre, you don't have to do it all in one day."

Defensive end Steve Conley left SEC quarterbacks with unpleasant memories.

Ford called it, even after the season, "Our best day of the year."

But he wouldn't trade the next week's 20-19 upset of Alabama on the field where he had played his college football.

That first win in six tries over Alabama came on a day when LSU upset Auburn and left the Hogs atop the SEC-West, a spot they never vacated.

It all came down to the season's signature play, a fourth-down pass from the three-yard line from Lunney to Meadors with 0:06 to play.

Did he catch it before it touched the ground?

"Only J. J. knows," Lunney liked to say. "For sure, he is the only man on the field who could have gotten low enough to make that play."

Then came the tie-breaking kick by Todd Latourette, who, as is the life of a good kicker, put in a workmanlike, effective season in virtual privacy. Good kickers draw attention only when they miss.

Lunney had faced a third and 24 at his 30 under three minutes. He got 15 back with a safety-valve pass to Hill, then scrambled and found the big Lucas coming back and then going with the ball down the sidelines for 31 to the Alabama 24. Hill's 10-yard sweep and a 16-yard pass to Meadors gained a first down at the three.

Alabama had to swallow the fourth down call when Meadors turned back and caught the ball maybe an inch above the turf. But Gene Stallings lamented a no-call when Arkansas had 12 men on the field on the previous down. In fact, the SEC suspended the crew that officiated the game. However, as Arkansas has learned the hard way, when a game is over, it's over.

The Tide got two touchdown passes in the second period and took a 19-10 lead in the third period when a questionable safety was ruled on a Hill run starting in the end zone.

The key play of the game was Mark Smith's interception of a Gary Burgdoff pass down the middle at 7:53 in the third period. His 48-yard runback and a personal foul penalty on the end set up Latourette's second field goal, a 21-yarder.

Arkansas's pulling to within six points on a poor pass down field by his shaky quarterback forced Stallings to become (as is his nature) awfully cautious. On a passing down, Burgdoff would throw to the sidelines and, most often, way long or wide (to the safe side) of the receiver.

Thus, Arkansas could load up for the run. The Tide made just one first down in the last half and never threatened to score with its offense.

Alabama fans who had seen the Tide win all of the close ones under Stallings at Tuscaloosa for four years, whatever it took, sat stunned.

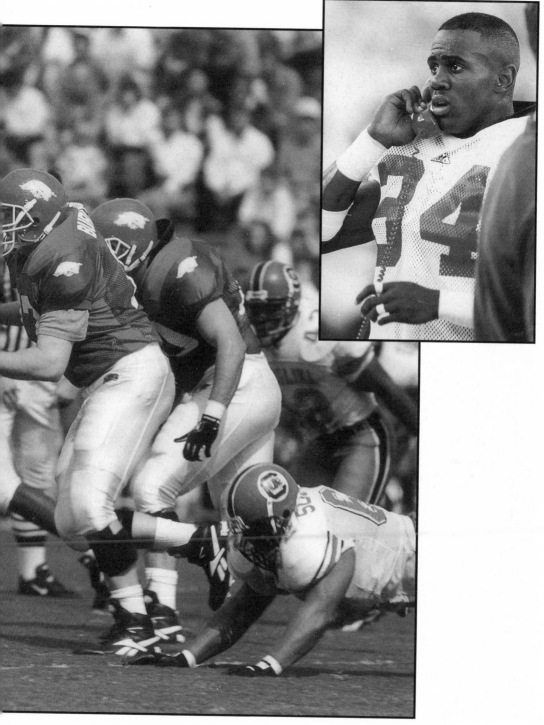

Madre Hill

Hill had a 26-114 day against the best defense in the league, a confidence builder for him and his blockers.

Ford acknowledged the difference in this and his other homecoming game, a 43-3 whipping in 1993, but he declined all truculence. Like Bryant, he tended to let the fans celebrate while he immediately took note of the next opponent.

It became a year of firsts.

The next week, however flat, the Hogs rallied in the fourth quarter to beat Memphis, 27-20, for the first time, and before a full house in Little Rock, the only one ever for that rivalry.

Felker found that they could run as well as pass with three wideouts to one side and a fourth to the other. Lucas began to make big plays, and then Eubanks, and then, with Lucas getting double-covered, Meadors again.

In fact, before a fired-up 52,728 for Tennessee in Fayetteville the following week, Lunney threw to Hill for one touchdown and to Lucas for two en route to a 24-14 lead with 6:07 left in the first half.

The Vols, with Peyton Manning throwing bullets to seven receivers and Jay Graham ripping the middle, sauntered to five straight touchdowns, getting it to 42-24 with 14:53 to play. Tennessee's coaches had spent two, three weeks getting ready, and this paid off.

Madre Hill hit 200 yards even in a wild 35-7 win at Vanderbilt. With that, the Hogs won for the first time in the Liberty Bowl at Memphis, 13-7 over Ole Miss. The Rebs made two big plays on fake kicks to stay even at 6-6. Then they fumbled. On the next play, Madre burst for 71 yards and the tie-breaker.

This brought the Hogs to 5-2 and 4-1 (in the SEC). They knew they'd get back into the bowls for the first time since 1991 (a 6-6 overall finish, Independence Bowl). They also knew that if they could split or sweep Auburn and Mississippi State in Little Rock, they'd win the SEC-West.

The Ole Miss game gave the first indication that this team, which had played five games in September, was showing fatigue. Luckily, the blessed open date before Auburn left Lunney and the team freshened for another team Arkansas had not defeated.

ESPN showcased the showdown with the Tigers and a crowd of 55,630 in War Memorial Stadium for the most important Razorback game there since a 45-39 shootout with Houston in 1989.

Just before halftime, a young reporter in the press box asked an old one how you could tell when a team like Arkansas had finally, really turned everything around. The old guy said, "They just did it."

Arkansas was leading by 24-0 with 6:17 showing in the half. Auburn's offense had been on the field for just 4:45. The Razorbacks went on to lead by 27-0 at intermission.

To coaches, players, and fans watching all over the country, Danny Ford's team had already delivered a message, delivered at the end of ESPN's prime-time telecast, "The Razorbacks are BACK!"

Coach-analyst Mike Gottfried, said, "Every button Danny Ford pushes is the right one."

Some thought the first play tipped the balance. The Hogs' kick coverage was their best of the decade. So was the kicking. Latourette hit the first kickoff deep. Robert Baker, Auburn's brilliant freshman receiver and return man, got sandwiched on the 14, lost the ball, and Marcus Campbell recovered back at the 5.

On third down at the 4, Lunney put four receivers out and saw that Auburn had each one matched closely with a defender. He checked off to a quick slant-in pass that Eubanks caught diving, his back shielding the ball from his man, just across the goal line.

Terry Bowden knew what Rockey Felker had spotted. Auburn's defense had been suspect all year. Bowden had decided to go with his gee-whiz true freshmen at four positions on defense, including nose guard and middle linebacker.

Arkansas could and would run up the middle, throw up the middle, attacking the linebackers. If you can run up the middle, you can run any play—or pass.

Lunney called Madre Hill's number 45 times. Hill delivered 131 yards on 25 carries by halftime.

"It's what I've always dreamed of," said the practically perfect sophomore who had run for 6,000-plus yards at Malvern High. (His Malvern coach, David Alpe, had teased Ford, "Quit fussing at Madre. Just keep giving him the ball.")

For the half, Lunney had completed 12 of 18 precise passes for 125 yards, 6 to Eubanks inside for 53 yards. He converted all seven first downs.

The Hogs scored touchdowns their first three possessions, then two field goals, five for five.

They had run 53 plays for 300 yards.

"We just knocked 'em on their butts," said Mike Bender, something no Arkansas line coach could say until then in a big game in the nineties. "Did you ever see a more perfect half?"

No, but there was a problem. They had to play 30 more minutes.

From the field, ESPN's Mike Adamle said, "Terry Bowden has had nothing to do this half but chomp double time on his Doublemint."

Bowden arguably panicked at the Hogs' immediate touchdown. Arkansas had feared the Tigers' power attack with Stephen Davis, the Heisman trophy candidate who had run roughshod in a three-touch-down final quarter in their previous meeting.

Davis did not appear until Auburn trailed, 14-0. He carried just 7 times for 49 yards, usually on a first down from in front of the goal.

Bowden went with his father's Florida State attack in the hands of his veteran quarterback, Patrick Nix. The no-huddle, four-wide attack didn't get untracked for a half, but it seldom was stopped after halftime.

Arkansas's concern was that Lunney, his face driven into the turf when a late man flung himself full-length on the passer's back just before halftime, might have to play with a broken nose, or worse.

Lunney missed one play. Some thought he lost some effectiveness, but, as he put it, "Our strategy changed. Auburn wasn't taking any time off the clock even when they scored. We had to keep the ball, use up time."

Barry Lunney scrambles to deliver the touchdown pass that J. J. Meadors caught diving in the end zone . . .

And they did. Lunney's short passes and runs and Hill's gutty slashes went into three long second-half drives that resulted in Latourette's third —and tell-tale—field goal and eventually left Auburn with little time and no timeouts.

On the final play, Lunney kneeled behind a mate on the sidelines and saw the snap go high to Auburn's previously perfect kicker. Furthermore, Junior Soli tipped Matt Hawkins's field-goal try awry.

Arkansas had finished its sweep of the state of Alabama, 30-28.

Ford said, "Lunney showed a lot of poise. He snapped it 85 times. Even with a broken nose, no turnovers. I'm proud of Madre. We had to have him in there. He came out with 186 yards on 45 carries, no fumbles.

"This is about as good as we've ever played. I just wish we'd done it for 60 minutes."

"That was a pretty thing to see," he said of Latourette's 44-yarder that made it 30-7 with 23:14 to play.

Bowden said, "This isn't Auburn's year. Maybe it's Arkansas's year. I know that Lunney is just sensational. He will not turn the ball over. We needed him to do it just once, but he wouldn't."

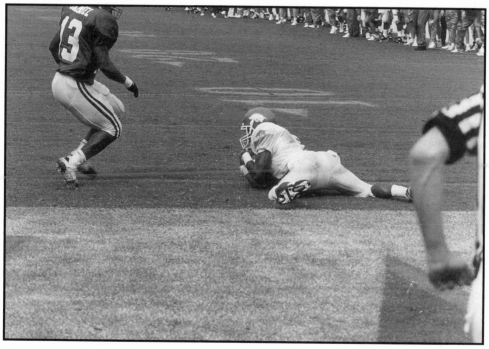

. . . with six seconds left to make possible a 20-19 victory over Alabama that turned around the 1995 season.

The next week, in that 11:30 A.M. Jefferson Pilot time slot that can be unfortunate for the favored home team, Lunney did the unthinkable on the very first play. He threw a hitch pass on a long line drive out to the corner, and Walt Harris, the veteran MSU safety, read it all the way for a pick and a solo 37-yard runback.

Lunney's next two passes went for touchdowns—for Arkansas, 64 yards to Kotto Cotton and 29 yards to Eubanks. When Conley tackled the MSU passer for a safety and a 26-21 lead at 1:34, the game looked safe. But Phillip Hayes had to break up a last-play Hail Mary pass in the end zone to save it.

It was another big first, putting the Hogs (7-2 and 6-1) into the SEC championship game against Florida.

Jackie Sherrill made the definitive statement after the game. Answering a question, the MSU coach said, "No, Arkansas doesn't have the best players, but it is playing the best football."

However, that spell had been broken.

The Hogs became the hunted, not the hunters. The other teams paid much more attention. They went to man-to-man coverage.

Danny Ford, finding the going tough, . . .

"They took a lot of our passing away," Lunney noted.

Turnovers always tell the tale. For the first eight games, through Auburn, Arkansas was plus 11 in turnovers, 16 takeaways (interceptions, recovered fumbles) and only 5 turnovers. So, the Razorbacks turned the ball over 14 times in their last four games.

Del Delco, Mike Nunnerly, and Conley for the defense broke the backs of little Southwestern Louisiana, 24-13.

With the SEC's best defense, LSU stifled the Hogs at Baton Rouge, 28-0 (the halftime score). Florida made no errors but many big plays, and Arkansas turned it over four times in the title game at Atlanta. The Gators took a 34-3 ticket to the college championship game. Early in the game at Atlanta, Madre Hill went down with the dreaded ACL joint tear in a knee. And North Carolina cashed in on two freak plays to rally for a 20-10 win in a blah Carquest Bowl game at Fort Lauderdale.

Arkansas lost eight turnovers in the first half against LSU and against Florida and Carolina—and achieved just one takeaway in the three games.

Turnovers represent physical and mental breakdowns.

The Hogs ran out of emotion, ran out of physical energy, fans said.

. . . urges the tough to get going.

This happens to most turn-around teams, over-achievers usually lacking in depth.

John Barnhill's 1946 team changed 3-7 to 6-3-1 and the Cotton Bowl, but it lapsed at the end. Bowden Wyatt's 1954 team changed 3-7 to 8-3 and the Cotton Bowl in 1954, but had started 7-0. Frank Broyles changed 4-6 to 9-2 and a championship in 1959, but with lapses.

Arkansas had played 13 games stretching from September 2 through December 30, its most arduous path ever.

Lunney set career school records for passing yards, most starts, completions, attempts, and touchdown passes. His most impressive feat might have been in taking part in a single-year record 400 runs/passes.

By the same token, Hill carried his load with three school records, 307 carries; 45 carries in one game; 1,387 yards rushing for the season (with not one lost fumble).

Emphasizing the long, hard route they followed, Joe Lee Dunn said

Barry Lunney and Madre Hill embrace after one of 1995's improbable wins.

just before departing for Jackie Sherrill's staff at Mississippi State, "Schedules determine what kind of year you have. Arkansas had 10 road games. I know the fans help at Little Rock, but we went through the same travel schedule there that our opponents did."

Arkansas had played all four powers of the SEC, Tennessee and Florida from the East as well as Alabama and Auburn (and now well-manned LSU) of the West.

Florida would replace Vandy on the Arkansas schedule for the next two years.

Ford said after the SEC title game in Atlanta, "Thank you for letting us come, Commissioner [Roy] Kramer. We'll be back."

He blurted out softly, "We hope."

He noted wryly, "We're looking forward to playing Florida again four games ahead, but first we get Alabama."

Before the season, Ford had said, "We are four or five years away from competing with Notre Dame and Southern Cal and everybody else, like [Nolan Richardson's] basketball does. One day, we'll be like basketball. First, we've got to get our highway [540 from Alma to Fayetteville] done and our airport [regional, near Rogers] built."

By then, with another round of very good recruits indicated, he may have what he lacked his first few years, enough solid players to rotate two at each position.

When Frank Broyles arrived in 1958, there was that deep-seated need "to beat all those Texas teams." The Razorbacks under Broyles (and in all sports) did that.

Danny Ford arrived 35 years later to handle a greater challenge, one posed by the national championship basketball and track programs. Ford has accepted his task—that of recruiting more magnificent players from all over and beating all those storied teams from everywhere. This is not impossible anymore.

"We've only scratched the surface," Ford told fans after the winning of the SEC-West.

For Razorback football fans, thwarted in the 1980s when they thought their heroes were ready for such as Miami, Oklahoma, and UCLA, the best may be yet to come.

RAZORBACK LETTERMEN, 1894–1995

A

Abernathy, Chad '95
Adair, Marcus '93, '94, '95
Adams, Dave '61, '62, '63
Adams, Gary '66, '67, '68
Adams, Gary '89, '90, '91, '92
Adams, O'Neal '39, '40, '41
Adams, Oliver '27, '28
Adams, Tim '76, '77, '78
Adkins, Jim '56
Akerfelds, Darrel '81
Akers, Freddy '58, '59
Akins, Chris '95
Akins, Terry '92
Alberty, Brett '87
Alberty, Joe Paul '58, '59, '60
Alcorn, E. '23
Alcorn, Hal '17, '18, '20
Alcorn, R. E. '17, '18, '19, '20
Alderson, Winston '94, '95
Alexander, Brother '84, '85
Alexander, Marion '43
Alexander, Tim '76
Allen, Clint '76
Allen, Jason '91, '92, '93, '94
Allen, Joe '09
Allen, V. V. 1896
Allison, Robert '39
Alworth, Lance '59, '60, '61
Amis, William '21, '22
Anderson, Gary '79, '80, '81, '82
Anderson, Ken '94, '95
Anderson, Kevin '84, '85
Anderson, Paul '44, '45
Apolskis, Rick '86, '87, '88, '89
Armendariz, Richard '84
Atkinson, Drexel '48, '49
Atteberry, Dwight '90, '91
Atwater, Steve '85, '86, '87, '88
Atwood, Ralph '37, '38, '39
Audas, Stan '73, '75
Avery, Steve '73, '75
Avlos, Nick '73
Ayers, James '25, '26

B

Bagby, Herman '23, '24
Bailey, Jack '50
Bain, James '15, '16, '19
Baker, Mark '94, '95
Baker, Pat '93, '94
Baker, Victor '80
Baldridge, Joe '49
Baldwin, Alton '43, '44, '45, '46
Baldwin, Jake '45, '49
Banks, Curtis '88, '89, '90, '91
Banks, Tim '65
Barker, Hubert '40, '41
Barnes, Charlie '58
Barnes, J. J. '01
Barnes, Jim '66, '67, '68
Barnes, Teddy '73, '74, '75
Barrow, Bubba '86, '87, '88, '89
Barwegen, Doug '75, '76, '77
Basore, George '19, '20, '21
Bass, Bill '47, '48, '49
Baxter, Robert '79
Bayne, Louis '44
Bazzel, David '81, '82, '84, '85
Beachum, Rodney '82, '83, '84, '85
Beane, Colmore '44
Beard, Abner H. 1900, '02
Beard, Chip '82
Beard, Scott Oscar '03
Beavers, Garland '26, '27, '28
Belknap, Ray '19
Bell, Geno '93, '94, '95
Bell, Mark '87, '88, '89
Bell, Richard '57, '58
Bender, Mike '64, '65
Bennett, Archie '70, '71
Bennett, Richard '55, '56, '57
Bennett, Ronnie '69, '70
Benoit, Steve '70
Benson, Buddy Bob '54, '55
Benson, Ken '89, '90
Benson, Mike '86, '87
Benton, James '35, '36, '37
Benton, Jim '70, '71, '72
Benton, W. R. '32, '33, '34
Bentz, J. L. 1895

Bequette, Chris '84, '85, '86, '87
Bequette, George '54, '55, '56
Bequette, Jay '80, '81, '82
Bercher, Martine '64, '65, '66
Berner, Dennis '67, '68, '69
Berry, Benny '54, '56
Berry, Charlie '56
Berry, Greg '83
Berry, Homer '22, '23, '24
Berryhill, Stuart '64, '65, '66
Beutelschies, Gene '62
Bickerstaff, Ray '45
Biddle, Joe '32, '33
Billings, Fred M. '02
Billingsley, Mickey '74, '76, '77
Binnion, Scott '70, '71, '72
Biocic, Jerry '86, '87
Birdwell, Steve '69, '70, '71
Black, Charles '32, '33
Black, Joe '64, '65, '66
Blackburn, Claud '24
Blackburn, Clifford '23, '24
Blackmer, E. '01
Blakely, Gervis T. '10
Blakely, Ronnie '61
Bland, John '85, '86, '87, '88
Blevins, Paul '69
Bloom, John R. '03, '04
Boatwright, William 1897, 1898
Bobo, Donny '76, '77, '78
Boepple, Emil '32, '33
Bogard, Jerry '51, '52, '53
Bohanon, Alex '93
Boles, John '56, '57
Bolton, Andy '73
Bonneau, Rob '89
Booth, Marc '91
Boozman, H. '24, '25, '26
Boozman, John '71, '72
Boren, Phillip '79, '81, '82, '83
Boschetti, Mike '68, '69, '70
Botkin, Kirk '90, '91, '92, '93
Boulware, David '93
Bowles, Darryl '79, '80, '81, '82
Boyd, Bill '54
Brabham, Danny '60, '61, '62

Bracey, Bill '51
Bradford, Bill '09, '10, '11, '12
Bradford, Carl '85, '86, '87
Bradford, Eddie '52, '53, '54
Bradford, Eric '85, '86, '87, '88
Bradford, Mike '78, '80
Bradford, Vincent '93, '94, '95
Bradford, William '21
Bradley, Freddie '91
Bradley, Melvin '95
Bradsher, Bobby '71
Branch, Jesse '61, '62
Branch, Job '84, '85
Brand, Rodger '71, '72
Brand, Rodney '67, '68, '69
Brandt, Jason '88, '89, '90
Brannon, Robert '83, '84
Brasher, Tommy '61, '62, '63
Brasuell, Jackie '63, '64, '65
Braswell, J. C. 1894
Brawner, Jim '71, '72
Bray, Don '94, '95
Brazil, Ernest '17, '18
Briggs, Oscar Garner 1899
Britt, Maurice '38, '39, '40
Britt, Tommy '51
Brittenum, Jon '63, '65, '66
Brooks, John '91
Brooks, Sam '94, '95
Brooks, Wm. Bud '52, '53, '54
Brothers, Richard '85, '86, '87, '88
Brown, Charlie '74
Brown, Fred I. 1900, '01
Brown, J. R. '86, '87
Brown, Justin '95
Brown, Larry '73, '75
Brown, Russ '95
Brown, Spencer '92, '93, '94, '95
Brown, Thomas '78, '81, '82
Brown, Vann '34, '35, '36
Brown, Wm. Buddy '48, '49, '50
Browne, Leshon '86
Browning, Eric '89, '90, '91, '92
Bruick, Kevin '85
Bryan, Frank '10
Bryan, Lemuel B. '01, '02
Bryant, Larry Gunn '83
Bryant, Trent '77, '78, '79, '80
Bryant, Wesley '61, '62, '63
Buckalew, Hollis '28, '29, '30
Buckingham, Earl '80, '81, '82
Bull, Scott '72, '74, '75
Bumpas, Dick '68, '69, '70
Burchfield, Mike '77, '78, '79
Burks, Pete '95

Burleson, C. H. '43
Burlingame, Mike '77, '78, '79
Burlsworth, Brandon '95
Burnett, Bill '68, '69, '70
Burnett, Bobby '64, '65
Burnett, Tommy '65, '66
Burns, Billy '72, '73, '74
Burns, Keith '80, '81, '82
Burns, Olan '54, '55, '56
Burris, Pat '89, '90
Busby, Bo '73, '74, '75, '76
Butler, Steve '58, '59, '60
Butz, Sam '49
Bynum, Firman '40, '41

C

Cain, Terrance '88
Calcagni, Mark '84, '85
Calcagni, Ron '75, '76, '77, '78
Caldwell, Ravin '82, '83, '84, '85
Caldwell, Tracy '90, '91, '92, '93
Calvin, Carlton '91, '92, '93, '94
Cameron, Pat '89, '90
Campbell, Charles '15, '16
Campbell, Joe '39
Campbell, Leon '46, '47, '48, '49
Campbell, Louis '70, '71, '72
Campbell, Marcus '94, '95
Campbell, Mike '73, '74, '75
Campbell, R. Roy 1894
Canada, Eugene Bud '45, '46, '47, '48
Cantlope, Tracy '92, '93, '94, '95
Capshaw, Gary '72
Carpenter, J. P. '43
Carpenter, Lewis '50, '51, '52
Carpenter, Preston '53, '54, '55
Carroll, J. J. '15
Carson, Bill '94, '95
Carter, Bill '69, '70, '71
Carter, Bubba '83
Carter, Elmo 1896, 1897
Carter, Harry '42, '46
Carter, J. L. (Nick) '13
Carter, Jan '38, '39, '40
Caruthers, Ernie '78
Castillo, Eric '89
Castleberry, Mike '83
Cato, Daryl '39, '40, '41
Cauthron, Jim '52, '53
Caveness, Ronnie '62, '63, '64
Cawood, Jim Brown 1894
Centers, Donnie '83, '85, '86
Chalene, Scott '81, '83
Chambers, Anthony '85, '86, '87, '88
Chambers, Joe '29, '30, '32

Chapman, Johnson '01, '02
Chatman, Tyrone '90, '91, '92, '93
Cherico, Tony '84, '85, '86, '87
Cherry, Mike '93, '94
Cheyne, Bob '73
Cheyne, Tommy '73, '74, '75
Childress, Bob '56, '57
Childress, Freddie '85, '86, '87, '88
Childress, John '59, '60, '61
Childs, E. '02
Childs, James L. '04
Chinn, John '32
Chipman, Marvin '25, '26
Christenbury, Tom '80, '81
Christian, Don '55, '56, '57
Chunn, Del '90
Cialone, Felice '42
Cissell, Mickey '60, '61
Claborn, Joe '45, '48
Clark, Elbert 1900, '01, '02
Clark, Jack '40, '41
Clark, Jessie '81, '82
Clark, L. '94
Clark, W. H. '30
Clay, Billy '60, '63
Clay, Charles '75, '76, '77, '78
Cleveland, Jay '86
Clyde, Steve '77, '79, '80, '81
Coats, Jeff '39, '40, '41
Cochran, Maurice '15, '16
Cody, Russell '67, '68, '69
Cole, Bob '93
Cole, Charles '56
Cole, George '25, '26, '27
Cole, Johnny '50, '51, '52
Cole, Nathan '95
Cole, Ray '37, '38, '39
Coleman, Eusell '25, '26, '27
Coleman, James W. '16, '17, '18, '19
Coleman, Richard '68, '69
Coleman, Sam '21, '22, '23, '24
Collier, Jimmy '59, '60, '61
Collins, Kirk '88, '89, '90, '91
Collins, Ronnie '76
Conger, Marvin '44
Conley, Steve '92, '93, '94, '95
Connor, Paul '65, '66, '67
Cook, Jake '13, '14
Cooks, Mark '95
Cooney, Anthoney '86, '87, '88, '89
Cooney, Mike '58
Cooper, David '65, '66, '67
Cope, Robert '43, '44
Corbett, Lundy '36
Cordell, Corkey '70, '71

Cordelli, Mark '86
Corgan, Charles '23
Cornelius, Jesse '94, '95
Cornish, Bryan '91, '92, '93, '94
Corrotto, Leo '23
Cory, A. B. 1894
Cory, Henry J. 1894
Cotton, Kotto '91, '92, '93, '95
Counce, Dale '45, '46, '47
Courtney, J. G. 1898
Covington, Pete '56
Cowger, James '25, '26, '27
Cowins, Ben '75, '76, '77, '78
Cox, Curtis '59, '60
Cox, David '68, '69
Cox, Harold Earl '43, '48
Cox, Harold Eugene '52
Cox, James '47
Cox, Steve '71
Cox, Steve '79, '80
Crabaugh, Alfred J. '21, '22, '23
Crabaugh, Quentin '27, '28, '29
Crafton, James '47, '48
Craig, Reggie '72, '73, '74
Crawford, Danny '73, '74
Crawford, Kerry '85, '86, '87, '88
Creekmore, Steve '08, '09, '10
Creighton, Milan '28, '29, '30
Criswell, Oliver '33, '34
Crocker, Patrick '89, '90
Crockett, Bobby '63, '64, '65
Cross, Bob '50
Crow, Olan '45
Crowley, L. G. 1896
Culpepper, Oren '54, '55, '56
Culwell, J. D. '04, '05, '06, '07
Cunningham, Dick '64, '65, '66
Curry, Ken '70
Cypert, Boyd '10, '11, '12

D

Daily, Marvin '73, '74, '75
Dale, Jack '28, '29, '30
Dalton, Dallas '50
Dameron, Kim '79, '80, '81, '82
Daniel, Charles '63, '64
Danielowicz, Mark '84, '85
Darr, Earl '29, '30, '31
Daugherty, Ray '47
Daves, Joe Paul '66, '67
David, Richard '90, '91, '92
Davidson, Gene Sodie '15, '16, '17, '18, '19
Davis, Elijah '73, '74, '75, '76
Davis, Isaac '90, '91, '92, '93
Davis, Jeff '91

Davis, Mike '71, '72
Davis, Raymond L. '07, '08, '09, '10
Davis, Vincent '91
Davis, Walter '43
Davis, Wm. Jake '46, '49
Deason, Jess '55
DeBorde, Skipper '71
Delco, Del '92, '93, '94, '95
Delmonego, Frank '41, '42
Deloney, Ernest D. '05
Derry, Lee '23, '24
DeSalvo, Henry '47
Dew, Robert '69
Dew, Tommy '67, '68, '69
Dewey, Mark '78, '79
Dhonau, Lloyd '25, '26
Dickerson, Ron Jr. '89, '90, '91, '92
Dickey, David '66, '67, '68
Dickson, Earnest '07, '08
Dickson, Enos H. '06
Dicus, Chuck '68, '69, '70
Dingler, Lamar '43, '44
Dixon, Tommy '67, '68
Donalson, John '35, '37
Donathan, Jay '55, '56, '57
Donathan, Jeff '26, '27
Donoho, Tommy '44
Dossey, Jerry '67, '68, '69
Douglas, Freddie '72, '73, '74, '75
Douglas, Mark '79, '80, '81, '82
Douglas, Steve '79, '80, '81
Douglass, Bill '65
Downey, Tim '73
Drake, Randy '72, '73, '74
Drover, W. H. '10, '11
Drummond, Lamar '57
Dubs, Ford '13, '15
Duckworth, Bobby '77, '78, '79, '80
Dudley, David '83, '84, '85, '86
Dudley, Paul '59, '61
Duffy, Richard '84
Dugan, Joe '49
Duke, Alvin C. '46, '47, '48, '49
Dumas, Sammy '51, '52
Dunagin, Sean '80
Duncan, Wm. Robert '53
Dunkelgod, Dennis '73

E

Eakin, Kay '37, '38, '39
Eason, Alcuin P. '02, '03, '04
Eason, Darrel '83, '84
East, Jack '22
Eckert, George '48, '49, '50
Eckwood, Jerry '75, '76, '78

Edmonds, Bobby Joe '83, '84, '85
Edmondson, Jim '30, '31, '32
Edwards, Fred '69, '70
Edwards, Ross '17
Edwards, T. A. 1895, 1896
Egan, Bob '50
Eichler, John '67, '68, '69
Eidson, Gus '32, '33, '34
Ellington, T. E. '05, '06, '07, '08, '09
Elliott, Jim '77, '78, '79, '80
Elliott, Marcus '82, '83, '84
Ellis, William Y. 1900, '01
Ellison, Lance '91, '92, '93, '94
Elton, Murry '51, '52
Epp, Marlin '58, '59, '60
Erwin, J. L. Buzz '68
Erwin, Judson L. '30, '31, '32
Estes, Dan '08, '10, '11, '13
Ettinger, Jack '71, '72, '73
Eubanks, Anthony '94, '95
Evans, Hoover '60, '61, '62
Evans, Kevin '76, '78, '79, '80
Ewart, James B. '17, '19, '20

F

Farrell, Robert '76, '77, '78, '79
Faulkinberry, Charles '52
Faurot, Ron '80, '81, '82, '83
Ferguson, Jerry '56, '57
Ferguson, Joe '70, '71, '72
Ferguson, John '48, '49
Fergusson, John "Bubba" '60
Field, Bobby '68, '69, '70
Fields, Johnny '59, '60
Fields, Milton '80, '81, '82, '83
Fillmore, Sedric '89
Finch, James '62, '63, '64
Finney, Tom '30
Fischel, Frank '49, '50, '51
Fishback, Herbert 1894, 1895, 1896, 1897
Fleming, Bert R. '07, '08, '09
Fletcher, Marion '36, '37, '38
Fletcher, Reed '13
Floor, Ben '87, '88, '89
Flores, Shon '88, '89
Fong, John '58
Ford, Henry '43, '44, '45, '46
Ford, Henry '90, '91, '92, '93
Ford, Jerry '54, '56, '57
Foreman, Jim '53
Foreman, Marshall '84, '85, '86
Forrest, Michael '75, '76, '77, '78
Forrester, Wm. Ron '52, '53
Forsythe, Charles '45
Forte, Robert '40, '41, '42

Forte, Robert (Ike) '74, '75
Forte, Rod '84, '85
Foster, Barry '87, '88, '89
Fowler, Aubrey '46, '47
Fowler, Tommy '61
Franklin, Bill '46, '47
Franklin, Kenny '86
Franklin, Luther '82, '83, '84, '85
Frappia, L. A. '15
Frazier, E. H. '12, '15
Freeland, Stuart '71, '72
Freeman, Reggie '75, '76, '77
Freeman, Stan '78, '79
Freeman, Wm. A. 1897, 1898, 1899, 1900
French, Keith '71
Frieberger, John '38, '39, '40
Fryer, Jimmy '70
Fuchs, Rolland '73, '74, '75
Fulbright, J. Wm. '21, '22, '23, '24
Fulbright, Jack '18
Fulcher, Don '75, '76
Fulcher, Ron '73, '74, '75
Fuller, Bill '53, '54, '55
Fuller, Dick '70
Fulton, Earl '33
Furo, Sammy '49, '50
Futrall, Byron '23, '24

G

Galloway, Bob '76
Galloway, Neal '81, '82
Garber, Russ '69, '70, '71
Gardner, Carnall '27, '28, '29
Gardner, Ellis '34
Gardner, Gerald '58, '59
Garlington, Tom '51, '52
Garner, Lynn '67, '68, '69
Garrett, Dean '59, '60, '61
Garrett, Grant '95
Garrett, Wayne '55
Garrison, Greg '81, '82, '83, '84
Gaston, James '59, '60
Gatson, Carlos '88
Gatson, Greg '82, '83, '84, '85
Geis, Clarence '27, '28, '29
Geiser, Elvin O. '32, '33, '34
Gentry, William '26
Geoghagen, Danny '68
Gibbs, Melvin '64, '65, '66
Gifford, Todd '88, '89, '90
Gilbow, Billy '56, '57, '58
Gilliam, Bobby '53, '54
Gilmore, George '35, '36, '37
Ginn, Charles '80, '81, '82
Ginn, Tom '76, '78, '79

Glover, Steve '72
Goff, Jeff '78, '79, '80, '81
Gold, Paul '17, '18
Goodman, John Ed '83
Gordon, Minor '16
Gordon, Nathan '36, '37
Gotto, Bill '71, '73
Grabiel, Kent '21
Gramlich, Billy '60
Graves, Cecil Buster '51, '52, '53
Gray, Bill '62, '63, '64
Gray, Kenneth '49
Gray, Oscar '92, '93, '94
Green, Jerry '58, '59
Green, Robert '41, '42
Griffin, Mike '70, '71, '72
Griffin, Robert '49, '50, '51
Grizzle, Jim '61, '62, '63
Grooms, Richard '88
Grovey, Quinn '87, '88, '89, '90
Guest, Gordon '63
Guillot, David '84
Gunn, David '86
Gunn, Johnson '52
Gunnell, G. W. 1896
Guynes, W. M. '10, '11

H

Haden, Jack '33, '34, '35
Hagan, Chester Earl '33
Hagler, James '46
Hale, Harvey '15, '16
Hale, Ryan '95
Hales, Mike '62
Hall, DeAnthony '95
Hall, George '78, '79, '80, '81
Hall, Reggie '85, '86, '87, '88
Hallum, Charles '51, '52, '53
Halstead, Glen '44, '49
Ham, H. H. 1897, 1899
Hamberg, Harold '40
Hamberg, Walter '38, '39
Hamilton, Ed '46, '48
Hamilton, Hartford '65, '66, '67
Hamilton, Norman '23, '24, '25
Hamilton, Ray '35, '36, '37
Hammers, Ronnie '68, '69, '70
Hampton, Dan '75, '76, '77, '78
Hampton, Harvey '73, '74, '75, '76
Hampton, William '75, '76, '77, '78
Hanner, Dave '49, '50, '51
Hansard, Harry '20, '21, '22
Hardin, T. H. '15, '16, '17, '18
Hardwick, Richard '54
Harmon, Neil '27

Harnish, Roger '69, '70
Harper, Harb '12
Harper, LaSalle '87, '88
Harrington, Leroy '21, '22
Harris, Al '34
Harris, Albert '86, '87, '89, '90
Harris, Alex '95
Harris, Leotis '74, '75, '76, '77
Harris, Mike '81, '82, '83
Harris, Muskie '73, '74, '76
Harris, Tommy '72, '73, '74, '75
Harris, Wayne '58, '59, '60
Harrison, Charles D. 1898, 1899, 1900
Harrison, Galloway C. '11
Harrison, Ralph '25, '26
Harrison, William Ringold '19
Harshaw, Juju '87, '88, '89
Hartsfield, Eddie '73
Hatfield, Dick '62, '63, '64
Hatfield, Ken '62, '63, '64
Haun, Bobby '82, '83
Hawkins, Waymon '74, '75
Hay, Bruce '76, '77, '78
Hayden, Kenneth '40, '41
Hayden, W. W. 1894
Hayes, Phil '94
Hayes, Rockie '82
Haynes, Bratton '40, '41
Haynes, David '80
Haynie, Bracy '21, '22
Hays, Orren '28, '29, '30
Hebert, Dexter '93, '95
Hedgepeth, Steve '71, '72, '73
Heim, Steve '75, '76, '77
Henderson, Charles '14
Henderson, DeMatt 1899, 1900
Henderson, Ed '48
Henderson, Gerald '56
Henderson, Paul '58, '59, '60
Hendren, Mike '67, '69
Henry, Cliff '79, '80, '81
Henry, Mark '88, '89, '90, '91
Henry, Michael '95
Henry, Tyrone '94, '95
Henson, David '87
Henson, Harold (Sonney) '45, '46, '47
Heringer, Al '95
Herman, Chuck '77, '78, '79
Hickey, Howard '38, '39, '40
Hicks, Anthony '93, '94, '95
Higgins, Mike '94
Hile, Kevin '93, '94
Hill, J. W. '03
Hill, Madre '94, '95
Hill, Tom '84, '85

Hill, Wade '91
Hines, Glen Ray '63, '64, '65
Hinson, Dock Newton '18
Hinton, L. E. Percy '10, '11, '12
Hirschfield, Hal '73
Hix, Billy '48, '49
Hixson, Guy '07, '08, '09
Hobbs, Wilburn D. 1898, 1899
Hockersmith, Glen '67, '68
Hockersmith, Steve '69
Hodge, Jim '70, '71, '72
Hoehn, Steve '65, '66, '67
Hoffman, John '45, '46
Hogan, Brad '93
Hogan, Floyd '73, '74
Hogue, David '69, '70, '71
Hogue, Larry '50, '51, '52
Holderby, R. H. '20
Holland, Kenneth '46, '47
Hollander, Jim '58, '59
Hollingsworth, Mark '71, '72
Holloway, Derek '80, '81, '82
Holly, Zeylon '40
Holmes, O. Wendell '28, '30, '31
Holmes, Tony '86, '87
Holt, Jack '35, '36, '37
Hooper, Tommy '68
Hopkins, Terry '69, '70
Hopson, E. E. '06
Horne, Greg '83, '84, '85, '86
Horner, John '84
Horsfall, Frank 1895, 1896, 1897
Horton, Don '55, '57, '58
Horton, Harold '60, '61
Horton, Tim '86, '87, '88, '89
Houfek, Keith '79, '80
Houston, Rex '30
Howard, Dexter '91, '92, '93
Howard, Gary '61, '62, '63
Howard, Jim '77, '78, '79
Howard, Shedrick '89
Howell, Jim Lee '33, '34, '35
Hubbell, Webb '67, '68
Hudson, Bryan '95
Hudson, Steve '88, '89, '90
Hudson, W. '94
Hughes, Howard '47, '48
Hughes, Max '80
Hunter, Billy '36
Hunter, Chris '86, '87, '88, '89
Huntley, Bruce W. '11, '12
Huntley, P. C. '08, '09, '10, '11
Hust, A. S. 1898
Hutton, Counts '04, '05
Hyatt, Robert F. '06

I

Ihrie, Mike '82, '84
Ireland, Darwin '90, '91, '92, '93
Irwin, Clark '71, '72
Irwin, Jim '71, '72
Irwin, Terry '74

J

Jackson, Aaron '86, '88, '89, '90
Jackson, Alfred '91, '92, '93, '94
Jackson, Carl '43
Jackson, E. D. '89, '90, '91, '92
Jackson, Ed '79, '80, '81, '82
Jackson, Elmer '46, '47
Jackson, Larry '76, '77, '78
Jackson, Nick '95
Jackson, O. C. '76, '77, '78
Jacobs, Mike '68
Jamerson, Charlie '19, '20, '21
James, Bruce '68, '69, '70
James, Frank D. 1894, 1896, 1899
James, Michael '89, '90, '91
Japp, Gus '24, '25, '26
Jefferies, Elrod B. '34, '35
Jeffers, Solomon L. 1897
Jeffery, Tony '91, '92
Jenkins, J. R. '84
Jenkins, John '71
Jernigan, Hugh '78, '79, '80
Jett, William '04, '05
John, Jim '61, '62, '63
Johnson, Carl '91, '92, '94, '95
Johnson, Charles '43, '44
Johnson, Cordale '92, '94
Johnson, James '62, '63, '64
Johnson, Joe '85, '86, '87, '88
Johnson, Lee '64, '65, '66
Johnson, Lewis '31, '32, '33
Johnson, Marius '92, '93, '94, '95
Johnson, Ray Lee '90, '91, '92
Johnson, Robert '35
Johnson, Virgil '41, '42
Johnson, Willie '91, '92, '93, '94
Jones, Alvin '65, '66, '67
Jones, Ben '42, '43
Jones, Carroll '44
Jones, David Paul '41, '42
Jones, Guy '64, '65
Jones, Harry '64, '65, '66
Jones, Herschel '52
Jones, Jamie '71
Jones, Jerry '62, '63, '64
Jones, Jeryl '83, '84, '85
Jones, Meredith '41, '42
Jones, Nathan '81, '82, '83, '84

Jones, Ricky '82
Jones, Ronnie '69, '70, '71
Jones, Steve '71
Jones, Steve '84, '85, '86, '87
Jones, Todd '87, '88
Jones, Tom '79, '80, '81, '82
Jones, Tommy '91
Jordan, Clark '32, '33, '34
Jordan, George '32, '33
Jordan, George '58
Jordan, Ivan '72, '73, '74, '75
Jordan, Jim '68
Jordan, Mike '64, '65, '66
Jurecka, Mike '75
Jurney, Bill '50, '51

K

Kaiser, Earl '52
Karr, Elwin '31
Keen, Allen '35, '36
Keith, Lee '91
Kelly, M. LeRoy '29, '30, '31
Kelly, Owen '89, '90, '91, '92
Kelson, Mike '69, '70, '71
Kempf, Kevin '92
Kennedy, Bill '70, '71
Kennedy, Kerry '90, '91, '92
Kenney, James S. '13, '14
Kerby, Kent '27, '28
Kersey, Rick '68, '69, '70
Kessinger '84, '86, '87
Kestner, Troy '91, '92
Ketcher, William '66, '67
Keyser, Dick '52
Kidd, Carl '93, '94
Kidd, Keith '81, '82, '83
Kilbourn, Rex '21, '22
Kilgore, Larry '70, '71
King, Bobby '82, '83
King, Cyrus '24
King, Lee '72, '73, '74
King, Les '77
King, Steve '72
Kingsby, Jim '82
Kinnebrew, Chris '92, '93, '94
Kinyo, John '89
Kirby, Chris '90, '91
Kirek, Paul '79
Kirkland, Mike '72, '73, '74, '75
Knapp, Trent '92, '93, '94
Kobel, Raleigh 1894
Kobza, Marty '82
Koch, Greg '73, '74, '75, '76
Kolb, Jim '54
Kolenda, Greg '76, '77, '78, '79

Korte, Steve '81, '82
Kyle, Winton '29, '30
Kyser, Billy '57, '58, '59

L

Lackey, Greg '68
LaFargue, Richard '73, '74, '75
LaForge, Ralph '32, '33, '34
Lahay, Bruce '78, '79, '81
Lairmore, F. G. '38
Lake, Howard '33, '34
Lalman, Ed '36, '37
Lamb, Jerry '62, '63, '64
Lambert, Eugene '27, '28
Lambright, Frank '44, '46, '47
Lane, Calvin '44, '45
Langston, Tim '60, '61, '62
Lashley, David '51, '52, '53
Lasker, Greg '82, '83, '84, '85
Latourette, Todd '95
Lawhon, Jay '40, '41, '42
Ledbetter, Homer '29, '30, '31
Lee, Mark '81, '82, '83, '84
Lemond, Martin '76
Lenz, Bill '85
Letsinger, Leslie '58, '59, '60
Leverett, Charles D. '06
Leverett, G. V. '14
Lewis, Mark '74, '75, '77
Lewis, Robert '69
Lindsey, Jim '63, '64, '65
Lindsey, Lyndy '88, '89, '90, '91
Lindsey, Marvin '43
Lindsey, Wright 1894
Linebarier, Bob '51, '52
Linebarier, Chester '49
Lineberger, Jerry '60, '61, '62
Lisko, Frankie '83, '84
Little, Emmett 1900, '01
Little, Steve '74, '75, '76, '77
Lively, Bill '71
Lively, Charles '42, '46, '47
Lloyd, Odis '85, '86, '87, '88
Locke, Birt '77, '78, '79
Logsden, Robert '50
Logue, Donald '49, '50
Long, Francis '52
Long, Gordon '44, '46, '47, '48
Long, Scott '89, '90, '91, '92
Looney, Stacy '47, '49
Loudermilk, J. W. '52
Lowe, Glen '70, '71, '72
Lubker, Herman '42, '46
Lucas, Anthony '95
Lucky, Art '75

Lueders, Jamie '84, '85
Lunday, Kenneth '35, '36
Lunney, Barry Jr. '92, '93, '94, '95
Lunney, John '46, '47, '48, '49
Luplow, Billy '58, '59
Luplow, Rollie '55, '56, '57
Lusby, Vaughn '74, '76, '77, '78
Lyons, Bill '54, '55
Lyons, Floyd '37, '38, '39

M

Mabry, Jim '86, '87, '88, '89
Mabry, Tom '69, '70, '71
Mallet, James '91
Malone, Oscar '92, '93, '94
Manor, Brison '73, '74
Marlow, Ronnie '89
Maroney, Mickey '65, '66
Marshall, Fred '62, '63, '64
Marshall, Herbert '51, '52
Marshall, Steven '88
Marshall, Wayne '42
Martin, Drew '36, '37
Martin, E. G. 1897, 1898
Martin, Finis '32
Martin, Lee '12
Martin, Neil '54, '55, '56
Martin, Patrick '75, '76, '77
Martin, Robert '34, '35, '36
Martin, Wayne '85, '86, '87, '88
Mason, Darryl '78, '79, '80, '81
Mason, Ty '88, '89, '90, '91
Massa, Kenn '86
Massey, Mike '76, '77, '78, '79
Massey, Shane '86
Matheney, Ronald '79, '80, '81
Matthews, Walter '54, '55
Matthews, Wilson '42
Mauldin, Travis '65, '66
Maxwell, Bruce '66, '68, '69
May, Pat '67, '68
May, Russell '10, '11, '12, '13
Mays, Dudley '37, '38, '39
Mazza, Carl '52
Mazzanti, Francis '55
Mazzanti, Geno '48, '49
Mazzanti, Jerry '60, '61, '62
McAfee, Hal '73, '74, '75
McAndrews, Joe A. 1898, 1900
McCall, J. K. 1899
McClard, Bill '69, '70, '71
McCollough, William '22
McConkey, Homer '21
McCoy, James '87, '88, '89
McDaniel, Arthur J. 1894, 1895, 1896

McDaniel, Estes '39, '40
McElvogue, Don '66, '67
McFadden, Gerald '54, '55
McGaha, Melvin '44, '46, '47
McGaughey, Chris '90
McGee, David '83, '84, '85
McGill, J. Tate '16, '19, '20
McGill, Leighton '25, '26
McGowan, James '83
McHan, Lamar '51, '52, '53
McIntosh, Ellis '43
McKinney, Chuck '74
McKinney, George '59, '60, '61
McKnelly, Tom '62, '63, '64
McLain, C. J. '95
McMurray, Gerald '81
McNair, Bill '42
McNulty, Gordon '68, '69
McQuay, Ken '87, '88, '89
Meacham, Allen '88, '89
Meadors, J. J. '92, '93, '94, '95
Meadors, Johnnie '74, '75, '76
Measel, John '33, '34
Meyer, Percy B. 1899
Meyers, J. C. '02, '03
Michael, Billy '56, '57, '58
Michael, Edward '45
Milam, Charles '43, '48, '49, '50
Miles, Wayne '72
Milford, C. C. '04, '05, '06, '07, '08, '09
Miller, Carl '82, '83, '84, '85
Miller, Chris '95
Miller, Mark '73, '74, '75
Miller, Nick '83, '84, '85
Miller, Richard '27, '28, '29
Miller, Richie '85, '86, '87, '88
Miller, Scott '90
Mills, E. F. '13
Minor, James '46, '47
Miros, Greg '85
Mistler, Mark '81, '82, '83
Mitcham, Marty '77, '78, '79
Mitchell, Bruce '73, '74, '76
Mitchell, James 1895, 1896
Mitchell, Monroe '83
Mitchell, Verl '92, '93, '94, '95
Mobra, Frank '49
Mohammed, Alfred '78, '79, '81, '82
Mohr, Mike '84
Monday, James '84
Monroe, James '56, '58, '59
Montgomery, Bill '68, '69, '70
Montgomery, Lloyd '36, '37
Moody, Billy Joe '60, '61, '62
Mook, Ed 1894

Moon, Phillip '78, '79, '80
Moore, Billy '60, '61, '62
Moore, Charlie '60, '61
Moore, George J. '05
Moore, H. Dade 1894
Moore, Henry '53, '54, '55
Moore, James L. 1895
Moore, Jerry '61
Moore, Jerry '68, '69, '70
Moore, Jess '03, '04
Moore, Joe Faye '27, '28, '29
Moore, Tommy '61, '62, '63
Mooty, Jerry '65
Mooty, Jim '57, '58, '59
Moran, Jack '65, '66
Moranz, George '52
Morgan, Claud '23
Morris, Jack '70
Morris, James '85, '87, '88
Morris, Teddy '78, '79, '80, '81
Morrison, Matt '72, '73, '74
Morrison, Pat '68, '69, '70
Morton, Dickey '71, '72, '73
Morton, Lock '23
Moseley, John '72
Mosier, Cody '88, '91
Mosley, Eddie '95
Mosley, Frank '37, '38
Mullins, Jim '67, '68, '69
Mullins, T. C. '04, '05
Mulrenin, Cass '17
Munson, Mike '85
Murphy, Tom '31, '32, '33
Murrey, J. T. '14
Murrey, Joe H. '13

N

Nagy, Tony '92, '94
Nalley, Louis '66, '67, '68
Nations, Leslie '31, '32
Neal, Aubrey '38, '40, '41
Nealon, Richard '50
Neely, Walter '31
Nelson, Walter '71, '72
Nelson, Willis '07, '08, '09
Nero, Norman '95
Nesbit, Robert '50
Nesbitt, Gerald '55, '56, '57
Newby, Jack '33, '34
Nicholas, Rhody '43
Nichols, Bobby '69, '70, '71
Nichols, Cory '95
Nichols, Q. B. '12
Nix, Edsel '51, '52, '53
Nix, Robert '64, '65

Norman, W. S. 1894
Norton, Delbert A. '05
Norwood, Gordon '67, '68
Norwood, Ray '10
Nunnerly, Mike '92, '93, '94, '95
Nutt, Danny '84
Nutt, Houston '76, '77

O

O'Brien, Kelvin '73, '74
Okoli, Ramon '93
Oliver, Chris '90, '91, '92, '93
Ollison, Tony '87, '88, '89, '90
Olney, Lee S. '03, '04, '05
Ordonez, Ish '78, '79, '80
Orrick, C. E. '07, '08, '09
Overby, Rogers '55, '56
Owen, B. A. '36, '37
Owens, Kerry '85, '86, '87, '88
Owens, Lewis F. 1896, 1897, 1898
Owens, W. B. '38

P

Painter, Zac '95
Paladino, Paul '41, '42
Palmer, Courtney '90
Palmer, L. L. '05, '06
Papageorge, George '48, '49
Parchman, O. D. '13, '14
Parker, Curtis '24, '25
Parker, Dudley '75
Parker, Guy '68, '69, '70
Parker, J. H. 1895
Parker, Mike '62, '63
Parker, Sam '38, '39
Parks, Limbo '85, '86
Parks, Ray '48, '49, '50
Parmer, Mike '73, '75
Parrish, Norm '77
Parson, Gary '68, '69
Peacock, Max '67, '68
Pearce, Howard '40
Pearson, Bobby '55
Peevy, Dean '90, '92, '93, '94
Pennington, Don '48
Pense, Leon '43, '44
Perdue, Gordon '17
Perdue, Monroe '19
Perry, James '93, '94
Perry, Pat '52
Perry, Stuart '55, '56, '57
Perryman, S. S. 1898
Peters, Raymond '47, '48
Petray, Allen '73, '74, '75
Phillip, H. E. '06, '07, '09, '10, '11

Phillip, Stanley '07, '08, '09
Phillips, Chief '12
Phillips, Danny '77, '78, '79, '80
Phillips, Harold Jiggs '50
Phillips, Loyd '64, '65, '66
Phillips, MacKenzie '88, '89, '91
Phillips, Terry Don '66, '68, '69
Phillips, William H. '30, '31, '32
Pickens, Billy '51, '52, '53
Pickett, Daryal '80, '81
Pierce, Bill '80
Pinkston, Greg '55, '56, '57
Pipkin, Joyce '46, '47
Pitner, Matt '89, '90
Pitts, R. C. '41
Plafcan, Cole '94
Poff, A. A. '12
Polk, Tommy '61, '62
Pollard, J. W. 1895, 1896
Poole, H. L. Ike '33, '34, '35
Potts, Thomas O. 1896
Powell, Cliff '67, '68, '69
Powell, William '69
Prescott, Mark '80
Preston, Doyle '92, '93
Price, John '82
Price, Kerwin '88, '89, '90, '91
Prince, Donny '73
Pritchard, Ross '46, '47, '48, '50
Proctor, Bobby '53, '54
Pruett, John R. '05
Pryor, Jerry '92
Pryor, R. Dean '50, '51, '52
Ptak, James V. '19
Putnam, L. E. 1896

R

Raether, Pete '90, '91, '92
Ragland, H. S. '01, '02, '03
Rainwater, Elmer '22, '23
Ramey, Paul '67
Ramsey, Charles '53
Ramsey, Louis '40, '41
Randolph, Billy R. '43
Rankin, Roxie '43
Ratcliff, E. M. '12, '13
Rawlings, Ralph '36, '37
Ray, Herman '34
Reavis, David '70, '71, '72
Reber, Kent '81, '82, '83
Reed, Don '56
Reed, J. L. '12
Reed, R. G. '12
Reed, Robert '94
Reed, Scott '83

Reed, Tom '70, '71, '72
Rees, John '68, '69, '70
Reginelli, Phillip '51, '53
Reichardt, Chris '14, '15, '16
Reichert, James '47, '48
Reid, Jim '56
Reinig, Mike '76
Renfro, Elza '23
Reppond, Mike '70, '71, '72
Reuter, Buddy '58, '59
Revard, Ron '71, '72
Reynolds, Bobby '62
Rhiddlehoover, Jon '72, '73, '74
Rhodes, Danny '71, '72, '73
Rhyne, Jake O. '12
Richards, Don '47
Richards, Jack S. '48, '50
Richardson, Ernie '65
Richardson, Jon '70, '71, '72
Richardson, Richard '79, '80, '81, '82
Riederer, Don '48, '49, '50
Riley, Ozzie '77, '78, '79
Rinehart, Jim '49, '50, '51
Ritschel, Don '56, '57, '58
Rivers, Scott '94, '95
Robbins, Jack '35, '36, '37
Roberts, Odus '37
Roberts, Theron '46, '47, '49
Roberts, Wayland '53, '54, '55
Robinson, Gary '64
Robinson, Jack '29, '30, '31
Robinson, Robert '19, '20, '21
Roebuck, Gene '58
Rogers, Tommy H. 1894, 1895
Rogers, William Buddy '48, '49, '50
Rogers, Yandell '22, '23, '24
Rolen, Chad '87, '88, '89, '90
Roper, Bobby '64, '65
Roper, Gary '74
Rose, Glen '25, '26, '27
Ross, J. R. '76, '77
Ross, Leslie '41
Rosson, Sam '26, '27
Roth, Jim '52, '53, '54
Rouse, James '85, '87, '88, '89
Rowland, Eckel '49
Rownd, Ed '71, '72, '73
Rucker, Choice '33, '34, '35
Rucker, Jeff '24, '25
Rucker, Paul '32, '34
Ruckers, Madison '42
Rudasill, Bill '83
Rudd, James T. '12, '13, '14, '15
Ruggles, William A. 1900, '01, '02
Ruple, Ernest '65, '66, '67
Rusher, Gus '69, '70, '71

Rushing, Gerald '20, '21, '22
Rushing, Jack '48, '49, '50
Russell, Derek '87, '88, '89, '90
Russell, Randy '89
Rutherford, R. P. 1895, 1896
Rystrom, Tom '76

S

Sadler, Nelson '27
Sadler, William P. '14, '15
Sagely, Floyd '51, '52, '53
Sain, Tommy '64, '65
Saint, Mike '70, '71, '72
Sales, Roland '77, '78, '79
Saliba, Eddie '37
Salley, Bryan '79
Sampson, Howard '74, '75, '76, '77
Sanders, C. F. 1895
Sanders, Carrel '17
Sanders, David '94, '95
Sanders, Percy '35, '36
Savage, Jeff '92
Saxton, Jerry '77, '78
Scalet, Joe '38
Scanlon, Kevin '78, '79
Scarbrough, David '41, '42
Schalchlin, George '12
Schaufele, Louis '48, '49, '50
Schaufele, Mike '67
Scheel, Doug '71, '73
Schell, David '84, '85, '86, '87
Schmidt, Harold '40
Schoolcraft, Jim '82, '83
Schoonover, Wear Jake '27, '28, '29
Schumchyk, Frank '44
Schumchyk, Mike '44, '45, '48
Scott, Brad '24, '25, '26
Scott, Clyde '46, '47, '48
Scott, Earl '92, '93, '94, '95
Scott, John T. 1900
Scott, Mike '76, '77, '78
Scott, Tracy '49
Seamster, Savoy '35
Seawell, A. C. 1895
Seawell, W. L. 1895
Secrest, Earl '30, '31
Secrest, Jack '29
Shaddox, John '46, '49
Shakelford, J. M. '16
Shantz, Bobby '80, '81, '82
Shantz, Joe '78, '79, '80
Shaw, Calvin '80, '81, '82, '83
Shaw, Homer '26
Shaw, Thurman '79, '80, '81
Shelby, Shannon '93, '94, '95
Shepherd, Mike '86, '87, '88, '89

Sherland, Mark '32, '33, '34
Shibest, James '83, '84, '85, '86
Shimer, Ted '87, '88, '89, '90
Shofner, Jim '45
Shoup, Brad '76, '77, '78
Showers, Carlos '94, '95
Shumaker, Rick '76, '77, '78
Sidney, Shannon '94, '95
Sigman, Mike '66, '67, '68
Silliman, W. E. '11
Simington, Milton '38, '39, '40
Simpson, Jim '86, '87, '88
Simpson, Travis '48, '49, '50
Sims, Buddy '64, '65
Sims, Chuck '72, '73
Singer, Saul '38, '39
Sisson, Walter '41
Skillern, James '15
Skinner, Gerald '73, '74, '75, '76
Skinner, Jerol '91
Sloan, Chester C. 1898, 1899
Sloan, Dwight Paddlefoot '36, '37
Smart, David '85, '86
Smith, Arlis '17, '20, '21
Smith, Billy Ray '54, '56
Smith, Billy Ray '79, '80, '81, '82
Smith, Calvin '45
Smith, Carl C. '99
Smith, Clarence '20, '21, '22
Smith, Cornelius '76, '77
Smith, Demetrius '90, '91, '93, '94
Smith, DeWitt '67, '68, '69
Smith, Elmer '49
Smith, Fred '24
Smith, Gerald '86, '87
Smith, James H. '49, '50, '51
Smith, James R. '45
Smith, Jarrette D. '48, '49
Smith, L. P. '16, '17, '18, '19
Smith, Mark '86
Smith, Mark '93, '94
Smith, Martin '82
Smith, Minor '24, '25, '26
Smith, Rollen '73, '74
Smith, Ronnie Mac '62, '63, '64
Smith, Tim '87
Smith, Trey '82
Smith, Wm. Joseph '51
Smith, Zack '38
Smithey, Claud '64, '65, '66
Soli, Junior '92, '93, '94, '95
Souter, Ted '54, '55, '56
South, Ronny '65, '67
Southerland, William '38
Spain, Harold '51, '52, '53
Spangler, Shannon '89

Spann, Dwayne '88
Sparks, Claude '08, '09
Sparks, Stan '62, '63
Spencer, Edward '54
Spencer, Terry '90, '91, '92
Sperring, James '51, '52
Spillers, Ray '34, '35, '36
Spivey, Bill '33, '34
Spriggs, David '74
St. Pierre, Bob '52
Stallings, Max '41, '42
Stallings, Randall '36, '37, '38
Stancil, William '48, '49
Stankovitch, Bob '68, '69
Stanley, Tom E. '02, '03, '05
Stansberry, E. E. '14, '15, '16
Steelman, Harold '54, '55
Steger, Curtis '84
Stendel, Marvin '50
Stevenson, James E. '16
Stewart, George '78, '79, '80
Stewart, Randy '63, '64, '65
Stewart, Terry '67, '68, '69
Stewart, Wayne '86, '87, '88
Stiggers, Gary '77, '78, '79, '80
Stitten, John '84, '85, '86, '87
Stockdell, Cary '68, '69
Stockton, Harold '48, '50
Stone, Donnie '56, '57, '58
Storey, Shane '87
Stout, Louis '30, '31, '32
Stout, Robert '37, '38, '39
Stover, Donald '12
Strain, Ray '72
Straschinske, Ray '90, '91, '92, '93
Strickland, J. S. 1897
Stringer, Tom '51
Struebing, Don '93
Sullivan, Jerry '77, '78
Summerall, Pat '49, '50, '51
Sutherland, Bruce '78, '81
Sutton, John '40, '41
Sutton, John '75
Sutton, Wm. Buddy '50, '51, '52
Swanson, Bill '53
Swartz, Anthony '94, '95
Switzer, Barry '57, '58, '59
Switzer, Greg '88, '89, '90, '91

T

Tackett, Buddy '62, '63
Tallent, Major '48
Tanner, Terry '80
Tatum, Terry '82, '83, '84, '85
Taylor, Brad '81, '82, '83, '84
Taylor, Jim '71, '72

Taylor, John '75, '76
Tegethoff, Carl '81, '82
Temple, Charlie '49
Thielemann, R. C. '73, '74, '75, '76
Thomas, Barry '82, '83
Thomas, Billy Ray '44, '46, '47, '48
Thomas, Brad '73, '74, '75
Thomas, Champ '67
Thomas, Curtis '91, '93, '94
Thomas, Derrick '83, '84, '85, '86
Thomas, Floyd '47
Thomas, Greg '84, '85, '86, '87
Thomas, Kevin '95
Thomas, Mick '89, '90, '91
Thomas, Travis '22, '23, '24
Thomas, Will '01
Thomason, George '50, '51, '52
Thomason, Joe '53, '54, '55
Thompson, Dan '95
Thompson, Derrick '92
Thompson, Skip '87, '88
Thornton, Duval '47, '48, '49
Thorpe, Wilfred '37, '38, '39
Tibbits, Joe '41, '42
Tolbert, James '79, '80, '81
Toole, Drew '71, '72
Towler, George F. 1898
Townsend, Curtis '75, '76
Trail, Ray '60, '61, '62
Trail, Richard '64, '65, '66
Trainor, Kendall '85, '86, '87, '88
Trantham, Tommy '65, '66, '67
Tranum, Billy '57, '58, '59
Travis, Tony '92
Tribble, Russ '73, '75
Triesch, Conrad '14
Troillett, Ralph '52, '53
Troxell, Billy F. '48
Troxell, Jack '51, '52
Trusty, Reggie '88, '89
Trusty, Ronnie '80, '81
Tunnah, B. '10
Turner, A. S. '11, '13, '14
Turner, John '70

U

Underwood, Ronnie '54, '55, '56
Upchurch, Andy '83, '84, '85
Uptmoor, Bernard '28, '29, '30

V

Valentine, Paul '13
Van Dover, Jimmy '56, '58
Van Dyke, Sammy '84, '85, '86, '87
Van Sickle, Clifford '34, '35, '36
Van Sickle, Clyde '27, '28, '29

Vanderventer, James 1899
Vanvalkenburgh, Horace '04, '05
Vanvalkenburgh, Wm. M. '06
Vernon, Thomas Jerry '51
Vestal, Steve '70
Vickers, Rick '70
Villarreal, Ernie '84, '86
Vincenheller, Ashton 1897, 1898, 1899, 1900

W

Wade, Vernon '92, '93, '94
Wait, Matt '94, '95
Walker, George '54, '55, '57
Walker, George Rea '62, '63
Walker, Jimmy '75, '76, '77, '78
Walls, Stephen '90, '91, '92
Walston, Dave '62, '63
Walters, Danny '80, '81, '82
Walters, Steve '69, '70
Ward, Bill '50
Warren, Billy '83, '84
Warren, Chris '75, '76
Warren, Earl '53
Warren, Robert '52, '53
Washington, Charles '83, '84, '85, '86
Watkins, James '06
Watkins, Larry '64, '65, '67
Watkins, Wayne '52
Watson, Alan '73, '74
Watson, John R. '03
Watters, Orlando '91, '92, '93
Weatherford, Z. '94
Weatherton, Carl Jr. '44
Webb, Charles W. '02
Webster, Tim '68, '69, '70
Weems, Orson '81, '82, '83
Welch, Charles '23
Welch, Jerry '62, '63, '64
Wells, Ira '83, '84
Wells, John A. '48
Wessinger, Randy '78, '79, '80
West, A. L. 1898
Westerman, Bruce '90
Westphal, Bennie '73, '75
Wewetzer, Jeff '88, '89
Wheat, John '71, '72
Wheeler, Earl '43, '44, '46
Whisenhunt, Jim '66
White, Barnabas '74, '76, '77
White, Bob '66, '67, '68
White, Bryan '84, '85, '86, '87
White, Dale '75, '76, '77, '78
White, Eddie '81, '82, '84
White, Larry '75, '76
White, Marsh '72, '73, '74

White, Nathaniel '82, '84, '85, '86
White, Steed '46, '47
Whittaker, Leon '47
Whitted, Erik '84, '85, '86, '87
Whitworth, Charles '55, '56, '57
Wilber, Rusty '76, '77
Wilcoxen, Robert '82, '83, '84
Wilkins, Charles '25
Williams, Bobby '60
Williams, Calvin '84, '85
Williams, Dale '84, '85
Williams, Darrell '59, '60, '61
Williams, Jarrell '59, '60
Williams, Jim '63, '64, '65
Williams, Jimmy '88, '89
Williams, John '20
Williams, Les '70, '71, '72
Williams, Patrick '87, '88, '89
Williams, Paul X. '28
Williams, Ray E. '20, '21, '22
Williams, Rickey '84, '85, '86, '87
Williams, Stanley '77, '78
Williams, Tom '23
Williamson, John '89
Wilson, Clint '83
Wilson, Joe Bill '54
Wilson, Richard '80

Wilson, William '15, '16, '17
Wilson, William O. '02, '03
Wingfield, Greg '85
Winkleman, Ben '17, '18, '19, '20, '21
Winkleman, Charles '24
Winston, Billy '86, '87, '88, '89
Winston, Dennis '73, '74, '75, '76
Winston, Rodney '88, '89, '90
Winters, Alva '26, '27, '28
Wise, Floyde '28
Wishon, Waylon '93, '94
Withers, Art '37
Witty, Eldo '24
Wood, Charles Fox 1900, '01, '02
Wood, Clark 1900, '01, '02
Wood, John Shirley '04, '05, '06
Wood, Stanley '22
Woodbury, Derrick '92
Woodell, Lloyd '36, '37, '38
Woodlee, Eddie '64, '65, '66
Woods, Gary '79
Woolfolk, Kirk '77, '78, '80
Worrell, Darren '86, '87, '88
Worthington, Jim '61, '62
Wren, Hudson '27, '28
Wren, Ronnie '74
Wright, A. E. '08, '09

Wright, Sam '06
Wright, Shannon '89, '90, '92
Wright, Todd '89, '90, '91, '92
Wunderly, Don '71, '72
Wyatt, Kevin '82, '83, '84, '85
Wynn, Robert '88
Wynn, Roger '76
Wynne, Clayton '40, '41, '42
Wynne, Tommy '35

Y

Yager, Richard '91, '92, '93
Yarborough, Bryon '84, '85, '86
Yates, A. J. '38, '39, '40
Yeager, Kelly '91, '92, '93
Yoder, Douglas '72, '73, '74, '75
Yoes, Oran C. '20
Young, Charles '49
Young, Clint '10, '11
Young, Henderson '19
Young, James '43, '44
Young, Theo '83, '84, '85, '86

Z

Zinamon, Bert '80, '81, '82, '83
Zoll, Alan A. '15, '16

THE FIRST 100 YEARS, GAME BY GAME

JOHN C. FUTRALL

Three years (5-2-0)

1894 (2-1-0)
Wright Lindsey, Capt.

Date		Opponent		Location
Oct. 13	42	Fort Smith High	0	Fayetteville
Oct. 27	38	Fort Smith High	0	Fort Smith
Nov. 22	0	Texas	54	Austin

1895 (1-0-0)
Herbert Fishback, Capt.

Date		Opponent		Location
Oct. 12	30	Fort Smith High	0	Fayetteville

1896 (2-1-0)
Herbert Fishback, Capt.

Date		Opponent		Location
Oct. 3	10	Fort Smith High	0	Fayetteville
Oct. 10	6	Fort Smith High	0	Fort Smith
Oct. 24	0	Drury College	34	Springfield

B. N. WILSON

Two Years (4-1-1)

1897 (2-0-1)
Herbert Fishback, Capt.

Date		Opponent		Location
Nov. 6	12	Fort Smith High	0	Fayetteville
Nov. 20	6	Drury College	6	Springfield
Nov. 25	24	Ouachita College	0	Arkadelphia

1898 (2-1-0)
Edward Martin, Capt.

Date		Opponent		Location
Oct. 22	17	Drury College	0	Fayetteville
Nov. 5	12	Drury College	6	Springfield
Nov. 19	8	Fort Scott High	36	Fort Scott

COLBERT SEARLES

Two Years (5-2-2)

1899 (3-1-1)
Chester Sloan, Capt.

Date		Opponent		Location
Oct. 14	10	Drury College	0	Fayetteville
Oct. 28	11	Tulsa	0	Fayetteville
Nov. 3	0	Tulsa	0	Muskogee
Nov. 4	5	Oklahoma	11	Shawnee
Nov. 18	11	Joplin High	10	Fayetteville

1900 (2-1-1)
Ashton Vincenheller, Capt.

Date		Opponent		Location
Oct. 27	15	Webb City High	0	Fayetteville
Nov. 3	6	Joplin High	6	Joplin
Nov. 10	10	Pierce City Col.	0	Fayetteville
Nov. 24	5	Drury College	17	Springfield

CHARLES THOMAS

Two Years (9-8-0)

1901 (3-5-0)
Fred Brown, Capt.

Date		Opponent		Location
Oct. 12	0	Pierce City Col.	5	Fayetteville
Oct. 19	22	Drury College	0	Fayetteville
Oct. 26	6	Fort Scott High	17	Fayetteville
Nov. 2	0	Little Rock H.	5	Little Rock
Nov. 9	48	Tulsa	0	Fayetteville
Nov. 16	6	Kansas City Med.	6	Fayetteville
Nov. 22	0	Louisiana Tech	15	Baton Rouge
Nov. 23	16	Louisiana Tech	0	Ruston

1902 (6-3-0)
Lemuel Bryan, Capt.

Date		Opponent		Location
Oct. 4	5	Neosho High	0	Neosho
Oct. 11	15	Kingfisher C.	6	Kingfisher
Oct. 13	0	Oklahoma	28	Norman
Oct. 22	33	Tulsa	0	Muskogee
Nov. 1	50	Tahlequah Sem.	0	Fayetteville
Nov. 8	5	SW Missouri	15	Springfield
Nov. 10	2	Pierce City Col.	24	Pierce City
Nov. 17	16	Fort Scott High	0	Fayetteville
Nov. 27	11	Missouri-Rolla	0	Fayetteville

D. A. McDANIEL

One Year (3-4-0)

1903 (3-4-0)
Henry Ragland, Capt.

Date		Opponent		Location
Oct. 10	5	SW Missouri	10	Fayetteville
Oct. 16	6	Missouri-Rolla	17	Rolla
Oct. 17	10	Drury College	6	Springfield
Oct. 30	0	Texas	15	Austin
Oct. 31	0	Texas A&M	6	College Station
Nov. 7	17	Fort Smith High	9	Fayetteville
Nov. 21	12	Oklahoma	0	Fayetteville

A. D. BROWN

Two Years (6-9-0)

1904 (4-3-0)
Jess Moore, Capt.

Date		Opponent		Location
Oct. 15	0	Drury College	12	Fayetteville
Oct. 22	22	Fort Scott High	0	Fayetteville
Nov. 4	0	Dallas Medics	5	Dallas
Nov. 5	6	Baylor	17	Waco
Nov. 12	12	Fairmount	6	Fayetteville
Nov. 19	11	Fort Smith High	5	Fort Smith
Nov. 26	11	Missouri-Rolla	10	Fayetteville

1905 (2-6-0)
William Jett, Capt.

Oct. 7	0	Kansas	6	Fayetteville
Oct. 14	0	Washington-St.L.	6	St. Louis
Oct. 16	0	Drury College	12	Springfield
Oct. 26	6	Chiloco Indians	0	Fayetteville
Oct. 31	0	Texas	4	Fayetteville
Nov. 12	0	Kentucky	6	Fayetteville
Nov. 17	0	Missouri-Rolla	16	Rolla
Nov. 30	26	Kansas City Med.	0	Fayetteville

F. C. LONGMAN

Two Years (5-8-3)

1906 (2-4-2)
John S. Wood, Capt.

Sept. 29	0	Chilico College	6	Fayetteville
Oct. 8	0	Drury College	0	Fayetteville
Oct. 13	5	Kansas	37	Lawrence
Oct. 30	0	Texas	11	Fayetteville
Nov. 6	12	SE Missouri	0	Hot Springs
Nov. 10	0	Missouri	11	Columbia
Nov. 24	22	Tulane	0	New Orleans
Nov. 30	6	LSU	6	Baton Rouge

1907 (3-4-1)
Clinton Milford, Capt.

Oct. 5	0	Haskell Indians	0	Fayetteville
Oct. 12	23	Drury College	0	Fayetteville
Oct. 19	17	Drury College	6	Springfield
Oct. 26	6	St. Louis U.	42	St. Louis
Nov. 2	6	Texas	26	Fayetteville
Nov. 9	12	LSU	17	Little Rock
Nov. 16	2	Tennessee	14	Memphis
Nov. 23	7	Missouri-Rolla	5	Fayetteville

HUGO BEZDEK

Five Years (29-13-1: .674)

1908 (5-4-0)
Willis Nelson, Capt.

Oct. 3	6	Haskell College	0	Fayetteville
Oct. 10	33	Ole Miss	0	Fayetteville
Oct. 17	0	St. Louis U.	24	St. Louis
Oct. 24	51	Henderson State	0	Fayetteville
Oct. 31	5	Oklahoma	27	Norman
Nov. 7	0	Texas	21	Austin
Nov. 14	42	Pittsburg St.	12	Fayetteville
Nov. 21	73	Ouachita College	0	Fayetteville
Nov. 26	4	LSU	36	Little Rock

1909 (7-0-0)
Stanley Phillip, Capt.

Oct. 2	24	Henderson State	0	Fayetteville
Oct. 9	12	Drury College	6	Springfield
Oct. 16	23	Fairmount	6	Fayetteville
Oct. 23	21	Oklahoma	6	Fayetteville
Oct. 30	16	LSU	0	Memphis
Nov. 13	56	Ouachita College	0	Arkadelphia
Nov. 25	34	Washington-St.L.	0	Little Rock

1910 (7-1-0)
Steve Creekmore, Capt.

Oct. 1	33	Drury College	0	Fayetteville
Oct. 9	63	Henderson State	0	Fayetteville
Oct. 15	0	Kansas State	5	Fayetteville
Oct. 22	13	Tex-SWestern	12	Fayetteville
Oct. 29	5	Texas A&M	0	Fayetteville
Nov. 5	50	Washington-St.L.	0	St. Louis
Nov. 15	6	Missouri-Rolla	2	Fayetteville
Nov. 24	51	LSU	0	Little Rock

1911 (6-2-1)
Dan Estes, Capt.

Sept. 30	100	SW Missouri	0	Fayetteville
Oct. 7	65	Drury College	5	Fayetteville
Oct. 14	45	Hendrix	0	Fayetteville
Oct. 21	0	Texas	12	Austin
Oct. 28	0	Tex-SWestern	0	Georgetown
Nov. 4	44	Missouri-Rolla	3	Joplin
Nov. 11	0	Kansas State	3	Kansas City
Nov. 18	3	Washington-St.L.	0	St. Louis
Nov. 23	11	LSU	0	Little Rock

1912 (4-6-0)
Percy Hinton, Capt.

Sept. 28	39	Henderson State	6	Fayetteville
Oct. 5	52	Hendrix	0	Fayetteville
Oct. 12	7	Oklahoma State	13	Fayetteville
Oct. 18	0	Texas A&M	27	Dallas
Oct. 19	0	Baylor	7	Waco
Oct. 26	25	Tex-SWestern	0	Fayetteville
Nov. 2	7	Wisconsin	64	Madison
Nov. 9	6	LSU	7	Little Rock
Nov. 16	13	Washington-St.L.	7	St. Louis
Nov. 21	0	Texas	48	Austin

E. T. PICKERING

Two Years ((11-7-0)

1913 (7-2-0)
Russell May, Capt.

Oct. 3	3	Henderson State	0	Fayetteville
Oct. 11	26	Hendrix	0	Fayetteville
Oct. 18	3	Oklahoma State	0	Fayetteville
Oct. 25	34	Baylor	0	Fayetteville
Nov. 1	26	Austin College	7	Fort Smith
Nov. 8	7	LSU	12	Shreveport
Nov. 15	10	Ole Miss	21	Little Rock
Nov. 17	14	Ouachita	3	Arkadelphia
Nov. 27	14	Tulane	0	New Orleans

1914 (4-5-0)
James Rudd, Capt.

Oct. 3	13	Hendrix	7	Fayetteville
Oct. 10	9	Ouachita	15	Fayettteville
Oct. 17	26	St. Louis U.	0	Fayetteville
Oct. 24	0	Missouri-Rolla	44	Fayetteville
Oct. 31	0	Oklahoma State	46	Stillwater
Nov. 7	20	LSU	12	Shreveport
Nov. 14	1	Ole Miss	0	Little Rock*
Nov. 21	7	Oklahoma	35	Oklahoma City

| Nov. 28 | 7 | Drury College | 28 | Springfield |

*Ole Miss won on the field, 13-6. Arkansas claimed Ole Miss used an ineligible player and has always listed the game as a 1-0 forfeit win.

T. T. McCONNELL

Two Years (8-6-1)

1915 (4-2-1)
James Rudd, Capt.

Oct. 2	41	Hendrix	0	Fayetteville
Oct. 9	13	Ouachita	9	Fayetteville
Oct. 16	14	Oklahoma State	9	Fort Smith
Oct. 30	0	St. Louis U.	0	St. Louis
Nov. 6	7	LSU	13	Shreveport
Nov. 14	0	Oklahoma	24	Fayetteville
Nov. 20	46	Missouri-Rolla	0	Fayetteville

1916 (4-4-0)
Chris Reichardt, Capt.

Sept. 30	34	Pittsburg State	20	Fayetteville
Oct. 7	58	Hendrix	0	Fayetteville
Oct. 14	82	Oklahoma Mines	0	Fayetteville
Oct. 21	60	Missouri-Rolla	0	Fayetteville
Nov. 4	7	LSU	17	Shreveport
Nov. 18	0	Texas	52	Austin
Nov. 23	13	Oklahoma	14	Fort Smith
Nov. 25	7	Miss. State	20	Memphis

NORMAN PAINE

Two Years (8-3-1)

1917 (5-1-1)
Gene (Sodie) Davidson, Capt.

Oct. 6	34	Central Missouri	0	Fayetteville
Oct. 13	19	Hendrix	0	Fayetteville
Oct. 20	32	Missouri-Rolla	0	Fayetteville
Oct. 27	19	Tulsa	7	Fayetteville
Nov. 3	14	LSU	0	Shreveport
Nov. 10	0	Oklahoma	0	Fort Smith
Nov. 17	0	Texas	20	Austin

1918 (3-2-0)
Paul Gold, Capt.

Sept. 28	0	Camp Pike	6	Fayetteville
Oct. 5	6	Missouri-Rolla	0	Fayetteville
Oct. 19	0	Oklahoma	103	Norman
Oct. 26	23	Tulsa	6	Fayetteville
Nov. 2	12	SW Missouri	6	Springfield

J. B. CRAIG

One Year (3-4-0-0)

1919 (3-4-0)
James Coleman, Capt.

Oct. 11	7	Hendrix	0	Fayettevlle
Oct. 18	20	Missouri-Rolla	0	Fayetteville
Oct. 25	0	LSU	20	Shreveport
Nov. 1	7	Tulsa	63	Fayetteville
Nov. 8	7	Texas	35	Austin
Nov. 15	7	Oklahoma	6	Fayetteville
Nov. 22	7	Rice	40	Houston

GEORGE W. MCCLAREN

Two Years (8-5-3)

1920 (3-2-2)
J. Tate McGill, Capt.

Oct. 9	0	Hendrix	0	Fayetteville
Oct. 16	2	TCU	19	Fayetteville
Oct. 23	6	SMU	0	Dallas
Oct. 30	14	Missouri-Rolla	0	Fayetteville
Nov. 6	0	LSU	3	Shreveport
Nov. 13	20	Phillips	0	Enid
Nov. 20	0	Rice	0	Houston

1921 (5-3-1)
Ben Winkleman, Capt.

Oct. 1	28	Hendrix	0	Fayetteville
Oct. 8	40	Drury College	0	Fayetteville
Oct. 15	28	Ouachita	0	Little Rock
Oct. 22	0	Oklahoma State	7	Stillwater
Oct. 29	14	SMU	0	Fort Smith
Nov. 5	7	LSU	10	Shreveport
Nov. 12	0	Phillips	0	Fayetteville
Nov. 19	13	Baylor	12	Fayetteville
Nov. 24	14	TCU	19	Fort Worth

FRANCIS SCHMIDT

Seven Years (42-20-3: .646)

1922 (5-4-0)
Clarence Smith, Capt.

Sept. 30	39	Hendrix	0	Fayetteville
Oct. 7	22	Drury College	0	Fayetteville
Oct. 14	7	Ouachita	13	Little Rock
Oct. 21	13	Baylor	60	Waco
Oct. 28	40	LSU	6	Shreveport
Nov. 4	1	Tulsa (forfeit)	0	Fayetteville
Nov. 11	7	Rice	31	Houston
Nov. 18	9	SMU	0	Fayetteville
Nov. 30	0	Oklahoma State	13	Fort Smith

1923 (6-2-1)
Sam Coleman, Capt.

Sept. 29	32	UCA	0	Fayetteville
Oct. 6	26	Drury College	0	Fayetteville
Oct. 13	23	Rice	0	Fayetteville
Oct. 20	0	Baylor	14	Fayetteville
Oct. 27	26	LSU	13	Shreveport
Nov. 3	0	Ouachita	0	Fayetteville
Nov. 10	6	SMU	13	Dallas
Nov. 24	32	Phillips	0	Muskogee
Dec. 1	13	Oklahoma State	0	Fort Smith

1924 (7-2-1)
Yandell Rogers, Capt.

Sept. 27	54	NE Oklahoma	6	Fayetteville
Oct. 4	47	SW Missouri	0	Fayetteville
Oct. 11	34	Hendrix	3	Fayetteville
Oct. 18	0	Baylor	13	Waco
Oct. 25	20	Ole Miss	0	Little Rock
Nov. 1	10	LSU	7	Shreveport
Nov. 8	14	SMU	14	Fayetteville
Nov. 15	28	Phillips	6	Fort Smith

Date		Opponent		Location
Nov. 21	0	Oklahoma State	20	Stillwater
Nov. 27	20	TCU	0	Fayetteville

1925 (4-4-1)
Brad Scott, Capt.

Date		Opponent		Location
Oct. 3	0	Iowa	26	Iowa City
Oct. 10	0	Okla. Bapt.	6	Fayetteville
Oct. 17	9	Rice	13	Houston
Oct. 24	45	Phillips	0	Fayetteville
Oct. 31	12	LSU	0	Shreveport
Nov. 7	0	SMU	0	Dallas
Nov. 14	0	TCU	3	Fort Worth
Nov. 21	9	Oklahoma State	7	Fayetteville
Nov. 26	20	Tulsa	7	Tulsa

1926 (5-5-0)
Herman Boozman, Capt.

Date		Opponent		Location
Sept. 25	60	UCA	0	Fayetteville
Oct. 2	21	Ole Miss	6	Fayetteville
Oct. 9	6	Oklahoma	13	Norman
Oct. 16	14	Hendrix	7	Little Rock
Oct. 23	33	Centenary	6	Fayetteville
Oct. 30	7	Kansas State	16	Manhattan
Nov. 6	0	LSU	14	Shreveport
Nov. 12	7	TCU	10	Fayetteville
Nov. 19	24	Oklahoma State	2	Stillwater
Nov. 25	7	Tulsa	14	Tulsa

1927 (8-1-0)
Eusell Coleman, Capt.

Date		Opponent		Location
Oct. 1	32	Ozarks	0	Fayetteville
Oct. 8	13	Baylor	6	Fayetteville
Oct. 15	6	Texas A&M	40	College Station
Oct. 22	34	Missouri-Rolla	0	Fayetteville
Oct. 29	28	LSU	0	Shreveport
Nov. 5	10	TCU	3	Fort Worth
Nov. 12	33	Oklahoma State	20	Fayetteville
Nov. 19	42	Austin Coll.	0	Fayetteville
Nov. 26	20	Hendrix	7	Little Rock

1928 (7-2-0)
Alva Winters, Capt.

Date		Opponent		Location
Sept. 29	0	Ole Miss	25	Oxford
Oct. 6	21	Ozarks	0	Fayetteville
Oct. 13	14	Baylor	0	Texarkana
Oct. 20	7	Texas	20	Austin
Oct. 29	27	Texas A&M	12	Fayetteville
Nov. 3	7	LSU	0	Shreveport
Nov. 17	45	Missouri-Rolla	6	Fayetteville
Nov. 24	57	Okla. Bapt.	0	Fayetteville
Nov. 29	73	Tex-SWestern	0	Memphis

FRED THOMSEN

13 Years (56-61-10: .440)

1929 (7-2-0)
Clarence Geis, Capt.

Date		Opponent		Location
Sept. 28	37	Ozarks	0	Fayetteville
Oct. 5	30	Henderson State	7	Fayettevlle
Oct. 12	0	Texas	27	Fayetteville
Oct. 19	20	Baylor	31	Waco
Oct. 26	14	Texas A&M	13	College Station
Nov. 2	32	LSU	0	Shreveport

Date		Opponent		Location
Nov. 9	52	E. Central Okla.	7	Fayetteville
Nov. 16	13	Centenary	2	Fayetteville
Nov. 28	32	Oklahoma State	6	Stillwater

1930 (3-6-0)
Milan Creighton, Capt.

Date		Opponent		Location
Sept. 27	27	Ozarks	0	Fayetteville
Oct. 4	6	Tulsa	26	Tulsa
Oct. 11	0	TCU	40	Fort Worth
Oct. 18	7	Rice	6	Fayetteville
Oct. 25	13	Texas A&M	0	Little Rock
Nov. 1	12	LSU	27	Shreveport
Nov. 8	0	Oklahoma State	26	Fayetteville
Nov. 15	7	Baylor	22	Fayeteville
Nov. 22	6	Centenary	2	Shreveport

1931 (3-5-1)
Earl Secrest, Capt.

Date		Opponent		Location
Sept. 26	13	Ozarks	6	Fayetteville
Oct. 3	19	Hendrix	0	Fayetteville
Oct. 10	6	SMU	42	Fayetteville
Oct. 17	7	Baylor	19	Waco
Oct. 24	6	LSU	13	Shreveport
Oct. 31	0	TCU	7	Fayetteville
Nov. 7	13	Chicago	13	Chicago
Nov. 21	12	Rice	26	Houston
Nov. 26	6	Centenary	0	Shreveport

1932 (1-6-2)
Judson Irwin, Capt.

Date		Opponent		Location
Sept. 24	0	Hendrix	0	Fayetteville
Oct. 1	19	Missouri-Rolla	20	Fayetteville
Oct. 8	12	TCU	34	Fort Worth
Oct. 15	20	Baylor	6	Little Rock
Oct. 22	0	LSU	14	Shreveport
Nov. 5	7	Rice	12	Fayetteville
Nov. 12	7	SMU	13	Dallas
Nov. 18	0	Texas	34	Fayetteville
Nov. 26	0	Centenary	0	Shreveport

1933 (7-3-1)
Louis Johnson, Capt.

Date		Opponent		Location
Sept. 23	40	Ozarks	0	Fayetteville
Sept. 30	42	Okla. Bapt.	7	Fayetteville
Oct. 7	13	TCU	0	Fayetteville
Oct. 14	19	Baylor	7	Little Rock
Oct. 21	0	LSU	20	Shreveport
Oct. 28	3	SMU	0	Fayetteville
Nov. 11	6	Rice	7	Houston
Nov. 18	63	Hendrix	0	Fayetteville
Nov. 24	20	Texas	6	Austin
Nov. 30	0	Tulsa	7	Tulsa
Jan. 1*	7	Centenary	7	Dallas

*Dixie Classic

1934 (4-4-2)
W. R. Benton, Capt.

Date		Opponent		Location
Sept. 29	13	Ozarks	0	Fayetteville
Oct. 6	24	TCU	10	Fort Worth
Oct. 13	6	Baylor	0	Little Rock
Oct. 20	0	LSU	16	Shreveport
Oct. 27	20	Missouri-Rolla	0	Fayetteville
Nov. 3	7	Texas A&M	7	College Station

Nov. 10	0	Rice	7	Fayetteville
Nov. 17	6	SMU	10	Dallas
Nov. 23	12	Texas	19	Fayetteville
Nov. 29	7	Tulsa	7	Tulsa

1935 (5-5-0)
Choice Rucker, Capt.

Sept. 28	12	Pittsburg State	0	Fayetteville
Oct. 5	7	TCU	13	Fayetteville
Oct. 12	6	Baylor	13	Waco
Oct. 19	7	LSU	13	Shreveport
Oct. 26	51	Ozarks	6	Fayetteville
Nov. 2	14	Texas A&M	7	Little Rock
Nov. 8	7	Rice	20	Houston
Nov. 16	6	SMU	17	Fayetteville
Nov. 22	28	Texas	13	Austin
Nov. 28	14	Tulsa	7	Tulsa

1936 (7-3-0)
Clifford Van Sickle, Capt.

Sept. 26	53	Pittsburg	0	Fayetteville
Oct. 3	14	TCU	18	Fort Worth
Oct. 10	14	Baylor	10	Fayetteville
Oct. 16	6	Geo. Washington	13	Wash., D.C.
Oct. 24	7	LSU	19	Shreveport
Oct. 31	18	Texas A&M	0	College Station
Nov. 7	20	Rice	14	Fayetteville
Nov. 14	17	SMU	0	Dallas
Nov. 26	23	Tulsa	13	Tulsa
Dec. 5	6	Texas	0	Little Rock

1937 (6-2-2)
Jack Robbins, Jim Benton, Capts.

Sept. 25	25	Cent. Okla	0	Fayetteville
Oct. 2	7	TCU	7	Fayetteville
Oct. 9	14	Baylor	20	Waco
Oct. 16	21	Texas	10	Austin
Oct. 23	13	SMU	0	Fort Smith
Oct. 30	26	Texas A&M	13	Fayetteville
Nov. 6	20	Rice	26	Houston
Nov. 13	32	Ole Miss	6	Memphis
Nov. 20	0	Geo. Wash.	0	Little Rock
Nov. 25	28	Tulsa	7	Tulsa

1938 (2-7-1)
Lloyd Woodell, Capt.

Sept. 24	27	Oklahoma State	7	Fayetteville
Oct. 1	14	TCU	21	Fort Worth
Oct. 8	6	Baylor	9	Fayetteville
Oct. 15	42	Texas	6	Little Rock
Oct. 22	6	Santa Clara	21	San Francisco
Oct. 29	7	Texas A&M	13	College Station
Nov. 5	0	Rice	3	Fayetteville
Nov. 12	6	SMU	19	Dallas
Nov. 16	14	Ole Miss	20	Memphis
Nov. 24	6	Tulsa	6	Tulsa

1939 (4-5-1)
Kay Eakin, Ray Cole, Capts.

Sept. 23	32	E. Central Okla.	6	Fayetteville
Sept. 30	0	Mississippi St.	19	Memphis
Oct. 7	14	TCU	13	Fayetteville
Oct. 14	7	Baylor	19	Waco
Oct. 21	13	Texas	14	Austin
Oct. 28	0	Villanova	7	Philadelphia
Nov. 4	0	Texas A&M	27	Fayetteville
Nov. 11	12	Rice	12	Houston
Nov. 17	14	SMU	0	Little Rock
Nov. 30	23	Tulsa	0	Tulsa

1940 (4-6-0)
A. J. Yates, Howard Hickey, Capts.

Sept. 28	38	E. Cent. Okla.	0	Fayetteville
Oct. 5	0	TCU	20	Fort Worth
Oct. 12	12	Baylor	6	Fayetteville
Oct. 19	0	Texas	21	Little Rock
Oct. 26	21	Ole Miss	20	Memphis
Nov. 2	0	Texas A&M	17	College Station
Nov. 9	7	Rice	14	Fayetteville
Nov. 16	0	SMU	28	Dallas
Nov. 21	7	Fordham	27	New York
Nov. 28	27	Tulsa	21	Tulsa

1941 (3-7-0)
Daryl Cato, Capt.

Sept. 27	56	E. Cent. Okla.	0	Fayetteville
Oct. 4	0	TCU	9	Fayetteville
Oct. 11	7	Baylor	20	Waco
Oct. 18	14	Texas	48	Austin
Oct. 24	9	Detroit	6	Detroit
Nov. 1	0	Texas A&M	7	Little Rock
Nov. 8	12	Rice	21	Houston
Nov. 15	7	SMU	14	Fayetteville
Nov. 22	0	Ole Miss	18	Memphis
Nov. 27	13	Tulsa	6	Tulsa

GEORGE COLE

One Year (3-7-0)

1942 (3-7-0)
Clayton Wynne, Robert Forte, Capts.

Sept. 26	27	Wichita State	0	Fayetteville
Oct. 3	6	TCU	13	Fort Worth
Oct. 10	7	Baylor	20	Fayetteville
Oct. 17	6	Texas	47	Little Rock
Oct. 24	7	Ole Miss	6	Memphis
Oct. 31	0	Texas A&M	41	College Station
Nov. 7	9	Rice	40	Fayetteville
Nov. 14	6	SMU	14	Dallas
Nov. 21	14	Detroit	7	Detroit
Nov. 26	7	Tulsa	40	Tulsa

JOHN TOMLIN

One Year (2-7-0)

1943 (2-7-0)
Lamar Dingler, Ben Jones, Capts.

Sept. 25	59	Missouri-Rolla	0	Fayetteville
Oct. 2	0	TCU	13	Little Rock
Oct. 9	12	Monticello NAS	20	Fayetteville
Oct. 16	0	Texas	34	Austin
Oct. 30	0	Texas A&M	13	Fayetteville
Nov. 6	7	Rice	20	Houston
Nov. 13	14	SMU	12	San Antonio
Nov. 19	13	Oklahoma State	19	Fort Smith
Nov. 25	0	Tulsa	61	Tulsa

GLEN ROSE

Two Years (8-12-1: .380)

1944 (5-5-1)
Lamar Dingler, James Young, Capts.

Sept. 23	7	Missouri	6	St. Louis
Sept. 29	0	Oklahoma State	19	Oklahoma City
Oct. 7	6	TCU	6	Fort Worth
Oct. 14	7	Norman Navy	27	Fayetteville
Oct. 21	0	Texas	19	Little Rock
Oct. 28	26	Ole Miss	18	Memphis
Nov. 4	7	Texas A&M	6	College Station
Nov. 11	12	Rice	7	Fayetteville
Nov. 18	12	SMU	20	Dallas
Nov. 23	2	Tulsa	33	Tulsa
Dec. 2	41	Arkansas A&M	0	Fayetteville

1945 (3-7)
Earl Wheeler, Henry Ford, Capts.

Sept. 22	12	Barksdale Field	6	Shreveport
Sept. 29	14	Oklahoma State	19	Fayetteville
Oct. 6	27	TCU	14	Fayetteville
Oct. 13	13	Baylor	23	Waco
Oct. 20	7	Texas	34	Little Rock
Oct. 27	19	Ole Miss	0	Memphis
Nov. 3	0	Texas A&M	34	Fayetteville
Nov. 10	7	Rice	26	Houston
Nov. 17	0	SMU	21	Dallas
Nov. 22	13	Tulsa	45	Tulsa

JOHN BARNHILL

Four Years (22-17-3: .559)

1946 (6-3-2)
Joyce Pipkin, Capt.

Sept. 21	21	NW Louisiana	14	Fayetteville
Sept. 28	21	Oklahoma State	21	Stillwater
Oct. 5	34	TCU	14	Fort Worth
Oct. 12	13	Baylor	0	Fayetteville
Oct. 19	0	Texas	20	Austin
Oct. 26	7	Ole Miss	9	Memphis
Nov. 2	7	Texas A&M	0	College Station
Nov. 9	7	Rice	0	Little Rock
Nov. 16	13	SMU	0	Fayetteville
Nov. 28	13	Tulsa	14	Tulsa
Jan. 1*	0	LSU	0	Dallas

*Cotton Bowl

1947 (6-4-1)
James Minor, Capt.

Sept. 20	64	NW Louisiana	0	Fayetteville
Sept. 27	12	North Texas	0	Little Rock
Oct. 4	6	TCU	0	Fayetteville
Oct. 11	9	Baylor	17	Waco
Oct. 18	6	Texas	21	Memphis
Oct. 25	19	Ole Miss	14	Memphis
Nov. 1	21	Texas A&M	21	Fayetteville
Nov. 8	0	Rice	26	Houston
Nov. 15	6	SMU	14	Dallas
Nov. 27	27	Tulsa	13	Tulsa
Jan. 1*	21	William & Mary	19	Birmingham

*Dixie Bowl

1948 (5-5-0)
Clyde Scott, Capt.

Sept. 18	40	Abilene Christ.	6	Little Rock
Sept. 25	46	East Texas	7	Fayetteville
Oct. 2	27	TCU	14	Fort Worth
Oct. 9	7	Baylor	23	Fayetteville
Oct. 16	6	Texas	14	Austin
Oct. 30	28	Texas A&M	6	College Station
Nov. 6	6	Rice	25	Little Rock
Nov. 13	12	SMU	14	Fayetteville
Nov. 20	55	Tulsa	18	Little Rock
Nov. 27	0	William & Mary	9	Little Rock

1949 (5-5-0)
Alvin Duke, Capt.

Sept. 24	33	North Texas	19	Little Rock
Oct. 1	27	TCU	7	Fayetteville
Oct. 8	13	Baylor	35	Waco
Oct. 15	14	Texas	27	Little Rock
Oct. 22	7	Vanderbilt	6	Nashville
Oct. 29	27	Texas A&M	6	Fayetteville
Nov. 5	0	Rice	14	Houston
Nov. 12	6	SMU	34	Dallas
Nov. 19	0	William & Mary	20	Little Rock
Nov. 26	40	Tulsa	7	Fayetteville

OTIS DOUGLAS

Three Years (9-21-1: .300)

1950 (2-8-0)
George Eckert, Capt.

Sept. 23	7	Oklahoma State	12	Little Rock
Sept. 30	50	North Texas	6	Fayetteville
Oct. 7	6	TCU	13	Fort Worth
Oct. 14	27	Baylor	6	Fayetteville
Oct. 21	14	Texas	19	Austin
Oct. 28	13	Vanderbilt	14	Little Rock
Nov. 4	13	Texas A&M	42	College Station
Nov. 11	6	Rice	9	Fayetteville
Nov. 18	7	SMU	14	Little Rock
Nov. 23	13	Tulsa	28	Tulsa

1951 (5-5-0)
Dave Hanner, Pat Summerall, Capts.

Sept. 22	42	Oklahoma State	7	Stillwater
Sept. 29	30	Arizona State	13	Fayetteville
Oct. 6	7	TCU	17	Little Rock
Oct. 13	7	Baylor	9	Waco
Oct. 20	16	Texas	14	Fayetteville
Oct. 27	12	Santa Clara	21	Little Rock
Nov. 3	33	Texas A&M	21	Fayetteville
Nov. 10	0	Rice	6	Houston
Nov. 17	7	SMU	47	Dallas
Nov. 24	24	Tulsa	7	Little Rock

1952 (2-8-0)
Dean Pryor, Buddy Sutton, Capts.

Sept. 20	22	Oklahoma State	20	Little Rock
Sept. 27	7	Houston	17	Fayetteville
Oct. 4	7	TCU	13	Fort Worth
Oct. 11	20	Baylor	17	Little Rock
Oct. 18	7	Texas	44	Austin

Oct. 25	7	Ole Miss	34	Little Rock
Nov. 1	12	Texas A&M	31	College Station
Nov. 8	33	Rice	35	Fayetteville
Nov. 15	17	SMU	27	Fayetteville
Nov. 22	34	Tulsa	44	Tulsa

BOWDEN WYATT

Two Years (11-10-0: .523)

1953 (3-7-0)
Jim Sperring, Ralph Troillett, Capts.

Sept. 26	6	Oklahoma State	7	Little Rock
Oct. 3	13	TCU	6	Fayetteville
Oct. 10	7	Baylor	14	Waco
Oct. 17	7	Texas	16	Fayetteville
Oct. 24	0	Ole Miss	28	Memphis
Oct. 31	41	Texas A&M	14	Little Rock
Nov. 7	0	Rice	47	Houston
Nov. 14	7	SMU	13	Dallas
Nov. 21	8	LSU	9	Little Rock
Nov. 28	27	Tulsa	7	Fayetteville

1954 (8-3-0)
Bobby Proctor, Jim Roth, Capts.

Sept. 25	41	Tulsa	0	Fayetteville
Oct. 2	20	TCU	13	Fort Worth
Oct. 9	21	Baylor	20	Fayetteville
Oct. 16	20	Texas	7	Austin
Oct. 23	6	Mississippi	0	Little Rock
Oct. 30	14	Texas A&M	7	College Station
Nov. 6	28	Rice	15	Little Rock
Nov. 13	14	SMU	21	Fayetteville
Nov. 20	6	LSU	7	Shreveport
Nov. 27	19	Houston	0	Houston
Jan. 1*	6	Georgia Tech	14	Dallas

*Cotton Bowl

JACK MITCHELL

Three Years (17-12-1: .566)

1955 (5-4-1)
Preston Carpenter, Henry Moore, Capts.

Sept. 17	21	Tulsa	6	Fayetteville
Sept. 24	21	Oklahoma State	0	Little Rock
Oct. 1	0	TCU	26	Fayetteville
Oct. 8	20	Baylor	25	Waco
Oct. 15	27	Texas	20	Little Rock
Oct. 22	7	Ole Miss	17	Oxford
Oct. 29	7	Texas A&M	7	Fayetteville
Nov. 5	10	Rice	0	Houston
Nov. 12	6	SMU	0	Dallas
Nov. 19	7	LSU	13	Little Rock

1956 (6-4-0)
Neil Martin, Ted Souter, Capts.

Sept. 22	21	Hardin-Simmons	6	Fayetteville
Sept. 29	19	Oklahoma State	7	Little Rock
Oct. 6	6	TCU	41	Fort Worth
Oct. 13	7	Baylor	14	Fayetteville
Oct. 20	32	Texas	14	Austin
Oct. 27	14	Ole Miss	0	Little Rock
Nov. 3	0	Texas A&M	27	College Station
Nov. 10	27	Rice	12	Fayetteville
Nov. 17	27	SMU	13	Little Rock
Nov. 24	7	LSU	21	Shreveport

1957 (6-4-0)
George Walker, Gerald Nesbitt, Jay Donathan, Capts.

Sept. 21	12	Oklahoma State	0	Little Rock
Sept. 28	41	Tulsa	14	Fayetteville
Oct. 5	20	TCU	7	Little Rock
Oct. 12	20	Baylor	17	Waco
Oct. 19	0	Texas	17	Fayetteville
Oct. 26	12	Ole Miss	6	Memphis
Nov. 2	6	Texas A&M	7	Fayetteville
Nov. 9	7	Rice	13	Houston
Nov. 16	22	SMU	27	Dallas
Nov. 23	47	Texas Tech	26	Little Rock

FRANK BROYLES

19 Years (144-58-5: .708)

1958 (4-6-0)

Sept. 20	0	Baylor	12	Little Rock
Sept. 27	14	Tulsa	27	Fayetteville
Oct. 4	7	TCU	12	Fort Worth
Oct. 11	0	Rice	24	Fayetteville
Oct. 18	6	Texas	24	Austin
Oct. 25	12	Ole Miss	14	Little Rock
Nov. 1	21	Texas A&M	8	College Station
Nov. 8	60	Hardin-Simmons	15	Little Rock
Nov. 15	13	SMU	6	Fayetteville
Nov. 22	14	Texas Tech	8	Lubbock

1959 (9-2-0)
James Monroe, Barry Switzer, Billy Luplow, Capts.

Sept. 19	28	Tulsa	0	Fayetteville
Sept. 26	13	Oklahoma State	7	Little Rock
Oct. 3	3	TCU	0	Fayetteville
Oct. 10	23	Baylor	7	Waco
Oct. 17	12	Texas	13	Little Rock
Oct. 24	0	Ole Miss	28	Memphis
Oct. 31	12	Texas A&M	7	Fayetteville
Nov. 7	14	Rice	10	Houston
Nov. 14	17	SMU	14	Dallas
Nov. 21	27	Texas Tech	8	Little Rock
Jan. 1*	14	Georgia Tech	7	Jacksonville

*Gator Bowl

1960 (8-3-0)
Wayne Harris, Steve Butler, Capts.

Sept. 17	9	Oklahoma State	0	Little Rock
Sept. 24	48	Tulsa	7	Fayetteville
Oct. 1	7	TCU	0	Fort Worth
Oct. 8	14	Baylor	28	Fayetteville
Oct. 15	24	Texas	23	Austin
Oct. 22	7	Ole Miss	10	Little Rock
Oct. 29	7	Texas A&M	3	College Station
Nov. 5	3	Rice	0	Little Rock
Nov. 12	26	SMU	3	Fayetteville
Nov. 19	34	Texas Tech	6	Lubbock
Jan. 1*	6	Duke	7	Dallas

*Cotton Bowl

1961 (8-3-0)

Harold Horton, John Childress, George McKinney, Capts.

Sept. 23	0	Ole Miss	16	Jackson
Sept. 30	6	Tulsa	0	Fayetteville
Oct. 7	28	TCU	3	Little Rock
Oct. 14	23	Baylor	13	Waco
Oct. 21	7	Texas	33	Fayetteville
Oct. 28	42	NW Louisiana	7	Little Rock
Nov. 4	15	Texas A&M	8	Fayetteville
Nov. 11	10	Rice	0	Houston
Nov. 18	21	SMU	7	Dallas
Nov. 25	28	Texas Tech	0	Little Rock
Jan. 1*	3	Alabama	10	New Orleans

*Sugar Bowl

1962 (9-2-0)

Billy Moore, Ray Trail, Capts.

Sept. 22	34	Oklahoma State	7	Little Rock
Sept. 29	42	Tulsa	14	Fayetteville
Oct. 6	42	TCU	14	Fort Worth
Oct. 13	28	Baylor	21	Fayetteville
Oct. 20	3	Texas	7	Austin
Oct. 27	49	Hardin-Simmons	7	Little Rock
Nov. 3	17	Texas A&M	7	College Station
Nov. 10	28	Rice	14	Fayetteville
Nov. 17	9	SMU	7	Little Rock
Nov. 24	34	Texas Tech	0	Lubbock
Jan. 1*	13	Ole Miss	17	New Orleans

*Sugar Bowl

1963 (5-5-0)

Mike Parker, Jim Grizzle, Capts.

Sept. 21	21	Oklahoma State	0	Little Rock
Sept. 28	6	Missouri	7	Little Rock
Oct. 5	18	TCU	3	Fayetteville
Oct. 12	10	Baylor	14	Waco
Oct. 19	13	Texas	17	Little Rock
Oct. 26	56	Tulsa	7	Little Rock
Nov. 2	21	Texas A&M	7	Little Rock
Nov. 9	0	Rice	7	Houston
Nov. 16	7	SMU	14	Dallas
Nov. 23	27	Texas Tech	20	Fayetteville

1964 (11-0-0)

Seniors, Capts.: Ken Hatfield, Jerry Jones, Jimmy Johnson, Jerry Lamb, Dick Hatfield, Jerry Welch, Fred Marshall, Billy Gray, Gary Robinson, Jim Finch, Ronnie Mac Smith, Ronnie Caveness, Charles Daniel, Tom McKnelly

Sept. 19	14	Oklahoma State	10	Little Rock
Sept. 26	31	Tulsa	22	Fayetteville
Oct. 3	29	TCU	6	Fort Worth
Oct. 10	17	Baylor	6	Little Rock
Oct. 17	14	Texas	13	Austin
Oct. 24	17	Wichita State	0	Little Rock
Oct. 31	17	Texas A&M	0	College Station
Nov. 7	21	Rice	0	Fayetteville
Nov. 14	44	SMU	0	Fayetteville
Nov. 21	17	Texas Tech	0	Lubbock
Jan. 1*	10	Nebraska	7	Dallas

*Cotton Bowl and National Champions

1965 (10-1-0)

Seniors, Capts.

Sept. 18	28	Oklahoma State	14	Little Rock
Sept. 25	20	Tulsa	12	Fayetteville
Oct. 2	28	TCU	0	Little Rock
Oct. 9	38	Baylor	7	Waco
Oct. 16	27	Texas	24	Fayetteville
Oct. 23	55	North Texas	20	Little Rock
Oct. 30	31	Texas A&M	0	Little Rock
Nov. 6	31	Rice	0	Houston
Nov. 13	24	SMU	3	Dallas
Nov. 20	42	Texas Tech	24	Fayetteville
Jan. 1*	7	LSU	14	Dallas

*Cotton Bowl

1966 (8-2-0)

Seniors, Capts.

Sept. 17	14	Oklahoma State	10	Little Rock
Sept. 24	27	Tulsa	8	Fayetteville
Oct. 1	21	TCU	0	Fort Worth
Oct. 8	0	Baylor	7	Fayetteville
Oct. 15	12	Texas	7	Austin
Oct. 22	41	Wichita State	0	Little Rock
Oct. 29	34	Texas A&M	0	College Station
Nov. 5	31	Rice	20	Little Rock
Nov. 12	22	SMU	0	Fayetteville
Nov. 19	16	Texas Tech	21	Lubbock

1967 (4-5-1)

Hartford Hamilton, Larry Watkins, Ernest Ruple, Capts.

Sept. 23	6	Oklahoma State	7	Little Rock
Sept. 30	12	Tulsa	14	Fayetteville
Oct. 7	26	TCU	0	Fayetteville
Oct. 14	10	Baylor	10	Waco
Oct. 21	12	Texas	21	Little Rock
Oct. 28	28	Kansas State	7	Little Rock
Nov. 4	21	Texas A&M	33	Fayetteville
Nov. 11	23	Rice	9	Houston
Nov. 18	35	SMU	17	Dallas
Nov. 25	27	Texas Tech	31	Little Rock

1968 (10-1-0)

Jim Barnes, Gary Adams, Capts.

Sept. 21	32	Oklahoma State	15	Little Rock
Sept. 28	56	Tulsa	13	Fayetteville
Oct. 5	17	TCU	7	Fort Worth
Oct. 12	35	Baylor	19	Fayetteville
Oct. 19	29	Texas	39	Austin
Oct. 26	17	North Texas	15	Little Rock
Nov. 2	25	Texas A&M	22	College Station
Nov. 9	46	Rice	21	Fayetteville
Nov. 16	35	SMU	29	Little Rock
Nov. 23	42	Texas Tech	7	Lubbock
Jan. 1*	16	Georgia	2	New Orleans

*Sugar Bowl

1969 (9-2-0)

Terry Stewart, Cliff Powell, Rodney Brand, Bruce Maxwell, Capts.

Sept. 20	39	Oklahoma State	0	Little Rock
Sept. 27	55	Tulsa	0	Fayetteville
Oct. 4	24	Texas Christian	6	Little Rock
Oct. 11	21	Baylor	7	Waco

Oct. 25	52	Wichita State	14	Little Rock
Nov. 1	35	Texas A&M	13	Fayetteville
Nov. 8	30	Rice	6	Houston
Nov. 15	28	SMU	15	Dallas
Nov. 27	33	Texas Tech	0	Little Rock
Dec. 6	14	Texas	15	Fayetteville
Jan. 1*	22	Ole Miss	27	New Orleans

*Sugar Bowl

1970 (9-2-0)
Bill Burnett, Bill Montgomery, Dick Bumpas, Mike Boschetti, Capts.

Sept. 12	28	Stanford	34	Little Rock
Sept. 19	23	Oklahoma State	7	Little Rock
Sept. 26	49	Tulsa	7	Fayetteville
Oct. 3	49	TCU	14	Fort Worth
Oct. 10	41	Baylor	7	Waco
Oct. 24	62	Wichita State	0	Little Rock
Oct. 31	45	Texas A&M	6	College Station
Nov. 7	38	Rice	14	Fayetteville
Nov. 14	36	SMU	3	Fayetteville
Nov. 21	24	Texas Tech	10	Lubbock
Dec. 5	7	Texas	42	Austin

1971 (8-3-1)
David Hogue, Ronnie Jones, Mike Kelson, Bobby Nichols, Tom Mabry, Capts.

Sept. 11	51	California	20	Little Rock
Sept. 18	31	Oklahoma State	10	Little Rock
Sept. 25	20	Tulsa	21	Fayetteville
Oct. 2	49	TCU	15	Fayetteville
Oct. 9	35	Baylor	7	Waco
Oct. 16	31	Texas	7	Little Rock
Oct. 23	60	North Texas	21	Fayetteville
Oct. 30	9	Texas A&M	17	Little Rock
Nov. 6	24	Rice	24	Houston
Nov. 13	18	SMU	13	Dallas
Nov. 20	15	Texas Tech	0	Fayetteville
Dec. 20*	13	Tennessee	14	Memphis

*Liberty Bowl

1972 (6-5-0)
Louis Campbell, Jim Hodge, Tom Reed, Don Wunderly, Capts.

Sept. 9	10	Southern Cal	31	Little Rock
Sept. 23	24	Oklahoma State	23	Little Rock
Sept. 30	21	Tulsa	20	Fayetteville
Oct. 7	27	TCU	13	Fort Worth
Oct. 14	31	Baylor	20	Fayetteville
Oct. 21	15	Texas	35	Austin
Oct. 28	42	North Texas	16	Little Rock
Nov. 4	7	Texas A&M	10	College Station
Nov. 11	20	Rice	23	Little Rock
Nov. 18	7	SMU	22	Fayetteville
Nov. 25	24	Texas Tech	14	Lubbock

1973 (5-5-1)
Nick Avlos, Jack Ettinger, Steve Hedgepeth, Dickey Morton, Danny Rhodes, Capts.

Sept. 15	0	Southern Cal	17	Los Angeles
Sept. 22	6	Oklahoma State	38	Little Rock
Sept. 29	21	Iowa State	19	Fayetteville
Oct. 6	13	TCU	5	Little Rock
Oct. 13	13	Baylor	7	Waco
Oct. 20	6	Texas	34	Fayetteville
Oct. 27	20	Tulsa	6	Little Rock
Nov. 3	14	Texas A&M	10	Fayetteville
Nov. 10	7	Rice	17	Houston
Nov. 17	7	SMU	7	Dallas
Nov. 24	17	Texas Tech	24	Little Rock

1974 (6-4-1)
Billy Burns, Rollen Smith, Capts.

Sept. 14	22	Southern Cal	7	Little Rock
Sept. 21	7	Oklahoma State	26	Little Rock
Sept. 28	60	Tulsa	0	Fayetteville
Oct. 5	49	TCU	0	Fort Worth
Oct. 12	17	Baylor	21	Fayetteville
Oct. 19	7	Texas	38	Austin
Oct. 26	43	Colorado State	9	Little Rock
Nov. 2	10	Texas A&M	20	College Station
Nov. 9	25	Rice	6	Fayetteville
Nov. 16	24	SMU	24	Little Rock
Nov. 23	21	Texas Tech	13	Lubbock

1975 (10-2-0)
Scott Bull, Ike Forte, Mike Campbell, Hal McAfee, Capts.

Sept. 13	35	Air Force	0	Little Rock
Sept. 20	13	Oklahoma State	20	Stillwater
Sept. 27	31	Tulsa	15	Fayetteville
Oct. 4	19	TCU	8	Little Rock
Oct. 11	41	Baylor	3	Waco
Oct. 18	18	Texas	24	Fayetteville
Oct. 25	31	Utah State	0	Little Rock
Nov. 8	20	Rice	16	Houston
Nov. 15	35	SMU	7	Dallas
Nov. 22	31	Texas Tech	14	Fayetteville
Dec. 6	31	Texas A&M	6	Little Rock
Jan. 1*	31	Georgia	10	Dallas

*Cotton Bowl

1976 (5-5-1)
Seniors, Capts.

Sept. 11	33	Utah State	16	Little Rock
Sept. 18	16	Oklahoma State	10	Little Rock
Sept. 25	3	Tulsa	9	Fayetteville
Oct. 2	46	TCU	14	Fayetteville
Oct. 23	14	Houston	7	Houston
Oct. 30	41	Rice	16	Fayetteville
Nov. 6	7	Baylor	7	Waco
Nov. 13	10	Texas A&M	31	Little Rock
Nov. 20	31	SMU	35	Shreveport
Nov. 27	7	Texas Tech	30	Little Rock
Dec. 4	12	Texas	29	Austin

LOU HOLTZ

Seven Years (60-21-2: .711)

1977 (11-1-0)
Leotis Harris, Howard Sampson, Steve Little, Capts.

Sept. 10	53	New Mexico St.	10	Little Rock
Sept. 17	28	Oklahoma State	6	Little Rock
Sept. 24	37	Tulsa	3	Fayetteville
Oct. 1	42	TCU	6	Fort Worth
Oct. 15	9	Texas	13	Fayetteville

Oct. 22	34	Houston	0	Little Rock
Oct. 29	30	Rice	7	Houston
Nov. 5	35	Baylor	9	Little Rock
Nov. 12	26	Texas A&M	20	College Station
Nov. 19	47	SMU	7	Fayetteville
Nov. 24	17	Texas Tech	14	Lubbock
Jan. 2*	31	Oklahoma	6	Miami

*Orange Bowl

1978 (9-2-1)
Ben Cowins, Jimmy Walker, Ron Calcagni, Larry Jackson, Capts.

Sept. 16	48	Vanderbilt	17	Little Rock
Sept. 23	19	Oklahoma State	7	Stillwater
Sept. 30	21	Tulsa	13	Fayetteville
Oct. 7	42	TCU	3	Little Rock
Oct. 21	21	Texas	28	Austin
Oct. 28	9	Houston	20	Houston
Nov. 4	37	Rice	7	Fayetteville
Nov. 11	27	Baylor	14	Waco
Nov. 18	26	Texas A&M	7	Little Rock
Nov. 25	27	SMU	14	Dallas
Dec. 2	49	Texas Tech	7	Fayetteville
Dec. 25*	10	UCLA	10	Phoenix

*Fiesta Bowl

1979 (10-2-0)
Roland Sales, Jim Howard, Capts.

Sept. 15	36	Colorado State	3	Little Rock
Sept. 22	27	Oklahoma State	7	Little Rock
Sept. 29	33	Tulsa	8	Fayetteville
Oct. 6	16	TCU	13	Fort Worth
Oct. 13	20	Texas Tech	6	Lubbock
Oct. 20	17	Texas	14	Little Rock
Oct. 27	10	Houston	13	Fayetteville
Nov. 3	34	Rice	7	Houston
Nov. 10	29	Baylor	20	Fayetteville
Nov. 17	22	Texas A&M	10	College Station
Nov. 24	31	SMU	7	Little Rock
Jan. 1*	9	Alabama	24	New Orleans

*Sugar Bowl

1980 (7-5-0)
George Stewart, Keith Houfek, Capts.

Sept. 1	17	Texas	23	Austin
Sept. 20	33	Oklahoma State	20	Little Rock
Sept. 27	13	Tulsa	10	Fayetteville
Oct. 4	44	TCU	7	Fayetteville
Oct. 11	27	Wichita State	7	Little Rock
Oct. 25	17	Houston	24	Houston
Nov. 1	16	Rice	17	Little Rock
Nov. 8	15	Baylor	42	Waco
Nov. 15	27	Texas A&M	24	Fayetteville
Nov. 22	7	SMU	31	Dallas
Nov. 29	22	Texas Tech	16	Little Rock
Dec. 27*	34	Tulane	15	Birmingham

*Hall of Fame Bowl

1981 (8-4-0)
Darryl Mason, Teddy Morris, Capts.

Sept. 12	14	Tulsa	10	Fayetteville
Sept. 19	38	Northwestern	7	Little Rock

Sept. 26	27	Ole Miss	13	Jackson
Oct. 3	24	TCU	28	Fort Worth
Oct. 10	26	Texas Tech	14	Lubbock
Oct. 17	42	Texas	11	Fayetteville
Oct. 24	17	Houston	20	Little Rock
Oct. 31	41	Rice	7	Houston
Nov. 7	41	Baylor	39	Little Rock
Nov. 14	10	Texas A&M	7	College Station
Nov. 21	18	SMU	32	Fayetteville
Dec. 28*	27	North Carolina	31	Jacksonville

*Gator Bowl

1982 (9-2-1)
Billy Ray Smith, Richard Richardson, Gary Anderson, Jessie Clark, Capts.

Sept. 11	38	Tulsa	0	Fayetteville
Sept. 18	29	Navy	17	Little Rock
Sept. 25	14	Ole Miss	12	Little Rock
Oct. 2	35	TCU	0	Little Rock
Oct. 9	21	Texas Tech	3	Fayetteville
Oct. 23	38	Houston	3	Houston
Oct. 30	24	Rice	6	Fayetteville
Nov. 6	17	Baylor	24	Waco
Nov. 13	35	Texas A&M	0	Little Rock
Nov. 20	17	SMU	17	Dallas
Dec. 4	7	Texas	33	Austin
Dec. 31*	28	Florida	24	Houston

*Bluebonnet Bowl

1983 (6-5-0)
Bert Zinamon, Mark Mistler, Ron Faurot, Capts.

Sept. 10	17	Tulsa	14	Fayetteville
Sept. 17	17	New Mexico	0	Little Rock
Sept. 24	10	Ole Miss	13	Jackson
Oct. 1	38	TCU	21	Fort Worth
Oct. 15	3	Texas	31	Little Rock
Oct. 22	24	Houston	3	Fayetteville
Oct. 29	35	Rice	0	Little Rock
Nov. 5	21	Baylor	24	Fayetteville
Nov. 12	23	Texas A&M	36	College Station
Nov. 19	0	SMU	17	Little Rock
Nov. 26	16	Texas Tech	13	Lubbock

KEN HATFIELD

Six Years (55-17-1: .746)

1984 (7-4-1)
Mark Lee, Marcus Elliott, Capts.

Sept. 15	14	Ole Miss	14	Little Rock
Sept. 22	18	Tulsa	9	Fayetteville
Sept. 29	33	Navy	10	Little Rock
Oct. 6	31	TCU	32	Fayetteville
Oct. 13	24	Texas Tech	0	Little Rock
Oct. 20	18	Texas	24	Austin
Oct. 27	17	Houston	3	Houston
Nov. 3	28	Rice	6	Little Rock
Nov. 10	14	Baylor	9	Waco
Nov. 17	28	Texas A&M	0	Fayetteville
Nov. 24	28	SMU	31	Dallas
Dec. 27*	15	Auburn	21	Memphis

*Liberty Bowl

1985 (10-2-0)
Greg Lasker, Nick Miller, Andy Upchurch, Capts.

Sept. 14	24	Ole Miss	19	Jackson
Sept. 21	24	Tulsa	0	Little Rock
Sept. 28	45	New Mexico State	13	Little Rock
Oct. 5	41	TCU	0	Fort Worth
Oct. 12	30	Texas Tech	7	Lubbock
Oct. 19	13	Texas	15	Fayetteville
Oct. 26	57	Houston	27	Little Rock
Nov. 2	30	Rice	15	Houston
Nov. 9	20	Baylor	14	Little Rock
Nov. 16	6	Texas A&M	10	College Station
Nov. 23	15	SMU	9	Fayetteville
Dec. 22*	18	Arizona State	17	San Diego

*Holiday Bowl

1986 (9-3-0)
James Shibest, Derrick Thomas, Theo Young, Capts.

Sept. 13	21	Ole Miss	0	Little Rock
Sept. 20	34	Tulsa	17	Fayetteville
Sept. 27	42	New Mexico State	11	Little Rock
Oct. 4	34	TCU	17	Fayetteville
Oct. 11	7	Texas Tech	17	Fayetteville
Oct. 18	21	Texas	14	Austin
Oct. 25	30	Houston	13	Houston
Nov. 1	45	Rice	14	Fayetteville
Nov. 8	14	Baylor	29	Waco
Nov. 15	14	Texas A&M	10	Little Rock
Nov. 22	41	SMU	0	Dallas
Jan. 1*	8	Oklahoma	42	Miami

*Orange Bowl

1987 (9-4-0)
Chris Bequette, Tony Cherico, Greg Thomas, Rickey
Williams, Capts.

Sept. 12	31	Ole Miss	10	Jackson
Sept. 19	30	Tulsa	15	Fayetteville
Sept. 26	7	Miami	51	Little Rock
Oct. 3	20	TCU	10	Fort Worth
Oct. 10	31	Texas Tech	0	Lubbock
Oct. 17	14	Texas	16	Little Rock
Oct. 24	21	Houston	17	Fayetteville
Oct. 31	38	Rice	14	Houston
Nov. 7	10	Baylor	7	Fayetteville
Nov. 14	0	Texas A&M	14	College Station
Nov. 28	43	New Mexico	25	Little Rock
Dec. 5	38	Hawaii	20	Honolulu
Dec. 29*	17	Georgia	20	Memphis

*Liberty Bowl

1988 (10-2-0)
Steve Atwater, John Bland, Odis Lloyd, Kerry Owens,
Capts.

Sept. 3	63	Pacific	14	Little Rock
Sept. 10	30	Tulsa	26	Fayetteville
Sept. 17	21	Ole Miss	13	Little Rock
Oct. 1	53	TCU	10	Little Rock
Oct. 8	31	Texas Tech	10	Little Rock
Oct. 15	27	Texas	24	Austin
Oct. 22	26	Houston	21	Houston
Oct. 29	21	Rice	14	Little Rock
Nov. 5	33	Baylor	3	Waco

Nov. 12	25	Texas A&M	20	Fayetteville
Nov. 26	16	Miami	18	Miami
Jan. 2*	3	UCLA	17	Dallas

*Cotton Bowl

1989 (10-2-0)
Anthoney Cooney, Elbert Crawford, Tim Horton,
Michael Shepherd, Capts.

Sept. 16	26	Tulsa	7	Fayetteville
Sept. 23	24	Ole Miss	17	Jackson
Sept. 30	39	Texas-El Paso	7	Little Rock
Oct. 7	41	TCU	19	Fort Worth
Oct. 14	45	Texas Tech	13	Lubbock
Oct. 21	20	Texas	24	Fayetteville
Oct. 28	45	Houston	39	Little Rock
Nov. 4	38	Rice	17	Houston
Nov. 11	19	Baylor	10	Fayetteville
Nov. 24	23	Texas A&M	22	College Station
Dec. 2	38	SMU	24	Little Rock
Jan. 1*	27	Tennessee	31	Dallas

*Cotton Bowl

JACK CROWE

Two Years (9-15-0: .375)

1990 (3-8-0)
Quinn Grovey, Chad Rolen, Capts.

Sept. 15	28	Tulsa	3	Fayetteville
Sept. 22	17	Ole Miss	21	Little Rock
Sept. 29	31	Colorado State	20	Little Rock
Oct. 6	26	TCU	54	Little Rock
Oct. 13	44	Texas Tech	49	Fayetteville
Oct. 20	17	Texas	49	Austin
Oct. 27	28	Houston	62	Houston
Nov. 3	11	Rice	19	Little Rock
Nov. 10	3	Baylor	34	Waco
Nov. 17	16	Texas A&M	20	Fayetteville
Nov. 24	42	SMU	29	Dallas

1991 (6-6-0)
Kirk Collins, Mark Henry, Capts.

Aug. 31	3	Miami	31	Little Rock
Sept. 7	17	SMU	6	Little Rock
Sept. 21	9	SW Louisiana	7	Fayetteville
Sept. 28	17	Ole Miss	24	Jackson
Oct. 5	22	TCU	21	Fort Worth
Oct. 12	29	Houston	17	Fayetteville
Oct. 19	14	Texas	13	Little Rock
Nov. 2	5	Baylor	9	Fayetteville
Nov. 9	21	Texas Tech	38	Lubbock
Nov. 16	3	Texas A&M	13	College Station
Nov. 23	20	Rice	0	Little Rock
Dec. 29*	15	Georgia	24	Shreveport

*Independence Bowl

JOE KINES

One Year* (3-5-1)

1992 (3-7-1)
Darwin Ireland, E. D. Jackson, Owen Kelly, Capts.

Sept. 5	3	The Citadel	10	Fayetteville
Sept. 12	45	South Carolina	7	Columbia

Sept. 19	11	Alabama	38	Little Rock
Sept. 26	6	Memphis State	22	Memphis
Oct. 3	3	Georgia	27	Fayetteville
Oct. 10	25	Tennessee	24	Knoxville
Oct. 17	3	Ole Miss	17	Little Rock
Oct. 31	24	Auburn	24	Auburn
Nov. 7	3	Mississippi State	10	Starkville
Nov. 21	19	SMU	24	Little Rock
Nov. 27	30	LSU	6	Fayetteville

*Kines replaced Jack Crowe after the first game

DANNY FORD

Three Years (17-17-1: .500)

1993 (5-5-1)
Kirk Botkin, Tyrone Chatman, Capts.

Sept. 4	10	SMU	6	Dallas
Sept. 11	18	South Carolina	17	Fayetteville
Sept. 18	3	Alabama	43	Tuscaloosa
Sept. 25	0	Memphis State	6	Little Rock
Oct. 2	20	Georgia	10	Athens
Oct. 9	14	Tennessee	28	Little Rock
Oct. 16	0	Ole Miss	19	Jackson
Oct. 30	21	Auburn	31	Fayetteville
Nov. 6	13	Mississippi State	13	Little Rock
Nov. 13	24	Tulsa	11	Fayetteville
Nov. 27	42	LSU	24	Baton Rouge

1994 (4-7-0)
Jason Allen, Willie Johnson, Capts.

Sept. 3	34	SMU	14	Little Rock
Sept. 10	0	South Carolina	14	Columbia
Sept. 17	6	Alabama	13	Fayetteville
Sept. 24	15	Memphis	16	Memphis
Oct. 1	42	Vanderbilt	6	Little Rock
Oct. 8	21	Tennessee	38	Knoxville
Oct. 15	31	Ole Miss	7	Fayetteville
Oct. 29	14	Auburn	31	Auburn
Nov. 5	7	Miss. State	17	Starkville
Nov. 12	30	Northern Illinois	27	Fayetteville
Nov. 26	12	LSU	30	Little Rock

1995 (8-5-0)
Barry Lunney, Steven Conley, Capts.

Sept. 2	14	SMU	17	Dallas
Sept. 9	51	South Carolina	21	Fayetteville
Sept. 16	20	Alabama	19	Tuscaloosa
Sept. 23	27	Memphis	20	Little Rock
Sept. 30	35	Vanderbilt	7	Nashville
Oct. 7	31	Tennessee	49	Fayetteville
Oct. 14	13	Ole Miss	6	Memphis
Oct. 28	30	Auburn	28	Little Rock
Nov. 4	26	Miss. State	21	Little Rock
Nov. 11	24	SW Louisiana	13	Fayetteville
Nov. 18	0	LSU	28	Baton Rouge
Dec. 2*	3	Florida	34	Atlanta
Dec. 30**	10	North Carolina	20	Fort Lauderdale

*SEC Championship
**Carquest Bowl, Fort Lauderdale

TWO-DEEP PLAYER LISTS IN RECENT YEARS

1958 (4-6)

OFFENSE AND DEFENSE

LE   Billy Tranum, 6-2, 194
       Steve Butler, 6-1, 172
LT   Billy Michael, 5-11, 196
       Jim Hollander, 6-1, 194
LG   Billy Gilbow, 5-9, 180
       Barry Switzer, 6-1, 190
C   Wayne Harris, 6-0, 182
       Gerald Gardner, 6-0, 184
RG   Jerry Green, 6-0, 189
       Billy Luplow, 6-2, 201
RT   Marlin Epp, 6-0, 196
       Paul Henderson, 5-11, 205
RE   Richard Bell, 6-2, 191
       Les Letsinger, 6-2, 182
QB   James Monroe, 6-0, 182
       Mike Cooney, 6-1, 174
LH   Jim Mooty, 5-10, 174
       Freddy Akers, 5-9, 166
RH   Billy Kyser, 6-0, 171
       Don Ritschel, 5-10, 168
       Don Horton, 5-9, 178
FB   Joe Paul Alberty, 6-0, 177
       Donnie Stone, 6-1, 192

COACHES

Frank Broyles, Doug Dickey, Merrill Green, Jim Mackenzie, Wilson Matthews, Dixie White, Steed White

1959 (9-2)

OFFENSE AND DEFENSE

LE   Steve Butler, 6-1, 187
       Jim Gaston, 6-1, 196
LT   Marlin Epp, 6-0, 198 /
       Paul Henderson, 5-11, 196
LG   Billy Luplow, 6-2, 208
       Jerry Green, 6-0, 185
C   Wayne Harris, 6-0, 187
       Barry Switzer, 6-1, 191
RG   Gerald Gardner, 6-2, 185
       Johnny Fields, 6-1, 190
RT   Jim Hollander, 6-1, 212
       Dean Garrett, 6-0, 190

RE   Billy Tranum, 6-2, 195
       Les Letsinger, 6-2, 192
QB   James Monroe, 6-0, 186
       George McKinney, 5-11, 180
LH   Jim Mooty, 5-10, 165
       Darrell Williams, 5-11, 165
RH   Lance Alworth, 6-0, 175
       Jarrell Williams, 5-11, 170
FB   Joe Paul Alberty, 6-0, 178
       Curtis Cox, 6-0, 195

COACHES

Frank Broyles, Doug Dickey, Merrill Green, Mervin Johnson, Jim Mackenzie, Wilson Matthews, Dixie White, Steed White

1960 (8-3)

LE   Steve Butler, 6-1, 180
       Jim Gaston, 6-1, 187
LT   Marlin Epp, 6-0, 198
       Jerry Mazzanti, 6-2, 198
LG   Dean Garrett, 6-0, 196
       Ray Trail, 5-11, 200
C   Wayne Harris, 6-2, 185
       Jerry Lineberger, 6-0, 192
RG   Johnny Fields, 6-1, 187
       Danny Brabham, 6-4, 214
RT   Paul Henderson, 5-11, 220
       John Childress, 6-2, 204
RE   Jimmy Collier, 6-1, 187
       Les Letsinger, 6-2, 194
QB   George McKinney, 5-11, 181
       Billy Moore, 5-10, 175
LH   Lance Alworth, 6-0, 178
       Jarrell Williams, 5-11, 170
RH   Darrell Williams, 5-11, 168
       Harold Horton, 5-8, 160
FB   Joe Paul Alberty, 6-0, 179
       Curtis Cox, 6-0, 192
K   Mickey Cissell, 6-1, 190

COACHES

Frank Broyles, Doug Dickey, Merrill Green, Jim Mackenzie, Wilson Matthews, Dixie White, Steed White

1961 (8-3)

OFFENSE AND DEFENSE

LE	Tim Langston, 6-1, 188
	Jim John, 6-0, 193
LT	Jerry Mazzanti, 6-2, 210
	Wes Bryant, 6-2, 212
LG	Ray Trail, 5-11, 202
	Gary Howard, 6-1, 182
C	Danny Brabham, 6-4, 215
	Jerry Lineberger, 6-0, 192
RG	Dean Garrett, 6-0, 200
	Tommy Brasher, 5-11, 192
RT	John Childress, 6-2, 207
	Dave Adams, 6-2, 210
RE	Jimmy Collier, 6-1, 188
	Hoover Evans, 6-1, 190
QB	George McKinney, 5-11, 178
	Billy Moore, 5-10, 174
LH	Lance Alworth, 6-0, 177
	Darrell Williams, 5-11, 168
RH	Paul Dudley, 6-0, 183
	Harold Horton, 5-8, 167
FB	Billy Joe Moody, 6-1, 195
	Jesse Branch, 5-11, 183
K	Mickey Cissell, 6-1, 190

COACHES

Frank Broyles, Doug Dickey, Hayden Fry, Jim Mackenzie, Wilson Matthews, Dixie White, Steed White

1962 (9-2)

OFFENSE (BIG RED, TUSH HOGS)

Big Red, first teamers, played offense and defense; Tush Hogs, listed second, offense only

WE	Gary Howard, 6-1, 193
	James Finch, 6-1, 193
WT	Jerry Mazzanti, 6-2, 220
	Jerry Welch, 6-0, 205
WG	Tommy Brasher, 5-11, 196
	Jerry Jones, 6-0, 192
C	Ronnie Caveness, 6-0, 206
	Dick Hatfield, 6-0, 183
SG	Ray Trail, 5-11, 209
	Jimmy Johnson, 5-11, 202
ST	Dave Adams, 6-2, 225
	Gene Beutelschies, 6-2, 200
SE	Jerry Lamb, 6-1, 180
	Hoover Evans, 6-1, 192
QB	Billy Moore, 5-10, 176
	Billy Gray, 6-1, 164
TB	Jesse Branch, 5-11, 186
	Dwayne Cox, 6-0, 169
WB	George Rea Walker, 5-11, 182
FB	Danny Brabham, 6-4, 218
	Charles Daniel, 5-11, 196
K	Tom McKnelly, 6-0, 190

DEFENSE (WILD HOGS)

LE	Jim Grizzle, 6-1, 191
LT	Buddy Tackett, 6-1, 200
LB	Tommy Polk, 6-0, 188
LB	Ronnie Mac Smith, 6-0, 191
MG	Mike Hales, 5-11, 188
RT	Wes Bryant, 6-2, 220
RE	Tim Langston, 6-1, 186
S	Ken Hatfield, 5-11, 169
LH	Mike Parker, 6-1, 174
RH	Tommy Moore, 6-0, 179
MM	Stan Sparks, 6-0, 188

COACHES

Frank Broyles, Doug Dickey, Mervin Johnson, Jim Mackenzie, Wilson Matthews, Bill Pace, Barry Switzer, Steed White

1963 (5-5)

OFFENSE AND DEFENSE

WE	Jim John, 6-1, 194
	Jim Finch, 6-1, 203
WT	Wes Bryant, 6-2, 221
	Jerry Welch, 6-0, 206
WG	Gary Howard, 6-1, 200
	Ronnie Mac Smith, 6-0, 195
C	Ronnie Caveness, 6-0, 215
	Randy Stewart, 6-0, 200
SG	Jimmy Johnson, 5-11, 195
	Jerry Jones, 6-0, 204
ST	Dave Adams, 6-2, 216
	Glen Ray Hines, 6-5, 240
SE	Jerry Lamb, 6-1, 184
	Jim Grizzle, 6-1, 196
QB	Billy Gray, 6-1, 167
	Fred Marshall, 6-0, 184
	Jon Brittenum, 6-0, 177
TB	Jack Brasuell, 5-9, 170
	Tommy Moore, 6-0, 181
FB	Charles Daniel, 5-11, 185
	Stan Sparks, 6-0, 190
WB	Jim Lindsey, 6-2, 198
	Ken Hatfield, 5-11, 167
	Mike Parker, 6-1, 182
K	Tom McKnelly, 6-0, 190

COACHES

Frank Broyles, Doug Dickey, Mervin Johnson, Jim Mackenzie, Wilson Matthews, Bill Pace, Barry Switzer, Steed White

1964 (11-0)

OFFENSE

WE	Bobby Crockett, 6-1, 189	
	Richard Trail, 6-3, 200	
WT	Glen Ray Hines, 6-5, 235	
	Claud Smithey, 6-1, 206	
WG	Jerry Welch, 6-0, 210	
	Melvin Gibbs, 5-11, 200	
C	Randy Stewart, 6-0, 204	
	Dick Hatfield, 6-0, 185	
SG	Jerry Jones, 6-0, 190	
	Ernie Richardson, 6-2, 194	
ST	Mike Bender, 6-3, 215	
	Dick Cunningham, 6-3, 209	
SE	Jerry Lamb, 6-1, 184	
	Tommy Burnett, 6-1, 194	
QB	Fred Marshall, 6-0, 181	
	Billy Gray, 6-1, 172	
TB	Jack Brasuell, 5-9, 174	
	Bobby Burnett, 6-1, 190	
WB	Jim Lindsey, 6-2, 198	
	Gary Robinson, 6-0, 196	
FB	Bobby Nix, 6-0, 193	
	Eddie Woodlee, 5-11, 196	
K	Tom McKnelly, 6-0, 190	

DEFENSE

LE	Jim Finch, 6-1, 204
	Mickey Maroney, 6-3, 200
LT	Loyd Phillips, 6-3, 220
	Jack Moran, 6-2, 208
LLB	Ronnie Mac Smith, 6-0, 191
	Joe Black, 6-0, 201
MG	Jimmy Johnson, 5-11, 203
	Guy Jones, 5-9, 180
RLB	Ronnie Caveness, 6-0, 212
	Buddy Sims, 6-1, 213
RT	Jim Williams, 6-2, 204
	Tommy Sain, 6-1, 201
RE	Bobby Roper, 6-3, 193
	Lee Johnson, 5-11, 192
MM	Charles Daniel, 5-11, 183
	Mike Jordan, 5-11, 183
LH	Billy Gray, 6-1, 172
	Larry Watkins, 6-1, 187
RH	Ken Hatfield, 5-11, 69
	Stu Berryhill, 5-10, 174
S	Harry Jones, 6-2, 192
	Garland Ridenour, 5-11, 182
PK	Tom McKnelly, 6-2, 206

COACHES

Broyles, Mervin Johnson, Jim Mackenzie, Johnny Majors, Wilson Matthews, Bill Pace, Barry Switzer, Steed White, Lon Farrell, Jack Davis

1965 (10-1)

OFFENSE

WE	Richard Trail, 6-2, 202
	Tommy Burnett, 6-1, 195
WT	Glen Ray Hines, 6-5, 235
	Phil Livingston, 6-2, 210
WG	Melvin Gibbs, 5-11, 212
	Travis Mauldin, 6-5, 190
C	Randy Stewart, 6-0, 205
	Tim Banks, 5-11, 196
SG	Mike Bender, 6-3, 215
	Ernie Richardson, 6-2, 199
ST	Dick Cunningham, 6-2, 210
	Ernest Ruple, 6-4, 225
SE	Bobby Crockett, 6-1, 195
	Martine Bercher, 6-0, 165
QB	Jon Brittenum, 6-0, 182
	Ronny South, 6-1, 179
TB	Bobby Burnett, 6-1, 192
	Jerry Mooty, 5-10, 171
WB	Jim Lindsey, 6-2, 200
	Harry Jones, 6-2, 193
FB	Bobby Nix, 6-0, 200
	Alvin Jones, 5-10, 190
K	Ronny South, 6-0, 180

DEFENSE

LE	Lee Johnson, 5-10, 190
	Hartford Hamilton, 6-3, 196
LT	Loyd Phillips, 6-3, 221
	Bill Douglass, 6-3, 205
LLB	Joe Black, 6-0, 205
	David Cooper, 6-1, 200
MG	Guy Jones, 5-9, 180
	Bill Douglass, 6-3, 205
RLB	Buddy Sims, 6-1, 215
	Tommy Sain, 6-1, 205
RT	Jim Williams, 6-2, 205
	Claud Smithey, 6-1, 212
RE	Bobby Roper, 6-3, 195
	Jack Moran, 6-2, 212
MM	Steve Hoehn, 6-3, 201
	Mickey Maroney, 6-3, 200
LH	Martine Bercher, 6-0, 165
	Paul Conner, 6-1, 185
RH	Tommy Trantham, 6-3, 190
	Paul Conner, 6-1, 185
S	Jack Brasuell, 5-9, 175
	Martine Bercher, 6-0, 165

COACHES

Frank Broyles, Mervin Johnson, Johnny Majors, Wilson Matthews, Bill Pace, Barry Switzer, Steed White, Jack Davis, Lon Farrell

1966 (8-2)

OFFENSE

WE	Richard Trail, 6-2, 213
	Mike Sigman, 6-2, 213
WT	Ernest Ruple, 6-4, 242
	Larry Reynolds, 6-4, 234
WG	Travis Mauldin, 6-0, 197
	Tom Spradlin, 6-2, 234
C	Melvin Gibbs, 5-11, 211
	Louis Nalley, 6-1, 188
SG	Jim Barnes, 6-3, 225
	John Evans, 5-11, 212
ST	Dick Cunningham, 6-2, 225
	Webb Hubbell, 6-4, 216
SE	Tommy Burnett, 6-2, 200
	Tommy Trantham, 6-3, 196
	Tommy Dixon, 5-11, 182
QB	Jon Brittenum, 6-0, 187
	Ronny South, 6-3, 195
	Gordon Norwood, 6-3, 195
TB	David Dickey, 6-1, 204
	Glen Hockersmith, 5-10, 202
WB	Harry Jones, 6-2, 200
	Jim Whisenhunt, 5-11, 183
FB	Eddie Woodlee, 5-10, 201
	Glen Hockersmith, 5-10, 202
K	Bob White, 5-9, 190

DEFENSE

LE	Hartford Hamilton, 6-3, 205
	William Ketcher, 6-3, 215
LT	Loyd Phillips, 6-3, 233
	Champ Thomas, 6-0, 201
LLB	Joe Black, 6-0, 210
	Joe Paul Daves, 6-0, 189
MG	David Cooper, 6-1, 218
	Pat May, 6-0, 200
RLB	Lee Johnson, 5-10, 207
	Alvin Jones, 5-10, 196
	Joe Smelser, 5-11, 190
RT	Terry Don Phillips, 6-1, 207
	Don McElvogue, 5-10, 207
	Lyndel Bland, 6-1, 222
RE	Mickey Maroney, 6-3, 205
	Jack Moran, 6-2, 219
	Bill Douglass, 6-3, 205
MM	Mike Jordan, 5-11, 195
	Steve Hoehn, 6-3, 207
LH	Gary Adams, 5-10, 175
	Stu Berryhill, 5-10, 171
RH	Tommy Trantham, 6-3, 196
	George Calhoun, 6-0, 189
S	Martine Bercher, 6-0, 177
	Terry Stewart, 6-0, 178
P	Paul Conner, 6-1, 180

COACHES

Frank Broyles, Charlie Coffey, Mervin Johnson, Johnny Majors, Wilson Matthews, Bill Pace, Gordon Smith, Steed White, Jack Davis, Lon Farrell

1967 (4-5-1)

OFFENSE

WE	Mike Sigman, 6-2, 193
	DeWitt Smith, 6-3, 211
WT	Webb Hubbell, 6-4, 225
	Larry Reynolds, 6-4, 223
WG	Pat May, 6-0, 220
	Jud Erwin, 6-4, 210
C	Rodney Brand, 6-3, 209
	Louis Nalley, 6-1, 195
SG	Jim Barnes, 6-3, 221
	Jim Mullins, 6-1, 209
ST	Ernest Ruple, 6-5, 245
	Jim Jordan, 6-2, 208
SE	Max Peacock, 6-2, 175
	Dennis Berner, 6-1, 185
QB	Ronny South, 6-0, 193
	John Eichler, 6-1, 189
	Gordon Norwood, 6-3, 196
TB	Russell Cody, 5-11, 181
	Mike Hendren, 6-3, 193
WB	David Dickey, 6-1, 201
	David Cox, 6-0, 179
	Tommy Dixon, 5-11, 183
FB	Glen Hockersmith, 5-10, 188
	Richard Coleman, 5-11, 201
	Larry Watkins, 6-1, 187
K	Bob White, 5-9, 194

DEFENSE

LE	Hartford Hamilton, 6-3, 200
	Tommy Dew, 6-0, 202
LT	Jerry Dossey, 6-4, 221
	Champ Thomas, 6-0, 197
LLB	Lynn Garner, 6-2, 191
	Guy Parker, 5-10, 196
MLB	David Cooper, 6-1, 218
	John Curtis, 5-11, 207
RLB	Cliff Powell, 6-1, 202
	Joe Paul Daves, 6-0, 189
RT	Alvin Jones, 5-10, 194
	Don McElvogue, 5-10, 202
RE	William Ketcher, 6-3, 210
	Tommy Harper, 6-1, 204
MM	Steve Hoehn, 6-4, 204
	Max Peacock, 6-2, 175
LH	Gary Adams, 5-10, 174
	Gary Harrell, 6-1, 173
RH	Tommy Trantham, 6-3, 194
	Mike McClendon, 6-1, 181
S	Terry Stewart, 6-0, 184
	Danny Geohagen, 6-0, 174
P	Paul Conner, 6-1, 184

COACHES

Frank Broyles, Charley Coffey, Hootie Ingram, Mervin Johnson, Johnny Majors, Wilson Matthews, Gordon Smith, Steed White, Jack Davis, Lon Farrell

1968 (10-1)

OFFENSE

SE	Max Peacock, 6-2, 175	
	David Cox, 6-0, 180	
LT	Webb Hubbell, 6-4, 229	
	Ronnie Hammers, 6-3, 228	
LG	Jerry Dossey, 6-3, 225	
	Jim Mullins, 6-1, 220	
C	Rodney Brand, 6-3, 209	
	Louis Nalley, 6-1, 196	
RG	Jim Barnes, 6-3, 227	
	DeWitt Smith, 6-3, 208	
RT	Bob Stankovich, 6-4, 235	
	Pat May, 6-0, 217	
TE	Mike Sigman, 6-2, 208	
	Pat Morrison, 6-1, 212	
QB	Bill Montgomery, 6-1, 174	
	John Eichler, 6-1, 196	
	Gordon Norwood, 6-3, 198	
TB	Bill Burnett, 6-0, 184	
	David Dickey, 6-1, 205	
FL	Chuck Dicus, 6-0, 171	
	John Rees, 6-1, 178	
FB	Bruce Maxwell, 6-1, 218	
	Glen Hockersmith, 5-10, 197	
K	Bob White, 5-9, 195	
	Tim Webster, 6-1, 179	

DEFENSE

LE	Bruce James, 6-3, 214
	Tommy Dew, 6-0, 199
LT	Rick Kersey, 5-11, 200
	Terry Don Phillips, 6-1, 209
RT	Dick Bumpas, 6-1, 216
	Gary Parson, 6-9, 255
RE	Gordon McNulty, 6-4, 214
	Greg Lackey, 6-1, 206
RLB	Lynn Garner, 6-2, 197
	Steve Birdwell, 6-3, 194
MLB	Cliff Powell, 6-1, 204
	Guy Parker, 5-10, 195
LLB	Mike Boschetti, 6-1, 189
	Mike Jacobs, 6-2, 206
MM	Bobby Field, 5-11, 170
	Steve Birdwell, 6-3, 194
LH	Gary Adams, 5-10, 175
	Dennis Berner, 6-2, 180
RH	Jerry Moore, 6-3, 198
	Tommy Dixon, 5-11, 182
S	Terry Stewart, 6-0, 187
	Dennis Berner, 6-2, 180
P	Cary Stockdell, 6-5, 225

COACHES

Frank Broyles, Don Breaux, Charlie Coffey, Harold Horton, Hootie Ingram, Mervin Johnson, Wilson Matthews, Richard Williamson, Jack Davis, Lon Farrell

1969 (9-2)

OFFENSE

SE	Chuck Dicus, 6-0, 170
	Steve Hockersmith, 5-11, 180
LT	Mike Kelson, 6-4, 230
	DeWitt Smith, 6-3, 212
LG	Jerry Dossey, 6-3, 235
	Jim Mullins, 6-1, 216
C	Rodney Brand, 6-3, 226
	Terry Hopkins, 6-0, 200
	Bill Carter, 6-1, 193
RG	Ronnie Hammers, 6-3, 230
	Ronnie Bennett, 6-3, 245
RT	Bob Stankovich, 6-4, 237
	Tom Mabry, 6-6, 248
TE	Pat Morrison, 6-2, 220
	Bobby Nichols, 6-1, 204
QB	Bill Montgomery, 6-1, 180
	John Eichler, 6-1, 198
TB	Bill Burnett, 6-0, 189
	Russell Cody, 5-11, 180
FL	John Rees, 6-1, 174
	David Cox, 6-0, 180
FB	Bruce Maxwell, 6-1, 214
	Russ Garber, 6-0, 220
K	Bill McClard, 6-0, 190
	Tim Webster, 6-1, 190

DEFENSE

LE	Bruce James, 6-3, 221
	Roger Harnish, 6-2, 216
LT	Rick Kersey, 5-11, 200
	Terry Don Phillips, 6-1, 216
RT	Dick Bumpas, 6-1, 225
	Gary Parson, 6-9, 250
RE	Gordon McNulty, 6-4, 215
	Fred Edwards, 6-1, 200
RLB	Mike Boschetti, 6-1, 195
	Tommy Dew, 6-0, 204
MLB	Cliff Powell, 6-1, 215
	Robert Lewis, 6-3, 208
LLB	Lynn Garner, 6-2, 205
	Ronnie Jones, 6-2, 200
MM	Bobby Field, 5-11, 175
	Steve Birdwell, 6-0, 202
LH	Terry Stewart, 6-0, 191
	David Hogue, 6-1, 185
RH	Jerry Moore, 6-3, 198
	Robert Dew, 5-11, 174
S	Dennis Berner, 6-2, 187
	Gus Rusher, 6-2, 180
P	Cary Stockdell, 6-5, 200

COACHES

Frank Broyles, Don Breaux, Charlie Coffey, Harold Horton, Hootie Ingram, Mervin Johnson, Wilson Matthews, Richard Williamson, Lon Farrell, Jack Davis

1970 (9-2)

OFFENSE

SE	Chuck Dicus, 6-0, 175	
	Mike Reppond, 6-0, 175	
LT	Mike Kelson, 6-4, 238	
	Rick Vickers, 6-2, 215	
LG	Tom Reed, 6-3, 227	
	Mike Griffin, 6-3, 250	
C	Terry Hopkins, 6-0, 200	
	Archie Bennett, 6-1, 243	
	Bill Carter, 6-1, 193	
RG	Ronnie Hammers, 6-3, 230	
	Ronnie Bennett, 6-3, 245	
RT	Tom Mabry, 6-6, 248	
	Glen Lowe, 6-4, 251	
TE	Pat Morrison, 6-2, 220	
	Bobby Nichols, 6-1, 204	
QB	Bill Montgomery, 6-1, 180	
	Joe Ferguson, 6-2, 175	
FL	Jim Hodge, 5-11, 170	
	John Rees, 6-1, 178	
FB	Russ Garber, 6-0, 218	
	Scott Binnion, 6-0, 200	
TB	Bill Burnett, 6-0, 190	
	Jon Richardson, 5-10, 175	
	Mike Saint, 6-0, 202	
K	Bill McClard, 6-0, 200	

DEFENSE

LE	Bruce James, 6-3, 230
	Jim Benton, 6-1, 205
LT	Rick Kersey, 6-0, 200
	Roger Harnish, 6-2, 216
RT	Dick Bumpas, 6-1, 225
	Steve Benoit, 6-2, 209
RE	David Reavis, 6-4, 240
	Fred Edwards, 6-0, 200
LLB	Guy Parker, 5-11, 209
	Steve Vestal, 5-11, 194
MLB	Mike Boschetti, 6-1, 195
	Bill Kennedy, 6-2, 201
RLB	Ronnie Jones, 6-2, 202
	Les Williams, 5-11, 195
MM	Bobby Field, 5-11, 175
	Louis Campbell, 6-1, 180
LH	Jerry Moore, 6-3, 198
	Jim Irwin, 5-11, 165
RH	Jack Morris, 6-1, 180
	David Hogue, 6-1, 185
S	Corky Cordell, 6-1, 179
	Steve Walters, 6-1, 190
P	Ken Curry, 6-2, 170

COACHES

Frank Broyles, Raymond Berry, Billy Kinard, Wilson Matthews, Don Breaux, Charlie Coffey, Harold Horton, Mervin Johnson, Lon Farrell, Jack Davis

1971 (8-3-1)

OFFENSE

SE	Mike Reppond, 6-0, 175
	Jack Ettinger, 6-3, 175
LT	Mike Kelson, 6-4, 238
	J. Jones, 6-2, 220
LG	Tom Reed, 6-3, 230
	Rodger Brand, 6-1, 220
C	Ron Revard, 6-2, 225
	Stuart Freeland, 6-3, 235
RG	Glen Lowe, 6-4, 245
	Mike Griffin, 6-3, 240
RT	Tom Mabry, 6-6, 248
	John Boozman, 6-3, 318
TE	Bobby Nichols, 6-2, 220
	Steve Hedgepeth, 6-4, 210
QB	Joe Ferguson, 6-2, 175
	Walter Nelson, 6-0, 180
FB	Mike Saint, 6-0, 200
	Skipper DeBorde, 6-0, 212
TB	Dickey Morton, 5-11, 175
	Jon Richardson, 5-11, 180
FL	Jim Hodge, 5-11, 170
	Mark Hollingsworth, 6-1, 190
K	Bill McClard, 6-0, 200

DEFENSE

LE	Les Williams, 5-11, 190
	Steve Cox, 6-3, 205
LT	Archie Bennett, 6-1, 245
	Don Wunderly, 6-4, 220
RT	David Reavis, 6-4, 240
	Bobby Bradsher, 6-2, 215
RE	Ronnie Jones, 6-2, 200
	Jim Brawner, 6-1, 195
SLB	Danny Rhodes, 6-2, 210
	Bill Kennedy, 6-2, 205
MLB	Jim Benton, 6-1, 207
	John Wheat, 6-2, 205
WLB	Scott Binnion, 6-0, 220
	Doug Scheel, 6-0, 190
LC	Jack Morris, 6-1, 175
	David Hogue, 6-1, 185
FS	Corky Cordell, 6-1, 180
	Jim Taylor, 6-1, 182
SS	Clark Irwin, 6-0, 180
	Mike Davis, 6-1, 177
RC	Louis Campbell, 6-1, 182
	Jim Irwin, 5-11, 170
P	Drew Toole, 5-11, 205

COACHES

Frank Broyles, Mervin Johnson, Harold Horton, Joe Gibbs, Don Breaux, Buddy Bennett, Raymond Berry, Wilson Matthews, Jack Davis, Lon Farrell

1972 (6-5)

OFFENSE

SE   Mike Reppond, 6-0, 172
       Jack Ettinger, 6-2, 184
LT   Mike Griffin, 6-2, 244
       Steve Glover, 6-1, 236
LG   Tom Reed, 6-3, 235
       Rodger Brand, 6-1, 212
C   Stuart Freeland, 6-3, 232
       Ron Revard, 6-2, 235
RG   Glen Lowe, 6-3, 240
       Randy Drake, 6-4, 230
RT   Lee King, 6-3, 244
       John Boozman, 6-3, 229
TE   Steve Hedgepeth, 6-3, 212
       Matt Morrison, 6-2, 193
QB   Joe Ferguson, 6-1, 182
       Walter Nelson, 6-0, 185
       Scott Bull, 6-4, 203
RB   Dickey Morton, 5-10, 170
       Jon Richardson, 5-11, 188
FB   Mike Saint, 6-0, 200
       Marsh White, 6-2, 209
FL   Jim Hodge, 5-11, 167
       Reggie Craig, 6-0, 182
K   Mike Kirkland, 6-2, 187

DEFENSE

LE   Ivan Jordan, 6-2, 200
       Les Williams, 5-10, 197
LT   Jon Rhiddlehoover, 6-0, 226
       Don Wunderly, 6-3, 221
RT   David Reavis, 6-3, 240
       Chuck Sims, 6-3, 223
RE   Ray Strain, 6-1, 198
       Douglas Yoder, 6-3, 205
SLB Danny Rhodes, 6-1, 217
       Ed Rownd, 6-1, 204
MLB John Wheat, 6-1, 210
       Jim Benton, 6-0, 212
WLB Scott Binnion, 5-11, 210
       Billy Burns, 6-1, 215
LC   Jim Irwin, 5-11, 177
       Mike Davis, 6-0, 184
FS   Tommy Harris, 6-1, 182
SS   Clark Irwin, 6-0, 187
       Mark Hollingsworth, 6-1, 191
RC   Louis Campbell, 6-1, 182
       Freddie Douglas, 5-10, 170
P   Drew Toole, 5-11, 207

COACHES

Frank Broyles, Buddy Bennett, Raymond Berry, Jack Davis, Lon Farrell, Joe Gibbs, Harold Horton, Wilson Matthews, Richard Williamson

1973 (5-5-1)

OFFENSE

SE   Jack Ettinger, 6-2, 180
       Reggie Craig, 6-0, 180
LT   Gerald Skinner, 6-5, 255
       Mike Parmer, 6-3, 217
LG   Greg Koch, 6-4, 227
       Russ Tribble, 6-4, 220
C   Richard LaFargue, 6-4, 220
       Stan Audas, 6-4, 220
       Randy Drake, 6-3, 221
RG   R. C. Thielemann, 6-3, 224
       Ron Fulcher, 6-0, 209
RT   Lee King, 6-2, 236
       Allen Petray, 6-3, 221
TE   Matt Morrison, 6-2, 197
       Nick Avlos, 6-4, 217
       Steve Hedgepeth, 6-3, 205
QB   Mike Kirkland, 6-1, 185
       Mark Miller, 6-2, 180
TB   Dickey Morton, 5-10, 180
       Rolland Fuchs, 5-10, 185
WB   Freddie Douglas, 5-10, 170
       Teddy Barnes, 5-9, 180
FB   Alan Watson, 6-0, 205
       Marsh White, 6-2, 209
K   Mike Kirkland

DEFENSE

LE   Ivan Jordan, 6-2, 200
       Eddie Hartsfield, 6-1, 200
LT   Brison Manor, 6-4, 232
       Chuck Sims, 6-3, 225
NG   Harvey Hampton, 6-1, 230
       Mike Campbell, 5-11, 200
RT   Jon Rhiddlehoover, 6-0, 220
       Dennis Dunkelgod, 6-2, 204
RE   Dennis Winston, 6-2, 218
       Danny Crawford, 6-3, 195
LB   Danny Rhodes, 6-1, 210
       Eddie Rownd, 6-1, 205
LB   Billy Burns, 6-1, 198
       Hal McAfee, 6-3, 200
CB   Bruce Mitchell, 6-3, 188
       Brad Thomas, 5-9, 172
SS   Bo Busby, 6-2, 185
       Tommy Harris, 6-1, 175
FS   Floyd Hogan, 6-0, 165
       Donny Prince, 5-11, 180
CB   Rollen Smith, 6-1, 180
       Elijah Davis, 5-11, 180

COACHES

Frank Broyles, Frank Falks, Harold Horton, Jimmy Johnson, Mervin Johnson, Bill Lewis, Ken Turner, Don Trull, Richard Williamson, Mike Bender, Jack Davis, Borys Malczycki

1974 (6-4-1)

OFFENSE

SE	Freddie Douglas, 5-10, 170	
	Reggie Craig, 6-0, 180	
LT	Gerald Skinner, 6-6, 255	
	Steve Heim, 6-4, 260	
LG	Greg Koch, 6-4, 228	
	Randy Drake, 6-4, 230	
C	Richard LaFargue, 6-4, 225	
	Sam Pope, 6-0, 210	
RG	R. C. Thielemann, 6-3, 230	
	Ron Fulcher, 6-0, 210	
RT	Lee King, 6-2, 237	
	Allen Petray, 6-3, 220	
TE	Doug Yoder, 6-3, 205	
	Mickey Billingsley, 6-2, 204	
QB	Mike Kirkland, 6-1, 185	
	Mark Miller, 6-2, 180	
	Scott Bull, 6-5, 205	
FB	Ike Forte, 6-0, 195	
	Marsh White, 6-2, 210	
RB	Rolland Fuchs, 5-10, 182	
	Vaughn Lusby, 5-9, 182	
RB	Teddy Barnes, 5-9, 172	
	Jerry Eckwood, 6-1, 175	
	Elijah Davis, 5-11, 180	
K	Steve Little, 6-0, 175	

DEFENSE

LE	Ivan Jordan, 6-2, 207	
	Ronnie Wren, 6-0, 200	
LT	Brison Manor, 6-4, 235	
	Harvey Hampton, 6-1, 230	
NG	Mike Campbell, 5-11, 200	
	Leotis Harris, 6-2, 245	
RT	Jon Rhiddlehoover, 6-0, 220	
	Gary Roper, 6-0, 215	
RE	Johnnie Meadors, 6-1, 212	
	Danny Crawford, 6-3, 198	
LB	Dennis Winston, 6-1, 210	
	Billy Burns, 6-1, 197	
LB	Hal McAfee, 6-3, 200	
	Terry Irwin, 6-0, 210	
LC	Brad Thomas, 5-9, 174	
	Muskie Harris, 5-11, 170	
RC	Rollen Smith, 6-1, 180	
	Howard Sampson, 5-10, 175	
SS	Bo Busby, 6-2, 185	
	Tommy Harris, 6-1, 175	
FS	Floyd Hogan, 6-0, 165	
P	Mike Kirkland, 6-1, 189	
PK	Steve Little, 6-1, 180	

COACHES

Frank Broyles, Richard Williamson, Jimmy Johnson, Ken Turner, Mervin Johnson, Bill Lewis, Harold Horton, Frank Falks, Jesse Branch

1975 (10-2)

OFFENSE

SE	Freddie Douglas, 5-10, 178	
	Chris Warren, 6-1, 190	
LT	Gerald Skinner, 6-5, 260	
	Stan Audas, 6-5, 241	
LG	Leotis Harris, 6-2, 246	
	Russ Tribble, 6-4, 225	
C	Richard LaFargue, 6-4, 245	
	Allen Petray, 6-3, 230	
RG	R. C. Thielemann, 6-3, 234	
	Mike Parmer, 6-3, 244	
RT	Greg Koch, 6-4, 240	
	Steve Heim, 6-4, 262	
TE	Doug Yoder, 6-3, 206	
	Marvin Daily, 6-0, 220	
QB	Scott Bull, 6-5, 202	
	Mike Kirkland, 6-1, 189	
	Ron Calcagni, 6-0, 187	
FL	Teddy Barnes, 5-9, 174	
	Charles Clay, 6-0, 195	
	Doug Barwegen, 5-11, 176	
RB	Ike Forte, 6-0, 199	
	Micheal Forrest, 6-2, 225	
RB	Jerry Eckwood, 6-0, 185	
	Rolland Fuchs, 5-10, 195	
	Ben Cowins, 6-1, 185	
K	Steve Little, 6-0, 181	

DEFENSE

LE	Ivan Jordan, 6-1, 215	
	Don Fulcher, 5-11, 206	
LT	Mark Lewis, 6-2, 246	
	Jimmy Walker, 6-2, 245	
NG	Mike Campbell, 5-11, 206	
	Dale White, 6-3, 235	
RT	Harvey Hampton, 5-11, 229	
	Dan Hampton, 6-5, 235	
RE	Johnnie Meadors, 6-1, 214	
	Dennis Winston, 6-1, 210	
LB	Curtis Townsend, 6-0, 220	
	Reggie Freeman, 6-0, 209	
LB	Hal McAfee, 6-0, 196	
	William Hampton, 6-1, 225	
LC	Brad Thomas, 5-9, 175	
	Larry White, 6-0, 160	
RC	Howard Sampson, 5-10, 178	
	Brad Shoup, 6-1, 175	
SS	Tommy Harris, 6-2, 186	
	Elijah Davis, 5-10, 172	
FS	Bo Busby, 6-1, 192	
	Mark Miller, 6-2, 190	
P	Tommy Cheyne, 5-10, 175	

COACHES

Frank Broyles, Jesse Branch, Bo Rein, Don Boyce, Jimmy Johnson, Harold Horton, Bill Lewis, Ken Turner, Pat Jones, Frank Falks, Steve Sprayberry, Joe Fred Young

1976 (5-5-1)

OFFENSE

SE	Kevin Evans, 6-1, 188
	Robert Farrell, 6-5, 196
LT	Gerald Skinner, 6-4, 260
	Rusty Wilber, 6-4, 256
LG	Steve Heim, 6-4, 270
	Roger Wynn, 6-1, 256
C	R. C. Thielemann, 6-4, 247
	Rick Shumaker, 6-0, 228
	Greg Kolenda, 6-1, 252
RG	Leotis Harris, 6-1, 261
	Tom Ginn, 6-4, 225
RT	Greg Koch, 6-4, 249
	Mike Reinig, 6-5, 228
TE	Charles Clay, 6-0, 199
	Tim Adams, 6-1, 211
QB	Ron Calcagni, 6-0, 187
	Houston Nutt, 6-0, 197
	Mike Scott, 5-11, 180
FL	Barnabas White, 5-11, 164
	Chris Warren, 6-0, 198
RB	Ben Cowins, 6-1, 187
	Donny Bobo, 5-11, 187
RB	Micheal Forrest, 6-2, 231
	Jerry Eckwood, 6-0, 196
K	Steve Little, 6-0, 180

DEFENSE

LE	Johnnie Meadors, 6-0, 214
	Don Fulcher, 5-11, 198
LT	Dan Hampton, 6-5, 240
	Jimmy Walker, 6-1, 242
NG	Dale White, 6-2, 240
	Reggie Freeman, 6-0, 205
RT	Harvey Hampton, 5-11, 224
	Cornelius Smith, 6-0, 202
RE	Dennis Winston, 6-1, 224
LB	Curtis Townsend, 6-0, 218
	Mike Massey, 6-2, 220
LB	William Hampton, 6-0, 218
	Larry Jackson, 6-0, 216
LC	Patrick Martin, 5-8, 180
	Vaughn Lusby, 5-9, 186
RC	Howard Sampson, 5-10, 178
	Brad Shoup, 6-0, 180
SS	Elijah Davis, 5-10, 180
	Bruce Mitchell, 6-3, 190
FS	Bo Busby, 6-1, 195
	Larry White, 5-11, 164
P	Steve Little

COACHES

Frank Broyles, Don Boyce, Jesse Branch, Frank Falks, Harold Horton, Ken Turner, Jimmy Johnson, Bill Lewis, Bob Gatling

1977 (11-1)

OFFENSE

SE	Robert Farrell, 6-5, 201
	Bobby Duckworth, 6-3, 195
	Bruce Hay, 5-11, 179
LT	Steve Heim, 6-3, 262
	Rusty Wilber, 6-4, 257
LG	Mark Lewis, 6-2, 252
	Chuck Herman, 6-3, 234
C	Rick Shumaker, 6-0, 228
	Tom Ginn, 6-4, 234
RG	Leotis Harris, 6-1, 254
	Jerry Sullivan, 6-4, 237
RT	Greg Kolenda, 6-1, 259
	Birt Locke, 6-2, 242
TE	Curtis Clay, 6-0, 198
	Tim Adams, 6-1, 211
QB	Ron Calcagni, 6-0, 188
	Houston Nutt, 6-1, 192
FL	Donny Bobo, 5-11, 181
	Gary Stiggers, 5-9, 169
RB	Ben Cowins, 6-0, 186
	Trent Bryant, 5-10, 171
RB	Micheal Forrest, 6-4, 210
	Roland Sales, 6-1, 192
K	Steve Little, 6-0, 180

DEFENSE

LE	Marty Micham, 6-4, 206
	Jim Howard, 6-2, 211
LT	Jimmy Walker, 6-0, 232
	Danny Phillips, 6-3, 220
MG	Reggie Freeman, 6-0, 210
	George Stewart, 6-3, 238
RT	Dan Hampton, 6-5, 242
	Jim Elliott, 6-0, 237
RE	Jerry Saxton, 6-1, 209
	Cornelius Smith, 6-1, 202
LB	Larry Jackson, 5-11, 210
	Marshall Cowley, 6-2, 219
LB	William Hampton, 6-1, 209
	Mike Massey, 6-2, 228
LC	Patrick Martin, 5-8, 172
	J. R. Ross, 5-10, 185
RC	Vaughn Lusby, 5-9, 169
	O. C. Jackson, 5-7, 167
SS	Brad Shoup, 6-0, 186
	Kirk Woolfolk, 5-10, 184
FS	Howard Sampson, 5-10, 185
	Les King, 6-2, 189
PK	Steve Little

COACHES

Lou Holtz, Larry Beightol, Jesse Branch, Don Breaux, Bob Cope, Harold Horton, Monte Kiffin, John Mitchell, Ken Turner

1978 (9-2-1)

OFFENSE

SE	Gary Stiggers, 5-9, 170	
	Bruce Hay, 5-11, 183	
LT	Phillip Moon, 6-1, 247	
	Birt Locke, 6-2, 248	
LG	Chuck Herman, 6-3, 244	
	Tom Ginn, 6-4, 234	
C	Rick Shumaker, 6-0, 231	
	Mike Burlingame, 6-2, 220	
RG	Jerry Sullivan, 6-4, 243	
	George Stewart, 6-3, 252	
RT	Greg Kolenda, 6-1, 259	
	Joe Shantz, 6-3, 265	
TE	Charles Clay, 6-0, 205	
	Tim Adams, 6-1, 215	
QB	Ron Calcagni, 6-0, 190	
	Kevin Scanlon, 6-0, 180	
RB	Ben Cowins, 6-0, 189	
	Roland Sales, 6-1, 205	
RB	Jerry Eckwood, 6-0, 199	
	Micheal Forrest, 6-1, 210	
FL	Robert Farrell, 6-5, 198	
	Bobby Duckworth, 6-3, 197	
K	Ish Ordonez, 5-7, 157	

DEFENSE

LE	Jim Howard, 6-2, 213
	Ozzie Riley, 5-10, 214
LT	Jimmy Walker, 6-0, 240
	Alfred Mohammed, 6-3, 253
NG	Dale White, 5-11, 242
	Stan Freeman, 6-4, 234
RT	Dan Hampton, 6-5, 259
	Jim Elliott, 6-0, 240
RE	Marty Micham, 6-4, 208
	Jerry Saxton, 6-0, 215
LB	Larry Jackson, 5-11, 201
	Mike Massey, 6-2, 218
LB	William Hampton, 6-1, 213
	Bruce Sutherland, 6-2, 198
SC	Vaughn Lusby, 5-9, 173
	O. C. Jackson, 5-7, 167
WC	Hugh Jernigan, 5-11, 172
SS	Brad Shoup, 6-0, 189
	Kirk Woolfolk, 5-10, 188
FS	Trent Bryant, 5-10, 178
	Tom Rystrom, 6-1, 194
P	Bruce Lahay, 6-2, 205

COACHES

Lou Holtz, Larry Beightol, Jesse Branch, Don Breaux, Bob Cope, Harold Horton, Monte Kiffin, John Mitchell, Ken Turner, John Konstantinos

1979 (10-2)

OFFENSE

SE	Robert Farrell, 6-5, 192
	Bobby Duckworth, 6-3, 197
LT	Phillip Moon, 6-1, 252
	Birt Locke, 6-2, 259
LG	Chuck Herman, 6-3, 242
	Tom Ginn, 6-4, 252
C	Mike Burlingame, 6-2, 245
	Keith Houfek, 6-3, 237
RG	George Stewart, 6-3, 252
	Thurman Shaw, 6-2, 248
RT	Greg Kolenda, 6-1, 258
	Joe Shantz, 6-3, 267
TE	Steve Clyde, 6-1, 202
	Darryl Mason, 6-1, 217
QB	Kevin Scanlon, 6-0, 185
	Tom Jones, 6-1, 182
RB	Gary Anderson, 6-1, 185
	Gary Woods, 6-1, 200
RB	Roland Sales, 6-1, 202
	James Tolbert, 6-0, 198
	Darryl Bowles, 5-11, 190
FL	Gary Stiggers, 5-9, 175
	Danny Walters, 6-2, 188
	Derek Holloway, 5-8, 165

DEFENSE

LE	Jim Howard, 6-2, 218
	Mark Dewey, 6-2, 208
LT	Billy Ray Smith, 6-4, 217
	Danny Phillips, 6-3, 234
NG	Ricky Richardson, 5-11, 226
	Alfred Mohammed, 6-3, 234
RT	Jim Elliott, 6-0, 239
	Stan Freeman, 6-4, 234
RE	Marty Micham, 6-4, 212
	Jeff Goff, 6-1, 202
LB	Mike Massey, 6-2, 225
	Ozzie Riley, 5-10, 214
LB	Teddie Morris, 6-1, 211
	Steve Douglas, 6-1, 212
LC	Trent Bryan, 5-10, 180
	Ronald Matheney, 6-0, 176
RC	Hugh Jernigan, 5-11, 175
	David Haynes, 5-11, 195
SS	Randy Wessinger, 6-0, 180
	Keith Burns, 6-0, 186
FS	Kevin Evans, 6-1, 195
P	Bruce Lahay, 6-2, 205
PK	Ish Ordonez, 5-7, 157
	Steve Cox, 6-3, 199

COACHES

Lou Holtz, Don Breaux, Bob Cope, Monte Kiffin, Jesse Branch, Harold Horton, John Mitchell, John Konstantinos, John Stuckey, Ken Turner

1980 (7-5)

OFFENSE

SE Bobby Duckworth, 6-3, 197, Sr., Hamburg
      Derek Holloway, 5-8, 166, Soph., Palmyra, N.J.
LT Phillip Moon, 6-0, 252, Sr., Harrison
      Ronnie Trusty, 6-4, 255, Jr., Paris
LG Daryal Pickett, 6-2, 237, Frosh, Texarkana, Tex.
      Thurman Shaw, 6-2, 252, Jr., Pine Bluff
C Keith Houfek, 6-3, 242, Sr., Shawnee Mission, Kan.
      Neal Galloway, 6-1, 235, Soph., Stuttgart
RG George Stewart, 6-3, 260, Sr., LR Parkview
      Jay Bequette, 6-2, 260, Soph., Crystal City, Mo.
RT Joe Shantz, 6-3, 265, Sr., Buffalo, Mo.
      Mike Bradford, 6-2, 242, Jr., Arlington, Va.
TE Darryl Mason, 6-1, 227, Jr., LR Parkview
      Steve Clyde, 6-1, 202, Jr., Houston, Tex., Stratford
QB Tom Jones, 6-2, 184, Soph., Ruston, La.
      Bill Pierce, 6-0, 185, Frosh, Crossett
RB James Tolbert, 6-0,199, Jr., LR Parkview
      Darryl Bowles, 5-11, 195, Soph., Brownsville, Tenn.
RB Gary Anderson, 6-1, 184, Soph., Columbia, Mo.
      Mark Douglas, 5-11, 109, Soph., Van Buren
FL Gary Stiggers, 5-9, 176, Sr., Fort Worth, Tex., Arlington
K Ish Ordonez, 5-7, 154, Sr., Carson, Calif.
      Steve Cox, 6-3, 196, Sr., Charleston, Ark.

DEFENSE

LE Earl Buckingham, 6-2, 236, Soph., Pine Bluff
      Ron Faurot, 6-8, 238, Frosh, Hurst, Tex.
LT Billy Ray Smith, 6-3, 234, Soph., Plano, Tex.
      Bobby Shantz, 6-3, 250, Soph., Buffalo, Mo.
RT Richard Richardson, 5-11, 236, Soph., LR Central
      Max Hughes, 6-3, 268, Soph., Searcy Harding
RE Danny Phillips, 6-1, 234, Sr., Hermitage
      George Hall, 6-1, 220, Jr., LR Hall
SLB Teddy Morris, 6-1, 213, Jr., LR Central
      Calvin Shaw, 6-2, 190, Frosh, Pine Bluff
MLB Steve Douglas, 6-1, 206, Soph., Richardson, Tex.
      Bert Zinamon, 5-11, 220, Frosh, LR Central
WLB Jeff Goff, 6-1, 195, Jr., Benton
      Ed Jackson, 6-2, 195, Soph., NLR Sylvan Hills
LC Kim Dameron, 5-10, 157, Soph., Rogers
      Hugh Jernigan, 5-11, 172, Sr., Jacksonville
RC Trent Bryant, 5-9, 180, Sr., Arkadelphia
      Richard Wilson, 5-10, 188, Sr., Hope
FS Kevin Evans, 6-1, 192, Sr., NLR Northeast
      Cliff Henry, 6-0, 178, Jr., Conway
SS Randy Wessinger, 5-10, 181, Jr., Sherman, Tex.
      Keith Burns, 6-3, 191, Soph., Hurst, Tex.
P Steve Cox, 6-3, 196, Sr., Charleston, Ark.

COACHES

Lou Holtz, Harold Horton, John Konstantinos, Ken Turner, John Mitchell, Don Breaux, Jesse Branch, Bob Cope, Larry Beightol

1981 (8-4)

OFFENSE

SE Gerald McMurray, 5-11, 190, Sr., Pine Bluff
      Derek Holloway, 5-8, 163, Jr., Palmyra, N.J.
LT Ronny Trusty, 6-4, 265, Sr., Paris
      Mike Ihrie, 6-2, 255, Soph., Memphis, Tenn., Craigmont
LG Charles Ginn, 6-3, 254, Jr., Berryville
      Daryal Pickett, 6-2, 250, Soph., Texarkana, Tex.
C Jay Bequette, 6-2, 255, Jr., Crystal City, Mo.
      Neal Galloway, 6-1, 235, Jr., Stuttgart
RG Steve Korte, 6-2, 265, Jr., Littleton, Colo., Arapahoe
      Thurman Shaw, 6-2, 255, Sr., Pine Bluff
RT Alfred Mohammed, 6-3, 265, Jr., Youngstown, Ohio, Ursuline
      Carl Tegethoff, 6-4, 266, Jr., Des Perres, Mo., Chaminade
TE Darryl Mason, 6-4, 221, Sr., LR Parkview
      Steve Clyde, 6-1, 213, Sr., Houston, Tex., Stratford
QB Tom Jones, 6-2, 184, Jr., Ruston, La.
      Brad Taylor, 6-0, 175, Frosh, Danville
RB Gary Anderson, 6-1, 175, Jr., Columbia, Mo., Hickman
      James Tolbert, 6-0, 202, Sr., LR Parkview
      Thomas Brown, 5-10, 176, Jr., Montgomery, Ala., Davis
FB Jessie Clark, 6-1, 226, Jr., Crossett
      Darryl Bowles, 5-11, 187, Jr., Brownsville, Tenn.
      Mark Douglas, 5-11, 214, Jr., Van Buren
FL Mark Mistler, 6-1, 175, Soph., Tucson, Ariz., Sahauro
      Keith Kidd, 6-2, 181, Soph., Crossett
K Bruce Lahay, 6-2, 232, Sr., St. Louis, Mo., Oakville

DEFENSE

E Ron Faurot, 6-8, 248, Soph., Hurst, Tex.
      Earl Buckingham, 6-2, 236, Jr., Pine Bluff
NG Richard Richardson, 5-11, 246, Jr., LR Central
      George Hall, 6-1, 220, Sr., LR Hall
T Phillip Boren, 6-5, 255, Soph., Dallas, Tex., Carter
      Bobby Shantz, 6-3, 233, Sr., Buffalo, Mo.
E Billy Ray Smith, 6-3, 228, Jr., Plano, Tex.
      Calvin Shaw, 6-2, 195, Soph., Pine Bluff
OLB Jeff Goff, 6-1, 223, Sr., Benton
      Darrel Akerfelds, 6-2, 213, Soph., Littleton, Colo., Columbine
SLB Steve Douglas, 6-1, 217, Jr., Richardson, Tex.
      Bert Zinamon, 5-11, 206, Soph., LR Central
WLB Teddy Morris, 6-1, 208, Sr., LR Central
      Milton Fields, 6-2, 225, Soph., LR Central
LC Danny Walters, 6-2, 189, Jr., Chicago, Ill., Julian
      Kim Dameron, 5-10, 162, Jr., Rogers
RC Kent Reber, 6-1, 186, Soph., Moss Bluff, La.
      Nathan Jones, 6-0, 180, Frosh, Texarkana, Tex.
FS Kim Dameron, 5-10, 162, Jr., Rogers
      Ronald Matheney, 6-0, 178, Jr., Crossett
SS Keith Burns, 6-3, 191, Jr., Hurst, Tex.
      Mark Lee, 6-1, 185, Frosh, Creve Coeur, Mo., Parkway N.

COACHES

Lou Holtz, Larry Beightol, Rich Olson, John Mitchell, Ken Turner, Fred Von Appen, Sam Goodwin, Jesse Branch, Don Lindsey

1982 (9-2-1)

OFFENSE

SE	Derek Holloway, 5-8, 169, Sr., Palmyra, N.J.	
	Keith Kidd, 6-2, 189, Jr., Crossett	
LT	Orson Weems, 6-3, 255, Jr., NLR Northeast	
	Carl Tegethoff, 6-4, 265, Sr., Des Perres, Mo., Chaminade	
LG	Charles Ginn, 6-2, 265, Sr., Berryville	
	Marcus Elliott, 6-2, 265, Soph., LR Central	
C	Jay Bequette, 6-2, 275, Sr., Crystal City, Mo.	
	Neal Galloway, 6-1, 232, Sr., Stuttgart	
RG	Steve Korte, 6-2, 270, Sr., Littleton, Colo., Arapahoe	
	Mike Ihrie, 6-2, 255, Jr., Memphis, Tenn., Craigmont	
RT	Alfred Mohammed, 6-2, 285, Sr., Youngstown, Ohio, Ursiline	
	Robert Wilcoxen, 6-6, 275, Soph., NLR Sylvan Hills	
TE	Eddie White, 6-4, 218, Jr., Camden	
	Luther Franklin, 6-1, 218, Frosh, Houston, Tex., Aldine	
QB	Tom Jones, 6-2, 185, Sr., Ruston, La.	
	Brad Taylor, 6-0, 185, Soph., Danville	
RB	Gary Anderson, 6-1, 180, Sr., Columbia, Mo., Hickman	
	Darryl Bowles, 5-11, 198, Sr., Brownsville, Tenn.	
FB	Jessie Clark, 6-1, 226, Sr., Crossett	
	Mark Douglas, 5-11, 220, Sr., Van Buren	
K	Martin Smith, 5-11, 170, Sr., London, England	

DEFENSE

E	Billy Ray Smith, 6-3, 228, Sr., Plano, Tex.	
	Marty Kobza, 6-4, 224, Soph., Schuyler, Neb.	
T	Earl Buckingham, 6-2, 220, Sr., Pine Bluff	
	Bobby King, 6-4, 263, Frosh, LR McClellan	
NG	Richard Richardson, 6-11, 160, Sr., LR Central	
	Jim Kingsby, 6-6, 255, Frosh, NLR Northeast	
E	Ron Faurot, 6-8, 253, Jr., Hurst, Tex.	
	Bobby Shantz, 6-3, 221, Sr., Buffalo, Mo.	
OLB	Mark Lee, 6-2, 199, Soph., Creve Coeur, Mo., Parkway N	
	Ravin Caldwell, 6-3, 190, Frosh, FS Northside	
SLB	Bert Zinamon, 5-11, 221, Jr., LR Central	
	Calvin Shaw, 6-2, 208, Jr., Pine Bluff	
WLB	Milton Fields, 6-2, 220, Jr., LR Central	
	David Bazzel, 6-1, 204, Soph., Panama City, Fla.	
R	Keith Burns, 6-3, 201, Sr., Hurst, Tex.	
	Kent Reber, 6-1, 190, Jr., Moss Bluff, La.	
SC	Nathan Jones, 6-0, 190, Soph., Texarkana, Tex.	
	Kevin Wyatt, 5-10, 180, Frosh, Kansas City, Kan., Rockhurst	
WC	Danny Walters, 6-2, 191, Sr., Chicago, Ill., Julian	
	Greg Gatson, 5-10, 165, Frosh, Newton, Tex.	
S	Greg Lasker, 6-1, 180, Frosh, Conway	
	Mark Fields, 5-9, 165, Soph., LR Central	
P	Brad Taylor, 6-0, 185, Soph., Danville	

COACHES

Lou Holtz, John Mitchell, Rich Olson, Ken Turner, Bob Shaw, Larry Beightol, Sam Goodwin, Jesse Branch, Don Lindsey

1983 (6-5)

OFFENSE

SE	Keith Kidd, 6-2, 190, Sr., Crossett	
	James Shibest, 6-0, 180, Frosh, Houston, Tex., MacArthur	
LT	Phillip Boren, 6-5, 275, Sr., Dallas, Tex., Carter	
	Greg Garrison, 6-7, 274, Jr., Conway	
LG	Orson Weems, 6-3, 253, Sr., NLR Northeast	
	Ira Wells, 6-2, 275, Jr., LR Mills	
C	Andy Upchurch, 6-2, 263, Soph., FS Northside	
	Bill Lenz, 6-4, 240, Soph., Benton	
RG	Marcus Elliott, 6-2, 266, Jr., LR Central	
	David McGee, 6-2, 238, Soph., Garland, Tex.	
RT	Robert Wilcoxen, 6-6, 277, Jr., NLR Sylvan Hills	
	Orson Weems (Swing man)	
TE	Luther Franklin, 6-0, 220, Soph., Houston, Tex., Aldine	
	Theo Young, 6-3, 200, Frosh, Newport	
QB	Brad Taylor, 6-0, 188, Jr., Danville	
	Scott Reed, 5-10, 183, Sr., Jacksonville	
FB	Carl Miller, 5-11, 200, Soph., PB Dollarway	
	Derrick Thomas, 6-2, 215, Frosh, Paducah, Ky.	
TB	Bobby Joe Edmonds, 5-11, 170, Soph., St. Louis, Mo., Lutheran	
N	Terry Tatum, 6-0, 208, Soph., LR Mills	
K	Greg Horne, 6-0, 170, Frosh, Russellville	

DEFENSE

E	Ron Faurot, 6-8, 254, Sr., Hurst, Tex.	
	Calvin Williams, 6-5, 220, Frosh, Greenville, Tex.	
T	Bobby King, 6-4, 263, Soph., LR McClellan	
	Greg Berry, 6-4, 221, Soph., Higginsville, Mo.	
NG	Rodney Beachum, 6-3, 238, Soph., Dallas, Tex., Lake Highlands	
	John Morris, 6-5, 276, Soph., Dallas, Tex., Wilmer-Hutchins	
WE	Nick Miller, 6-3, 217, Soph., Clute, Tex., Brazoswood	
	Robert Brannon, 6-7, 240, Jr., Columbia, S.C., Flora	
OLB	Ravin Caldwell, 6-3, 217, Soph., FS Northside	
	David Dudley, 6-2, 210, Frosh, Houston, Tex., Alief Hastings	
SLB	Bert Zinamon, 5-11, 220, Sr., LR Central	
	Mike Castleberry, 6-0, 221, Sr., Denison, Tex.	
WLB	Milton Fields, 6-1, 219, Sr., LR Central	
	Calvin Shaw, 6-3, 209, Sr., Pine Bluff	
R	Mark Lee, 6-1, 200, Jr., Creve Coeur, Mo., Parkway N	
	Larry Gunn Bryant, 6-1, 192, Sr., England	
RC	Greg Lasker, 6-1, 197, Soph., Conway	
	Nathan Jones, 6-0, 189, Jr., Texarkana, Tex.	
LC	Greg Gatson, 5-10, 178, Soph., Newton, Tex.	
	Charles Washington, 5-11, 175, Frosh, Pine Bluff	
S	Kevin Wyatt, 5-10, 180, Soph., Kansas City, Kan., Rockhurst	
	Kent Reber, 6-1, 191, Sr., Moss Bluff, La.	
P	Brad Taylor, 6-0, 188, Jr., Danville	

COACHES

Lou Holtz, Ken Turner, Rich Olson, Bob Shaw, Jim Strong, Mike Tolleson, Jesse Branch, Pete Cordelli, Don Lindsey, Harvey Hampton

1984 (7-4-1)

OFFENSE

SE — James Shibest, 6-0, 182, Soph., Houston, Tex., MacArthur
Jamie Lueders, 5-10, 173, Jr., Siloam Springs

LT — Dale Williams, 6-1, 239, Soph., Austin, Tex., Lanier
Mark Danielowicz, 6-3, 215, Jr., NLR Sylvan Hills

LG — Mike Ihrie, 6-2, 262, Sr., Memphis, Tenn., Craigmont
John Stitten, 6-6, 291, Frosh, Jasper, Tex.

C — Andy Upchurch, 6-2, 250, Jr., FS Northside
Bryan White, 6-2, 267, Frosh, FS Northside

RG — Marcus Elliott, 6-2, 260, Sr., LR Central
Ira Wells, 6-3, 261, Sr., LR Mills

RT — David McGee, 6-3, 240, Jr., Garland, Tex.
Byron Yarbrough, 6-2, 255, Soph., Clute, Tex., Brazoswood

TE — Eddie White, 6-4, 230, Sr., Camden
Luther Franklin, 6-0, 230, Jr., Houston, Tex., Aldine

QB — Brad Taylor, 6-0, 192, Sr., Danville
Danny Nutt, 5-11, 185, Sr., LR Central

HB — Bobby Joe Edmonds, 5-11, 173, Jr., St. Louis, Mo., Lutheran

N — Terry Tatum, 6-0, 215, Jr., LR Mills

HB — Carl Miller, 5-11, 205, Jr., PB Dollarway
Sammy Van Dyke, 6-1, 185, Frosh, Dallas, Tex., Lake Highlands

FB — Marshall Foreman, 5-9, 187, Soph., Houston, Tex., CyFair
Derrick Thomas, 6-1, 217, Soph., Paducah, Ky.

K — Greg Horne, 6-0, 178, Soph., Russellville
Ernie Villareal, 5-7, 147, Soph., Carson, Calif., Torrance

DEFENSE

OLB — Mark Lee, 6-1, 210, Sr., Creve Coeur, Mo., Parkway N
David Dudley, 6-2, 190, Soph., Houston, Tex., Alief Hastings

DE — Ravin Caldwell, 6-3, 220, Jr., FS Northside
Calvin Williams, 6-3, 227, Soph., Greenville, Tex.

DT — Jeryl Jones, 6-4, 226, Jr., Cabot
Frankie Lisko, 6-1, 230, Sr., Hazen

NG — Tony Cherico, 6-2, 230, Frosh, Shawnee Mission, Kan., NW
Robert Brannon, 6-7, 235, Sr., Columbia, S.C., Flora

DT — Rodney Beachum, 6-3, 239, Jr., Dallas, Tex., Lake Highlands
Chris Bequette, 6-2, 251, Frosh, Crystal City, Mo.

LB — Nick Miller, 6-3, 221, Jr., Clute, Tex., Brazoswood
Erik Whitted, 6-1, 208, Frosh, Dallas, Tex., Lake Highlands

LB — David Bazzel, 6-1, 215, Jr., Panama City, Fla.
Rickey Williams, 6-1, 195, Frosh, LR Parkview

R — Nathan Jones, 6-0, 197, Sr., Texarkana, Tex.
Steve Jones, 6-2, 190, Frosh, LR Catholic

LC — Kevin Wyatt, 5-10, 188, Jr., Kansas City, Kan., Rockhurst
Charles Washington, 5-11, 175, Soph., Pine Bluff

RC — Kevin Anderson, 6-0, 186, Frosh, Morrilton
Greg Gatson, 5-10, 175, Jr., Newton, Tex.

S — Greg Lasker, 6-1, 200, Jr., Conway
Nathaniel White, 6-1, 183, Soph., Dallas, Tex., Wilmer-Hutchins

P — Greg Horne, 6-0, 178, Soph., Russellville

COACHES

Ken Hatfield, Larry Brinson, Fred Goldsmith, Roger Hinshaw,
Wally Ake, Larry Beckman, Jesse Branch, David Lee, Bobby Trott,
Ken Turner

1985 (10-2)

OFFENSE

SE — Donnie Centers, 5-10, 165, Soph., Longview, Tex.
James Shibest, 5-11, 185, Jr., Houston, Tex., MacArthur

LT — Dale Williams, 6-1, 247, Jr., Austin, Tex., Lanier
Mark Danielowicz, 6-3, 230, Sr., NLR Sylvan Hills

LG — Limbo Parks, 6-2, 285, Jr., Kansas City, Mo., Raytown S
John Stitten, 6-6, 295, Soph., Jasper, Tex.

C — Andy Upchurch, 6-1, 250, Sr., FS Northside
Bryan White, 6-2, 270, Soph., FS Northside

RG — Chris Bequette, 6-2, 256, Soph., Crystal City, Mo.
Freddie Childress, 6-4, 295, Frosh, West Helena

RT — David McGee, 6-2, 241, Sr., Garland, Tex.
David Smart, 6-3, 252, Frosh, Bryant

TE — Theo Young, 6-3, 227, Jr., Newport
Luther Franklin, 6-0, 218, Sr., Houston, Tex., Aldine

QB — Greg Thomas, 5-11, 185, Soph., San Angelo, Tex., Central
Mark Calcagni, 6-0, 183, Sr., Youngstown, Ohio, Chaney

LH — James Rouse, 6-2, 205, Frosh, LR Parkview
Carl Miller, 5-10, 209, Sr., Pine Bluff, Dollarway

RH — Bobby Joe Edmonds, 5-11, 175, Sr., St. Louis, Mo., Lutheran

N — Sammy Van Dyke, 5-11, 200, Soph., Dallas, Tex., Lake Highlands
Joe Johnson, 6-0, 190, Frosh, Longview, Tex.

FB — Marshall Foreman, 5-8, 191, Jr., Houston, Tex., Cy-Fair
Derrick Thomas, 6-0, 218, Jr., Paducah, Ky.

K — Kendall Trainor, 6-2, 195, Frosh, Fredonia, Kan.

DEFENSE

OLB — David Dudley, 6-3, 196, Jr., Houston, Tex., Alief Hastings
Steve Jones, 6-2, 194, Soph., LR Catholic

DE — Calvin Williams, 6-4, 231, Jr., Greenville, Tex.
Carl Bradford, 6-2, 230, Soph., Paris, Tex.
(Ravin Caldwell, starter until injured in fifth game)

DT — Rodney Beachum, 6-3, 245, Sr., Dallas, Tex., Lake Highlands
Calvin Williams, 6-4, 231, Jr., Greenville, Tex.

NG — Tony Cherico, 6-0, 231, Soph., Shawnee Mission, Kan., NW
Kerry Crawford, 6-0, 220, Frosh, NLR Old Main

DT — Jeryl Jones, 6-4, 233, Sr., Cabot
David Schell, 6-4, 233, Soph., Albuquerque, N.M., Del Norte

LB — Nick Miller, 6-3, 218, Sr., Clute, Tex., Brazoswood
Erik Whitted, 6-1, 207, Soph., Dallas, Tex., Lake Highlands

LB — David Bazzel, 6-0, 214, Sr., Panama City, Fla.
Rickey Williams, 6-0, 217, Soph., LR Parkview

R — Odis Lloyd, 5-9, 189, Frosh, Stuttgart
Nathaniel White, 6-1, 180, Jr., Dallas, Tex., Wilmer-Hutchins

LC — Kevin Wyatt, 5-10, 190, Sr., Kansas City, Kan., Rockhurst
Greg Gatson, 5-9, 180, Sr., Newton, Tex.

RC — Kevin Anderson, 5-11, 183, Soph., Morrilton
Richard Brothers, 6-1, 185, Frosh, Wilson Rivercrest

S — Greg Lasker, 6-1, 205, Sr., Conway
Steve Atwater, 6-2, 202, Frosh, St. Louis, Mo., Lutheran N

P — Greg Horne, 6-0, 188, Jr., Russellville

COACHES

Ken Hatfield, Wally Ake, Larry Beckman, Jesse Branch, David Lee,
Bob Trott, Ken Turner, Larry Brinson, Fred Goldsmith, Roger Hinshaw

---

TWO-DEEP PLAYER LISTS

1986 (9-3)

OFFENSE

SE	James Shibest, 5-11, 195, Sr., Houston, Tex., MacArthur
	Donnie Centers, 5-10, 170, Jr., Longview, Tex.
LT	David Smart, 6-3, 253, Soph., Bryant
	Jim Mabry, 6-4, 246, Frosh, Memphis Briarcrest
LG	Limbo Parks, 6-2, 275, Sr., Kansas City, Kan., Raytown S
	John Stitten, 6-6, 274, Jr., Jasper, Tex.
RG	Freddie Childress, 6-4, 310, Soph., West Helena
	Mike Benson, 6-2, 285, Frosh, Nashville
RT	Chris Bequette, 6-2, 265, Jr., Crystal City, Mo.
	James Morris, 6-3, 253, Soph., Eudora
TE	Theo Young, 6-3, 228, Sr., Newport
	Billy Winston, 6-2, 229, Frosh, Marianna
QB	Greg Thomas, 5-11, 195, Jr., San Angelo, Tex., Central
	John Bland, 5-10, 177, Soph., Knoxville, Tenn., Farragut
LH	Joe Johnson, 6-0, 200, Soph., Longview, Tex.
	(James Rouse, starter until injured in second game)
RH	Sammy Van Dyke, 5-11, 207, Jr., Dallas, Tex., Lake Highlands
	Aaron Jackson, 5-11, 192, Frosh, Denison, Tex.
FB	Derrick Thomas, 6-0, 223, Sr., Paducah, Ky.
	Marshall Foreman, 5-8, 189, Sr., Houston, Tex., Cy-Fair
K	Kendall Trainor, 6-2, 195, Soph., Fredonia, Kan.

DEFENSE

OLB	David Dudley, 6-3, 215, Sr., Houston, Tex., Alief Hastings
	Steve Jones, 6-2, 206, Jr., LR Catholic
	Bubba Barrow, 6-3, 206, Frosh, Benton
DE	Carl Bradford, 6-3, 235, Jr., Paris, Tex.
	Kerry Owens, 6-2, 222, Soph., Stuttgart
DT	Wayne Martin, 6-5, 240, Soph., Cherry Valley (Cross County)
	Elbert Crawford, 6-3, 246, Frosh, LR Hall
NG	Tony Cherico, 6-0, 239, Jr., Shawnee Mission, Kan., NW
	Kerry Crawford, 6-0, 231, Soph., NLR Old Main
DT	David Schell, 6-4, 240, Jr., Albuquerque, N.M., Del Norte
	Michael Shepherd, 6-4, 245, Frosh, Monroe, La., OC
LB	Rickey Williams, 6-0, 225, Jr., LR Parkview
	Reggie Hall, 5-11, 206, Soph., Stuttgart
LB	Erik Whitted, 6-1, 214, Jr., Dallas, Tex., Lake Highlands
	Albert Harris, 6-2, 230, Frosh, Browns Mills, N.J.
R	Odis Lloyd, 5-9, 180, Soph., Stuttgart
	Nathaniel White, 6-1, 185, Sr., Dallas, Tex., Wilmer-Hutchins
CB	Charles Washington, 5-11, 183, Sr., Pine Bluff
	Chris Hunter, 6-2, 185, Frosh, Arkadelphia
CB	Richard Brothers, 6-1, 186, Soph., Wilson Rivercrest
	Anthoney Cooney, 6-3, 203, Frosh, LR Mills
S	Steve Atwater, 6-4, 210, Soph., St. Louis, Mo., Lutheran
N	Eric Bradford, 6-1, 186, Soph., Fayetteville
P	Greg Horne, 6-0, 187, Sr., Russellville

COACHES

Ken Hatfield, David Lee, Bob Trott, Ken Turner, Wally Ake, Larry ity Brinson, Larry Beckman, Fred Goldsmith, Jim Goodman, Roger Hinshaw

1987 (9-4)

OFFENSE

SE	Tim Horton, 5-9, 171, Soph., Conway
	Derek Russell, 6-1, 185, Frosh, LR Central
LT	Jim Mabry, 6-4, 255, Soph., Memphis Briarcrest
	Todd Jones, 6-3, 289, Frosh, LR Central
LG	John Stitten, 6-6, 308, Sr., Jasper, Tex.
	Todd Gifford, 6-4, 286, Frosh, PB White Hall
C	Bryan White, 6-2, 287, Sr., FS Northside
	Darren Worrell, 6-4, 273, Soph., Bartlesville, Okla.
RG	Freddie Childress, 6-4, 345, Jr., Helena
	James Morris, 6-3, 265, Jr., Eudora
RT	Chris Bequette, 6-2, 268, Sr., Crystal City, Mo.
	Rick Apolskis, 6-4, 262, Soph., Houston, Tex., St. Thomas
TE	Billy Winston, 6-2, 238, Soph., Marianna
	Jim Kessinger, 6-4, 218, Sr., Fort Campbell, Ky.
QB	Greg Thomas, 5-11, 195, Sr., San Angelo, Tex., Central
	Quinn Grovey, 5-10, 176, Frosh, Duncan, Okla.
	John Bland, 5-10, 177, Jr., Knoxville, Tenn., Farragut
LH	Joe Johnson, 6-0, 196, Jr., Longview, Tex.
	Tony Holmes, 5-10, 198, Soph., LR Central
RH	James Rouse, 6-1, 217, Jr., LR Parkview
	Sammy Van Dyke, 5-11, 203, Sr., Dallas, Tex., Lake Highlands
FB	Barry Foster, 5-11, 190, Frosh, Duncanville, Tex.
	Juju Harshaw, 6-0, 200, Frosh, NLR Northeast
K	Kendall Trainor, 6-2, 205, Jr., Fredonia, Kan.

DEFENSE

OLB	Kerry Owens, 6-2, 222, Jr., Stuttgart
	Bubba Barrow, 6-3, 208, Soph., Benton
	Steve Jones, 6-2, 207, Sr., LR Catholic
RT	Wayne Martin, 6-5, 265, Jr., Cherry Valley (Cross County)
	Chad Rolen, 6-3, 257, Frosh, Denison, Tex.
	Tony Ollison, 6-3, 257, Frosh, Malvern
NG	Tony Cherico, 6-0, 242, Sr., Shawnee Mission, Kan., NW
	Kerry Crawford, 6-0, 235, Jr., NLR Old Main
CT	David Schell, 6-4, 248, Sr., Albuquerque, N.M., Del Norte
	Michael Shepherd, 6-4, 260, Soph., Monroe, La., OC
E	Albert Harris, 6-2, 233, Soph., Browns Mills, N.J.
	Carl Bradford, 6-2, 233, Sr., Paris, Tex.
LB	Erik Whitted, 6-1, 207, Sr., Dallas, Tex., Lake Highlands
	LaSalle Harper, 6-1, 235, Jr., LaPorte, Tex.
LB	Rickey Williams, 6-0, 221, Sr., LR Parkview
	Reggie Hall, 5-11, 213, Jr., Stuttgart
R	Odis Lloyd, 5-9, 194, Jr., Stuttgart
	Patrick Williams, 6-2, 190, Soph., McGehee
SC	Richard Brothers, 6-1, 190, Jr., Wilson Rivercrest
	Ben Floor, 6-0, 165, Frosh, Mesquite, Tex.
RC	Anthoney Cooney, 6-2, 193, Soph., LR Mills
	Chris Hunter, 6-2, 191, Soph., Arkadelphia
S	Steve Atwater, 6-4, 205, Jr., St. Louis, Mo., Lutheran N
	Eric Bradford, 6-1, 193, Jr., Fayetteville
P	Kendall Trainor, 6-2, 205, Jr., Fredonia, Kan.

COACHES

Ken Hatfield, David Lee, Bob Trott, Ken Turner, Fred Goldsmith, Jim Goodman, Roger Hinshaw, Wally Ake, Larry Beckman, Larry Brinson

1988 (10-2)

OFFENSE

SE Tim Horton, 5-9, 180, Jr., Conway
    Derek Russell, 6-0, 175, Soph., LR Central
LT Jim Mabry, 6-4, 265, Jr., Memphis Briarcrest
    Todd Jones, 6-3, 275, Soph., LR Central
LG James Morris, 6-3, 265, Sr., Eudora
    Mark Henry, 6-5, 260, Frosh, LR Central
C Elbert Crawford, 6-3, 260, Jr., LR Hall
    Dwayne Spann, 6-5, 260, Frosh, LaPorte, Tex.
RG Freddie Childress, 6-4, 310, Sr., Helena
    Todd Gifford, 6-4, 275, Soph., PB White Hall
RT Rick Apolskis, 6-4, 265, Jr., Houston, Tex., St. Thomas
    Todd Jones, 6-3, 175, Soph., LR Central
TE Billy Winston, 6-2, 235, Jr., Marianna
    Steve Hudson, 6-4, 230, Soph., Monroe, La., OC
    Lyndy Lindsey, 6-3, 225, Frosh, Fayetteville
QB Quinn Grovey, 5-10, 183, Soph., Duncan, Okla.
    John Bland, 5-10, 188, Sr., Knoxville, Tenn., Farragut
    Jimmy Williams, 6-0, 190, Jr., Houston, Tex., Jones
HB Joe Johnson, 6-0, 196, Sr., Longview, Tex.
    Kerwin Price, 6-0, 202, Frosh, E. St. Louis, Ill.
    (James Rouse, injured much of the season)
WB Aaron Jackson, 5-11, 199, Soph., Denison, Tex.
    Carlos Gatson, 6-4, 214, Soph., El Dorado
FB Barry Foster, 5-10, 205, Soph., Duncanville, Tex.
    Juju Harshaw, 6-0, 210, Soph., NLR Northeast
PK Kendall Trainor, 6-2, 205, Sr., Fredonia, Kan.

DEFENSE

OLB Odis Lloyd, 5-9, 198, Sr., Stuttgart
    Chris Hunter, 6-2, 190, Jr., Arkadelphia
RT Wayne Martin, 6-5, 263, Sr., Cherry Valley (Cross County)
    Tony Ollison, 6-3, 258, Soph., Malvern
NG Kerry Crawford, 6-0, 240, Sr., NLR Old Main
    Chad Rolen, 6-3, 255, Soph., Sherman, Tex.
CT Michael Shepherd, 6-4, 258, Jr., Monroe, La., OC
    MacKenzie Phillips, 6-5, 250, Frosh, Springdale
E Kerry Owens, 6-2, 232, Sr., Stuttgart
    Bubba Barrow, 6-3, 212, Jr., Benton
    James McCoy, 6-5, 215, Jr., Marianna
LB LaSalle Harper, 6-1, 235, Sr., LaPorte, Tex.
    Steven Marshall, 6-1, 230, Soph., Wilson Rivercrest
LB Reggie Hall, 5-11, 220, Sr., Stuttgart
    Ty Mason, 6-2, 218, Frosh, Decatur, Ill., MacArthur
SC Richard Brothers, 6-1, 195, Sr., Wilson Rivercrest
    Ben Floor, 6-0, 185, Soph., Mesquite, Tex.
R Patrick Williams, 6-2, 192, Jr., McGehee
    Eric Bradford, 6-1, 190, Sr., Fayetteville
S Steve Atwater, 6-4, 215, Sr., St. Louis, Mo., Lutheran N
    Kirk Collins, 6-0, 195, Frosh, LaMarque, Tex.
WC Anthoney Cooney, 6-2, 200, Jr., LR Mills
    Curtis Banks, 5-11, 195, Frosh, Dallas, Tex., Carter
P Allen Meacham, 6-1, 195, Jr., Flagstaff, Ariz.

COACHES

Ken Hatfield, David Lee, Ken Turner, Bob Trott, Fred Goldsmith, Roger Hinshaw, Jim Goodman, Wally Ake, Larry Brinson, Larry Beckman

1989 (10-2)

OFFENSE

SE Tim Horton, 5-9, 180, Sr., Conway
    Rodney Winston, 6-1, 202, Jr., Marianna
LT Jim Mabry, 6-4, 266, Sr., Memphis Briarcrest
    Reggie Trusty, 5-11, 265, Sr., Paris
LG Todd Gifford, 6-4, 270, Jr., Pine Bluff White Hall
    Shon Flores, 6-3, 290, Jr., Port Isabel, Tex.
C Elbert Crawford, 6-3, 262, Sr., LR Hall
    Eric Castillo, 6-4, 250, Frosh, Hialeah, Fla.
RG Mark Henry, 6-5, 262, Soph., LR Central
    Matt Pitner, 6-1, 268, Jr., Houston, Tex., Memorial
RT Rick Apolskis, 6-4, 270, Sr., Houston, Tex., St. Thomas
    Patrick Crocker, 6-4, 290, Soph., FS Northside
TE Billy Winston, 6-2, 235, Sr., Marianna
    Lyndy Lindsey, 6-3, 230, Soph., Fayetteville
    Steve Hudson, 6-4, 235, Jr., Monroe, La., OC
QB Quinn Grovey, 5-10, 185, Jr., Duncan, Okla.
    Jimmy Williams, 6-0, 188, Sr., Houston, Tex., Jones
    Gary Adams, 6-2, 185, Frosh, Springfield, Mo., Central
FL Derek Russell, 6-0, 178, Jr., LR Central
    Sedric Fillmore, 6-1, 185, Frosh, LR Central
TB James Rouse, 6-1, 220, Sr., LR Parkview
    E. D. Jackson, 5-10, 200, Frosh, Kilgore, Tex.
    Ron Dickerson Jr., 6-2, 205, Frosh, State College, Pa.
FB Barry Foster, 5-10, 217, Jr., Duncanville, Tex.
    Juju Harshaw, 6-0, 212, Jr., NLR Northeast
    Kerwin Price, 6-0, 210, Soph., E. St. Louis, Ill.
K Todd Wright, 5-11, 166, Frosh, Stillwater, Okla.

DEFENSE

OLB Ken Benson, 6-2, 207, Jr., Manhattan, Kan.
    Chris Hunter, 6-2, 198, Sr., Arkadelphia
RT Tony Ollison, 6-3, 258, Jr., Malvern
    Scott Long, 6-4, 243, Frosh, Benton
NG Chad Rolen, 6-3, 255, Jr., Sherman, Tex.
    Owen Kelly, 6-0, 250, Frosh, Wichita Falls, Tex., Rider
CT Michael Shepherd, 6-4, 261, Sr., Monroe, La., OC
    MacKenzie Phillips, 6-5, 260, Soph., Springdale
E Bubba Barrow, 6-3, 217, Sr., Benton
    James McCoy, 6-5, 215, Sr., Marianna
RLB Mick Thomas, 6-2, 230, Soph., Bakersfield, Calif., Garces
    Ted Shimer, 6-0, 218, Jr., Bentonville
KLB Ty Mason, 6-2, 216, Soph., Decatur, Ill., MacArthur
    Shannon Wright, 6-1, 220, Frosh, FS Southside
SC Curtis Banks, 5-11, 190, Soph., Dallas, Tex., Carter
    Michael James, 6-1, 180, Soph., Pine Bluff
R Patrick Williams, 6-2, 196, Sr., McGehee
    Kirk Collins, 6-0, 195, Soph., LaMarque, Tex.
FS Aaron Jackson, 5-11, 208, Jr., Denison, Tex.
    Rob Bonneau, 6-0, 185, Frosh, Spokane, Wash., Gonzaga
WC Anthoney Cooney, 6-2, 200, Sr., LR Mills
    Pat Burris, 5-11, 180, Jr., Rock Hill, S.C.
P Allen Meacham, 6-1, 195, Sr., Flagstaff, Ariz., Garcia

COACHES

Ken Hatfield, Bob Trott, Richard Wilson, Roger Hinshaw, Jack Crowe, J. B. Grimes, Dick Bumpas, Wally Ake, Larry Brinson, Larry Beckman

OFFENSE

SE   Derek Russell, 6-0, 190, Sr., LR Central
      Demetrius Smith, 6-1, 192, Frosh, LR Mills
LT   Shon Flores, 6-3, 285, Sr., Port Isabel, Tex.
      Dwight Atteberry, 6-3, 275, Jr., Conroe, Tex., Kingwood
LG   Ray Straschinske, 6-4, 280, Frosh, Cabot
      Matt Pitner, 6-1, 270, Sr., Houston, Tex., Memorial
C   Mark Henry, 6-5, 275, Jr., LR Central
      John Brooks, 6-2, 265, Soph., Arlington, Tex.
RG   Todd Gifford, 6-4, 285, Sr., Pine Bluff White Hall
      Tommy Jones, 6-4, 275, Frosh, Dallas, Tex., White
RT   Chris Oliver, 6-5, 270, Frosh, Fayetteville
      Patrick Crocker, 6-4, 290, Jr., FS Northside
TE   Lyndy Lindsey, 6-3, 240, Jr., Fayetteville
      Kirk Botkin, 6-2, 235, Frosh, Baytown, Tex., Lee
FL   Tracy Caldwell, 6-0, 175, Frosh, Pine Bluff
      Jason Brandt, 5-8, 185, Jr., Harrison
QB   Quinn Grovey, 5-10, 183, Sr., Duncan, Okla.
      Gary Adams, 6-2, 190, Soph., Springfield, Mo., Central
FB   Chris Kirby, 5-11, 215, Frosh, Pine Bluff Dollarway
      Kerwin Price, 6-0, 215, Jr., E. St. Louis, Ill.
TB   E. D. Jackson, 5-10, 205, Soph., Kilgore, Tex.
      Aaron Jackson, 5-11, 205, Sr., Denison, Tex.
      Ron Dickerson Jr., 6-2, 205, Soph., State College, Pa.
K   Todd Wright, 5-11, 180, Soph., Stillwater, Okla.

DEFENSE

WLB Darwin Ireland, 6-1, 215, Frosh, Pine Bluff
      Tyrone Chatman, 5-10, 205, Frosh, Dumas
LT   Chad Rolen, 6-3, 265, Sr., Sherman, Tex.
      Henry Ford, 6-4, 240, Frosh, Fort Worth, Tex., Trimble Tech
NG   Owen Kelly, 6-0, 250, Soph., Wichita Falls, Tex., Rider
      Stephen Walls, 6-3, 270, Frosh, LR Parkview
RT   Scott Long, 6-4, 260, Soph., Benton
      Ronnie Marlow, 6-3, 266, Soph., Wills Point, Tex.
RLB Ken Benson, 6-2, 220, Sr., Wichita, Kan., North
      Ray Lee Johnson, 6-3, 235, Soph., Fordyce
SLB Mick Thomas, 6-2, 230, Jr., Bakersfield, Calif., Garces
      Shannon Wright, 6-1, 225, Soph., FS Southside
MLB Ty Mason, 6-2, 225, Jr., Decatur, Ill., MacArthur
      Albert Harris, 6-2, 232, Sr., Browns Mills, N.J.
LC   Michael James, 6-1, 180, Jr., Pine Bluff
      Pat Burris, 5-11, 180, Sr., Rock Hill, S.C.
S   Curtis Banks, 5-11, 192, Jr., Dallas, Tex., Carter
      Richard David, 5-11, 195, Soph., New Orleans, La., Holy Cross
FS   Ben Floor, 6-0, 185, Sr., Mesquite, Tex., North
      Dean Peevy, 5-11, 185, Frosh, Montgomery, Ala., Lee
RC   Del Chunn, 5-11, 185, Frosh, Denton, Tex.
      Pat Burris, 5-11, 180, Sr., Rock Hill, S.C.
P   Pete Raether, 6-4, 200, Soph., Edina, Minn.

COACHES

Jack Crowe, Charlie Weatherbie, Ken Rucker, Jerry Pullen, Joe Pate, Houston Nutt, Bill Johnson, Louis Campbell, Scott Conley, J. B. Grimes

---

OFFENSE

SE   Ron Dickerson Jr., 6-2, 205, Jr., State College, Pa.
      Lee Keith, 6-4, 215, Jr., McAlester, Okla.
LT   Cody Mosier, 6-3, 285, Sr., Hope
      Dwight Atteberry, 6-3, 272, Sr., Conroe, Tex., Kingwood
LG   Ray Straschinske, 6-4, 280, Soph., Cabot
      Tommy Jones, 6-4, 265, Soph., Dallas, Tex., White
C   Mark Henry, 6-5, 270, Sr., LR Central
      Jerol Skinner, 6-3, 265, Sr., Salinas, Kan.
RG   Isaac Davis, 6-3, 305, Soph., Malvern
      John Brooks, 6-2, 260, Jr., Arlington, Tex.
RT   Chris Oliver, 6-5, 265, Soph., Fayetteville
      Dwight Atteberry, 6-3, 272, Sr., Conroe, Tex., Kingwood
TE   Lyndy Lindsey, 6-3, 235, Sr., Fayetteville
      Kirk Botkin, 6-3, 235, Soph., Baytown, Tex., Lee
QB   Jason Allen, 6-0, 190, Frosh, Edmond, Okla.
      Wade Hill, 6-3, 203, Soph., Waldron
      Gary Adams, 6-2, 192, Jr., Springfield, Mo., Central
FB   Kerwin Price, 6-0, 215, Sr., E. St. Louis, Ill.
      Chris Kirby, 5-11, 212, Soph., Pine Bluff Dollarway
TB   E. D. Jackson, 5-10, 205, Jr., Kilgore, Tex.
      Tony Jeffery, 5-8, 195, Jr., St. Louis, Mo.
FL   Tracy Caldwell, 6-0, 165, Soph., Pine Bluff
      Vincent Davis, 6-2, 185, Frosh, Birmingham, Ala.
K   Todd Wright, 5-11, 180, Jr., Stillwater, Okla.

DEFENSE

RE   Ray Lee Johnson, 6-3, 230, Jr., Fordyce
      Greg Switzer, 6-0, 212, Sr., LR Central
T   MacKenzie Phillips, 6-5, 265, Sr., Springdale
      Curtis Thomas, 6-3, 260, Frosh, Baytown, Tex., Lee
NG   Owen Kelly, 6-0, 250, Jr., Wichita Falls, Tex., Rider
      Scott Long, 6-4, 260, Jr., Benton
E   Henry Ford, 6-4, 262, Soph., Fort Worth, Tex., Trimble Tech
      James Mallet, 6-3, 230, Soph., Liberty, Tex.
WLB Darwin Ireland, 6-1, 218, Soph., Pine Bluff Dollarway
      Willie Johnson, 6-1, 205, Frosh, Lufkin, Tex.
SLB Tyrone Chatman, 5-10, 212, Soph., Dumas
      Demetrius Smith, 6-1, 215, Soph., LR Mills
MLB Mick Thomas, 6-6, 230, Sr., Bakersfield, Calif., Garces
      Ty Mason, 6-2, 220, Sr., Decatur, Ill., MacArthur
RC   Michael James, 6-1, 180, Sr., Pine Bluff
      Kotto Cotton, 6-0, 170, Frosh, NLR Old Main
SS   Curtis Banks, 5-11, 195, Sr., Dallas, Tex., Carter
      Alfred Jackson, 6-1, 185, Soph., Marshall, Tex.
FS   Kirk Collins, 6-0, 196, Jr., LaMarque, Tex.
      Ivan Pickett, 6-0, 190, Soph., Cincinnati, Ohio, Green Hills
LC   Orlando Watters, 6-0, 175, Soph., Anniston, Ala.
      Kerry Kennedy, 5-10, 185, Soph., Raleigh, N.C., Millbrook
P   Pete Raether, 6-4, 200, Soph., Edina, Minn.

COACHES

Jack Crowe, Joe Pate, Ken Rucker, Charlie Weatherbie, Bill Johnson, Joe Kines, Houston Nutt, Louis Campbell, Scott Conley, J. B. Grimes

---

THE RAZORBACKS

1992 (3-7-1)

OFFENSE

SE	Tracy Caldwell, 5-11, 175, Jr., Pine Bluff
	Kotto Cotton, 6-0, 175, Soph., NLR Old Main
LT	Chris Oliver, 6-5, 275, Jr., Fayetteville
	Terry Spencer, 6-3, 265, Jr., Terrell, Tex.
LG	Ray Straschinske, 6-4, 285, Jr., Cabot
	Tony Nagy, 6-4, 265, Frosh, Tulsa, Okla., Union
C	Earl Scott, 6-3, 265, Frosh, NLR Old Main
	Tony Nagy, 6-4, 265, Frosh, Tulsa, Okla., Union
RG	Isaac Davis, 6-3, 300, Jr., Malvern
	Tony Swartz, 6-3, 327, Frosh, Dickinson, Tex.
RT	Bryan Cornish, 6-4, 280, Soph., Warren
	Verl Mitchell, 6-3, 270, Frosh, Paragould Greene County Tech
TE	Kirk Botkin, 6-3, 237, Jr., Baytown, Tex., Lee
	Carl Johnson, 6-0, 226, Soph., PB Dollarway
QB	Barry Lunney Jr., 6-2, 175, Frosh, FS Southside
	Jason Allen, 6-1, 190, Soph., Edmond, Okla.
FL	Ron Dickerson Jr., 6-1, 200, Sr., State College, Pa.
	Derrick Thompson, 5-9, 160, Soph., Fort Worth, Tex., Dunbar
FB	E. D. Jackson, 5-10, 205, Sr., Kilgore, Tex.
	Oscar Gray, 6-2, 245, Soph., Houston, Tex., Smiley
TB	Oscar Malone, 6-9, 180, Frosh, Gadsen, Ala., Emma Sansom
	Marius Johnson, 5-8, 175, Frosh, Houston, Tex., Austin
K	Todd Wright, 5-10, 173, Sr., Stillwater, Okla.

DEFENSE

RE	Ray Lee Johnson, 6-3, 235, Sr., Fordyce
	Waylon Wishon, 6-4, 250, Frosh, Rogers
T	Scott Long, 6-3, 265, Sr., Benton
	Vernon Wade, 6-4, 260, So. Lufkin, Tex.
NG	Owen Kelly, 5-10, 250, Sr., Wichita Falls, Tex., Rider
	Junior Soli, 6-1, 265, Frosh, Columbus, Ga., Spencer
E	Henry Ford, 6-3, 265, Jr., Fort Worth, Tex., Trimble Tech
	Dexter Howard, 6-1, 245, Jr., LR Central
ELB	Tyrone Chatman, 5-9, 215, Jr., Dumas
	Willie Johnson, 5-11, 220, Soph., Lufkin, Tex.
WLB	Darwin Ireland, 6-1, 226, Jr., PB Dollarway
	Brad Hogan, 5-10, 206, Jr., Heidelberg, Germany
MLB	Kevin Kempf, 6-3, 240, Jr., Vermillion, Ohio
	Shannon Wright, 6-1, 230, Jr., FS Southside
FC	Orlando Watters, 5-11, 175, Jr., Anniston, Ala.
	Spencer Brown, 5-11, 175, Frosh, Morrilton
SS	Alfred Jackson, 6-0, 190, Jr., Marshall, Tex.
	Mike Nunnerley, 6-0, 200, Frosh, NLR, N. Pulaski
FS	Gary Adams, 6-0, 190, Sr., Springfield, Mo., Central
	Del Delco, 6-0, 190, Frosh, Houston, Tex., Mayde Creek
BC	Deen Peevy, 5-11, 185, Soph., Montgomery, Ala., Lee
	Tracy Cantlope, 5-10, 170, Frosh, Dothan, Ala., Northview
P	Pete Raether, 6-4, 205, Sr., Edina, Minn.

COACHES

Jack Crowe (One Game), Joe Kines (10 Games), Danny Ford (Consultant, last seven games), Louis Campbell, Scott Conley, Greg Davis, J. B. Grimes, Fitz Hill, Houston Nutt, Joe Pate, Ken Rucker

1993 (5-5-1)

OFFENSE

SE	J. J. Meadors, 5-8, 152, Soph., Ruston, La.
	Shannon Sidney, 6-1, 170, Frosh, Russellville
LT	Chris Oliver, 6-2, 275, Sr., Fayetteville
	Scott Rivers, 6-5, 260, Frosh, Benton
LG	Pat Baker, 6-3, 275, Jr., Owasso, Kan.
	Ray Straschinske, 6-4, 285, Sr., Cabot
C	Don Streubing, 6-3, 264, Frosh, Springdale
	Earl Scott, 6-3, 270, Soph., NLR Old Main
RG	Isaac Davis, 6-3, 305, Sr., Malvern
	Cole Plafcan, 6-4, 225, Soph., LR Catholic
RT	Verl Mitchell, 6-3, 270, Soph., Paragould Greene County Tech
	Ramon Okoli, 6-5, 313, Jr., LR Joe T. Robinson
	Bryan Cornish, 6-4, 275, Jr., Warren
TE	Kirk Botkin, 6-3, 225, Sr., Baytown, Tex., Lee
	Bob Cole, 6-2, 225, Frosh, Tulsa, Okla.
QB	Barry Lunney, 6-2, 185, Soph., FS Southside
	Jason Allen, 6-1, 190, Jr., Edmond, Okla.
	Mike Cherry, 6-5, 213, Frosh, Texarkana, Ark.
FL	Kotto Cotton, 6-0, 180, Jr., NLR Old Main
	Tracy Caldwell, 5-11, 182, Sr., Pine Bluff
K	Lance Ellison, 6-5, 230, Jr., Conway
	David Boulware, 5-8, 150, Frosh, Matthews, N.C.

DEFENSE

RE	Marcus Adair, 6-2, 225, Soph., Memphis, Tenn., East
	Steve Conley, 6-5, 215, Soph., Chicago, Ill., Luther S
DT	Vernon Wade, 6-4, 260, Jr., Lufkin, Tex.
	Curtis Thomas, 6-3, 260, Jr., Baytown, Tex., Lee
NG	Junior Soli, 6-1, 275, Soph., Columbus, Ga.
	Geno Bell, 6-5, 265, Frosh, Columbia, S.C.
DE	Henry Ford, 6-3, 260, Jr., Fort Worth, Tex., Trimble Tech
	Waylon Wishon, 6-4, 242, Soph., Rogers
WLB	Darwin Ireland, 6-2, 225, Sr., PB Dollarway
	Vincent Bradford, 6-2, 215, Frosh, Malvern
SLB	Demetrius Smith, 6-1, 218, Jr., LR Mills
	Willie Johnson, 5-11, 223, Jr., LR Mills
MLB	Mark Smith, 6-3, 225, Frosh, Webb City, Mo.
	Trent Knapp, 6-2, 225, Jr., Houston, Tex., Clements
	Shannon Wright, 6-0, 225, Sr., FS Southside
LC	Orlando Watters, 5-11, 165, Sr., Anniston, Ala.
	Spencer Brown, 5-11, 175, Soph., Morrilton
SS	Alfred Jackson, 6-0, 190, Sr., Marshall, Tex.
	Mike Nunnerley, 6-0, 200, Soph., NLR N. Pulaski
FS	Carl Kidd, 6-1, 200, Jr., Pine Bluff
	Del Delco, 6-0, 195, Soph., Houston, Tex., Mayde Creek
RC	Dean Peevy, 5-11, 185, Jr., Montgomery, Ala., Lee
	Tracy Cantlope, 5-10, 175, Soph., Dothan, Ala., Northview
P	Doyle Preston, 6-2, 190, Soph., Mount Vernon, Tex., Saltillo

COACHES

Danny Ford, Louis Campbell, Greg Davis, Rockey Felker, Fitz Hill, Buddy King, Joe Kines, Joe Pate, Scott Smith, Larry Van Der Heyden

OFFENSE

FL   J. J. Meadors, 5-6, Jr., Ruston, La.
     James Perry, 5-8, 173, Soph., Houston Northbrook
LT   Carlos Showers, 6-5, 278, Soph., Morrilton
     Scott Rivers, 6-5, 260, Soph., Benton
LG   Tony Nagy, 6-5, 277, Jr., Tulsa Union
     Tony Swartz, 6-3, 301, Soph., Dickinson, Tex.
C   Earl Scott, 6-2, 272, Jr., North Little Rock
     Chris Miller, 6-1, 278, Soph., Angleton, Tex.
RG   Pat Baker, 6-3, 310, Sr., Owasso, Okla.
     Cole Plafcan, 6-4, 270 , Jr., Little Rock Catholic
RT   Verl Mitchell, 6-3, 282, Paragould Greene County
     Winston Alderson, 6-4, 298, Soph., El Dorado
TE   Carl Johnson, 6-2, 240, Jr., Pine Bluff Dollarway
     Kevin Hile, 6-3, 230, Jr., Lee's Summit, Mo.
SE   Anthony Eubanks, 6-2, 290, Frosh, Spiro, Okla.
     Mike Higgins, 6-3, 205, Jr., Carrolton, Ga.
     Shannon Sidney, 6-1, 170, Frosh, Russellville
QB   Barry Lunney, 6-2, 187, Jr., Fort Smith Southside
     Robert Reed, 6-1, 190, Frosh, Brandon, Miss.
     Mike Cherry, 6-4, 219, Soph., Texarkana, Ark.
TB   Oscar Malone, 5-8, 192, Jr., Gadsden, Ala.
     Madre Hill, 6-1, 182, Frosh, Malvern
     Marius Johnson, 5-8, 179, Jr., Houston, Tex., Austin
FB   Carlton Calvin, 6-0, 236, Sr., Keller, Tex.
     Tyrone Henry, 5-11, 216, Frosh, Wilson Rivercrest
     Oscar Gray, 6-1, 150, Sr., Houston Smiley
K   Lance Ellison, 6-5, 242, Sr., Conway

DEFENSE

RE   Marcus Adair, 6-3, 221, Jr., Memphis, Tenn., East
     David Sanders, 6-4, 279, Frosh, Jackson, Miss., Provine
T   Geno Bell, 6-2, 290, Soph., Columbia, S.C.
     Vernon Wade, 6-3, 270, Sr., Lufkin, Tex.
NG   Junior Soli, 6-1, 289, Jr., Columbus, Ga., Spencer
     Ken Anderson, 6-4, 280, Soph., Shreveport, La., Shreve
E   Steven Conley, 6-5, 229, Jr., Chicago Luther (South)
     Waylon Wishon, 6-4, 248, Jr., Rogers
WLB   Willie Johnson, 6-0, 228, Sr., Lufkin, Tex.
     Vincent Bradford, 6-2, 221, Soph., Malvern
     Anthony Hicks, 6-2, 217, Soph., Arkadelphia
SLB   Mark Smith, 6-3, 230, Soph., Webb City, Mo.
     Demetrius Smith, 6-2, 230, Sr., Little Rock Mills
MLB   Trent Knapp, 6-0, 230, Sr., Houston, Tex., Clements
     Don Bray, 6-2, 220, Jr., Carrollton, Ga.
LC   Dean Peevy, 5-11, 185, Sr., Montgomery, Ala., Lee
     Marcus Campbell, 6-0, 181, Frosh, North Little Rock
SS   Mike Nunnerley, 6-1, 203, Jr., North Little Rock, North Pulaski
     Carl Kidd, 6-1, 198, Sr., Pine Bluff Dollarway
FS   Del Delco, 6-0, 208, Jr., Houston, Tex., Mayde Creek
     Philip Hayes, 5-11, 178, Jr., Morrilton
RC   Tracy Cantlope, 5-10, 179, Jr., Dothan, Ala., Northview
     Spencer Brown, 5-11, 178, Jr., Morrilton
P   Matt Wait, 5-10, 227, Frosh, Lake Hamilton
S   Bill Carson, 5-9, 209, Frosh, Batesville

COACHES

Danny Ford, Louis Campbell, Rockey Felker, Fitz Hill, Buddy King, Joe Kines, Joe Pate, Larry Van Der Heyden, David Mitchell, Jim Washburn

OFFENSE

FL   J. J. Meadors, 5-6, 251, Sr., Ruston, La.
     Shannon Sidney, 6-1, 171, Soph., Russellville
LT   Carlos Showers, 6-5, 278, Jr., Morrilton
     Michael Henry, 6-2, 310, Frosh, Houston, Tex., Madison
LG   Russ Brown, 6-0, 273, Frosh, Bristow, Okla.
     Eddie Mosley, 6-4, 264, Jr., Memphis, Tenn., Trevezant
C   Earl Scott, 6-2, 284, Sr., North Little Rock
     Chris Miller, 6-1, 275, Jr., Angleton, Tex.
     Grant Garrett, 6-3, 262, Frosh, Lake Hamilton
RG   Verl Mitchell, 6-4, 285, Sr., Paragould Greene County
     Brandon Burlsworth, 6-3, 275, Frosh, Harrison
RT   Winston Alderson, 6-4, 288, Jr., El Dorado
     Scott Rivers, 6-5, 262, Jr., Benton
TE   Mark Baker, 6-3, 241, Soph., Osceola
     Carl Johnson, 6-2, 234, Sr., Pine Bluff Dollarway
     Al Heringer, 6-4, 249, Frosh, Jonesboro
SE   Anthony Lucas, 6-3, 187, Frosh, Talullah, La., McCall
     Shannon Sidney, 6-1, 171, Soph., Russellville
JR   Anthony Eubanks, 6-2, 194, Soph., Spiro, Okla.
     Kotto Cotton, 6-0, 184, Sr., North Little Rock
FB   Tyrone Henry, 5-11, 230, Soph., Wilson Rivercrest
     Dexter Hebert, 5-7, 205, Soph., Beaumont, Tex., Kelly
TB   Madre Hill, 6-1, 185, Soph., Malvern
     Marius Johnson, 5-8, 175, Sr., Houston, Tex., Austin
QB   Barry Lunney, 6-2, 190, Sr., Fort Smith Southside
     Lajun (Pete) Burks, 6-2, 190, Frosh, Houma, La., Terrebonne
K   Todd Latourette, 6-3, 205, Frosh, Pensacola, Fla., Tate
S   Bill Carson, 5-9, 209, Soph., Batesville

DEFENSE

TSE   Marcus Adair, 6-3, 240, Sr., Memphis, Tenn., East
     Justin Brown, 6-04, 236, Frosh, Newport
LT   Geno Bell, 6-2, 276, Jr., Columbia, S.C.
     Ryan Hale, 6-5, 278, Frosh, Rogers
NG   Junior Soli, 6-3, 275, Sr., Columbus, Ga., Spencer
     Kevin Thomas, 6-2, 288, Soph., Hammond, La.
     Melvin Bradley, 6-2, 258, Frosh, Barton
RT   David Sanders, 6-4, 270, Soph., Jackson, Miss., Provine
     Ken Anderson, 6-4, 274, Shreveport, La., Shreve
OE   Steven Conley, 6-5, 221, Sr., Chicago, Ill., Luther South
     C. J. McClain, 6-4, 225, Frosh, Madison, Miss., Central
     Norman Nero, 6-1, 221, Frosh, Escambia City, Ala.
TLB   Mark Smith, 6-3, 229, Jr., Webb City, Mo.
     Don Bray, 6-0, 230, Sr., Carrollton, Ga.
WLB   Vincent Bradford, 6-2, 217, Jr., Malvern
     Anthony Hicks, 6-2, 225, Jr., Arkadelphia
LCB   Spencer Brown, 5-11, 182, Sr., Morrilton
     Marcus Campbell, 6-0, 176, Soph., Russellville
HS   Del Delco, 6-0,. 200, Sr., Houston, Tex., Mayde Creek
     DeAnthony Hall, 5-10, 187, Frosh, Tuscaloosa, Ala., Central
FS   Mike Nunnerley, 6-1, 204, Sr., North Little Rock, North Pulaski
     Philip Hayes, 5-11, 186, Jr., Fort Wayne, Ind., Homestead
RC   Tracy Cantlope, 5-10, 177, Sr., Dothan, Ala., Northview
     Zac Painter, 5-9, 191, Frosh, Jonesboro
P   Matt Wait, 5-10, 221, Soph., Lake Hamilton

COACHES

Danny Ford, Mike Bender, Louis Campbell, Joe Lee Dunn, Rockey Felker, Fitz Hill, Charley North, Joe Pate, David Mitchell, Jim Washburn

INDEX

Hinton, Percy, 25, 28
Hitt, Dick, 133, 134, 137
Hixon, Chuck, 240, 246
Hodge, Jim, 254, 256, 261, 262, 265
Hoffman, John, 88, 94, 95, 136
Hogue, David, 256
Holieway, Jamelle, 359
Holland, Kenny, 88, 90, 101
Hollingsworth, Mike, 263
Holloway, Derek, 327, 330, 331, 333
Holtz, Anne, 293
Holtz, Lou, 276, 282, 291–97, 299, 302–5,
   309, 312–14, 316–21, 324–29, 331–39,
   341, 345, 347, 373, 376, 377, 379
Homan, Dennis, 234
Horton, Don, 143, 144, 149, 169
Horton, Harold, 181, 183, 193, 234, 254,
   386, 399
Horton, Tim, 360
Howard, Jim, 309
Howell, Jim Lee, 49
Hubble, Web, 236
Huerta, Carlos, 361
Humble, Weldon, 94
Hunt, Joel, 41
Hunter, Billy, 62
Huntley, Phil, 19, 20, 21, 25–29
Hutson, Mark, 345

Illes, Buddy, 189
Ingram, Hootie, 232, 241, 253, 367
Iselin, Phil, 291, 295

Jackson, Bo, 344
Jackson, E. D., 363, 364, 370
Jackson, Keith (athlete), 338, 345
Jackson, Keith (broadcaster), 337
Jackson, Ken, 116
Jackson, Larry, 295
Jackson, O. C., 309
James, Bruce, 236, 248, 256
James, Craig, 333
James, Frank D., 7
James, Tory, 397
Japp, Gus, 43
Jenkins, Dan, 4, 195, 222, 246
Jenkins, John, 360
John, Jim, 189
Johnson, Brad, 241
Johnson, Carl, 401, 403
Johnson, Gil, 105
Johnson, Jimmy, 203, 213, 274, 276,
   292, 293, 295, 341, 343, 348, 361
Johnson, Joe, 346, 361
Johnson, Johnie, 314, 317
Johnson, Marius, 396

Johnson, Ray Lee, 394
Jones, A. J. (Jam), 317, 330
Jones, Bert, 327
Jones, Gomer, 114
Jones, Harry, 200, 205, 209, 216–19,
   223, 226–29
Jones, Jerry, 203, 205
Jones, Johnny (Ham), 296
Jones, Johnny (Lam), 309
Jones, Nate, 334
Jones, Ronnie, 256, 259
Jones, Tom, 314, 316, 327, 328, 330,
   332, 333
Jones, Tommy, 386, 387
Jones, Tony, 353
Jordan, Clark, 49, 55
Jordan, George, 49, 50, 52, 55
Jordan, Leroy, 189
Jordan, Shug, 388
Judy, Steve, 244, 245
Jurney, Bill, 118

Keen, Allen, 62, 63
Keeney, Huey, 94
Kelly, Andy, 365
Kennedy, Cortez, 388
Kersey, Rick, 236, 239, 248, 256
Kettler, Elwood, 136
Kiffin, Monte, 295, 318, 325
Killenger, Glenn, 29
Kimbrough, John, 58
Kinard, Billy, 253, 254
Kines, Joe, 325, 370, 372, 373, 382–85,
   387, 392, 394, 403
King, J. T., 204, 230
King, Kenny, 302
Kirkland, Mike, 270, 272, 274, 277
Kitts, Jimmy, 45
Knight, Bobby, 342
Knight, Virgil, 402
Kobel, Raleigh, 7
Korte, Steve, 329
Koy, Ernie, 209, 212
Koy, Ted, 239, 248, 249
Kramer, Roy, 415
Kristynik, Marv, 208, 212, 218, 219
Krueger, Charley, 148
Kyser, Billy, 143–45, 148, 171, 178

Labruzzo, Joe, 226
Lacewell, Larry, 302, 303
LaForge, Ralph, 49–52
Lahay, Bruce, 330
Lain, Ernie, 69
Lake, Harold (Muddy), 49, 52
Lalman, Ed, 62

Lamb, Jerry, 194, 198–205, 208, 209,
   212, 213
Lambert, Eugene, 77
Lambright, Frank, 105
Lammons, Pete, 217
Landry, Tom, 293
Lasater, Marvin, 175
Lasker, Greg, 336
Latourette, Chuck, 228
Latourette, Todd, 392, 405, 411
Leach, Bobby, 334
Leeks, Roosevelt, 269
Lemke, Walt, 50, 57
Lester, Danny, 249, 260
Levias, Jerry, 229
Lewis, Bill, 274, 295
Lewis, Herschel, 79
Lewis, Tommy, 125
Lindsey, Don, 329–31, 333, 336, 337
Lindsey, Elmer (B), 205
Lindsey, Jim, 201, 205, 209, 213, 217,
   219, 233, 258
Lindsey, Wright, 7
Lilly, Bob, 182
Linebarrier, Bob, 118
Lineberger, Jerry, 188
Little, Donnie, 317
Little, Steve, 106, 279, 296, 302
Locke, Doug, 48
Logue, Don, 108
Long, Gordon, 105
Longman, F. C., 20, 21
Lott, Billy, 145
Lowery, Alan, 269
Loyd, Odis, 347
Lubker, Herman, 88
Lucas, Anthony, 392, 403, 405, 408
Lucas, Tommy, 198
Luckman, Sid, 159
Lujack, Johnny, 159
Luke, Milo, 167
Lunney, Barry Jr., 368, 391, 392, 396,
   397, 399–401, 403, 405, 408, 414
Lunney, Barry Sr., 392
Lunney, John, 88, 392
Luplow, Rollie, 144
Lusby, Vaughn, 296, 302, 309
Lyons, Billy, 130, 137

Mabry, Jim, 359
Mackenzie, Jim, 163, 166, 167, 169, 193,
   194, 203, 204, 208, 212, 214, 223,
   230, 232, 258, 297
Maegle, Dick, 125, 136
Majors, Bobby, 265
Majors, Johnny, 204, 232, 234